SQL FOR DATA ANALYTICS

THIRD EDITION

Harness the power of SQL to extract insights

from data

Jun Shan, Matt Goldwasser, Upom Malik, and Benjamin Johnston

SQL FOR DATA ANALYTICS
THIRD EDITION

Authors: Jun Shan, Matt Goldwasser, Upom Malik, and Benjamin Johnston

Reviewers: Haibin Li and Bharath Kumar Bolla

Development Editor: Padma K. Mohapatra

Acquisitions Editors: Anindya Sil and Sneha Shinde

Production Editor: Shantanu Zagade

Editorial Board: Megan Carlisle, Ketan Giri, Heather Gopsill, Bridget Kenningham, Manasa Kumar, Alex Mazonowicz, Monesh Mirpuri, Abhishek Rane, Brendan Rodrigues, Ankita Thakur, Nitesh Thakur, and Jonathan Wray

First published: August 2019

Second edition: February 2020

Third edition: August 2022

Production reference: 1250822

ISBN: 978-1-80181-287-0

Published by Packt Publishing Ltd.
Livery Place, 35 Livery Street
Birmingham B3 2PB, UK

Table of Contents

Chapter 4: Aggregate Functions for Data Analysis 151

Chapter 5: Window Functions for Data Analysis 187

Chapter 7: Analytics Using Complex Data Types   267

Chapter 8: Performant SQL 327

Chapter 9: Using SQL to Uncover the Truth: A Case Study 383

PREFACE

ABOUT THE BOOK

Every day, businesses operate around the clock, and a huge amount of data is generated at a rapid pace. This book helps you analyze this data and identify key patterns and behaviors that can help you and your business understand your customers at a deep, fundamental level.

SQL for Data Analytics, *Third Edition* is a great way to get started with data analysis, showing how to effectively sort and process information from raw data, even without any prior experience.

You will begin by learning how to form hypotheses and generate descriptive statistics that can provide key insights into your existing data. As you progress, you will learn how to write SQL queries to aggregate, calculate, and combine SQL data from sources outside of your current dataset. You will also discover how to work with advanced data types, like JSON. By exploring advanced techniques, such as geospatial analysis and text analysis, you will be able to understand your business at a deeper level. Finally, the book lets you in on the secret to getting information faster and more effectively by using advanced techniques like profiling and automation.

By the end of this book, you will be proficient in the efficient application of SQL techniques in everyday business scenarios and looking at data with the critical eye of analytics professional.

ABOUT THE AUTHORS

Jun Shan is an expert information technology professional who has been designing and implementing data management systems for more than 20 years. He also teaches SQL and Relational Database at Columbia University in the City of New York and Saint Peter's University. He completed his Master of Science in Computer Science from Virginia Tech and is currently a solution architect in a top 3 cloud computing service provider.

Matt Goldwasser is the Head of Applied Data Science at the T. Rowe Price NYC Technology Development Center. Prior to his current role, Matt was a data science manager at OnDeck, and prior to that, he was an analyst at Millennium Management. Matt holds a bachelor of science in mechanical and aerospace engineering from Cornell University.

Upom Malik is a data science and analytics leader who has worked in the technology industry for over 8 years. He has a master's degree in chemical engineering from Cornell University and a bachelor's degree in biochemistry from Duke University. As a data scientist, Upom has overseen efforts across machine learning, experimentation, and analytics at various companies across the United States. He uses SQL and other tools to solve interesting challenges in finance, energy, and consumer technology. Outside of work, he likes to read, hike the trails of the Northeastern United States, and savor ramen bowls from around the world.

Benjamin Johnston is a senior data scientist for one of the world's leading data-driven MedTech companies and is involved in the development of innovative digital solutions throughout the entire product development pathway, from problem definition to solution research and development, through to final deployment. He is currently completing his Ph.D. in machine learning, specializing in image processing and deep convolutional neural networks. He has more than 10 years of experience in medical device design and development, working in a variety of technical roles, and holds first-class honors bachelor's degrees in both engineering and medical science from the University of Sydney, Australia.

AUDIENCE

If you are a database engineer looking to transition into analytics or a backend engineer who wants to develop a deeper understanding of production data, you will find this book useful. This book is also ideal for data scientists or business analysts who want to improve their data analytics skills using SQL.

Basic familiarity with SQL (such as basic **SELECT**, **WHERE**, and **GROUP BY** clauses), a good understanding of linear algebra and statistics, and PostgreSQL 14 are necessary to make the most of this book.

ABOUT THE CHAPTERS

Chapter 1, Understanding and Describing Data, helps you learn the basics of data analytics. You will learn how to form hypotheses and generate descriptive statistics that can provide insights into your data. You will achieve this goal by using mathematical and graphical techniques to analyze data with Excel.

Chapter 2, The Basics of SQL for Analytics, helps you learn the basics of SQL in the world of data and CRUD operations. You will learn how to use basic SQL to manipulate data in a relational database.

Chapter 3, SQL for Data Preparation, shows you how to clean and prepare data for analysis using SQL techniques. You will begin by learning how to combine multiple tables and queries into a dataset before moving on to more advanced materials.

Chapter 4, Aggregate Functions for Data Analysis, covers SQL's aggregate functions, which are powerful techniques for summarizing data. You will be able to apply these functions to generate descriptive statistics and learn how to aggregate data across all rows and break out subpopulations for further analysis.

Chapter 5, Window Functions for Data Analysis, covers SQL's window functions, which take order into account for a group of data. You will be able to apply these functions to gain new insights into data and gain important knowledge about the data, such as orders and ranks.

Chapter 6, Importing and Exporting Data, provides you with the skills required to interact with your database from other software tools (such as Python).

Chapter 7, Analytics Using Complex Data Types, gives you a rich understanding of the various data types available in SQL and shows you how to extract insights from datetime data, geospatial data, arrays, JSON, and text.

Chapter 8, Performant SQL, helps you optimize your queries so that they run faster. In addition to learning how to analyze query performance, you will also learn how you can use additional SQL functionality, such as functions and triggers, to expand the default functionality.

Chapter 9, Using SQL to Uncover the Truth: A Case Study, reinforces your acquired skills to help you solve real-world problems outside of those described in this book. Using the scientific method and critical thinking, you will be able to analyze your data and convert it into actionable tasks and information.

CONVENTIONS

Code words in the text, database table names, folder names, filenames, file extensions, pathnames, dummy URLs, user input, and Twitter handles are shown as follows: "Three of the columns, `Year of Birth`, `Height`, and `Number of Doctor Visits`, are quantitative because they are represented by numbers."

Words that you see on the screen (for example, in menus or dialog boxes) also appear in the text like this: "Choose the `Delimited` option in the `Text Import Wizard` dialog box, and make sure that you start the import at row `1`."

A block of code is set as follows:

```
SELECT *
FROM products
WHERE production_end_date IS NULL;
```

New terms and important words are shown like this: "Statistics can be further divided into two subcategories: **descriptive statistics** and **inferential statistics**."

SETTING UP YOUR ENVIRONMENT

Before exploring the book in detail, you need to set up specific software and tools. In the following section, you shall see how to do that.

INSTALLING POSTGRESQL 14

The following sections list the instructions for installing and setting up PostgreSQL 14 on Windows, Linux, and macOS.

DOWNLOADING AND INSTALLING POSTGRESQL ON WINDOWS

First, download and install PostgreSQL on Windows:

1. Navigate to https://www.postgresql.org/download/. Select **Windows** from the list of **Packages and Installers**.

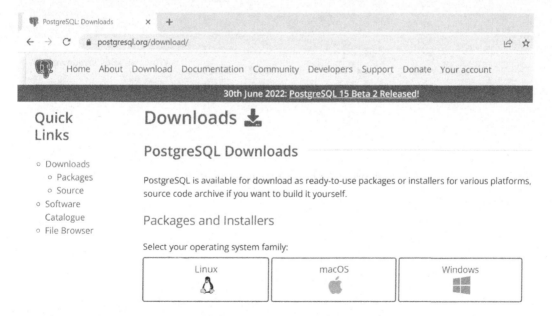

Figure 0.1: PostgreSQL Downloads page

2. Click **Download the installer**.

Figure 0.2: PostgreSQL interactive installer download

3. Select version **14.2** as this is the version that is used in this book.

Figure 0.3: PostgreSQL downloads page

4. Click **Next** for most of the installation steps. You will be asked to specify a data directory. It is recommended that you specify a path that you will easily remember in the future.

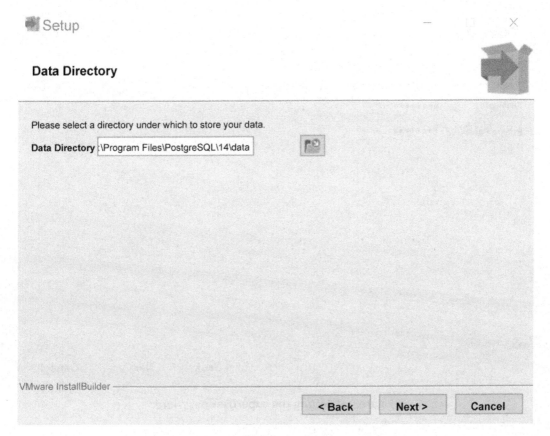

Figure 0.4: PostgreSQL installation – Windows

5. Specify a password for the **postgres** superuser.

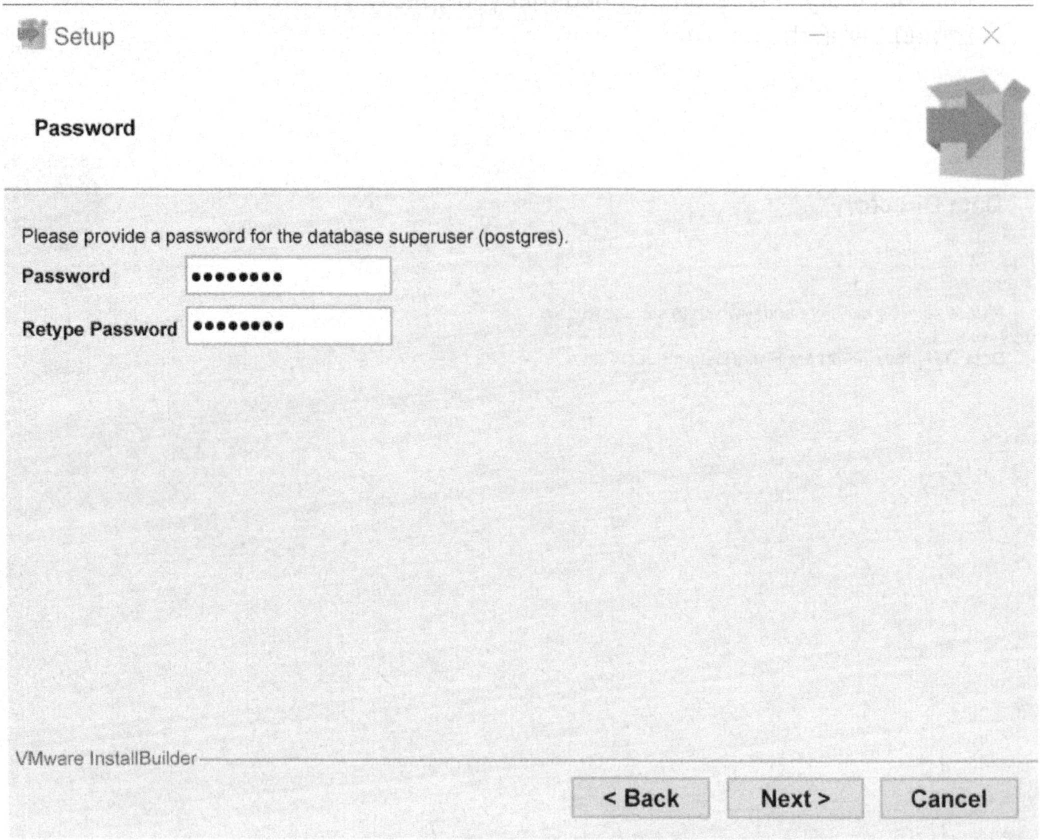

Setup — □ X

Password

Please provide a password for the database superuser (postgres).

Password ••••••••

Retype Password ••••••••

VMware InstallBuilder ——————————————————————————

< Back   Next >   Cancel

Figure 0.5: Setting the superuser password

6. Do not change the port number that is specified by default, unless it conflicts with an application that is already installed on your system.

Figure 0.6: PostgreSQL port settings

7. Click **Next** to proceed through the rest of the steps and wait for the installation to finish.

SETTING THE PATH VARIABLE

To validate whether the **PATH** variable has been set correctly, open the command line, type or paste the following command, and press the *return* key:

```
psql -U postgres
```

If you get the following error, you need to add the PostgreSQL binaries directory to the **PATH** variable:

```
Command Prompt

Microsoft Windows [Version 10.0.19044.1826]
(c) Microsoft Corporation. All rights reserved.

C:\Users\Dell>psql
'psql' is not recognized as an internal or external command,
operable program or batch file.
```

Figure 0.7: Error – Path variable not set

The following steps will help you do that:

1. Search for the term **environment variables** in Windows Search:

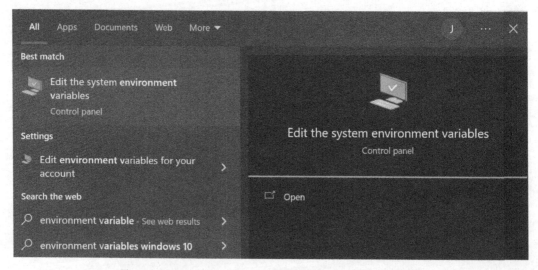

Figure 0.8: Windows Search for environment variables

2. Click **Environment Variables**:

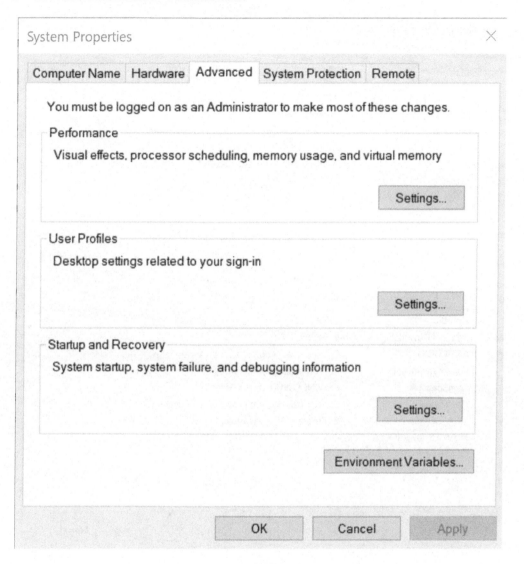

Figure 0.9: Windows System Properties

3. Click **Path** and then click `Edit`:

Figure 0.10: Setting the PATH variable

4. Click **New**:

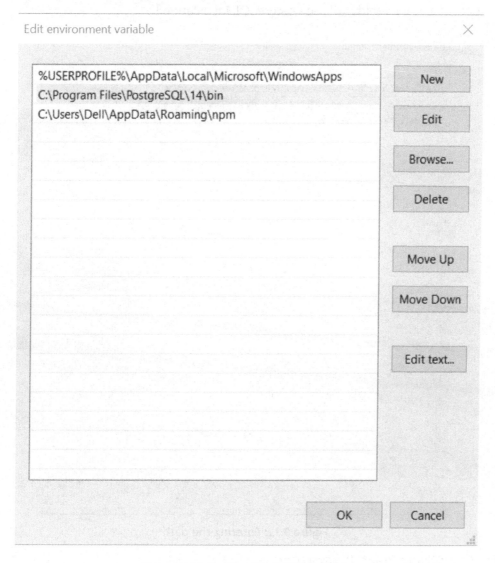

Figure 0.11: Setting the PATH variable

5. Using Windows Explorer, locate the path where PostgreSQL is installed. Add the path to the **bin** folder of the PostgreSQL installation:

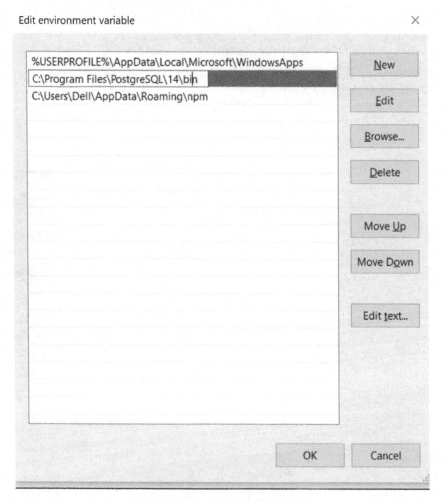

Figure 0.12: Entering the path

6. Click **OK** and restart the system.

7. Now, open the command line where you can either type or paste the following command. Press the *return* key to execute it:

```
psql -U postgres
```

8. Enter the password you set in *step 5* of the *Downloading and Installing PostgreSQL on Windows* section. Then, press the *return* key. You should be able to log in to the PostgreSQL console:

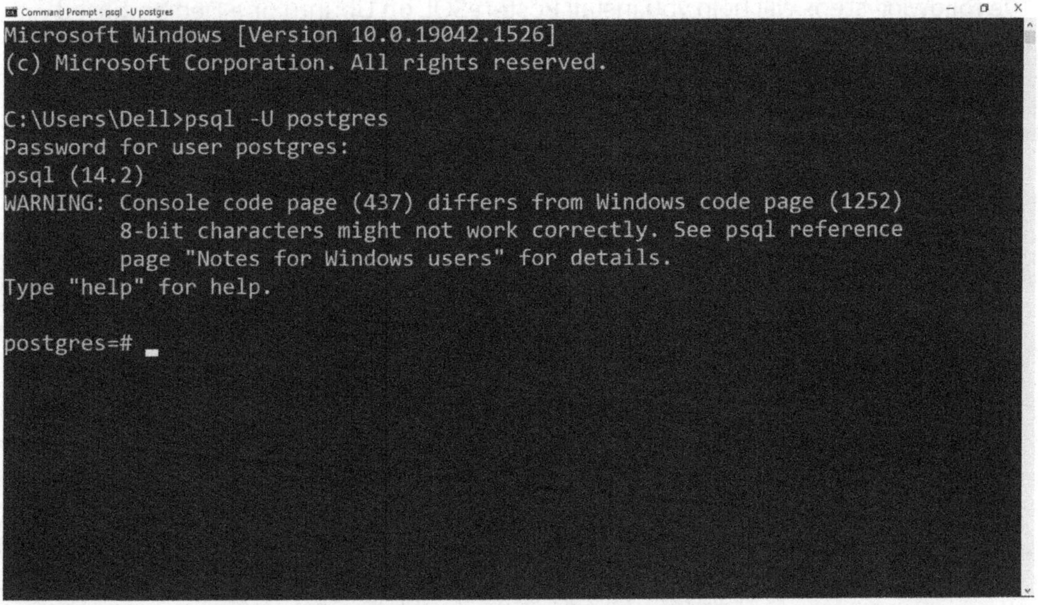

Figure 0.13: PostgreSQL shell

9. Type **\q** and press the *return* key to exit the shell:

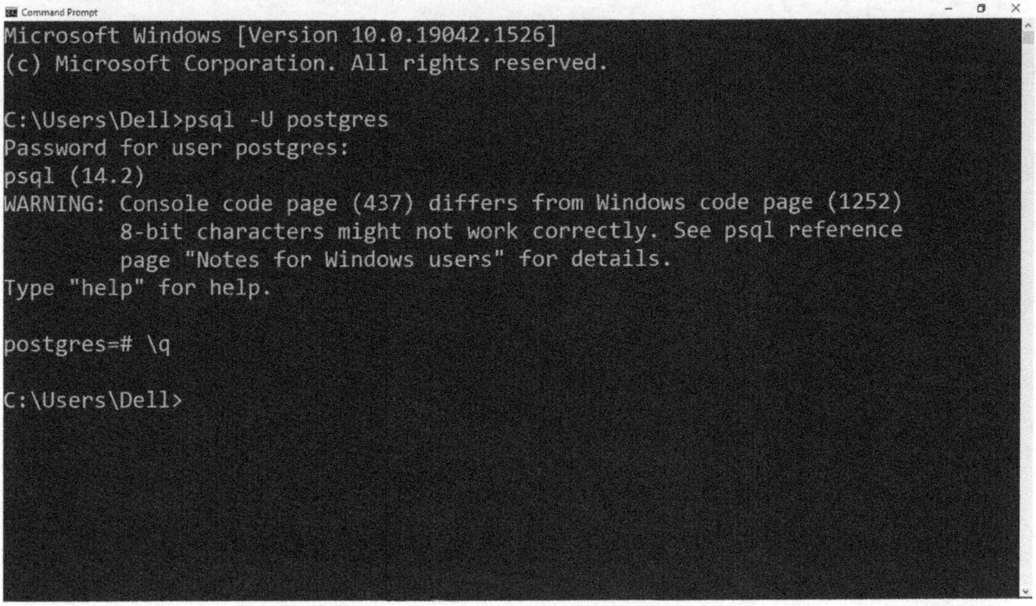

Figure 0.14: Exiting the PostgreSQL shell

The following steps will help you install PostgreSQL on Ubuntu or a Debian-based Linux system.

1. Open the Terminal. Then, type or paste the following command on a new line and press the *return* key:

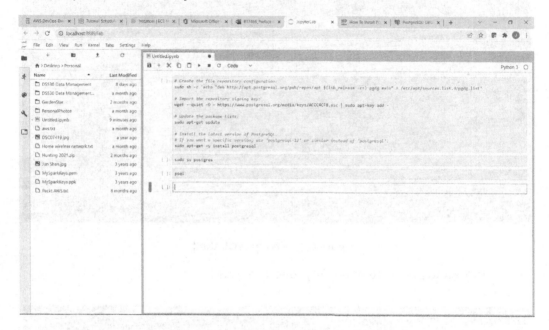

Figure 0.15: Commands on the Terminal

2. Upon installation, PostgreSQL will create a user called **postgres**. You will need to log in as that user to access the PostgreSQL shell:

```
sudo su postgres
```

You should see your shell prompt change as follows:

```
ubuntu@ip-172-31-80-15:~$ sudo su postgres
postgres@ip-172-31-80-15:/home/ubuntu$
postgres@ip-172-31-80-15:/home/ubuntu$ 
```

Figure 0.16: Accessing the PostgreSQL shell on Linux

3. Typing the following command will take you to the PostgreSQL shell:

```
psql
```

You can type **\l** (a backslash and a lowercase L) to see a list of all the databases that are loaded by default:

```
postgres@ip-172-31-80-15:/home/ubuntu$ psql
could not change directory to "/home/ubuntu": Permission denied
psql (14.4 (Ubuntu 14.4-0ubuntu0.22.04.1))
Type "help" for help.

postgres=# \l
                                List of databases
    Name    |  Owner   | Encoding | Collate |  Ctype  |   Access privileges
------------+----------+----------+---------+---------+-----------------------
 postgres   | postgres | UTF8     | C.UTF-8 | C.UTF-8 |
 template0  | postgres | UTF8     | C.UTF-8 | C.UTF-8 | =c/postgres          +
            |          |          |         |         | postgres=CTc/postgres
 template1  | postgres | UTF8     | C.UTF-8 | C.UTF-8 | =c/postgres          +
            |          |          |         |         | postgres=CTc/postgres
(3 rows)

postgres=# 
```

Figure 0.17: List of databases on Linux

> **NOTE**
>
> You have covered how to install PostgreSQL on Ubuntu and Debian-based systems here. For instructions to install it on other distributions, please refer to your distribution's documentation. The PostgreSQL download page for Linux can be found at https://www.postgresql.org/download/linux/.

INSTALLATION ON MACOS

This section will help you install PostgreSQL on macOS. Before you start installing the software, make sure you have the Homebrew package manager installed on your system. If you do not, head over to https://brew.sh/ and paste the script provided on the webpage in a macOS Terminal (the Terminal app) and press the *return* key.

Follow the prompts that appear and wait for the script to finish the installation.

> **NOTE**
>
> The following instructions are written based on macOS Catalina version 10.15.6, which was the latest version at the time of writing. For more help on using Terminal, refer to the following link: https://support.apple.com/en-in/guide/terminal/apd5265185d-f365-44cb-8b09-71a064a42125/mac.

Figure 0.18: Installing Homebrew

Once Homebrew is installed, follow these steps to install PostgreSQL:

1. Open a new Terminal window. Type in the following commands in succession followed by the *return* key to install the PostgreSQL package:

```
brew doctor brew update
brew install postgres
```

Wait for the installation to complete. Depending on your local setup and connection speed, you will see messages like those shown below (note that only the partial installation log is shown here):

```
(base) dineshreddy@Dineshs-MacBook-Pro ~ % brew install postgres
==> Downloading https://ghcr.io/v2/homebrew/core/icu4c/manifests/70.1
######################################################################## 100.0%
==> Downloading https://ghcr.io/v2/homebrew/core/icu4c/blobs/sha256:f124a30b9ecb4bfe6
==> Downloading from https://pkg-containers.githubusercontent.com/ghcr1/blobs/sha256:
######################################################################## 100.0%
==> Downloading https://ghcr.io/v2/homebrew/core/ca-certificates/manifests/2022-04-26
######################################################################## 100.0%
==> Downloading https://ghcr.io/v2/homebrew/core/ca-certificates/blobs/sha256:c05a44f
==> Downloading from https://pkg-containers.githubusercontent.com/ghcr1/blobs/sha256:
######################################################################## 100.0%
==> Downloading https://ghcr.io/v2/homebrew/core/openssl/1.1/manifests/1.1.1q
######################################################################## 100.0%
==> Downloading https://ghcr.io/v2/homebrew/core/openssl/1.1/blobs/sha256:9a130889462
==> Downloading from https://pkg-containers.githubusercontent.com/ghcr1/blobs/sha256:
######################################################################## 100.0%
==> Downloading https://ghcr.io/v2/homebrew/core/krb5/manifests/1.20
######################################################################## 100.0%
==> Downloading https://ghcr.io/v2/homebrew/core/krb5/blobs/sha256:8e6be25060a0223ec6
==> Downloading from https://pkg-containers.githubusercontent.com/ghcr1/blobs/sha256:
######################################################################## 100.0%
==> Downloading https://ghcr.io/v2/homebrew/core/readline/manifests/8.1.2
######################################################################## 100.0%
==> Downloading https://ghcr.io/v2/homebrew/core/readline/blobs/sha256:1eaadc077c1584
==> Downloading from https://pkg-containers.githubusercontent.com/ghcr1/blobs/sha256:
######################################################################## 100.0%
==> Downloading https://ghcr.io/v2/homebrew/core/postgresql/manifests/14.4
######################################################################## 100.0%
==> Downloading https://ghcr.io/v2/homebrew/core/postgresql/blobs/sha256:04247388a3fc
==> Downloading from https://pkg-containers.githubusercontent.com/ghcr1/blobs/sha256:
######################################################################## 100.0%
==> Installing dependencies for postgresql: icu4c, ca-certificates, openssl@1.1, krb5 and readline
```

Figure 0.19: Installation progress (partially shown) for PostgreSQL

2. Once the installation is complete, start the PostgreSQL process by typing the following command in Terminal and pressing the *return* key:

```
pg_ctl -D /usr/local/var/postgres start
```

You should see an output similar to the following:

```
(base) dineshreddy@Dineshs-MacBook-Pro ~ % pg_ctl -D /usr/local/var/postgres start
waiting for server to start....2022-07-18 22:47:21.386 IST [17819] LOG:  starting PostgreSQL 14.4 on x86_64-apple-darwin20.6.0, compiled by Apple clang version 13.0.0
 (clang-1300.0.29.30), 64-bit
2022-07-18 22:47:21.390 IST [17819] LOG:  listening on IPv6 address "::1", port 5432
2022-07-18 22:47:21.390 IST [17819] LOG:  listening on IPv4 address "127.0.0.1", port 5432
2022-07-18 22:47:21.393 IST [17819] LOG:  listening on Unix socket "/tmp/.s.PGSQL.5432"
2022-07-18 22:47:21.403 IST [17820] LOG:  database system was shut down at 2022-07-18 22:32:50 IST
2022-07-18 22:47:21.409 IST [17819] LOG:  database system is ready to accept connections
 done
server started
(base) dineshreddy@Dineshs-MacBook-Pro ~ % psql postgres
psql (14.4)
Type "help" for help.
```

Figure 0.20: Starting the PostgreSQL process

3. Once the process is started, log in to the PostgreSQL shell using the default superuser called **postgres** as follows (press the *return* key to execute the command):

```
psql postgres
```

4. You can type **\l** (a backslash and a lowercase L) followed by the *return* key to see a list of all the databases that are loaded by default:

```
(base) dineshreddy@Dineshs-MacBook-Pro ~ % psql postgres
psql (14.4)
Type "help" for help.

postgres=# \l
                                List of databases
   Name    |    Owner    | Encoding | Collate | Ctype |        Access privileges
-----------+-------------+----------+---------+-------+--------------------------------
 postgres  | dineshreddy | UTF8     | C       | C     |
 template0 | dineshreddy | UTF8     | C       | C     | =c/dineshreddy                +
           |             |          |         |       | dineshreddy=CTc/dineshreddy
 template1 | dineshreddy | UTF8     | C       | C     | =c/dineshreddy                +
           |             |          |         |       | dineshreddy=CTc/dineshreddy
(3 rows)
```

Figure 0.21: List of databases loaded by default

5. Enter **\q** and then press the *return* key to quit the PostgreSQL shell.

> **NOTE**
>
> pgAdmin will get installed automatically along with PostgreSQL 14.

INSTALLING PYTHON

INSTALLING PYTHON ON WINDOWS

1. Find your desired version of Python on the official installation page at https://www.anaconda.com/distribution/#windows.

2. Ensure that you select Python 3.9 from the download page.

3. Ensure that you install the correct architecture for your computer system—that is, either 32-bit or 64-bit. You can find out this information in the **System Properties** window of your OS.

4. After you download the installer, double-click on the file and follow the user-friendly prompts on screen.

INSTALLING PYTHON ON LINUX

To install Python on Linux, you have a couple of good options:

1. Open Command Prompt and verify that Python 3 is not already installed by running **python3 --version**.

2. To install Python 3, run this:

```
sudo apt-get update
sudo apt-get install python3.9
```

3. If you encounter problems, there are numerous sources online that can help you troubleshoot the issue.

4. You can also install Python by downloading the Anaconda Linux installer from https://www.anaconda.com/distribution/#linux and following the instructions.

INSTALLING PYTHON ON MACOS

Similar to Linux, you have a couple of methods for installing Python on a Mac.
To install Python on macOS, do the following:

1. Open the Terminal for Mac by pressing *CMD + Spacebar*, type **terminal** in the open search box, and hit *Enter*.

2. Install Xcode through the command line by running **xcode-select—install**.

3. The easiest way to install Python 3 is using **Homebrew**, which is installed through the command line by running **ruby -e "$(curl -fsSL https://raw. githubusercontent.com/Homebrew/install/master/install)"**.

4. Add Homebrew to your **$PATH** environment variable. Open your profile in the command line by running **sudo nano ~/.profile** and inserting **export PATH="/usr/local/opt/python/libexec/bin:$PATH"** at the bottom.

5. The final step is to install Python. In the command line, run **brew install python**.

6. Again, you can also install Python via the Anaconda installer, which is available at https://www.anaconda.com/distribution/#macos.

INSTALLING GIT

INSTALLING GIT ON WINDOWS OR MACOS

Git for Windows/Mac can be downloaded and installed via https://git-scm.com/. However, for improved user experience, it is recommended that you install Git through an advanced client such as GitKraken (https://www.gitkraken.com/).

INSTALLING GIT ON LINUX

Git can be easily installed via the command line:

```
sudo apt-get install git
```

If you prefer a graphical user interface, GitKraken (https://www.gitkraken.com/) is also available for Linux.

LOADING THE SAMPLE DATASETS – WINDOWS

Most exercises in this book use a sample database, **sqlda**, which contains fabricated data for a fictional electric vehicle company called ZoomZoom. Set it up by performing the following steps:

1. First, create a database titled **sqlda**. Open the command line and type or paste the following command. Then, press the *return* key to execute it:

```
createdb -U postgres sqlda
```

You will be prompted to enter the password that you set for the **postgres** superuser during installation:

```
C:\Users\Dell>createdb -U postgres sqlda
Password:
```

Figure 0.22: PostgreSQL shell password request

2. To check whether the database has been successfully created, log in to the shell by typing or pasting the following command and pressing the *return* key:

```
psql -U postgres
```

Enter your password when prompted. Press the *return* key to proceed.

3. Type **\l** (a backslash and a lowercase L) and then press the *return* key to check if the database has been created. The **sqlda** database should appear along with a list of the default databases:

```
postgres=# \l
                                              List of databases
   Name    |  Owner   | Encoding |          Collate           |           Ctyp
e          |    Access privileges
-----------+----------+----------+----------------------------+----------------
-----------+-----------------------
 postgres  | postgres | UTF8     | English_United States.1252 | English_United
 States.1252 |
 sqlda     | postgres | UTF8     | English_United States.1252 | English_United
 States.1252 |
 template0 | postgres | UTF8     | English_United States.1252 | English_United
 States.1252 | =c/postgres            +
```

Figure 0.23: PostgreSQL list of databases

4. Download the **data.dump** file from the **Datasets** folder in the GitHub repository of this book by clicking this link: http://packt.link/GuU31. Modify the highlighted path in the following command based on where the file is located on your system. Type or paste the command into the command line and press the *return* key to execute it:

```
psql -U postgres -d sqlda -f C:\<path>\data.dump
```

> **NOTE**
>
> Alternatively, you can use the command line and navigate to the local folder where you have downloaded the file using the **cd** command. For example, if you have downloaded it to the **Downloads** folders of your computer, you can navigate to it using **cd C:\Users\<your username>\ Downloads**. In this case, remove the highlighted path prefix in the step. The command should look like this: **psql -U postgres -d sqlda -f data.dump**.

You should get an output similar to the one that follows:

```
psql -U postgres -d sqlda -f data.dump
Password for user postgres:
SET
SET
SET
SET
SET
 set_config
------------

(1 row)


SET
SET
SET
SET
CREATE EXTENSION
COMMENT
CREATE EXTENSION
```

Figure 0.24: PostgreSQL database import

5. Check whether the database has been loaded correctly. Log in to the **PostgreSQL console** by typing or pasting the following command. Press the *return* key to execute it:

```
psql -U postgres
```

In the shell, type the following command to connect to the **sqlda** database:

```
\c sqlda
```

Then type **\dt**. This command should list all the tables in the database, as follows:

```
sqlda=# \dt
                     List of relations
 Schema |            Name            | Type  |  Owner
--------+----------------------------+-------+----------
 public | closest_dealerships        | table | postgres
 public | countries                  | table | postgres
 public | customer_sales             | table | postgres
 public | customer_survey            | table | postgres
 public | customers                  | table | postgres
 public | dealerships                | table | postgres
 public | emails                     | table | postgres
 public | products                   | table | postgres
 public | public_transportation_by_zip | table | postgres
 public | sales                      | table | postgres
 public | salespeople                | table | postgres
 public | top_cities_data            | table | postgres
(12 rows)
```

Figure 0.25: Validating that the database has been imported

> **NOTE**
>
> You are importing the database using the **postgres** superuser for demonstration purposes only. It is advised in production environments to use a separate account.

LOADING THE SAMPLE DATASETS – LINUX

Most exercises in this book use a sample database, **sqlda**, which contains fabricated data for a fictional electric vehicle company called ZoomZoom. Set it up by performing the following steps:

1. Switch to the **postgres** user by typing the following command in the terminal. Press the *return* key to execute it:

```
sudo su postgres
```

You should see your shell change as follows:

```
ubuntu@ip-172-31-82-195:~$ sudo su postgres
postgres@ip-172-31-82-195:/home/ubuntu$
```

Figure 0.26: Loading the sample datasets on Linux

2. Type or paste the following command to create a new database called **sqlda**. Press the *return* key to execute it:

```
createdb sqlda
```

You can then type the **psql** command to enter the PostgreSQL shell, followed by **\l** (a backslash followed by lowercase L) to check if the database was successfully created:

```
postgres=# \l
                                  List of databases
    Name    |   Owner  | Encoding |  Collate  |   Ctype  |   Access privileges
------------+----------+----------+-----------+----------+----------------------
 postgres   | postgres | UTF8     | C.UTF-8   | C.UTF-8  |
 sqlda      | postgres | UTF8     | C.UTF-8   | C.UTF-8  |
 template0  | postgres | UTF8     | C.UTF-8   | C.UTF-8  | =c/postgres          +
            |          |          |           |          | postgres=CTc/postgres
 template1  | postgres | UTF8     | C.UTF-8   | C.UTF-8  | =c/postgres          +
            |          |          |           |          | postgres=CTc/postgres
(4 rows)
```

Figure 0.27: Accessing the PostgreSQL shell on Linux

Enter **\q** and then press the *return* key to quit the PostgreSQL shell.

3. Download the **data.dump** file from the **Datasets** folder in the GitHub repository of this book by running this command:

```
wget "https://github.com/PacktPublishing/SQL-for-Data-Analytics-Third-Edition/tree/main/Datasets/data.dump"
```

4. Navigate to the folder where you have downloaded the file using the **cd** command. Then, type the following command:

```
psql -d sqlda < data.dump
```

5. Then, wait for the dataset to be imported:

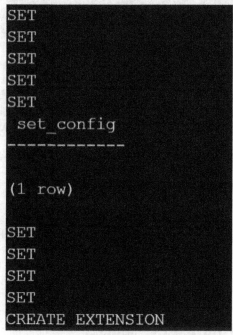

Figure 0.28: Importing the dataset on Linux

6. To test whether the dataset was imported correctly, type **ppsql postgres** and then press the *return* key to enter the PostgreSQL shell. Then, run **\c sqlda** followed by **\dt** to see the list of tables within the database:

```
Schema |              Name                  | Type  |   Owner
--------+------------------------------------+-------+-----------
 public | closest_dealerships                | table | postgres
 public | countries                          | table | postgres
 public | customer_sales                     | table | postgres
 public | customer_survey                    | table | postgres
 public | customers                          | table | postgres
 public | dealerships                        | table | postgres
 public | emails                             | table | postgres
 public | products                           | table | postgres
 public | public_transportation_by_zip      | table | postgres
 public | sales                              | table | postgres
 public | salespeople                        | table | postgres
 public | top_cities_data                    | table | postgres
(12 rows)
```

Figure 0.29: Validating the import on Linux

> **NOTE**
>
> You are importing the database using the **postgres** superuser for demonstration purposes only. It is advised in production environments to use a separate account.

LOADING THE SAMPLE DATASETS – MACOS

Most exercises in this book use a sample database, **sqlda**, which contains fabricated data for a fictional electric vehicle company called ZoomZoom. Now, set it up by performing the following steps:

1. Enter the PostgreSQL shell by typing the following command in Terminal. Press the *return* key to execute it:

```
psql postgres
```

2. Now, create a new database called **sqlda** by typing the following command and pressing *return* (do not forget the semicolon at the end):

```
create database sqlda;
```

3. You should see the following output. Type **\l** (a backslash followed by lowercase L) in Terminal and press the *return* key to check whether the database was successfully created (you should see the **sqlda** database listed there):

```
postgres=# create database sqlda;
CREATE DATABASE
postgres=# \l
                                 List of databases
    Name    |     Owner      | Encoding | Collate | Ctype |        Access privileges
------------+----------------+----------+---------+-------+---------------------------------------
 postgres   | brendanrodrigues | UTF8   | C       | C     |
 sqlda      | brendanrodrigues | UTF8   | C       | C     |
 template0  | brendanrodrigues | UTF8   | C       | C     | =c/brendanrodrigues               +
            |                |          |         |       | brendanrodrigues=CTc/brendanrodrigues
 template1  | brendanrodrigues | UTF8   | C       | C     | =c/brendanrodrigues               +
            |                |          |         |       | brendanrodrigues=CTc/brendanrodrigues
(4 rows)

postgres=#
```

Figure 0.30: Checking whether a new database is successfully created

4. Type or paste **\q** in the PostgreSQL shell and press the *return* key to exit.

5. Download the **data.dump** file from the **Datasets** folder in the GitHub repository of this book at https://packt.link/GuU31. Navigate to the folder where you have downloaded the file using the **cd** command. Then, type the following command:

```
psql sqlda < ~/Downloads/data.dump
```

> **NOTE**
>
> The preceding command assumes that the file is saved in the **Downloads** directory. Make sure you change the highlighted path based on the location of the **data.dump** file on your system.

6. Then, wait for the dataset to be imported:

```
SET
SET
SET
SET
SET
 set_config
------------

(1 row)

SET
SET
SET
SET
CREATE EXTENSION
```

Figure 0.31: Importing the dataset

7. To test if the dataset was imported correctly, type **psql postgres** and then press the *return* key to enter the PostgreSQL shell again. Then, run **\c sqlda** followed by **\dt** to see the list of tables within the database:

```
postgres=# \c sqlda
You are now connected to database "sqlda" as user "brendanrodrigues".
sqlda=# \dt
                            List of relations
 Schema |             Name              | Type  |      Owner
--------+-------------------------------+-------+------------------
 public | closest_dealerships           | table | brendanrodrigues
 public | countries                     | table | brendanrodrigues
 public | customer_sales                | table | brendanrodrigues
 public | customer_survey               | table | brendanrodrigues
 public | customers                     | table | brendanrodrigues
 public | dealerships                   | table | brendanrodrigues
 public | emails                        | table | brendanrodrigues
 public | products                      | table | brendanrodrigues
 public | public_transportation_by_zip  | table | brendanrodrigues
 public | sales                         | table | brendanrodrigues
 public | salespeople                   | table | brendanrodrigues
 public | top_cities_data               | table | brendanrodrigues
(12 rows)

sqlda=#
```

Figure 0.32: List of tables within the sqlda database

RUNNING SQL FILES

Commands and statements can be executed via a ***.sql** file from the command line using the following command:

```
psql -d your_database_name -U your_username < commands.sql
```

Alternatively, they can be executed via the SQL interpreter:

```
database=#
```

To get to the interactive interpreter, type the following command:

```
psql -d your_database_name -U your_username
```

ACCESSING THE CODE FILES

You can find the complete code files of this book at https://packt.link/wEkdN.

The high-quality color images used in this book can be found at https://packt.link/Ue9Qb.

If you have any issues or questions about installation, please email us at workshops@packt.com.

1

UNDERSTANDING AND
DESCRIBING DATA

OVERVIEW

By the end of this chapter, you will be able to explain data and statistics and classify data based on its characteristics. You will find out how to calculate basic univariate statistics of data and identify outliers. You will also learn how to use bivariate analysis to understand the relationship between two variables.

INTRODUCTION

Data collection and analysis is an old practice going back to the beginning of civilization. Records from ancient Egyptian papyrus suggest that pharaohs collected census information from villages, possibly to determine the number of soldiers that could be enlisted for the war. However, it was after the arrival of modern computers that the art of data analytics became a significant phenomenon that is changing people's lives every day.

This book, as its name suggests, teaches you how to use **Structured Query Language (SQL)** for data analytics. SQL is the tool that you will be focusing on in the rest of the book. But before diving into SQL, this chapter will provide an overview of data analytics. You will be introduced to fundamental concepts such as the definition and type of statistics and different methods of statistics, which will lay the foundation for the concepts that future chapters will be based on, define the purpose of the SQL operations that you will learn about, and set up the domain of analytics in which the SQL operations will run on. You will start the chapter by learning about data and statistics.

DATA ANALYTICS AND STATISTICS

Raw data is a group of values that you can extract from a source. It becomes useful when it is processed to find different patterns in the data that was extracted. These patterns, also referred to as information, help you to interpret the data, make predictions, and identify unexpected changes in the future. This information is then processed into knowledge.

Knowledge is a large, organized collection of persistent and extensive information and experience that can be used to describe and predict phenomena in the real world. Data analysis is the process by which you convert data into information and, thereafter, knowledge. **Data analytics** is when data analysis is combined with making predictions.

There are several data analysis techniques available to make sense of data. One of them is statistics, which uses mathematical techniques on datasets.

Statistics is the science of collecting and analyzing a large amount of data to identify the characteristics of the data and its subsets. For example, you may want to study the medical history of a country to identify the most common causes of illness-related fatality. You can also dive deeper into some subgroups, such as people from different geographic areas, to identify whether there are specific patterns for people from each area.

Statistics is performed on datasets. Different data inside datasets have different characteristics and require different methods of processing. Some types of data, such as name and label, may be **qualitative**, which means it provides descriptive information. Others, such as counts and amounts, are **quantitative**, which means you can perform numerical operations, such as addition or multiplication, on these values. For example, the following dataset is a collection of some biomedical information collected across a set of patients:

Year of Birth	Country of Birth	Height (cm)	Eye Color	Number of Doctor Visits in the Year 2018
1997	Egypt	182	Blue	1
1988	China	196	Hazel	2
1986	USA	180	Brown	2
1990	USA	166	Brown	1
1975	India	181	Green	3
1951	Germany	184	Brown	1
2000	Australia	174	Gray	5
1995	India	183	Brown	1
1992	China	187	Brown	2
1987	USA	169	Blue	2

Figure 1.1: Healthcare data

In this case, the unit of observation for the dataset is an individual patient because each row represents an individual observation, which is a unique patient. There are 10 data points, each with 5 variables. Three of the columns, `Year of Birth`, `Height`, and `Number of Doctor Visits in the Year 2018`, are quantitative because they are represented by numbers. Two of the columns, `Eye Color` and `Country of Birth`, are qualitative.

To get you familiar with the fundamental concepts of datasets and statistics, here is an activity.

ACTIVITY 1.01: CLASSIFYING A NEW DATASET

In this activity, you will classify the sales data of different cars in a dataset. You are about to start a job in a new city at a start-up. You are excited to start your new job, but you have decided to sell all your belongings before you head off, which includes your car. As you are not sure what price to sell it at, you decide to collect some data. You ask some friends and family who have recently sold their cars about the make of the car and how much they sold it for. Based on this information, you now have a dataset. The data is as follows:

Date	Make	Sales Amount (Thousands of $)
2/1/18	Ford	12
2/2/18	Honda	15
2/2/18	Mazda	19
2/3/18	Ford	20
2/4/18	Toyota	10
2/4/18	Toyota	10
2/4/18	Mercedes	30
2/5/18	Ford	11
2/6/18	Chevy	12.5
2/6/18	Chevy	19

Figure 1.2: Used car sales data

These are the steps to perform:

1. Determine the unit of observation.

2. Identify whether each column is quantitative or qualitative based on the definition provided in the text right before the activity. If you can apply arithmetical operations to it, it is quantitative. Otherwise, it is qualitative.

3. Use a numeric value to represent different string values if a column contains string values and the string values are fixed and limited. This is a common technique that makes it faster for computers to process data. For example, to process a day in the week column, you can use 0 to represent Sunday, 1 to represent Monday, and so on. Try to use this concept and convert the **Make** column into a numeric data column.

In this activity, you learned how to classify your data. In the next section, you will learn about various types of statistics.

> **NOTE**
>
> The solution for this activity can be found on page 432.

TYPES OF STATISTICS

Statistics can be further divided into two subcategories: **descriptive statistics** and **inferential statistics**.

Descriptive statistics are used to describe a collection of data. For example, the average age of people in a country is a descriptive statistics indicator that describes an aspect of the country's residents. Descriptive statistics on a single variable in a dataset are called **univariate analysis**, while descriptive statistics that look at two or more variables at the same time are called **multivariate analysis**. In particular, statistics that look at two variables are called **bivariate analysis**. The average age of a country is an example of univariate analysis, while an analysis examining the interaction between GDP per capita, healthcare spending per capita, and age is multivariate analysis.

In contrast, **inferential statistics** allows datasets to be collected as a sample or a small portion of measurements from a larger group, called a population. Inferential statistics are used to infer the properties of a population-based on the properties of a sample. For example, a survey of 10,000 people is a sample of the entire population of a country with 100 million people. Instead of collecting the age of every person in the country, you survey 10,000 people in the country and use their average age as the average age of the country.

> **NOTE**
>
> In this book, you will be primarily focusing on descriptive statistics.

METHODS OF DESCRIPTIVE STATISTICS

In this section, you will take a closer look at the basic mathematical techniques of univariate and bivariate analyses and how to use them to describe and understand a given dataset. You will be introduced to the following methods in this order:

Univariate Analysis Techniques

- Data Frequency Distribution

- Quantiles

- Central Tendency

- Dispersion

Bivariate Analysis Techniques

- Scatterplots

- Linear Trend Analysis and Pearson Correlation Coefficient

- Interpreting and Analyzing the Correlation Coefficient

- Time Series Data

UNIVARIATE ANALYSIS

As mentioned in the previous section, one of the main branches of statistics is univariate analysis. It consists of multiple methods that are used to understand a single aspect of a dataset. In this section, you will look at some of the most common univariate analysis techniques.

DATA FREQUENCY DISTRIBUTION

The distribution of data is simply a count of the number of values that are in a dataset. For example, say that you have a dataset of 1,000 medical records and one of the variables in the dataset is eye color. If you look at the dataset and find 700 people have brown eyes, 200 people have green eyes, and 100 people have blue eyes, then you have just described the distribution of the dataset. Specifically, because you used the absolute number to show the occurrence frequency of a certain pattern (eye color in this example), you have described the **absolute frequency distribution**.

If you were to describe the counts not by the actual number of occurrences in the dataset but by the proportion of the total number of data points, then you would be describing the **relative frequency distribution**. In the preceding eye color example, the relative frequency distribution would be 70% brown eyes, 20% green eyes, and 10% blue eyes. It is easy to calculate the distribution when the variable can take on several fixed values, such as eye color.

But what about a quantitative variable that can take on a range of continuous values, such as height? The general way to calculate distributions for these types of variables is to make interval "buckets" that these values can be assigned to, and then calculate distributions using these buckets. For example, height can be broken down into 5 cm interval buckets. A height of 172 will fall into the 170–174.99 bucket and a height of 181 will fall into the 180–184.99 bucket. You can then create a distribution based on the values of buckets derived from the heights. This distribution is based on the absolute number of heights in each bucket, so it is an absolute frequency distribution. You can then divide each row in the table by the total number of data points and get the relative frequency distribution.

Another useful thing to do with distributions is to put the numbers in a graph, which is called data visualization. Data visualization shows the relationship between data points visually, making it easier to spot patterns. In *Exercise 1.01*, *Creating a Histogram*, you will create a histogram, which is a graphical representation of the continuous distribution using interval buckets.

EXERCISE 1.01: CREATING A HISTOGRAM

In this exercise, you will use Microsoft Excel to create a histogram. Imagine, as a healthcare policy analyst, you want to see the distribution of heights to see whether it is possible to discover any patterns related to the quality of healthcare. To accomplish this task, you need to create a histogram.

> **NOTE**
>
> You can use spreadsheet software such as Excel or any data analysis scripting language, such as Python, to create histograms. For convenience, you will use Excel in this exercise.

Perform the following steps:

1. All the datasets used in this chapter can be found on GitHub. To access the files, open the following address in your preferred browser: http://packt.link/hW355.

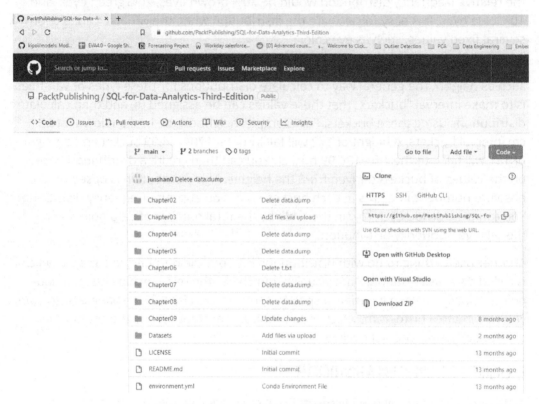

Figure 1.3: Download code files from Github

Click the **Code** drop-down menu in the upper right corner and click on the **Download ZIP** option. You will get a zip file containing all codes in this book. Unzip it and go to the **Datasets** folder. You will find the data files inside.

2. Open Microsoft Excel to a blank workbook:

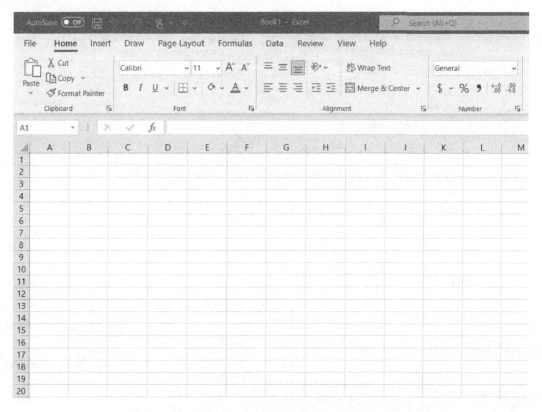

Figure 1.4: A blank Excel workbook

> **NOTE**
>
> The Excel version used in this book is Office 365 Excel v2203. If you are using another version of Excel, your screen and menu may look different, but the workflow is the same and you should be able to find the menus/ options related to the tasks in this book.

3. Go to the **Data** tab and click `Get Data | From File | From Text/CSV`.

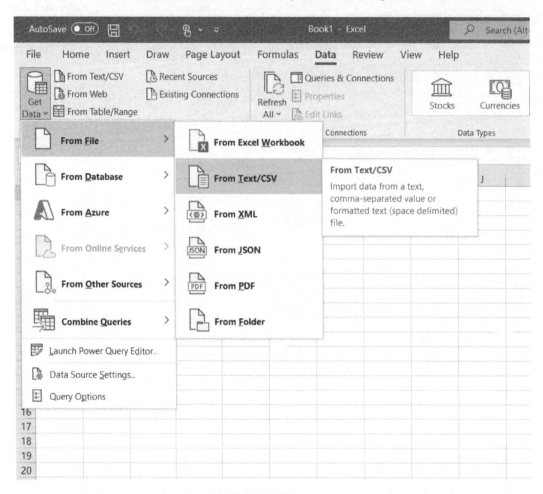

Figure 1.5: Opening a CSV file

4. Find the **heights.csv** dataset file in the **Datasets** folder of the GitHub repository. After navigating to it, click **Import**.

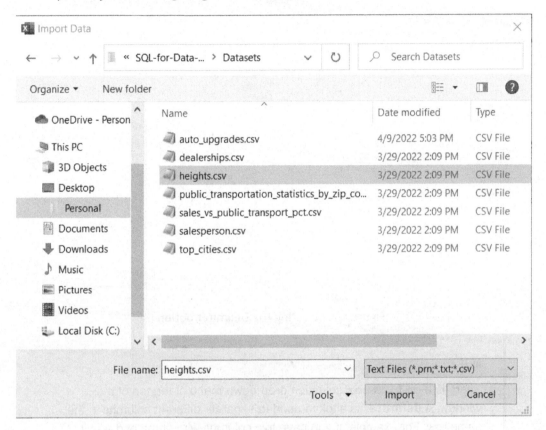

Figure 1.6: Selecting heights.csv

5. The **Text Import Wizard** dialog box will show up.

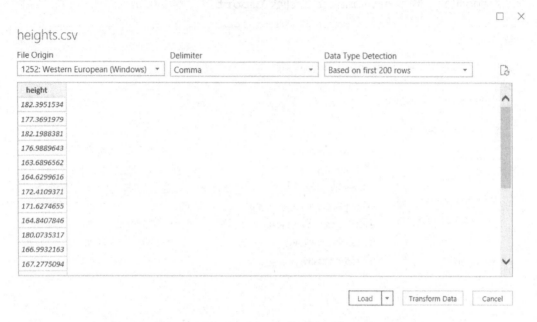

Figure 1.7: Selecting the Delimiter option

> **NOTE**
>
> There is a **delimiter** selection drop-down menu at the top of the window. A **delimiter** is a token used to separate different columns in the same row. For example, if you have two columns with name and age in a row, such as **Sarah** and **23**, you need to use a character to separate these two values so that computers know they belong to different columns. **Comma-Separated Values** (**CSVs**) traditionally use commas as delimiters (in the future, use whatever is appropriate for your dataset), which will result in the following row:
>
> `Sarah, 23`

The **heights.csv** file only has one column. So, it does not need a delimiter. You can leave the option as is. Now, click **Load**.

6. In column **C**, write the numbers **140**, **145**, **150**, and so on in increments of five all the way to **220** in cells **C2** to **C18**, as shown in *Figure 1.8*:

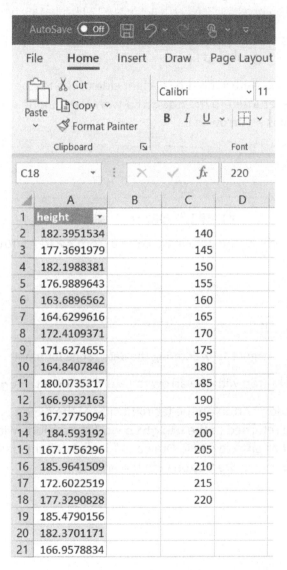

Figure 1.8: Entering the data into the Excel sheet

7. Click **Data Analysis** (if you do not see the **Data Analysis** option, follow these instructions to enable it: https://support.office.com/en-us/article/load-the-analysis-toolpak-in-excel-6a63e598-cd6d-42e3-9317-6b40ba1a66b4) on the **Data** tab.

8. Select **Histogram** and click **OK** from the selection box that pops up. The **Histogram** dialog will pop up.

9. Click the selection button on the far-right side of the textbox for **Input Range**. You should be returned to the **heights** worksheet along with a blank box with a button that has an arrow in it.

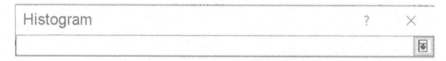

Figure 1.9: Input range dialog box

Drag and highlight all the data in **heights** from **A2** to **A10001**, which will result in:

Figure 1.10: Entering the data range for input

Now, click the button with the arrow to return to the **Histogram** window.

10. Click the selection button on the far-right side of the dialog box for **Bin Range**. You should be returned to the **heights** worksheet along with a blank box with a button that has an arrow in it. Drag and highlight all the data in **heights** from **C2** to **C18**. Now, click the button with the arrow.

11. Select **New Worksheet Ply** under **Output options** and make sure **Chart Output** is marked, as shown in *Figure 1.11*. Now, click **OK**:

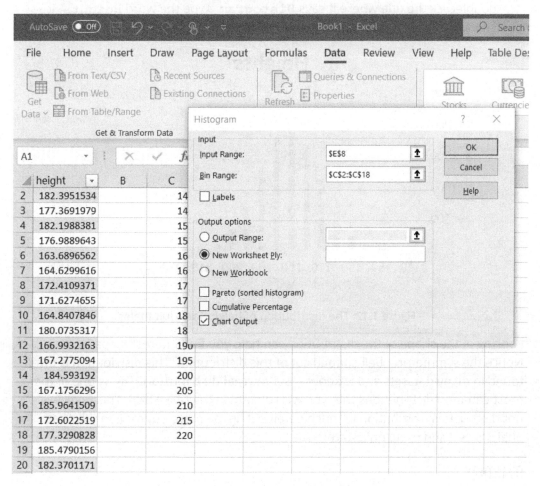

Figure 1.11: Selecting New Worksheet Ply

12. As you chose to output the histogram in a new worksheet ply, a new worksheet (usually called **Sheet2**) will be created. Click **Sheet2**. Find the graph and doubleclick the title where it says **Histogram**. Type the word **Heights**. It should produce a graph that is similar to the one in *Figure 1.12*:

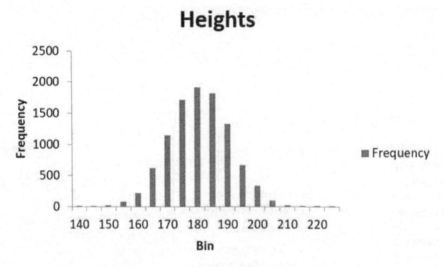

Figure 1.12: The distribution of height for adult males

Looking at the shape of the distribution can help you find interesting patterns. Notice the symmetrical bell-shaped cut of this distribution. This distribution is often found in many datasets and is known as a **normal distribution**. This is one of the most common distributions that you will run into in the real world. This book will not discuss this distribution in much detail but keep an eye out for it in your data analysis as it shows up quite often.

QUANTILES

In the previous section, *Data Frequency Distribution*, you learned how to compute the frequency of distribution as well as how to visualize it. However, there is more to study in the pattern of each distribution. For example, given any two normal distributions, one may be more concentrated around the middle, thus having a sharper peak. Another may spread out more and look flatter. You will need to use some quantitative metrics to evaluate the characteristics of each distribution.

One way to numerically quantify data distribution is to use quantiles. **N-quantiles** are a set of n-1 points used to divide a dataset into n groups based on the order of a variable. These points are often called **cut points**. For example, a 4-quantiles (also referred to as a quartile) has three cut points (n-1) that divide a variable into four approximately equal groups of numbers. There are several common names for quantiles used interchangeably, which are as follows:

N	Common Name
3	Terciles
4	Quartiles
5	Quintiles
10	Deciles
20	Ventiles
100	Percentiles

Figure 1.13: Common names for *n*-quantiles

The procedure for calculating quantiles varies from place to place. In one of the most common approaches, you can use the following procedure to calculate the *n*-quantiles for data points for a single variable:

1. Order the data points from lowest to highest based on the variable.

2. Determine the number, **n**, of *n*-quantiles you want to calculate and the number of cut points, n-1.

3. Determine the number of **k** cut points you want to calculate, that is, a number from 1 to n-1. If this is the first step of the calculation, set **k** to be equal to 1.

    Find the index, **i**, for the *k*th cut point using the following:

$$i = \left[\frac{k}{n}(d-1)\right] + 1$$

Figure 1.14: The index

4. If for the *k*th cut point the i calculated is a whole number, simply pick that numbered item from the ordered data points. If i is not a whole number, find the numbered item that is lower than i and the one higher than it. Multiply the difference between the numbered item and the one after it by the decimal portion of the index. Add this number to the lower-numbered item.

5. Repeat *Steps 1* to *4* with different values of **k** until you have calculated all the cut points.

Now that you have understood the steps of calculating quartiles, it would be helpful to work through an exercise for better understanding.

EXERCISE 1.02: CALCULATING THE QUARTILES FOR ADD-ON SALES

In this exercise, you will classify the data and calculate the quartiles for a car purchase using Excel. Your new boss wants you to look at some data before you start on Monday so that you have a better sense of one of the problems you will be working on—that is, the increasing sales of add-ons and upgrades for car purchases.

Your boss sends over a list of 11 car purchases and how much was spent on add-ons and upgrades to the base model of the new ZoomZoom Model Chi. The following are the values of **Add-on Sales ($)**: **5000**, **1700**, **8200**, **1500**, **3300**, **9000**, **2000**, **0**, **0**, **2300**, and **4700**.

> **NOTE**
>
> All the datasets used in this chapter can be found on GitHub:
>
> https://packt.link/skue4

Perform the following steps to complete the exercise:

1. Open Microsoft Excel to a blank workbook.

2. Go to the **Data** tab and click **Get Data | From File | From Text/CSV**. You can find the **auto_upgrades.csv** dataset file in the **Datasets** folder of the GitHub repository. Navigate to the file and click **Import**.

3. As this file has only one column, it has no delimiters, although CSVs traditionally use commas as delimiters (in the future, use whatever is appropriate for your dataset). For now, click the **auto_upgrades** tab and select **Sort** from the tab.

4. A sorted dialog box will pop up. Now, click **OK**. The values will now be sorted from lowest to highest. The list in *Figure 1.15* shows the sorted values:

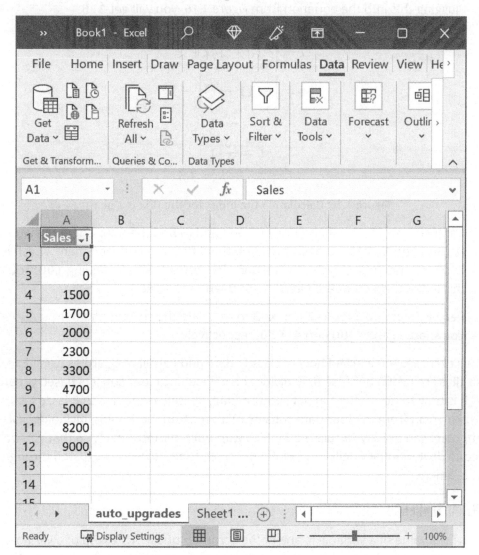

Figure 1.15: The add-on sales figures sorted

5. Now, determine the number of *n*-quantiles and cut points you need to calculate. Quartiles are equivalent to 4-quantiles, as shown in *Figure 1.13*. Because the number of cut points is just one less than the number of *n*-quantiles (n-1), you know there will be three cut points.

6. Calculate the index for the first cut point, in this case, **k=1; d**, the number of population-based values, equals **11**, and **n**, the number of n-quantiles, equals **4**. Plugging this into the equation from *Figure 1.16*, you will get **3.5**:

$$i = \left[\frac{k}{n}(d-1)\right] + 1$$

$$i = \left[\frac{1}{4}(11-1)\right] + 1$$

$$i = \frac{10}{4} + 1$$

$$i = \frac{10}{4} + 1$$

$$i = 2.5 + 1 = 3.5$$

Figure 1.16: Calculating the index for the first cut point

7. Because index **3.5** is a noninteger, you need to find the third and fourth items (**1,500** and **1,700**, respectively). Find the difference between them, which is **200**, and then multiply this by the decimal portion of **0.5**, yielding **100**. You add this to the third numbered item, **1,500**, and get **1,600**.

8. Repeat *Steps 2* to *5* for **k=2** and **k=3** to calculate the second and third quartiles. You should get **2,300** and **4,850**, respectively.

In this exercise, you learned how to classify data and calculate quartiles using Excel. Quartiles are useful because they divide the dataset into four subsets based on order, and it is easy to derive the top half, bottom half, as well as the half that is closest to the median from the four data subsets. With most modern tools, including SQL, computers can quickly calculate quantiles with built-in functionality so that you do not need to do it manually. Still, it is helpful to understand how it is calculated through this example.

CENTRAL TENDENCY

The typical value of a variable is one of the common questions asked of a variable in a dataset. This value is often described as the **central tendency** of the variable. There are several ways to describe the central tendency of a dataset. Each of these has its own advantages and disadvantages. Some of the ways to measure central tendency include the following:

- **Mode**: Mode is simply the value that comes up most often in the distribution of a variable. In *Figure 1.1*, the example on eye color, the mode would be "brown eyes" because it occurs most frequently in the dataset. If multiple values are tied for the most common variable, then the variable is called multimodal, and all the highest values are reported. If no value is repeated, then there is no mode for that set of values.

  Mode tends to be useful when a variable can take on a small, fixed number of values. However, it is problematic to calculate when a variable is a continuous quantitative variable, as seen in the example on height in *Figure 1.12*. With these variables, other calculations are more appropriate for determining the central tendency.

- **Average/mean**: The average of a variable (also called the mean) is the value calculated when you take the sum of all the values of the variable and divide it by the number of data points. For example, if you have a small dataset of ages, 26, 25, 31, 35, and 29, the average of these ages would be 29.2 because that is the number you get when you derive the sum of the five numbers and then divide by 5, that is, the number of data points.

  The mean is easy to calculate and, generally, does a good job of describing a "typical" value for a variable. No wonder it is one of the most reported descriptive statistics in the literature. However, using the average to determine the central tendency has one major drawback, that is, it is sensitive to outliers. An **outlier** is a data point that is significantly different in value from the rest of the data and occurs rarely. Outliers can often be identified by using graphical techniques (such as scatterplots and box plots). These techniques display the data visually and can help in identifying any data points that are very far from the rest of the data.

  When a dataset has an outlier, it is called a **skewed dataset**. Some common reasons why outliers occur include unclean data, extremely rare events (such as a month where you win a lottery versus the months where you receive a regular salary), and problems with measurement instruments. Outliers may change the average to a point where it is no longer representative of a typical value in the data.

- **Median**: The median (also called the 2nd quartile and the 50th percentile) is another measure of central tendency but has some advantages over the average. To calculate the median, take the numbers of a variable and sort them from the lowest to the highest, and then determine the middle number. For an odd number of data points, this number is simply the middle value of the ordered data. If there is an even number of data points, then take the average of the two middle numbers.

  While the median is a bit unwieldy to calculate, it is less affected by outliers, unlike the mean. To illustrate this fact, calculate the median of the skewed age dataset of 26, 25, 31, 35, 29, and 82. When you calculate the median of the dataset, you get the value of 30. This value is much closer to the typical value of the dataset than the average of 38. This robustness toward outliers is one of the major reasons the median is calculated.

> **NOTE**
>
> As a rule, it is a good idea to calculate both the mean and median of a variable. If there is a significant difference in the value of the mean and the median, then the dataset may have outliers.

Next, you will learn how to perform central tendency calculations in the following exercise.

EXERCISE 1.03: CALCULATING THE CENTRAL TENDENCY OF ADD-ON SALES

In this exercise, you will calculate the central tendency of the given data using Excel. To better understand the **Add-on Sales** data (the items that are sold in addition to the main purchase), you will need to gain an understanding of what a typical value for this variable is. Calculate the mode, mean, and median of the **Add-on Sales** data. Here is the data for the 11 cars purchased: **5000, 1700, 8200, 1500, 3300, 9000, 2000, 0, 0, 2300,** and **4700**.

Perform the following steps to implement the exercise:

1. Open an Excel workbook and type in the preceding numbers in a column.

2. Calculate the mode by finding the most common value. Because **0** is the most common value in the dataset, the mode is **0**.

3. Calculate the mean. Sum the numbers in **Add-on Sales**, which should equal 37,700. Then, divide by the number of values (11), and you get a mean of 3,427.27.

4. Select the entire range of data. In the **Data** menu, choose **Sort | AtoZ**. Calculate the median by identifying the middle value of the data, as shown in *Figure 1.17*:

	A	B	C
1	0		
2	0		
3	1500		
4	1700		
5	2000		
6	2300		
7	3300		
8	4700		
9	5000		
10	8200		
11	9000		
12			
13			
14			
15			

Figure 1.17: Add-on Sales figures sorted

Because there are 11 values, the middle value will be the sixth on the list. You now take the sixth element in the ordered data and get a median of **2300**.

> **NOTE**
>
> When you compare the mean and the median, you can see that there is a significant difference between the two. As previously mentioned in the *Central Tendency* section, it is a sign that you have outliers in your dataset. You will then need to determine whether you want to cleanse your data by removing the outliers or not. You will learn how to determine which values are outliers in the next section, *Dispersion*.

Now that you know about central tendency, you can learn about a different property of data, called dispersion.

DISPERSION

Another property of interest in a dataset is discovering how close together data points are in a variable. For example, the number sets [100, 100, 100] and [50, 100, 150] both have a mean of 100, but the numbers in the second group are spread out more than in the first. This property of describing how the data is spread is called dispersion.

There are many ways to measure the dispersion of a variable. Here are some of the most common ways to evaluate dispersion.

Range: The range is simply the difference between the highest and lowest values for a variable. For example, the range in *Exercise 1.03, Calculating the Central Tendency of Add-On Sales* is 0–9,000. It is easy to calculate but is very susceptible to outliers. It also does not provide much information about the spread of values in the middle of the dataset.

Standard deviation/variance: Standard deviation is simply the square root of the average of the squared difference between each data point and the mean. The value of standard deviation ranges from 0 to positive infinity. The closer the standard deviation is to 0, the less the numbers in the dataset vary. If the standard deviation is 0, it means all the values for a dataset variable are the same.

One subtle distinction to note is that there are two different formulas for standard deviation, which are shown in *Figure 1.18*. When the dataset represents the entire population, you should calculate the population standard deviation using formula A in *Figure 1.18*. The variable **ux** here is the mean (average) of the dataset. If your sample represents a portion of the observations, then you should use formula B for the sample standard deviation, as displayed in *Figure 1.18*. The variable **ux** here is also the mean (average) of the dataset. When in doubt, use the sample standard deviation as it is more conservative. Also, in practice, the difference between the two formulas is very small when there are several data points:

$$A) \sqrt{\frac{\sum_{i=1}^{n}(x_i - u_x)^2}{n}} \quad B) \sqrt{\frac{\sum_{i=1}^{n}(x_i - u_x)^2}{n-1}}$$

Figure 1.18: The standard deviation formulas for A) population and B) sample

The standard deviation is generally the quantity used most often to describe dispersion. Like the range, it can also be affected by outliers, though not in such an extreme way as the range. It can also be fairly involved to calculate. Modern tools make it easy to calculate the standard deviation. For example, for the dataset in *Exercise 1.03, Calculating the Central Tendency of Add-On Sales*, you can use the **STDEV()** function in Excel to calculate the sample standard deviation:

A13	▼ ⋮	✕	✓	*fx*	=STDEV(A1:A11)
	A	**B**	**C**	**D**	**E**	**F**
1	0					
2	0					
3	1500					
4	1700					
5	2000					
6	2300					
7	3300					
8	4700					
9	5000					
10	8200					
11	9000					
12						
13	3023.935					
14						
15						

Figure 1.19: Calculating standard deviation in Excel

One final note is that, occasionally, you may see a related value called variance. It is simply the square of the standard deviation.

Interquartile Range (**IQR**): IQR is the difference between the first quartile, Q1 (this is also called the lower quartile), and the third quartile, Q3 (this is also called the upper quartile).

> **NOTE**
>
> For more information on calculating quantiles and quartiles, refer to the *Data Frequency Distribution* section in this chapter.

IQR, unlike the range and standard deviation, is robust toward outliers. While it is one of the most complicated functions to calculate, it provides a more robust way to measure the spread of datasets. In fact, IQR is often used to define outliers. If a value in a dataset is smaller than *Q1 - 1.5 X IQR* or larger than *Q3 + 1.5 X IQR*, then the value is considered an outlier.

To better illustrate dispersion, you will work through an example in the next exercise.

EXERCISE 1.04: DISPERSION OF ADD-ON SALES

In this exercise, you will calculate the range, standard deviation, and IQR. To better understand the sales of additions and upgrades, you need to take a closer look at the dispersion of the data. Here is the data for the 11 cars purchased: **5000, 1700, 8200, 1500, 3300, 9000, 2000, 0, 0, 2300**, and **4700**. Follow these steps to perform the exercise:

1. Calculate the range by finding the minimum value of the data, **0**, and subtracting it from the maximum value of the data, **9000**, yielding **9000**.

2. Follow and execute the data. The standard deviation calculation requires you to determine whether you want to calculate the sample standard deviation or the population standard deviation. As these 11 data points only represent a small portion of all purchases, you will calculate the sample standard deviation.

3. Find the mean of the dataset, which you calculated in *Exercise 1.02, Calculating the Quartiles for Add-On Sales*, to be **3427.27**.

4. Subtract each data point from the mean and square the result. The results are summarized in the following figure:

Add-on Sales ($)	Difference with Mean	Difference with Mean Squared
5000	1572.727273	2473471.074
1700	-1727.272727	2983471.074
8200	4772.727273	22778925.62
1500	-1927.272727	3714380.165
3300	-127.2727273	16198.34711
9000	5572.727273	31055289.26
2000	-1427.272727	2037107.438
0	-3427.272727	11746198.35
0	-3427.272727	11746198.35
2300	-1127.272727	1270743.802
4700	1272.727273	1619834.711

Figure 1.20: The sum of the squared calculation

5. Sum up the **Difference with Mean Squared** values, yielding 91,441,818.

6. Divide the sum by the number of data points minus 1, which, in this case, is 10, and take its square root. This calculation should result in 3,023.93 as the sample standard deviation.

7. Find the first and third quartiles to calculate the IQR. This calculation can be found in *Exercise 1.02*, *Calculating the Quartiles for Add-On Sales*, to give you 1,600 and 4,850. Then, subtract the two to get the value of 3,250.

In this exercise, you calculated the range, standard deviation, and IQR using Excel. In the next section, you will learn how to use bivariate analysis to find patterns.

BIVARIATE ANALYSIS

So far, you have understood the methods for describing a single variable. Now, you will learn how to find patterns with two variables using bivariate analysis.

SCATTERPLOTS

One of the most effective ways to conduct bivariate analysis is using scatterplots. A general principle you will find in analytics is that graphs are incredibly helpful for finding patterns. Just as histograms can help you to understand a single variable, scatterplots can help you to understand two variables. Scatterplots can be produced easily using data analysis tools, such as Excel.

> ### NOTE
>
> Scatterplots are particularly helpful when there is only a small number of points, usually a number between 30 and 500. If you have many points and plotting them appears to produce a giant blob in your scatterplot, take a random sample of 200 of those points and plot them to help discern any interesting trends.

A lot of different patterns are worth looking out for within a scatterplot. The most common pattern people look for is an upward or downward trend between the two variables noting, as one variable increases, does the other variable increase or decrease? Such a trend indicates there may be a predictable mathematical relationship between the two variables. For example, there is an upward trend between age and the income a person makes. *Figure 1.21* shows an example of a linear trend:

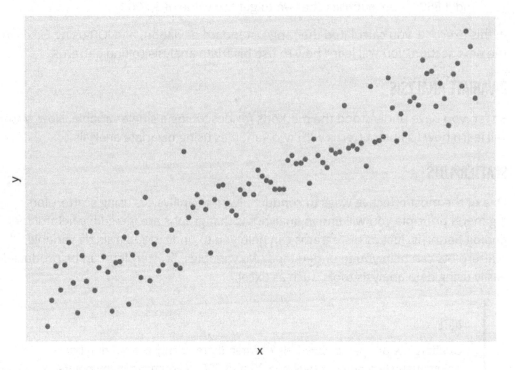

Figure 1.21: The upward linear trend between two variables, the age and the income of a person

There are also other trends that are worth looking out for that are not linear, including **quadratic**, **power**, **inverse**, and **logistic** trends. Look at the following figure to see what some of these trends look like:

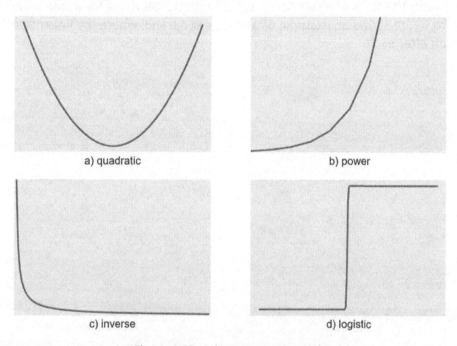

Figure 1.22: Other common trends

NOTE

The process of approximating a trend with a mathematical function is known as **regression analysis**. Regression analysis plays a critical part in analytics but is outside the scope of this book.

While trends are useful for understanding and predicting patterns, detecting changes in trends is often as important. Changes in trends usually indicate a critical change in whatever you are measuring and are worth examining further for an explanation. For example, the stock of a company begins to drop after rising for a long time. The following figure shows an example of a change in a trend, where the linear trend wears off after **x=50**:

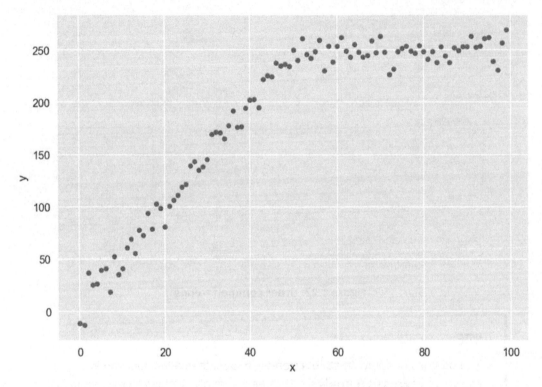

Figure 1.23: An example of a change in a trend

Another pattern that people tend to look for is periodicity—that is, repeating patterns in the data. Such patterns can indicate that two variables may have cyclical behavior and can be useful in making predictions. A very common example is the temperature, which goes higher during the day and goes lower during the night. *Figure 1.24* shows an example of periodic behavior:

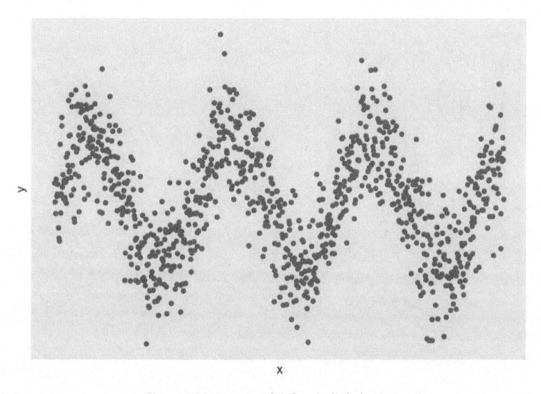

Figure 1.24: An example of periodic behavior

Scatterplots are also used to detect outliers. While most points in a graph appear to be in a specific region of the graph, some points, such as the two in the upper-left corner in the following figure (circled in red), are quite far away from the rest. It may indicate that these two points are outliers in regard to the two variables. When doing further bivariate analysis, it may be wise to remove these points to reduce any noise and produce better insights.

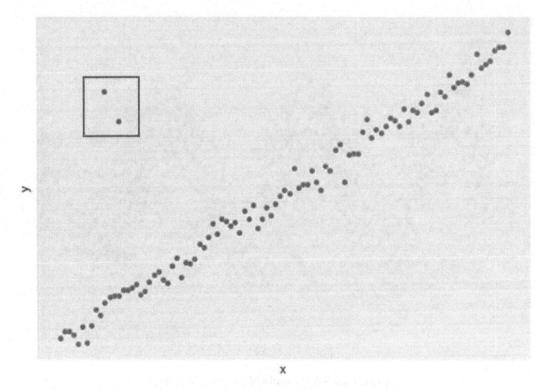

Figure 1.25: A scatterplot with two outliers

These techniques with scatterplots allow data professionals to understand the broader trends in their data and take the first steps to turn data into information.

LINEAR TREND ANALYSIS AND PEARSON CORRELATION COEFFICIENT

One of the most common trends in analyzing bivariate data is linear trends. The linear trend shows if there is a relationship in which when one variable increases, another variable shows a pattern of increase or decrease. Some linear trends are weak, while other linear trends are strong in terms of how well they fit the data. In *Figure 1.26* and *Figure 1.27*, you will see examples of scatterplots with their line of best fit. This is a line calculated using a technique known as **Ordinary Least Squares (OLS)** regression:

> **NOTE**
>
> OLS is beyond the scope of this book, but you need to understand that it indicates how well bivariate data fits a linear trend and is a valuable tool for understanding the relationship between two variables.

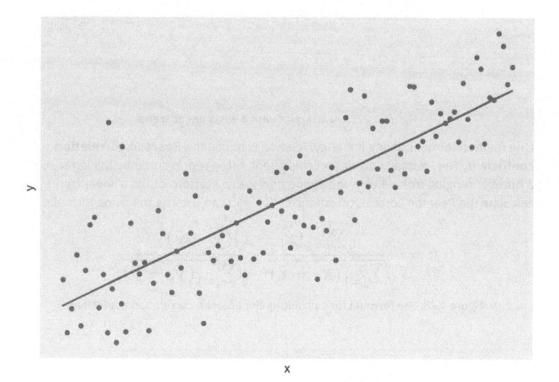

Figure 1.26: A scatterplot with a strong linear trend

The following figure shows a scatterplot with a weak linear trend:

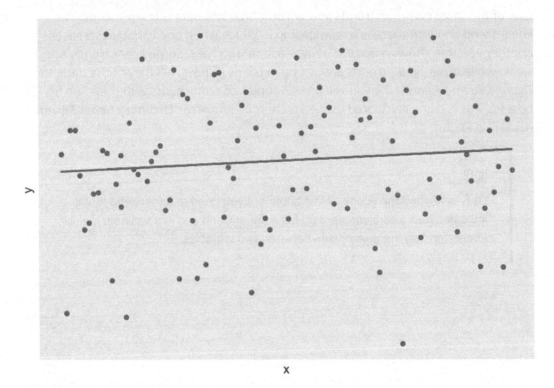

Figure 1.27: A scatterplot with a weak linear trend

One method for quantifying linear correlation is to use the **Pearson correlation coefficient**. The Pearson correlation coefficient, often represented by the letter **r**, is a number ranging from -1 to 1, indicating how well a scatterplot fits a linear trend. To calculate the Pearson correlation coefficient, **r**, you can use the following formula:

$$r = \frac{\sum_{i=1}^{n}(x_i - \bar{x})(y - \bar{y})}{\sqrt{\sum_{i=1}^{n}(x_i - \bar{x})^2}\ \sqrt{\sum_{i=1}^{n}(y_i - \bar{y})^2}}$$

Figure 1.28: The formula for calculating the Pearson correlation coefficient

Here, the denominator is the standard deviation of variables **x** and **y**. The nominator is the covariance between **x** and **y**. This formula is a bit heavy, so work through an example to turn the formula into specific steps.

EXERCISE 1.05: CALCULATING THE PEARSON CORRELATION COEFFICIENT FOR TWO VARIABLES

In this exercise, you will calculate the Pearson correlation coefficient for the relationship between `Hours Worked Per Week` and `Sales Per Week ($)`. In the figure, you can see some listed data for 10 salespeople at the ZoomZoom dealership in Houston and how much they netted in sales that week:

Hours Worked Per Week	Sales Per Week ($)
40	179480.58
56	2495037.37
50	2285369.51
82	2367896.33
41	1309745.16
51	623013.69
45	2989943.37
90	1970316.24
47	1845840.39
72	2553231.33

Figure 1.29: Data for 10 salespersons at a ZoomZoom dealership

> **NOTE**
>
> The `salesperson.csv` dataset can be directly downloaded from GitHub to perform this exercise. Here is the link to the **Datasets** folder: https://packt.link/mriXZ.

Perform the following steps to complete the exercise:

1. Create a scatterplot of the two variables in Excel by using the data given in the scenario. This will help you to get a rough estimate of what to expect for the Pearson correlation coefficient.

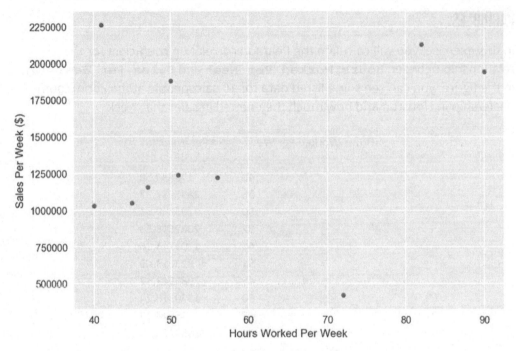

Figure 1.30: A scatterplot of Hours Worked Per Week and Sales Per Week ($)

There does not appear to be a strong linear relationship, but there does appear to be a general increase in **Sales Per Week ($)** versus **Hours Worked Per Week**.

2. Calculate the mean of each variable. You should get 57.40 for **Hours Worked Per Week** and 1,861,987.43 for **Sales Per Week ($)**. If you are not sure how to calculate the mean, refer to the *Central Tendency* section in this chapter.

3. Calculate four values for each row: the difference between each value and its mean and the square of the difference between each value and its mean. Then, find the product of these differences. You should get a table of values, as shown in the following figure:

Hours Worked Per Week	Sales Per Week ($)	x-mean(x)	(x-mean(x))^2	y-mean(y)	(y-mean(y))^2	[x-mean(x)][y-mean(y)]
40	179,480.58	-17.40	302.76	-1,682,506.85	2,830,829,303,631.31	29,275,619.21
56	2,495,037.73	-1.40	1.96	633,050.29	400,752,674,381.30	-886,270.41
50	2,285,369.51	-7.40	54.76	423,382.07	179,252,379,435.48	-3,133,027.34
82	2,367,896.33	24.60	605.16	505,908.90	255,943,812,657.79	12,445,358.88
41	1,309,745.16	-16.40	268.96	-552,242.27	304,971,527,314.18	9,056,773.27
51	623,013.69	-6.40	40.96	-1,238,973.75	1,535,055,945,620.25	7,929,431.98
45	2,989,943.37	-12.40	153.76	1,127,955.94	1,272,284,593,638.99	-13,986,653.61
90	1,970,316.24	32.60	1,062.76	108,328.81	11,735,131,115.82	3,531,519.21
47	1,845,840.39	-10.40	108.16	-16,147.04	260,726,862.48	167,929.20
72	2,553,231.33	14.60	213.16	691,243.90	477,818,127,736.76	10,092,160.92

Figure 1.31: Calculations for the Pearson correlation coefficient

4. Find the sum of the squared terms and the sum of the product of the differences. You should get 2,812.40 for **Hours Worked Per Week** (x), 7,268,904,226,420.96 for **Sales Per Week** (y), and 54,492,841.19 for the product of the differences.

5. Take the square root of the sum of the differences to get 53.03 for **Hours Worked Per Week** (x) and 2,696,090.55 for **Sales Per Week** (y).

6. Input the values into the equation from *Figure 1.32* to get 0.38. The calculation will be: 54492841.19/(53.03 * 2696090.55) = 0.38:

$$r = \frac{\sum_{i=1}^{n}(x_i - \bar{x})(y - \bar{y})}{\sqrt{\sum_{i=1}^{n}(x_i - \bar{x})^2}\ \sqrt{\sum_{i=1}^{n}(y_i - \bar{y})^2}} = \frac{54492841.32}{(53.03) * (2696090.54)} \approx 0.38$$

Figure 1.32: The final calculation of the Pearson correlation coefficient

You learned how to calculate the Pearson correlation coefficient for two variables in this exercise and got the final output of 0.38 after using the formula.

INTERPRETING AND ANALYZING THE CORRELATION COEFFICIENT

Manually calculating the correlation coefficient can be complicated. It is generally preferable to calculate it on the computer. As you will learn in *Chapter 3, SQL for Data Preparation*, it is possible to calculate the Pearson correlation coefficient using SQL.

To interpret the Pearson correlation coefficient, compare its value to the table in *Figure 1.33*. The closer to 0 the coefficient is, the weaker the correlation. The higher the absolute value of a Pearson correlation coefficient, the more likely it is that the points will fit a straight line:

Value of Correlation	Interpretation
-1.0 <= r <= -0.7	Very Strong Negative Correlation
-0.7 <= r <= -0.4	Strong Negative Correlation
-0.4 < r < -0.2	Moderate Negative Correlation
-0.2 < r < 0.2	Weak to Non-Existent Correlation
0.2 < r < 0.4	Moderate Positive Correlation
0.4 < r < 0.7	Strong Positive Correlation
0.7 < r < 1.0	Very Strong Positive Correlation

Figure 1.33: Interpreting the Pearson correlation coefficient

There are a couple of things to watch out for when examining the correlation coefficient. The first is that the correlation coefficient measures how well two variables fit a linear trend. Two variables may share a strong trend but have a relatively low Pearson correlation coefficient.

For example, look at the points in *Figure 1.34*. If you calculate the correlation coefficient for these two variables, you will find it is -0.08. However, the curve has a very clear quadratic relationship. Therefore, when you look at the correlation coefficients of bivariate data, be on the lookout for nonlinear relationships that may describe the relationship between the two variables:

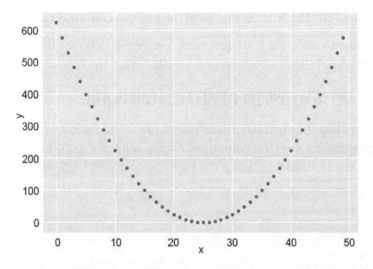

Figure 1.34: A strong nonlinear relationship with a low correlation coefficient

Another point of importance is the number of points used to calculate a correlation. It only takes two points to define a perfectly straight line. Therefore, you may be able to calculate a high correlation coefficient when there are fewer points. However, this correlation coefficient may not hold when more bivariate data is presented. As a rule of thumb, correlation coefficients calculated with fewer than 30 data points should be taken with a pinch of salt. Ideally, you should have as many good data points as you can to calculate the correlation.

Notice the use of the term "good data points." One of the recurring themes of this chapter was the negative impact of outliers on various statistics. Indeed, with bivariate data, outliers can impact the correlation coefficient. Look at the graph in *Figure 1.35*. It has 11 points, one of which is an outlier. Due to that outlier, the Pearson correlation coefficient, **r**, for the data is 0.59; however, without it, it equals 1.0. Therefore, care should be taken to remove outliers, especially from limited data.

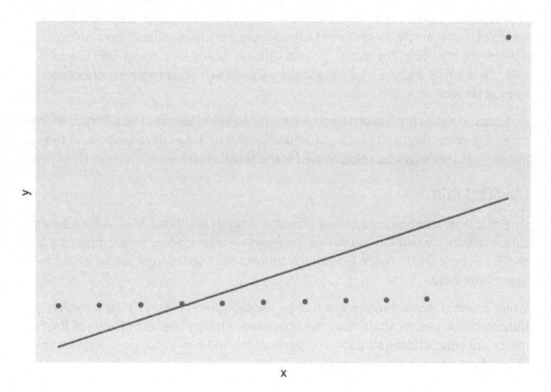

Figure 1.35: Calculating r for a scatterplot with an outlier

Finally, one of the major problems associated with calculating correlation is the logical fallacy of correlation implying causation. That is, just because **x** and **y** have a strong correlation, does not mean that **x** causes **y**. Take one example of the number of **Hours Worked Per Week** versus **Sales Per Week**. Imagine that, after adding more data points, it turns out the correlation is 0.5 between these two variables. Many beginner data professionals and experienced executives alike would conclude that more working hours cause more sales and start making their sales team work nonstop. While it is possible that working more hours causes more sales, a high correlation coefficient is not hard evidence for that.

Another possibility may be a reverse set of causation. It is possible that because of the increase in sales, there is more paperwork, therefore the need to stay longer at the office to complete it. In this scenario, working more hours may not cause more sales.

There may also exist a third factor responsible for the association between the two variables. For example, experienced salespeople work longer hours and also do a better job of selling. Therefore, the real cause is having employees with lots of sales experience, and the recommendation should be to hire more experienced sales professionals.

As a data analytics professional, you will be responsible for avoiding pitfalls such as confusing correlation and causation, and you need to think critically about all the possibilities that might be responsible for the results you see.

TIME SERIES DATA

One of the most important types of bivariate analysis is a time series. A time series is simply a bivariate relationship where the *x*-axis variable is time. An example of a time series can be found in *Figure 1.36*, which shows a time series from January 2010 to September 2012.

While at first glance it may not seem to be the case, date and time information is quantitative in nature. Understanding how things change over time is one of the most important types of analysis done in organizations and provides a lot of information about the context of the business.

All the patterns discussed in the previous section can also be found in time series data. Time series are also important in organizations because they can be indicative of when specific changes happened. Such time points can be useful in determining what caused these changes.

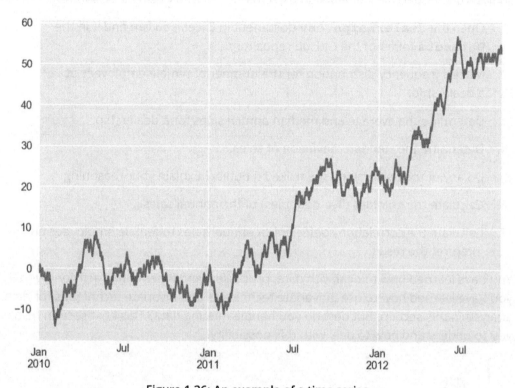

Figure 1.36: An example of a time series

You will now look at a small dataset to demonstrate how to perform basic statistical analysis.

ACTIVITY 1.02: EXPLORING DEALERSHIP SALES DATA

In this activity, you will explore a dataset using statistics. As a data analyst for ZoomZoom, a company specializing in electric vehicles, you are doing some high-level analysis on annual sales at dealerships across the country using a `.csv` file.

1. Open the `dealerships.csv` document in Excel. You can find it in the **Datasets** folder of the GitHub repository.

2. Make a frequency distribution for the number of female employees at a dealership.

3. Determine the average and median annual sales for a dealership.

4. Determine the standard deviation of sales.

5. Do any of the dealerships seem like an outlier? Explain your reasoning.

6. Calculate the quintiles (five-quantiles) of the annual sales.

7. Calculate the correlation coefficient of annual sales to female employees and interpret the result.

You have learned how to deal with data, processes, and types in this activity. Overall, you have learned how to use univariate techniques and bivariate techniques for data analysis in this section. But how do you handle missing data? This next section helps you to understand how to deal with this possibility.

> **NOTE**
>
> The solution for this activity can be found on page 432.

WORKING WITH MISSING DATA

In all the examples so far, you have been dealing with datasets that are clean and easy to decipher. However, datasets in real world are more complicated than these. One of the many problems you may have to deal with when working with datasets is missing values.

You will further learn the specifics of preparing data in *Chapter 3, SQL for Data Preparation*. However, in this section, you will learn several strategies that you can use to handle missing data. Some of your strategies include the following:

- **Deleting rows**: If a very small number of rows (that is, less than 5% of your dataset) is missing data, then the simplest solution may be to just delete the data points from your set. This would not impact your results too much.

- **Mean/median/mode imputation**: If 5% to 25% of your data for a variable is missing, another option is to take the mean, median, or mode of that column and fill in the blanks with that value. It may provide a small bias to your calculations, but it will allow you to complete more analysis without deleting valuable data.

- **Regression imputation**: If possible, you may be able to build and use a model to impute missing values. This skill may be beyond the capability of most data analysts, but if you are working with a data scientist, this option could be viable.

- **Deleting variables**: Ultimately, you cannot analyze data that does not exist. If you do not have a lot of data available, and a variable is missing most of its data, it may simply be better to remove that variable than to make too many assumptions and reach faulty conclusions.

You will also find that a decent portion of data analysis is more an art than a science. Working with missing data is one such area. With experience, you will find a combination of strategies that work well for different scenarios.

STATISTICAL SIGNIFICANCE TESTING

Often, an analyst is interested in comparing the statistical properties of two groups, or perhaps just one group before and after a change. Of course, the difference between these two groups may just be due to chance.

An example of where this comes up is in marketing A/B tests. Companies often test two different types of landing pages for a product and measure how many clicks it will receive on each of the landing pages. For example, if you make the image of a product two times larger, will this make people more likely to click it? You may find that 10% of the visitors for variation A of the landing page clicked on the product, and 11% for variation B. So, does that mean variation B is 10% better than A or is this just a result of day-to-day variance? You need a method based on statistics to determine just that.

Statistical significance testing is the method of determining whether the data that you have supports a certain hypothesis. To build such a method, there are several major parts you need to define first, see *Figure 1.40*. First, you have the test statistic you are examining. It may be a proportion, an average, the difference between two groups, or a distribution. The next necessary part is a null hypothesis, which is the idea that the results observed are the product of chance.

You will then need an **alternative hypothesis**, which is the idea that the results seen cannot be explained by chance alone. Finally, a test requires a **significance level**, which is the value the test statistic needs to take before it is decided that the null hypothesis cannot explain the difference.

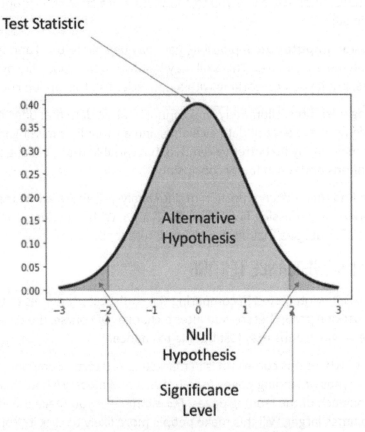

Figure 1.37: Parts of statistical significance testing

COMMON STATISTICAL SIGNIFICANCE TESTS

A statistical significance test is an important part of data analysis. In a typical data analysis scenario, data analysts will bring in data from the real world and create models that fit this data. But how accurate are these models? Can you accurately predict what will happen in the real world based on the models? To answer this question, you need to perform a statistical significance test.

All statistical significance tests have the four aspects discussed in the previous section. Different significance tests have different ways of calculating these components. Some common statistical significance tests include the following:

- **Two-sample Z-test**: This test is for determining whether the average of the two samples is different. This test assumes that both samples are drawn from a normal distribution with a known population standard deviation.

- **Two-sample T-test**: A test for determining whether the average of two samples is different when either the sample set is too small (that is, less than 30 data points per sample) or the population standard deviation is unknown. The two samples are also generally drawn from distributions assumed to be normal.

- **Pearson's Chi-squared test**: A test for determining whether the distribution of data points to categories is different than what would be expected due to chance. This is the primary test for determining whether the proportions in tests, such as those in an A/B test, are beyond what would be expected from chance.

SQL AND ANALYTICS

Throughout this chapter, you have learned about different techniques used in data analytics. All these analytics techniques inevitably lead to the storage and processing of massive data. While there are many tools in today's market that can help you with these tasks, a relational database is the most important one.

A relational database is a convenient and easy-to-understand way to store datasets. Modern relational database management systems, such as PostgreSQL databases, also provide a powerful tool for processing and analyzing data, which is SQL. Using SQL, you can clean data, transform data into more useful formats, and analyze data with statistics to find interesting patterns. The rest of this book will be dedicated to understanding how you can use SQL for these purposes productively and efficiently.

SUMMARY

Data analytics is a powerful method through which you analyze raw data to find patterns and gather predictions that help you to understand the world. The goal of analytics is to turn data into information and knowledge. To accomplish this goal, statistics, or **descriptive statistics** and **statistical significance testing**, are used to understand data.

Univariate analysis, a branch of descriptive statistics, can be utilized to understand a single variable of data. It can also be used to find outliers and the distribution of data by utilizing frequency distributions and quantiles. It is useful in finding the central tendency of a variable by calculating the mean, median, and mode of data and the dispersion of data using the range, standard deviation, and IQR.

Bivariate analysis is also used to understand the relationship between datasets. You can determine trends, changes in trends, periodic behavior, and anomalous points regarding two variables by using scatterplots. You can also use the **Pearson correlation coefficient** to measure the strength of a linear trend between the two variables. The Pearson correlation coefficient, however, is subject to scrutiny due to the outliers or the number of data points used to calculate the coefficient. Additionally, just because two variables have a strong correlation coefficient, does not mean that one variable causes the other variable to change.

Statistical significance testing also provides important information about data and allows you to determine how likely it is that certain outcomes would occur by chance. It also helps you to understand whether the changes seen between groups are of consequence rather than by chance.

As important as statistics are, they must be built on top of a significant amount of data. Both data storage and computation can be extremely demanding. Different tools have been built to utilize the power of computers for statistics. One of the most important tools is a relational database, as well as SQL. In the rest of this book, you will learn about the concept and use of SQL. This will start with the next chapter, which provides you with an introduction to relational databases and SQL. You will learn how to **Create**, **Read**, **Update**, and **Delete** (**CRUD**) a dataset.

2

THE BASICS OF SQL FOR ANALYTICS

OVERVIEW

In this chapter, you will learn about relational databases and basic data types in SQL. You will learn to read data from a database using the **SELECT** keyword and use basic keywords in a **SELECT** query. You will also learn how to create, modify, and delete tables in SQL. You will explore the purpose of SQL and learn how it can be used in an analytics workflow.

INTRODUCTION

Since the invention of the first commercial computer, the process of storing data has evolved considerably over the past 50 years. Easy access to computers plays an important role as companies and organizations have been able to change the way they work with large and complex datasets—from manual bookkeeping to intelligent and statistics-based data management. Using data, insights that would have been virtually impossible to derive 50 years ago can now be found with just a few lines of code. Two of the most important tools in this revolution are the relational database and its primary language, **Structured Query Language** (**SQL**). These two technologies have been cornerstones of data processing and continue to be the backbone of most companies that deal with substantial amounts of data. Companies use relational databases as the primary method for storing much of their data. Furthermore, companies take much of this data and put it into specialized databases called data warehouses to perform advanced analytics on their data. Virtually all these data warehouses are accessed using SQL.

Relational databases require data to be organized into a fixed format and processed following a predefined algorithm. In recent years, there has been an emergence of NoSQL databases. Originally created as an alternative way of data storage, these NoSQL databases utilize technologies that are different from relational operations and SQL and can achieve what traditional relational databases cannot do or are not good at, such as distributed compute/storage, unformatted data (such as tweets) processing, and non-atomic read/write.

However, these NoSQL databases usually focus on a specific usage scenario and have yet to provide a more generic platform that can meet the needs of the majority of common database usage patterns. As such, these databases quickly evolved from "No SQL" to "Not Only SQL," signifying that they are a part of a larger ecosystem for data management, together with relational databases and SQL.

Compared to NoSQL databases, relational databases have several advantages that make them the center of data management ecosystems. The core reason is that relational databases maintain a good balance of features and performances for a wide variety of data operations, which makes them good candidates for a generic data management platform. The second reason is that all relational databases use SQL, which has a solid mathematical theory behind it and is easy to learn. In general, relational databases and SQL serve as the best place to start your data analytics journey.

Most people will find that SQL alone is enough for their needs. Only a small fraction of people will need the functionalities provided by a NoSQL database. But even for the latter, SQL will still serve as a great foundation for data analytical purposes.

> **NOTE**
>
> It is assumed that every person following this book has had some basic exposure to SQL. However, for those users who have very limited exposure, or have not used it for some time, this chapter will provide a basic refresher of what relational databases and SQL are, along with a basic review of SQL operations and syntax. You will also go over practice exercises to help reinforce these concepts.

To begin with, it is important to understand data and its characteristics.

THE WORLD OF DATA

Start with a simple question: what is data? Data is the recorded description or measurements of something in the real world. For example, a list of heights is data; that is, height is a measure of the distance between a person's head and their feet. The data is used to describe a unit of observation. In the case of these heights, a person is a unit of observation.

As you can imagine, there is a lot of data you can gather to describe a person—including their age, weight, and smoking preferences. One or more of these measurements used to describe a specific unit of observation is called a data point, and each measurement in a data point is called a variable (often referred to as a feature). When you have several data points together, you have a dataset. For example, you may have Person A, who is a 45-year-old smoker, and Person B, who is a 24-year-old non-smoker. Here, age is a variable. The age of Person A is one measurement and the age of Person B is another. 45 and 24 are the values of measurement. A compilation of data points with measurements such as ages, weights, and smoking trends of various people is called a dataset.

TYPES OF DATA

Data can be broken down into three main categories: structured, semi-structured, and unstructured.

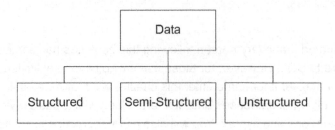

Figure 2.1: The classification of types of data

Structured data has an atomic definition for all the variables, such as the data type, value range, and meaning for values. In many cases, even the order of variables is clearly defined and strictly enforced. For example, the record of a student in a school registration card contains an identification number, name, and date of birth, each with a clear meaning and stored in order.

Unstructured data, on the other hand, does not have a definition as clear as structured data, and thus is harder to extract and parse. It may be some binary blob that comes from electronic devices, such as video and audio files. It may also be a collection of natural input tokens (words, emojis), such as social network posts and human speech.

Semi-structured data usually does not have a pre-defined format and meaning, but each of its measurement values is tagged with the definition of that measurement. For example, all houses have an address. But some may have a basement, or a garage, or both. It is also possible that owners may add upgrades that cannot be expected at the time when this house's information is recorded. All components in this data have clear definitions, but it is difficult to come up with a pre-defined list for all the possible variables, especially for the variables that may come up in the future. Thus, this house data is semi-structured.

RELATIONAL DATABASES AND SQL

A relational database is a database that utilizes the relational model of data. The relational model, invented by Dr. Edgar F. Codd in 1970, organizes data as relations, or sets of tuple. Tuple is the mathematical term for a series of attributes grouped together in a particular order. A more common (and more practical) name for a tuple is a record. Each record consists of a series of attributes that generally describe the record.

For instance, a fast-moving consumer goods company wants to track its customers. They can save the customer information in a relation called `customer_info`. Each record in this relation contains details about one customer. The attributes in each record include information such as the customer's last name, first name, age, date of signup, and delivery address. This relationship and its first two records will look like this:

ID	Last Name	First Name	Age	...
1	Smith	John	27	...
2	Higgins	Mary	53	...

Figure 2.2: An example customer_info relation

As you can see, each relation is indeed a two-dimensional table that looks like an Excel spreadsheet. Thus, when implemented in a relational database, these relations are called tables. Each table is made up of rows and columns. Each row of the table is a record, and the attributes are represented as columns of the table. There cannot be duplicate columns and the columns must follow the same order in all the rows. Every column also has a data type that describes the type of data in the column.

While not technically required, most tables in a relational database have a column (sometimes a group of columns) referred to as the primary key, which uniquely identifies a row of the database. In the example shown in *Figure* 2.2, each row contains a column called ID. This record, as the name suggests, is an attribute that can be used to uniquely identify this record. It is known as a relational key. In all other columns, you can have data duplicated across different rows. But in the primary key column(s), the data must be unique.

Most of the operations in a relational database, and in all data management systems, are organized around tables and the data inside them. They generally can be categorized into four groups—create, read, update, and delete. To utilize any data, you must create the definition of the dataset first, then create the individual data records one by one and put them into the dataset. Once a dataset is created, you can read all aspects of information from it. If there is any change to the data, you need to update the affected records.

Finally, when you do not need the data anymore, you will want to delete the records to save storage costs and increase performance. If you do not need this dataset, you can even delete the whole dataset by removing its definition from the database. These operations, by the order of each operation's position in a dataset's lifecycle, are generally called CRUD. **CRUD** stands for **create**, **read**, **update**, and **delete**.

In relational databases, all these operations are carried out using SQL. You will learn all the related SQL statements in this and the upcoming chapters.

> **NOTE**
>
> Virtually all relational databases that use SQL deviate from the relational model in some basic ways. For example, not every table has a specified relational key. Additionally, a relational model does not technically allow duplicate rows, but you can have duplicate rows in a relational database. These differences are minor and will not matter to most readers of this book.

ADVANTAGES AND DISADVANTAGES OF SQL DATABASES

As discussed in the previous sections, since relations are collections of records that have clearly defined attributes in a defined order, they are considered structured data. Relational databases are the main tool used for storing and processing structured data.

Since the release of Oracle Database in 1979, SQL has become an industry standard for structured data in nearly all computer applications—and for good reasons. SQL databases provide a range of advantages that make them the first choice for many applications:

- Intuitive: Relations represented as tables serve as a common data structure that almost everyone understands. As such, working with and reasoning about relational databases is much easier than doing so with other models.

- Efficient: Using a technique known as normalization, relational databases allow the representation of data without unnecessarily repeating it. As such, relational databases can represent large amounts of information while utilizing less space. This reduced storage footprint also allows the database to reduce operation costs, making well-designed relational databases quick to process.

- Declarative: SQL is a declarative language, meaning that when you write code, you only need to tell the computer what data you want, and the database takes care of determining how to execute the SQL code. You never have to worry about telling the computer how to access and pull data from the table.

- Robust: Most popular SQL databases have a property known as **atomicity**, **consistency**, **isolation**, and **durability** (**ACID**) compliance, which guarantees the validity of the data, even if the hardware fails.

That said, there are still some downsides to SQL databases, which are as follows:

- Relatively lower specificity: While SQL is declarative, its functionality can often be limited to what has already been programmed into it. Although most popular relational database software is updated constantly with new functionality being built all the time, it can be difficult to process and work with data structures and algorithms that are not programmed into a relational database.

- Limited scalability: SQL databases are incredibly robust, but this robustness comes at a cost. As the amount of information you have doubles, the cost of resources increases even more than double. When very large volumes of information are involved, other data stores such as NoSQL databases may be efficient.

- Sacrificing performance for consistency: Relational databases are generally designed for consistency, which means they will take extra steps to make sure multiple users will see the same data when they try to access/modify the data at the same time. To achieve this, relational databases implement some complex checking and data locking mechanisms into their operational logic. For usage scenarios that do not require consistency, especially for high-performance operations like search engines or social network sites, this is an unnecessary burden and will hurt the performance of the application.

- Lack of semi-structured and unstructured data processing ability: The fundamental theory that SQL is built on is the relational theory, which, by definition, handles only structured data. Relational databases can store and fetch semi-structured and unstructured data. But processing this data requires processing power and functionalities that are beyond standard SQL. Later chapters of this book will cover some examples of this type of processing.

POSTGRESQL RELATIONAL DATABASE MANAGEMENT SYSTEM (RDBMS)

In any production computer system, data constantly flows in and out and is eventually stored on storage hardware. It must be properly received, stored with the location recorded so that it can be retrieved later, retrieved as requested by the user, and sent out in the appropriate format. These tasks are handled by software commonly referred to as a **relational database management system** (**RDBMS**). SQL is the language utilized by users of an RDBMS to access and interact with a relational database.

There are many different types of RDBMS. They can be loosely categorized into two groups, commercial and open source. These RDBMSs differ slightly in the way they operate on data and even some minor parts in SQL syntax. There is an **American National Standards Institute (ANSI)** standard for SQL, which is largely followed by all RDBMSs. But each RDBMS may also have its own interpretations and extensions of the standard.

In this book, you will use one of the most popular open-source RDBMSs, PostgreSQL. You have installed a copy of PostgreSQL in the activities described in the preface. During that activity, you installed and enabled a PostgreSQL server application on your local machine. Your local machine's hard disk is the storage device on which data is stored. Once installation is complete, the PostgreSQL server software will be running in the backend of your computer and monitoring and handling requests from the user. Users communicate with the server software via a client tool. There are many popular client tools that you can choose from. PostgreSQL comes with two tools, a graphic user interface called **pgAdmin** (sometimes called pgAdmin4), and a command-line tool called psql. You used psql in the *Preface*. For the rest of this book, you will use **pgAdmin** for SQL operations.

NOTE

In *Exercise 2.01*, *Running Your First SELECT Query*, you will learn how to run a simple SQL query via pgAdmin in a sample database that is provided in this book, which is called the **ZoomZoom** database. But before the exercise, here is an explanation of how tables are organized in PostgreSQL and what tables the **ZoomZoom** database has.

In PostgreSQL, tables are collected in common collections in databases called schemas. One or several schemas form a database. For example, a **products** table can be placed in the **analytics** schema. Tables are usually referred to when writing queries in the format **[schema].[table]**. For example, a **products** table in the **analytics** schema would generally be referred to as **analytics.products**.

However, there is also a special schema called the public schema. This is a default schema. If you do not explicitly mention a schema when operating on a table, the database will assume the table exists in the **public** schema. For example, when you specify the **products** table without a schema name, the database will assume you are referring to the **public.products** table.

Here is the list of the tables in the **sqlda** database, as well as a brief description for each table:

- **closest_dealerships**: Contains the distance between each customer and dealership

- **countries**: An empty table with columns describing countries

- **customer_sales**: Contains raw data in a semi-structured format of some sales records

- **customer_survey**: Contains feedback with ratings from the customers

- **customers**: Contains detailed information for all customers

- **dealerships**: Contains detailed information for all dealerships

- **emails**: Contains the details of emails sent to each customer

- **products**: Contains the products sold by ZoomZoom

- **public_transportation_by_zip**: Contains the availability measure of public transportation in different zip codes in the United States

- **sales**: Contains the sales records of ZoomZoom on a per customer per product basis

- **salespeople**: Contains the details of salespeople in all the dealerships

- **top_cities_data**: Contains some aggregation data for customer counts in different cities

> **NOTE**
>
> Though you may run the examples provided in this book using another RDBMS, such as MySQL, it is not guaranteed this will work as described. To make sure your results match the text, it is highly recommended that you use PostgreSQL.

EXERCISE 2.01: RUNNING YOUR FIRST SELECT QUERY

In this exercise, you will use **pgAdmin** to connect to a sample database called ZoomZoom on your PostgreSQL server and run a basic SQL query.

> ### NOTE
>
> You should have set up the PostgreSQL working environment while studying the preface. If you set up your PostgreSQL on a Windows or Mac, the installation wizard would have installed pgAdmin on your machine. If you set up your PostgreSQL on a Linux machine, you will need to go to the official PostgreSQL website to download and install pgAdmin, which is a separate package. Once set up, the user interface of pgAdmin is consistent across different platforms. This book will use screenshots from pgAdmin version 14 installed on a Windows machine. Your pgAdmin interface should be very similar regardless of your operating system.

Perform the following steps to complete the exercise:

1. Go to **Start** > **PostgreSQL 14** > **pgAdmin 4**. The pgAdmin interface should pop up. Enter your user password when requested to do so. You will be directed to the pgAdmin **Welcome** page. If you are a first-time user, you will be prompted to set a password. Make sure to note down the password.

Figure 2.3: pgAdmin initial interface

2. Click on the **Servers** in the left panel to expand its contents. You should see an entry called **PostgreSQL 14**. This is the PostgreSQL RDBMS installed on your machine. Click to open its content. Enter your user password when requested to do so.

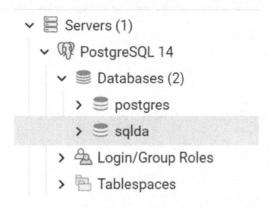

Figure 2.4: Databases in PostgreSQL 14 server

You should see a **Databases entry** under **PostgreSQL 14**, which contains two databases, **PostgreSQL default database postgres** and a sample database called **sqlda**. A database is a collection of multiple tables. The **sqlda** database is the database that you imported in this book's preface after installing PostgreSQL.

This database has been created with a sample dataset for a fictional company called ZoomZoom, which specializes in car and electronic scooter retail. ZoomZoom sells via both the internet and its fleet of dealerships. Each dealership has a salesperson. Customers will purchase a product and optionally participate in a survey. Periodically, ZoomZoom will also send out promotional emails with meaningful subjects to customers. The dates that the email is sent, opened, and clicked, as well as the email subject and the recipient customer are recorded.

3. Click the **sqlda** database to open its contents. Open **Schemas** > **public** > **Tables**. This shows you all the tables in the public schema.

4. Right-click on the **sqlda** database and choose the **Query Tool** option to open the SQL query editor. You will see the **query editor** on the right side of the pgAdmin interface.

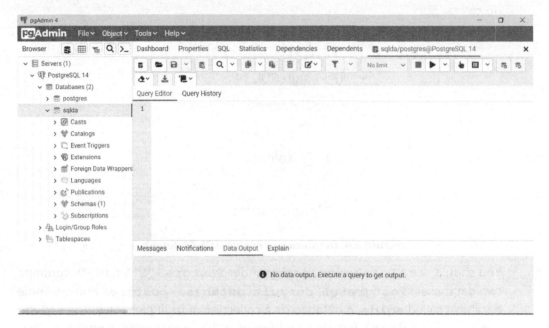

Figure 2.5: PostgreSQL SQL editor

5. Paste or type out the following query in the terminal. Click on the **Execute** button (marked with a red circle in the following screenshot) to execute the SQL:

```
SELECT first_name
FROM customers
WHERE state='AZ'
ORDER BY first_name;
```

The result of this SQL appears below the query editor:

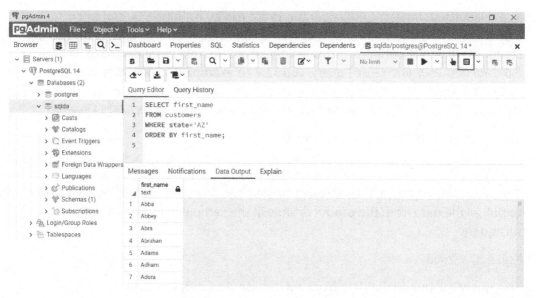

Figure 2.6: Sample SQL and result

NOTE

In this screenshot, as well as many screenshots later in this book, only the first few rows are shown due to the number of rows returned exceeding the number of rows that can be displayed in this book. In addition, there is a semicolon at the end of this statement. This semicolon is not a part of the SQL statement, but it tells the PostgreSQL server that this is the end of the current statement. It is also widely used to separate several SQL statements that are grouped together and should be executed one after another.

The SQL query you just executed in this exercise is a **SELECT** statement. You will learn further details about this statement in the next section.

SELECT STATEMENT

In a relational database, CRUD operations are run by running SQL statements. A SQL statement is a command that utilizes certain SQL keywords and follows certain standards to specify what result you expect from the relational database. In *Exercise 2.01, Running your first SELECT query*, you saw an example SQL **SELECT** statement. **SELECT** is probably the most common SQL statement; it retrieves data from a database. This operation is almost exclusively done using the **SELECT** keyword.

The most basic **SELECT** query follows this pattern:

```
SELECT...FROM <table_name>;
```

This query is a way to pull data from a single table. In its simplest form, if you want to pull all the data from the products table in the sample database, simply use this query:

```
SELECT * FROM products;
```

This query will pull all the data from a database. The output will be:

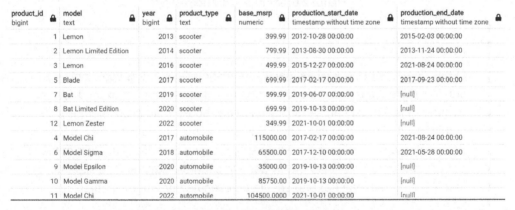

product_id bigint	model text	year bigint	product_type text	base_msrp numeric	production_start_date timestamp without time zone	production_end_date timestamp without time zone
1	Lemon	2013	scooter	399.99	2012-10-28 00:00:00	2015-02-03 00:00:00
2	Lemon Limited Edition	2014	scooter	799.99	2013-08-30 00:00:00	2013-11-24 00:00:00
3	Lemon	2016	scooter	499.99	2015-12-27 00:00:00	2021-08-24 00:00:00
5	Blade	2017	scooter	699.99	2017-02-17 00:00:00	2017-09-23 00:00:00
7	Bat	2019	scooter	599.99	2019-06-07 00:00:00	[null]
8	Bat Limited Edition	2020	scooter	699.99	2019-10-13 00:00:00	[null]
12	Lemon Zester	2022	scooter	349.99	2021-10-01 00:00:00	[null]
4	Model Chi	2017	automobile	115000.00	2017-02-17 00:00:00	2021-08-24 00:00:00
6	Model Sigma	2018	automobile	65500.00	2017-12-10 00:00:00	2021-05-28 00:00:00
9	Model Epsilon	2020	automobile	35000.00	2019-10-13 00:00:00	[null]
10	Model Gamma	2020	automobile	85750.00	2019-10-13 00:00:00	[null]
11	Model Chi	2022	automobile	104500.0000	2021-10-01 00:00:00	[null]

Figure 2.7: Simple SELECT statement

It is important to understand the syntax of the **SELECT** query in a bit more detail.

> **NOTE**
>
> In the statements used in this section, SQL keywords such as **SELECT** and **FROM** are in uppercase, while the names of tables and columns are in lowercase. SQL statements (and keywords) are case insensitive. However, when you write your own SQL, it is generally recommended to follow certain conventions on the usage of case and indentation. It will help you understand the structure and purpose of the statement.

Within the **SELECT** clause, the * symbol is shorthand for returning all the columns from a database. The semicolon operator (;) is used to tell the computer it has reached the end of the query, much as a period is used for a normal sentence. To return only specific columns from a query, you can simply replace the asterisk (*) with the names of the columns to be returned in the order you want them to be returned. For example, if you wanted to return the **product_id** column followed by the **model** column of the products table, you would write the following query:

```
SELECT product_id, model FROM products;
```

The output will be as follows:

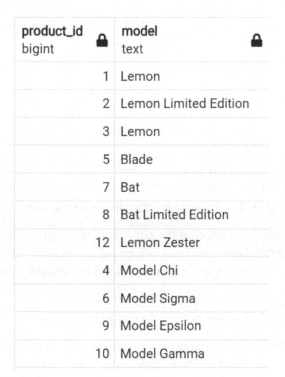

product_id 🔒 bigint	model 🔒 text
1	Lemon
2	Lemon Limited Edition
3	Lemon
5	Blade
7	Bat
8	Bat Limited Edition
12	Lemon Zester
4	Model Chi
6	Model Sigma
9	Model Epsilon
10	Model Gamma

Figure 2.8: SELECT statement with column names

To return the **model** column first and the **product_id** column second, you would write this:

```
SELECT model, product_id FROM products;
```

The output will be the following:

model text	product_id bigint
Lemon	1
Lemon Limited Edition	2
Lemon	3
Blade	5
Bat	7
Bat Limited Edition	8
Lemon Zester	12
Model Chi	4
Model Sigma	6
Model Epsilon	9
Model Gamma	10

Figure 2.9: SELECT statement with column names versus Figure 2.8

It is important to note that although the columns are output in the order you defined in the **SELECT** query, the rows will be returned in no specific order. You will learn how to output the result in a certain order in the **ORDER BY** section later in this chapter.

A **SELECT** query can be broken down into five parts:

1. **Operation**: The first part of a query describes what is going to be displayed. In this case, the word **SELECT** is followed by the names of columns combined with functions.

2. **Data**: The next part of the query is the data, which is the **FROM** keyword, followed by one or more tables connected with reserved keywords indicating which data should be scanned for filtering, selection, and calculation.

3. **Condition**: This is a part of the query that filters the data to show only rows that meet conditions usually indicated with **WHERE**.

4. **Grouping**: This is a special clause that takes the rows of a data source and assembles them together using a key created by a **GROUP BY** clause, and then calculates an output for all rows with the same value in the **GROUP BY** key. You will learn more about this step in *Chapter 4, Aggregate Functions for Data Analysis*.

5. **Postprocessing**: This is a part of the query that takes the results of the data and formats them by sorting and limiting the data, often using keywords such as **ORDER BY** and **LIMIT**.

Take, for instance, the statement that you ran in *Exercise 2.01, Running your first SELECT query*. Suppose that, from the **customers** table, you wanted to retrieve the first name of all customers in the state of Arizona. You also want these names listed alphabetically. You could write the following **SELECT** query to retrieve this information:

```
SELECT first_name
FROM customers
WHERE state='AZ'
ORDER BY first_name;
```

The first few rows of the result look like this:

| first_name 🔒 |
text
Abba
Abbey
Abra
Abrahan
Adams
Adham
Adora
Adore
Adrianna
Agnese

Figure 2.10: Sample SELECT statement

The operation of the query you executed in the preceding exercise follows a sequence:

1. Start with the data in the **customers** table.

2. Filter the **customers** table to where the **state** column equals **AZ**.

3. Capture the **first_name** column from the filtered table.

4. Check the **first_name** column, which is ordered alphabetically.

This demonstrates how a query can be broken down into a series of steps for the database to process. This breakdown is based on the keywords and patterns found in a **SELECT** query. There are many keywords that you can use while writing a **SELECT** query. To learn the keywords, you will start with the **WHERE** clause in the next section.

THE WHERE CLAUSE

The **WHERE** clause is a piece of conditional logic that limits the amount of data returned. You can use the **WHERE** clause to specify conditions based on which the **SELECT** statement will retrieve specific rows. In a **SELECT** statement, you will usually find this clause placed after the **FROM** clause.

The condition in the **WHERE** clause is generally a Boolean statement that can either be true or false for every row. In the case of numeric columns, these Boolean statements can use equals (**=**), greater than (**>**), or less than (**<**) operators to compare the columns against a value.

For example, say you want to see the model names of the products with the model year of 2014 from the sample dataset. You would write the following query:

```
SELECT model
FROM products
WHERE year=2014;
```

The output of this SQL is:

Figure 2.11: Simple WHERE clause

You were able to filter out the products matching a certain criterion using the **WHERE** clause. If you want a list of products before 2014, you could simply modify the **WHERE** clause to say **year<2014**. But what if you want to filter out rows using multiple criteria at once? Alternatively, you might also want to filter out rows that match either of two or more conditions. You can do this by adding an **AND** or **OR** clause in the queries.

THE AND/OR CLAUSE

The previous query, which outputs *Figure 2.11*, had only one condition. However, you might be interested in multiple conditions being met at once. For this, you need to put multiple statements together using **AND** or **OR** clauses. The **AND** clause helps us retrieve only the rows that match two or more conditions. The **OR** clause, on the other hand, retrieves rows that match one (or many) of the conditions in a set of two or more conditions.

For example, you want to return models that were not only built in 2014, but also have a **Manufacturer's Suggested Retail Price** (**MSRP**) of less than $1,000. You can write the following query:

```
SELECT model, year, base_msrp
FROM products
WHERE year=2014
AND base_msrp<=1000;
```

The result will look like this:

model text	year bigint	base_msrp numeric
Lemon Limited Edition	2014	799.99

Figure 2.12: WHERE clause with AND operator

Here, you can see that the **year** of the product is 2014 and **base_msrp** is lower than $1,000. This is exactly what you are looking for.

Suppose you want to return any models that were released in the **year** 2014 or had a **product type** of **automobile**. You would write the following query:

```
SELECT Model, product_type
FROM products
WHERE year=2014
OR product_type='automobile';
```

The result is as follows:

model text	product_type text
Lemon Limited Edition	scooter
Model Chi	automobile
Model Sigma	automobile
Model Epsilon	automobile
Model Gamma	automobile
Model Chi	automobile

Figure 2.13: WHERE clause with OR operator

You already know that there is one product, **Lemon Limited Edition**, with a **year** of **2014**. The rest of the products in the example have been listed with **automobile** as the **product_type**. You are seeing the combined dataset of **year=2014** together with **product_type='automobile'**. That is exactly what the **OR** operator does.

When using more than one **AND** or **OR** condition, you may need to use parentheses to separate and position pieces of logic together. This will ensure that your query works as expected and is as readable as possible. For example, if you wanted to get all products with models between the years **2016** and **2018**, as well as any products that are scooters, you could write the following:

```
SELECT *
FROM products
WHERE year> 2016
AND year<2018
OR product_type='scooter';
```

The result contains all the scooters as well as an automobile that has a year between **2016** and **2018**.

product_id bigint	model text	year bigint	product_type text	base_msrp numeric	production_start_date timestamp without time zone	production_end_date timestamp without time zone
1	Lemon	2013	scooter	399.99	2012-10-28 00:00:00	2015-02-03 00:00:00
2	Lemon Limited Edition	2014	scooter	799.99	2013-08-30 00:00:00	2013-11-24 00:00:00
3	Lemon	2016	scooter	499.99	2015-12-27 00:00:00	2021-08-24 00:00:00
5	Blade	2017	scooter	699.99	2017-02-17 00:00:00	2017-09-23 00:00:00
7	Bat	2019	scooter	599.99	2019-06-07 00:00:00	[null]
8	Bat Limited Edition	2020	scooter	699.99	2019-10-13 00:00:00	[null]
12	Lemon Zester	2022	scooter	349.99	2021-10-01 00:00:00	[null]
4	Model Chi	2017	automobile	115000.00	2017-02-17 00:00:00	2021-08-24 00:00:00

Figure 2.14: WHERE clause with multiple AND/OR operators

However, to clarify the **WHERE** clause, it would be preferable to write the following:

```
SELECT *
FROM products
WHERE (year>2016 AND year<2018)
OR product_type='scooter';
```

You will receive the same result as above. The logic of this SQL is easier to understand. You will find that the **AND** and **OR** clauses are used quite a lot in SQL queries. However, in some scenarios, they can be tedious, especially when there are more efficient alternatives for such scenarios.

THE IN/NOT IN CLAUSE

Now that you can write queries that match multiple conditions, you also might want to refine your criteria by retrieving rows that contain (or do not contain) one or more specific values in one or more of their columns. This is where the **IN** and **NOT IN** clauses come in handy.

For example, you are interested in returning all models from the years **2014**, **2016**, or **2019**. You could write a query such as this:

```
SELECT model, year
FROM products
WHERE year = 2014
OR year = 2016
OR year = 2019;
```

The result will look like the following image, showing three models from these three years:

model text	year bigint
Lemon Limited Edition	2014
Lemon	2016
Bat	2019

Figure 2.15: WHERE clause with multiple OR operator

However, this is tedious to write. Using **IN**, you can instead write the following:

```
SELECT model, year
FROM products
WHERE year IN (2014, 2016, 2019);
```

This is much cleaner and makes it easier to understand what is going on. It will also return the same result as above.

Conversely, you can also use the **NOT IN** clause to return all the values that are not in a list of values. For instance, if you wanted all the products that were not produced in the years **2014**, **2016**, and **2019**, you could write the following:

```
SELECT model, year
FROM products
WHERE year NOT IN (2014, 2016, 2019);
```

Now you see the products that are in years other than the three mentioned in the SQL statement.

model text	year bigint
Lemon	2013
Blade	2017
Bat Limited Edition	2020
Lemon Zester	2022
Model Chi	2017
Model Sigma	2018
Model Epsilon	2020
Model Gamma	2020
Model Chi	2022

Figure 2.16: WHERE clause with the NOT IN operator

In the next section, you will learn how to use the **ORDER BY** clause in your queries.

ORDER BY CLAUSE

SQL queries will order rows as the database finds them if they are not given specific instructions to do otherwise. For many use cases, this is acceptable. However, you will often want to see rows in a specific order.

For instance, you want to see all the products listed by the date when they were first produced, from earliest to latest. The method for doing this in SQL would be using the **ORDER BY** clause as follows:

```
SELECT model, production_start_date
FROM products
ORDER BY production_start_date;
```

As shown in the screenshot below, the products are ordered by the **production_start_date** field.

model text	production_start_date timestamp without time zone
Lemon	2012-10-28 00:00:00
Lemon Limited Edition	2013-08-30 00:00:00
Lemon	2015-12-27 00:00:00
Blade	2017-02-17 00:00:00
Model Chi	2017-02-17 00:00:00
Model Sigma	2017-12-10 00:00:00
Bat	2019-06-07 00:00:00
Model Epsilon	2019-10-13 00:00:00
Bat Limited Edition	2019-10-13 00:00:00
Model Gamma	2019-10-13 00:00:00
Model Chi	2021-10-01 00:00:00

Figure 2.17: SELECT statement with ORDER BY

If an order sequence is not explicitly mentioned, the rows will be returned in ascending order. Ascending order simply means the rows will be ordered from the smallest value to the highest value of the chosen column or columns. In the case of things such as text, this means arranging in alphabetical order. You can make the ascending order explicit by using the **ASC** keyword. For the last query, this could be achieved by writing the following:

```
SELECT model
FROM products
ORDER BY production_start_date ASC;
```

This SQL will return the same result in the same order as the SQL above.

If you want to extract data in descending order, you can use the **DESC** keyword. If you wanted to fetch manufactured models ordered from newest to oldest, you would write the following query:

```
SELECT model, production_start_date
FROM products
ORDER BY production_start_date DESC;
```

The result will be sorted by descending order of **production_start_date**, latest first.

model text	production_start_date timestamp without time zone
Model Chi	2021-10-01 00:00:00
Lemon Zester	2021-10-01 00:00:00
Bat Limited Edition	2019-10-13 00:00:00
Model Epsilon	2019-10-13 00:00:00
Model Gamma	2019-10-13 00:00:00
Bat	2019-06-07 00:00:00
Model Sigma	2017-12-10 00:00:00
Model Chi	2017-02-17 00:00:00
Blade	2017-02-17 00:00:00
Lemon	2015-12-27 00:00:00
Lemon Limited Edition	2013-08-30 00:00:00

Figure 2.18: SELECT statement with ORDER BY DESC

Also, instead of writing the name of the column you want to order by, you can refer to the position number of that column in the query's **SELECT** clause. For instance, you wanted to return all the models in the **products** table ordered by **product ID**. You could write the following:

```
SELECT product_id, model
FROM products
ORDER BY product_id;
```

The result will be like the following:

product_id bigint	model text
1	Lemon
2	Lemon Limited Edition
3	Lemon
4	Model Chi
5	Blade
6	Model Sigma
7	Bat
8	Bat Limited Edition
9	Model Epsilon
10	Model Gamma
11	Model Chi

Figure 2.19: SELECT statement with numbered ORDER BY

However, because **product_id** is the first column in the **SELECT** statement, you could instead write the following:

```
SELECT product_id, model
FROM products
ORDER BY 1;
```

This SQL will return the same result as *Figure 2.19*.

Finally, you can order by multiple columns by adding additional columns after **ORDER BY**, separated with commas. For instance, you want to order all the rows in the table first by the **year** of the model from newest to oldest, and then by the **MSRP** from least to greatest. You would then write the following query:

```
SELECT *
FROM products
ORDER BY year DESC, base_msrp ASC;
```

The following is the output of the preceding code:

product_id bigint	model text	year bigint	product_type text	base_msrp numeric	production_start_date timestamp without time zone	production_end_date timestamp without time zone
12	Lemon Zester	2022	scooter	349.99	2021-10-01 00:00:00	[null]
11	Model Chi	2022	automobile	104500.0000	2021-10-01 00:00:00	[null]
8	Bat Limited Edition	2020	scooter	699.99	2019-10-13 00:00:00	[null]
9	Model Epsilon	2020	automobile	35000.00	2019-10-13 00:00:00	[null]
10	Model Gamma	2020	automobile	85750.00	2019-10-13 00:00:00	[null]
7	Bat	2019	scooter	599.99	2019-06-07 00:00:00	[null]
6	Model Sigma	2018	automobile	65500.00	2017-12-10 00:00:00	2021-05-28 00:00:00
5	Blade	2017	scooter	699.99	2017-02-17 00:00:00	2017-09-23 00:00:00
4	Model Chi	2017	automobile	115000.00	2017-02-17 00:00:00	2021-08-24 00:00:00
3	Lemon	2016	scooter	499.99	2015-12-27 00:00:00	2021-08-24 00:00:00
2	Lemon Limited Edition	2014	scooter	799.99	2013-08-30 00:00:00	2013-11-24 00:00:00

Figure 2.20: Ordering multiple columns using ORDER BY

In the next section, you will learn about the **LIMIT** keyword in SQL.

THE LIMIT CLAUSE

Most tables in SQL databases tend to be quite large and, therefore, returning every single row is unnecessary. Sometimes, you may want only the first few rows. For this scenario, the **LIMIT** keyword comes in handy. Imagine that you wanted to only get the model of the first five products that were produced by the company. You could get this by using the following query:

```
SELECT model
FROM products
ORDER BY production_start_date
LIMIT 5;
```

The following is the output of the preceding query:

model text
Lemon
Lemon Limited Edition
Lemon
Blade
Model Chi

Figure 2.21: Query with LIMIT

When you are not familiar with a table or query, it is a common concern that running a **SELECT** statement will accidentally return many rows, which can take up a lot of time and machine bandwidth. As a common precaution, you should use the **LIMIT** keyword to only retrieve a small number of rows when you run the query for the first time.

IS NULL/IS NOT NULL CLAUSE

Often, some entries in a column may be missing. This could be for a variety of reasons. Perhaps the data was not collected or not available at the time that the data was collected. Perhaps the absence of a value is representative of a certain state in the row and provides valuable information.

Whatever the reason, you are often interested in finding rows where the data is not filled in for a certain value. In SQL, blank values are often represented by the **NULL** value. For instance, in the **products** table, the **production_end_date** column having a **NULL** value indicates that the product is still being made. In this case, to list all products that are still being made, you can use the following query:

```
SELECT *
FROM products
WHERE production_end_date IS NULL;
```

The following is the output of the query:

product_id bigint	model text	year bigint	product_type text	base_msrp numeric	production_start_date timestamp without time zone	production_end_date timestamp without time zone
7	Bat	2019	scooter	599.99	2019-06-07 00:00:00	[null]
8	Bat Limited Edition	2020	scooter	699.99	2019-10-13 00:00:00	[null]
12	Lemon Zester	2022	scooter	349.99	2021-10-01 00:00:00	[null]
9	Model Epsilon	2020	automobile	35000.00	2019-10-13 00:00:00	[null]
10	Model Gamma	2020	automobile	85750.00	2019-10-13 00:00:00	[null]
11	Model Chi	2022	automobile	104500.0000	2021-10-01 00:00:00	[null]

Figure 2.22: Products with NULL production_end_date

If you are only interested in products that are not being produced anymore, you can use the **IS NOT NULL** clause, as shown in the following query:

```
SELECT *
FROM products
WHERE production_end_date IS NOT NULL;
```

The following is the output of the code:

product_id bigint	model text	year bigint	product_type text	base_msrp numeric	production_start_date timestamp without time zone	production_end_date timestamp without time zone
1	Lemon	2013	scooter	399.99	2012-10-28 00:00:00	2015-02-03 00:00:00
2	Lemon Limited Edition	2014	scooter	799.99	2013-08-30 00:00:00	2013-11-24 00:00:00
3	Lemon	2016	scooter	499.99	2015-12-27 00:00:00	2021-08-24 00:00:00
5	Blade	2017	scooter	699.99	2017-02-17 00:00:00	2017-09-23 00:00:00
4	Model Chi	2017	automobile	115000.00	2017-02-17 00:00:00	2021-08-24 00:00:00
6	Model Sigma	2018	automobile	65500.00	2017-12-10 00:00:00	2021-05-28 00:00:00

Figure 2.23: Products with non-NULL production_end_date

Now, you will learn how to use these new keywords in the following exercise.

EXERCISE 2.02: QUERYING THE SALESPEOPLE TABLE USING BASIC KEYWORDS IN A SELECT QUERY

In this exercise, you will create various queries using basic keywords in a **SELECT** query. For instance, after a few days at your new job, you finally get access to the company database. Your boss has asked you to help a sales manager who does not know SQL particularly well. The sales manager would like a couple of different lists of salespeople.

First, you need to generate a list of the first 10 salespersons hired by dealership 17, that is, the salespersons with oldest **hire_date**, ordered by hiring date, with the oldest first. Second, you need to get all salespeople that were hired in 2021 and 2022 but have not been terminated, that is, the **hire_date** must be later than 2021-01-01, and **terminiation_date** is **NULL**, ordered by hire date, with the latest first. Finally, the manager wants to find a salesperson that was hired in 2021 but only remembers that their first name starts with "Nic." He has asked you to help find this person. You will use your SQL skill to help the manager to achieve these goals.

> **NOTE**
>
> For all future exercises in this book, you will be using pgAdmin 4.

Perform the following steps to complete the exercise:

1. Open pgAdmin, connect to the **sqlda** database, and open SQL query editor.

2. Examine the schema for the **salespeople** table from the schema drop-down list. Get familiar with the names of the columns in the following figure:

Figure 2.24: Schema of the salespeople table

3. Execute the following query to get the usernames of **salespeople** from **dealership_id** 17, sorted by their **hire_date** values, and then set **LIMIT** to **10**:

```
SELECT *
FROM salespeople
WHERE dealership_id = 17
ORDER BY hire_date
LIMIT 10;
```

The following is the output of the preceding code:

salesperson_id bigint	dealership_id bigint	title text	first_name text	last_name text	suffix text	username text	gender text	hire_date timestamp without time zone	termin timest
52	17	[null]	Bobbi	McKeon	[null]	bmckeon1f	Female	2017-12-08 00:00:00	[null]
88	17	[null]	Eldin	Addenbrooke	[null]	eaddenbrooke2f	Male	2018-03-03 00:00:00	[null]
189	17	[null]	Abby	Drewery	[null]	adrewery58	Male	2018-04-28 00:00:00	[null]
249	17	[null]	Tristan	Ainge	[null]	tainge6w	Male	2018-08-11 00:00:00	[null]
187	17	[null]	Tyson	Kerford	[null]	tkerford56	Male	2018-12-23 00:00:00	[null]
86	17	[null]	Willie	Gullen	[null]	wgullen2d	Male	2019-03-13 00:00:00	[null]
3	17	[null]	Ethyl	Sloss	IV	esloss2	Female	2019-04-07 00:00:00	[null]
150	17	[null]	Jermaine	Bamell	[null]	jbamell45	Female	2019-11-14 00:00:00	[null]
1	17	[null]	Electra	Elleyne	[null]	eelleyne0	Female	2020-01-26 00:00:00	[null]
84	17	Ms	Klemens	Schneidau	II	kschneidau2b	Male	2020-01-27 00:00:00	[null]

Figure 2.25: Usernames of 10 earliest salespeople in dealership 17 sorted by hire date

Now you have the list of the first 10 salespersons hired by dealership 17, that is, the salespersons with the oldest **hire_date**, ordered by hiring date, with the oldest first.

4. Now, to find all the salespeople that were hired in 2021 and 2022 but have not been terminated, that is, the **hire_date** must be later than 2021-01-01, and **termination_date** is null, ordered by hire date, with the latest first:

```
SELECT *
FROM salespeople
WHERE hire_date >= '2021-01-01'
AND termination_date IS NULL
ORDER BY hire_date DESC;
```

54 rows are returned from this SQL. The following are the first few rows of the output:

salesperson_id bigint	dealership_id bigint	title text	first_name text	last_name text	suffix text	username text	gender text	hire_date timestamp without time zone	termination_date timestamp withou
226	20	[null]	Moli	Kardos-Stowe	[null]	mkardosstowe69	Female	2021-10-20 00:00:00	[null]
72	13	[null]	Neron	Hamly	[null]	nhamly1z	Male	2021-10-17 00:00:00	[null]
163	1	[null]	Lyda	Prine	[null]	lprine4i	Female	2021-10-15 00:00:00	[null]
254	2	[null]	Pincus	Cowp	[null]	pcowp71	Male	2021-10-13 00:00:00	[null]
39	1	[null]	Massimiliano	McSpirron	[null]	mmcspirron12	Male	2021-10-09 00:00:00	[null]
259	11	[null]	Demetris	Gable	[null]	dgable76	Male	2021-10-08 00:00:00	[null]
243	17	[null]	Shandie	Allderidge	[null]	sallderidge6q	Female	2021-09-30 00:00:00	[null]
92	1	Rev	Sandye	Duny	[null]	sduny2j	Female	2021-08-30 00:00:00	[null]
2	6	[null]	Montague	Alcoran	[null]	malcoran1	Male	2021-08-27 00:00:00	[null]

Figure 2.26: Active salespeople hired in 2021/2022 sorted by hire date latest first

5. Now, find a salesperson that was hired in **2021** and whose first name starts with **Nic**.

```
SELECT *
FROM salespeople
WHERE first_name LIKE 'Nic%'
AND hire_date >= '2021-01-01'
AND hire_date <= '2021-12-31';
```

salesperson_id bigint	dealership_id bigint	title text	first_name text	last_name text	suffix text	username text	gender text	hire_date timestamp without time zone	termination_date timestamp without
279	19	[null]	Nicholle	Lisciandri	[null]	nlisciandri7q	Female	2021-03-10 00:00:00	[null]

Figure 2.27: Salespeople hired in 2021 and whose first name starts with Nic

> **NOTE**
>
> To access the source code for this specific section, please refer to
> https://packt.link/y2qsW.

In this exercise, you used various basic keywords in a **SELECT** query to help the sales manager get a list of salespeople that they needed.

ACTIVITY 2.01: QUERYING THE CUSTOMERS TABLE USING BASIC KEYWORDS IN A SELECT QUERY

The marketing department has decided that they want to run a series of marketing campaigns to help promote a sale. To do this, they need the email communication records for ZoomZoom customers in the state of Florida, and details of all customers in New York City. They also need the customer phone numbers with specific orders. The following are the steps to complete the activity:

1. Open pgAdmin, connect to the **sqlda** database, and open SQL query editor.

2. Examine the schema for the **customers** table from the schema drop-down list. Get yourself familiar with the columns in this table.

3. Write a query that retrieves all emails for ZoomZoom customers in the state of Florida in alphabetical order.

4. Write a query that pulls all first names, last names, and emails for ZoomZoom customers in New York City in the state of New York. They should be ordered alphabetically, with the last name followed by the first name.

5. Write a query that returns all customers with a phone number ordered by the date the customer was added to the database.

The output in *Figure 2.30* will help the marketing manager to carry out campaigns and promote sales.

> **NOTE**
>
> To access the source code for this specific section, please refer to https://packt.link/8bQ6n.

In this activity, you used various basic keywords in a **SELECT** query and helped the marketing manager to get the data they needed for the marketing campaign.

> **NOTE**
>
> The solution for this activity can be found on page 435.

CREATING TABLES

Now that you know how to read data from tables, you will look at how to create new tables. There are two ways to do this—by creating blank tables or by using **SELECT** queries.

CREATING BLANK TABLES

To create a new blank table, you use the **CREATE TABLE** statement. This statement takes the following structure:

```
CREATE TABLE {table_name} (
{column_name_1} {data_type_1} {column_constraint_1},
{column_name_2} {data_type_2} {column_constraint_2},
{column_name_3} {data_type_3} {column_constraint_3},
...
{column_name_last} {data_type_last} {column_constraint_last}
);
```

Here, `{table_name}` is the name of the table, `{column_name}` is the name of the column, `{data_type}` is the data type of the column, and `{column_constraint}` is one or more optional keywords giving special properties to the column. Before discussing how to use the **CREATE TABLE** query, you should first learn about column data types and column constraints.

BASIC DATA TYPES OF SQL

Each column in a table has a data type. You will explore the major data types of PostgreSQL here. These types include:

- Numeric
- Character
- Boolean
- Datetime
- Data structures (array and JSON)

> **NOTE**
>
> Although the ANSI SQL standard defines a list of data types, different RDBMSs may have their own interpretations and extensions. The data types discussed in this book are based on the PostgreSQL definition. If you use a different RDBMS, you may see some differences in implementation. Furthermore, all RDBMSs, including PostgreSQL, are actively evolving. They constantly add support for new data types, and slightly adjust data type implementations if necessary. So, it is always prudent to use the data type definitions in this book as general guidance and double-check your RDBMS for the exact data type definitions it has.

NUMERIC

Numeric data types represent numbers. The following figure provides an overview of some of the main types:

Name	Storage Size	Description	Range
smallint	2 bytes	Small-range integer	-32.768 to +32.767
integer	4 bytes	Typical choice for integer	-2,147,483,648 to +2,147,483,647
bigint	8 bytes	Large-range integer	-9,223,372,036,854,775,808 to +9,223,372,036,854,775,807
decimal	variable	User-specified precision, exact	Up to 131,072 digits before the decimal point; up to 16,383 digits after the decimal point
numeric	variable	User-specified precision, exact	Up to 131,072 digits before the decimal point; up to 16,383 digits after the decimal point
real	4 bytes	Variable precision, inexact	6 decimal digits precision
double precision	8 bytes	Variable precision, inexact	15 decimal digits precision
smallserial	2 bytes	Small autoincrementing integer	1 to 32,767
serial	4 bytes	Autoincrementing integer	1 to 2,147,483,647
bigserial	8 bytes	Large autoincrementing integer	1 to 9,223,372,036,854,775,807

Figure 2.28: Major numeric data types

CHARACTER

Character data types store text information. The following figure summarizes character data types:

Name	Description
character varying(n), varchar(n)	variable-length with limit
character(n), char(n)	fixed-length, blank padded
text	variable unlimited length

Figure 2.29: Major character data types

Under the hood, all character data types use the same underlying data structure in PostgreSQL (and in many other RDBMSs). The most common character data type is **varchar(n)**.

BOOLEAN

Booleans are a data type used to represent **True** or **False**. The following table summarizes values that are represented as Boolean when used in a query with a data column type of Boolean:

Boolean Value	Accepted Values
True	t, true, y, yes, on, 1
False	f, false, n, no, off, 0

Figure 2.30: Accepted Boolean values

While all these values are accepted, the values of **True** and **False** are compliant with best practices. Booleans can also take on **NULL** values.

DATETIME

The **datetime** data type is used to store time-based information, such as dates and times. The following are some examples of **datetime** data types:

Name	Storage Size	Description
timestamp without time zone	8 bytes	both date and time (no time zone)
timestamp with time zone	8 bytes	both date and time, with time zone
date	4 bytes	date (no time of day)
time without time zone	8 bytes	time of day (no date)
time with time zone	12 bytes	time of day (no date), with time zone
interval	16 bytes	time interval

Figure 2.31: Popular datetime data types

You will explore this data type further in *Chapter 7, Analytics Using Complex Data Types*.

DATA STRUCTURES: JSON AND ARRAYS

Many versions of modern SQL also support data structures, such as **JavaScript Object Notation (JSON)** and arrays. Arrays are simply lists of data usually written as members enclosed in square brackets. For example, `['cat', 'dog', 'horse']` is an array. A JSON object is a series of key-value pairs that are separated by commas and enclosed in curly braces. For example, `{'name': 'Bob', 'age': 27, 'city': 'New York'}` is a valid JSON object. These data structures show up constantly in technology applications, and being able to use them in a database makes it easier to perform many kinds of analysis work.

You will explore data structures in more detail in *Chapter 7, Analytics Using Complex Data Types*. Before that, you will learn about some basic operations in an RDBMS using SQL.

COLUMN CONSTRAINTS

Column constraints are keywords that help you specify the properties you want to attribute to a particular column. In other words, you can ensure that all the rows in that column adhere to your specified constraint. Some major column constraints are as follows:

- **NOT NULL**: This constraint guarantees that no value in a column can be **NULL**.

- **UNIQUE**: This constraint guarantees that every single row for a column has a unique value and that no value is repeated.

- **PRIMARY KEY**: This is a special constraint that is unique for each row and helps you to find a specific row more quickly. If the primary key of this table contains only one column, you can add this **PRIMARY KEY** constraint to the column definition of the primary key column. If the primary key of this table consists of multiple columns, you need to use a table constraint to define the key in the **CREATE** statement.

SIMPLE CREATE STATEMENT

Now that you know about data types and column constraints, you can start creating your first table. Suppose you want to create a table called **state_populations** with columns for the initials and populations of states. The query would look as follows:

```
CREATE TABLE state_populations (
  state VARCHAR(2) PRIMARY KEY,
  population NUMERIC
);
```

Once you execute this statement, you can run a simple **SELECT** statement to verify that the table is created. However, you cannot see any row in the output as you have not run any statements to populate it.

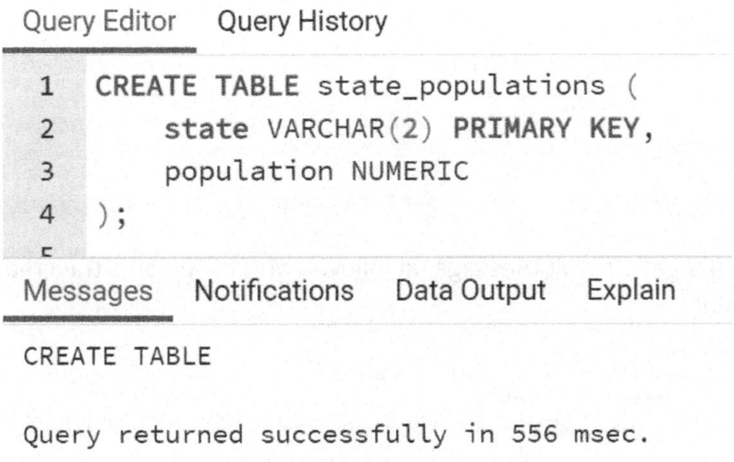

Figure 2.32: Simple CREATE statement

> **NOTE**
>
> Sometimes, you may run a **CREATE TABLE** query and get the error relation **{table_name} already exists**. This simply means that a table with the same name already exists. You either must delete the table with the same name or change the name of your table. You will learn how to delete a table later in this chapter.

You will soon be exploring the second way to create a table, which is by using a SQL query. But first, you will do an exercise to create a blank table in SQL.

EXERCISE 2.03: CREATING A TABLE IN SQL

In this exercise, you will create a table using the **CREATE TABLE** statement. The marketing team at ZoomZoom would like to create a table called **countries** to analyze the data of different countries. It should have four columns: an integer key column, a unique name column, a founding year column, and a capital column.

Follow these steps to complete the exercise:

1. Open pgAdmin, connect to the **sqlda** database, and open SQL query editor.

2. Execute the following query to drop the **countries** table since it already exists in the database:

```
DROP TABLE IF EXISTS countries;
```

3. Run the following query to create the **countries** table:

```
CREATE TABLE countries (
  key INT PRIMARY KEY,
  name text UNIQUE,
  founding_year INT,
  capital text
);
```

You should get a result message as follows, which indicates the creation of a blank table:

```
Query Editor    Query History

1    CREATE TABLE countries (
2        key INT PRIMARY KEY,
3        name text UNIQUE,
4        founding_year INT,
5        capital text
6    );
7

Messages    Notifications    Data Output    Explain

CREATE TABLE

Query returned successfully in 205 msec.
```

Figure 2.33: CREATE statement for the countries table

> **NOTE**
>
> To access the source code for this specific section, please refer to
> https://packt.link/COMnA.

In this exercise, you learned how to create a table using different column constraints and the **CREATE TABLE** statement. In the next section, you will create tables using the **SELECT** query.

CREATING TABLES WITH SELECT

You already know how to create a table. However, say you wanted to create a table using data from an existing table. This can be done by using a modification of the **CREATE TABLE** statement:

```
CREATE TABLE {table_name} AS (
   {select_query}
);
```

Here, **{select_query}** is any **SELECT** query that can be run in your database. For instance, say you wanted to create a table based on the **products** table that only had products from the year 2014. Suppose the title of the table is **products_2014**; you could write the following query:

```
CREATE TABLE products_2014 AS (
   SELECT *
FROM products
WHERE year=2014
);
```

Running this SQL will yield the following result:

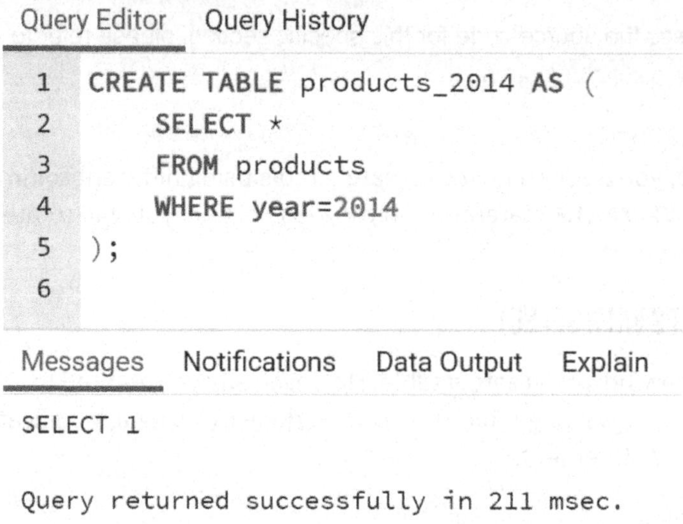

```
Query Editor    Query History

1   CREATE TABLE products_2014 AS (
2       SELECT *
3       FROM products
4       WHERE year=2014
5   );
6

Messages    Notifications    Data Output    Explain

SELECT 1

Query returned successfully in 211 msec.
```

Figure 2.34: CREATE from a SELECT query

This can be done with any query, and the table will inherit all the properties of the output query.

PostgreSQL also provides another way to create a table from a query, which utilizes a **SELECT** ... **INTO** ... syntax. An example of this syntax is shown below:

```
SELECT *
INTO products_2014
FROM products
WHERE year=2014;
```

> **NOTE**
>
> Before running this query, please check the table list in the `sqlda` database and make sure this table does not exist. If it does, please drop the table from the console.

This query achieves the same result as the **CREATE** ... **AS** statement. In this book, you will use the **CREATE** ... **AS** statement because the syntax inside the parenthesis is a complete **SELECT** statement, thus it is easier to create and modify the query without changing the structure of the statement. You can choose either based on your personal preference.

One issue with creating a table with a query is that the data types of the query are not explicitly specified and can be confusing. Luckily, PostgreSQL stores the table definitions in a set of system tables, and you can read the table definition from the system tables. For example, to check the column definitions of the **products_2014** table, you can run the following SQL:

```
SELECT COLUMN_NAME, DATA_TYPE
FROM INFORMATION_SCHEMA.COLUMNS
WHERE TABLE_NAME = 'products_2014';
```

From the result, you can identify all the columns and their data types in the **products_2014** table:

column_name	data_type
name	character varying
production_start_date	timestamp without time zone
production_end_date	timestamp without time zone
year	bigint
product_id	bigint
base_msrp	numeric
product_type	text
model	text

Figure 2.35: Query table definition from information schema

UPDATING TABLES

Over time, you may also need to modify a table by adding columns, adding new data, or updating existing rows. This section will help you understand how to do this.

ADDING AND REMOVING COLUMNS

To add new columns to an existing table, you use the **ALTER TABLE** ... **ADD COLUMN** statement, as shown in the following query:

```
ALTER TABLE {table_name}
ADD COLUMN {column_name} {data_type};
```

For example, if you wanted to add a new column to the **products_2014** table that you will use to store the products' weights in kilograms called **weight**, you could do this by using the following query:

```
ALTER TABLE products_2014
ADD COLUMN weight INT;
```

This query will make a new column called **weight** in the **products_2014** table and will give it the integer data type so that only integers can be stored in it.

product_id bigint	model text	year bigint	product_type text	base_msrp numeric	production_start_date timestamp without time zone	production_end_date timestamp without time zone	weight integer
2	Lemon Limited Edition	2014	scooter	799.99	2013-08-30 00:00:00	2013-11-24 00:00:00	[null]

Figure 2.36: ALTER statement that adds a column to a table

If you want to remove a column from a table, you can use the **ALTER TABLE** ... **DROP COLUMN** statement:

```
ALTER TABLE {table_name}
DROP COLUMN {column_name};
```

Here, **{table_name}** is the name of the table you want to change, and **{column_name}** is the name of the column you want to drop. Imagine that you decide to delete the **weight** column you just created. You could get rid of it using the following query:

```
ALTER TABLE products_2014
DROP COLUMN weight;
```

As you can see from the screenshot below, the column is dropped:

product_id bigint	model text	year bigint	product_type text	base_msrp numeric	production_start_date timestamp without time zone	production_end_date timestamp without time zone
2	Lemon Limited Edition	2014	scooter	799.99	2013-08-30 00:00:00	2013-11-24 00:00:00

Figure 2.37: ALTER statement that drops a column from a table

ADDING NEW DATA

You can add new data to a table using several methods in SQL. One of those methods is to simply insert values straight into a table using the **INSERT INTO...** **VALUES** statement. It has the following structure:

```
INSERT INTO {table_name} (
    {column_1], {column_2}, ...{column_last}
)
VALUES (
    {column_value_1}, {column_value_2}, ... {column_value_last}
);
```

Here, **{table_name}** is the name of the table you want to insert your data into, **{column_1}, {column_2}, ... {column_last}** is a list of the columns whose values you want to insert, and **{column_value_1}, {column_value_2}, ... {column_value_last}** is the list of values you want to insert into the table. If a column in the table is not put into the **INSERT** statement, the column is assumed to have a **NULL** value.

For example, say you want to insert a new entry for a scooter into the **products_2014** table. This can be done with the following query:

```
INSERT INTO products_2014 (
product_id, model, year,
    product_type, base_msrp,
    production_start_date, production_end_date
)
VALUES (
    13, 'Nimbus 5000', 2014,
    'scooter', 500.00,
    '2014-03-03', '2020-03-03'
);
```

This query adds a new row to the **products_2014** table accordingly. You can run a **SELECT** query to see all the rows in the table:

product_id bigint	model text	year bigint	product_type text	base_msrp numeric	production_start_date timestamp without time zone	production_end_date timestamp without time zone
2	Lemon Limited Edition	2014	scooter	799.99	2013-08-30 00:00:00	2013-11-24 00:00:00
13	Nimbus 5000	2014	scooter	500.00	2014-03-03 00:00:00	2020-03-03 00:00:00

Figure 2.38: INSERT statement adding one row to table

Another way to insert data into a table is to use the **INSERT** statement with a **SELECT** query using the following syntax:

```
INSERT INTO {table_name} ({column_1}, {column_2}, ...{column_last})
{select_query};
```

Here, **{table_name}** is the name of the table into which you want to insert the data, **{column_1}, {column_2}, ... {column_last}** is a list of the columns whose values you want to insert, and **{select query}** is a query with the same structure as the values you want to insert into the table.

Take the example of the **products_2014** table. You have created it with a **SELECT** query with one row. Earlier in this section, you have inserted one row into it. So, now it contains two rows. If you also want to insert the products from 2016, you could use the following query, which inserts one more row into the table:

```
INSERT INTO products_2014(
    product_id, model, year, product_type, base_msrp,
    production_start_date, production_end_date
)
SELECT*
FROM products
WHERE year=2016;
```

This query produces the following result:

product_id bigint	model text	year bigint	product_type text	base_msrp numeric	production_start_date timestamp without time zone	production_end_date timestamp without time zone
2	Lemon Limited Edition	2014	scooter	799.99	2013-08-30 00:00:00	2013-11-24 00:00:00
13	Nimbus 5000	2014	scooter	500.00	2014-03-03 00:00:00	2020-03-03 00:00:00
3	Lemon	2016	scooter	499.99	2015-12-27 00:00:00	2021-08-24 00:00:00

Figure 2.39: The Products_2014 table after a successful INSERT INTO query

Now it contains three rows from three different ways of inserting data: one row from **CREATE** as the result of a **SELECT** query, one row from an **INSERT** with data, and one row from **INSERT** using the result of a **SELECT** query.

Next, you will learn how to update the content in a row.

UPDATING EXISTING ROWS

Sometimes, you may need to update the values of the data present in a table. To do this, you can use the **UPDATE** statement:

```
UPDATE {table_name} SET
   {column_1} = {column_value_1},
   {column_2} = {column_value_2},
   ...
   {column_last} = {column_value_last}
WHERE {conditional};
```

Here, **{table_name}** is the name of the table with data that will be changed, **{column_1}**, **{column_2}**,... **{column_last}** is the list of columns whose values you want to change, **{column_value_1}**, **{column_value_2}**, ... **{column_value_last}** is the list of new values you want to update into those columns, and **{WHERE}** is a conditional statement like the one you would find in a **SELECT** query.

To illustrate its use of the **UPDATE** statement, imagine that, for the rest of the year, the company has decided to sell all scooter models before 2018 for $299.99. You could change the data in the **products_2014** table using the following query:

```
UPDATE Products_2014 SET
   base_msrp = 299.99
WHERE product_type = 'scooter'
AND year<2018;
```

This query produces the following output. You can see that the **base_msrp** column of all three records has been updated to **299.99** because they are all scooters manufactured before 2018.

product_id bigint	model text	year bigint	product_type text	base_msrp numeric	production_start_date timestamp without time zone	production_end_date timestamp without time zone
2	Lemon Limited Edition	2014	scooter	299.99	2013-08-30 00:00:00	2013-11-24 00:00:00
13	Nimbus 5000	2014	scooter	299.99	2014-03-03 00:00:00	2020-03-03 00:00:00
3	Lemon	2016	scooter	299.99	2015-12-27 00:00:00	2021-08-24 00:00:00

Figure 2.40: Successful update of the products_2014 table

In the following exercise, you will take a closer look at how to use **UPDATE** statements in a SQL database.

EXERCISE 2.04: UPDATING THE TABLE TO INCREASE THE PRICE OF A VEHICLE

In this exercise, you will update the data in a table using the **UPDATE** statement. Due to an increase in the cost of the rare metals needed to manufacture an electric vehicle, the 2022 Model Chi will need to undergo a price hike of 10%. The current price is $95,000.

In a real-world scenario, you will update the **products** table to increase the price of this product. However, because you will use the same **sqlda** database throughout the book, it would be better to keep the values in the original tables unchanged so that your SQL results remain consistent. For this reason, you will create new tables for all the **INSERT**, **ALTER**, **UPDATE**, **DELETE**, and **DROP** statement examples.

Perform the following steps to complete the exercise:

1. Open **pgAdmin**, connect to the **sqlda** database, and open SQL query editor.

2. Run the following query to create a **product_2022** table from the **products** table:

```
CREATE TABLE products_2022 AS (
SELECT *
FROM products
WHERE year=2022
);
```

3. Run the following query to update the price of Model Chi by 10% in the **products_2022** table:

```
UPDATE Products_2022 SET
   base_msrp = base_msrp*1.10
WHERE model='Model Chi'
AND year=2022;
```

4. Write the **SELECT** query to check whether the price of Model Chi in 2022 has been updated:

```
SELECT *
FROM products_2022
WHERE model='Model Chi'
AND year=2022;
```

The following is the output of the preceding code:

product_id bigint	model text	year bigint	product_type text	base_msrp numeric	production_start_date timestamp without time zone	production_end_date timestamp without time zone
11	Model Chi	2022	automobile	104500.0000	2021-10-01 00:00:00	[null]

Figure 2.41: The updated price of Model Chi in 2022

As you see from the output, the price of Model Chi is now $104,500; it was previously $95,000.

> **NOTE**
>
> To access the source code for this specific section, please refer to https://packt.link/fOQgA.

In this exercise, you learned how to update a table using the **UPDATE** statement. Next, you will learn how to delete data from tables and drop tables.

DELETING DATA AND TABLES

You often discover that data in a table is out of date and, therefore, can no longer be used. At such times, you might need to delete data from a table.

DELETING VALUES FROM A ROW

Often, you might be interested in deleting a value from a row. The easiest way to accomplish this is to use the **UPDATE** structure that has already been discussed, and by setting the column value to **NULL**:

```
UPDATE {table_name} SET
  {column_1} = NULL,
  {column_2} = NULL,
  ...
  {column_last} = NULL
WHERE {conditional};
```

Here, **{table_name}** is the name of the table with the data that needs to be changed, **{column_1}, {column_2},... {column_last}** is the list of columns whose values you want to delete, and **{WHERE}** is a conditional statement like the one you would find in a **SELECT** query.

For instance, you have the wrong email address on file for the customer with the **customer ID** equal to **3**. To fix that, you can use the following query:

```
UPDATE customers SET
  email = NULL
WHERE customer_id=3;
```

However, there might be cases where you might need to delete rows from a table. For example, in the database, you have a row labeled **test customer**, which is no longer needed and needs to be deleted. In the next section, you will learn how to delete rows from a table.

DELETING ROWS FROM A TABLE

Deleting a row from a table can be done using the **DELETE** statement, which looks like this:

```
DELETE FROM {table_name}
WHERE {condition};
```

For instance, you must delete the products whose **product_type** is **scooter** from the **products_2014** table. To do that, you can use the following query:

```
DELETE FROM products_2014
WHERE product_type='scooter';
```

In the past few sections, you have inserted three products into this table, all scooters. After running the **DELETE** statement, PostgreSQL shows that there was no product in this table anymore as all records are deleted.

product_id 🔒	model	year 🔒	product_type 🔒	base_msrp 🔒	production_start_date	production_end_date 🔒
bigint	text	bigint	text	numeric	timestamp without time zone	timestamp without time zone

Figure 2.42: DELETE statement example

If you want to delete all the data in the **products_2014** table without deleting the table, you could write the following query, which is **DELETE** without any conditions:

```
DELETE FROM products_2014;
```

Alternatively, if you want to delete all the data in a query without deleting the table, you could use the **TRUNCATE** keyword like so:

```
TRUNCATE TABLE products_2014;
```

Now you have learned how to delete rows from a table, the next section will teach you how to delete a table entirely.

DELETING TABLES

To delete all the data in a table and the table itself, you can just use the **DROP TABLE** statement with the following syntax:

```
DROP TABLE {table_name};
```

Here, **{table_name}** is the name of the table you want to delete. If you wanted to delete all the data in the **products_2014** table along with the table itself, you would write the following:

```
DROP TABLE products_2014;
```

If you want to read from this table, you will receive an error message from PostgreSQL telling you that the table does not exist:

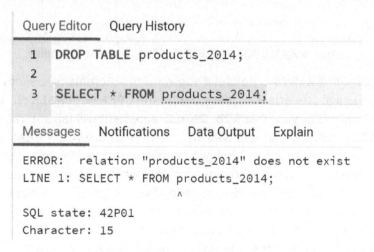

Figure 2.43: DROP statement example

As seen in *Figure 2.46*, once the table is dropped, all aspects of this table are gone, and you cannot perform any operations on it. For example, if you try to run the **DROP TABLE products_2014** statement again, you will run into an error. A PostgreSQL enhancement of the **DROP** statement is **DROP TABLE IF EXISTS**. This statement will check the existence of the table. If the table is not in the database, PostgreSQL will skip this statement with a notification, but without reporting an error, as shown below:

```
DROP TABLE IF EXISTS products_2014;
```

Query Editor   Query History

```
1   DROP TABLE IF EXISTS products_2014;
```

Messages   Notifications   Data Output   Explain

```
NOTICE:  table "products_2014" does not exist, skipping
DROP TABLE

Query returned successfully in 87 msec.
```

Figure 2.44: DROP TABLE IF EXISTS statement example

DROP TABLE IF EXISTS is helpful if you want to automate SQL script execution. One common usage scenario is to use it before the **CREATE TABLE** statement. If the table already exists, your **CREATE TABLE** statement will fail and raise an error. But if your **DROP TABLE IF EXISTS** statement is before your **CREATE TABLE** statement, pre-existing tables would have been dropped before you tried to recreate them. This is useful in automated computing operations where you constantly create temporary tables that you do not need after the current computing job is completed. The catch is that you must make sure that the table is truly temporary and is not used by anyone else. Otherwise, you may accidentally drop tables that are used by some other users without knowing. For this reason, the **DROP TABLE IF EXISTS** statement is usually only used in environments designated for automated data processing.

Now test what you have learned by performing an exercise to delete or drop the table using the **DROP TABLE** statement.

EXERCISE 2.05: DELETING AN UNNECESSARY REFERENCE TABLE

In this exercise, you will learn how to delete a table using SQL. For instance, the marketing team has finished analyzing the potential number of customers they have in every state, and they no longer need the **state_populations** table. To save space in the database, delete the table. If you have not created this table, please go back to the *Simple CREATE Statement* section in this chapter and create it now.

Perform the following steps to complete the exercise:

1. Open pgAdmin, connect to the **sqlda** database, and open **SQL query editor**.

2. Run the following query to drop the **state_populations** table:

```
DROP TABLE state_populations;
```

3. Check that the **state_populations** table has been deleted from the database.

4. Since the table has just been dropped, a **SELECT** query on this table throws an error, as expected:

```
SELECT *
FROM state_populations;
```

You will find the error shown in the following figure:

```
ERROR:   relation "state_populations" does not exist
LINE 1: select * from state_populations;
                      ^
```

Figure 2.45: Error shown as the state_populations table was dropped

5. Also, drop the **products_2022** table that was created above to keep the database clean:

```
DROP TABLE products_2022;
```

> **NOTE**
>
> To access the source code for this specific section, please refer to https://packt.link/kJVag.

In this exercise, you learned how to delete a table using the **DROP TABLE** statement. In the next activity, you will test the skills you learned by creating and modifying tables using SQL.

ACTIVITY 2.02: CREATING AND MODIFYING TABLES FOR MARKETING OPERATIONS

In this activity, you will test your ability to create and modify tables using SQL.

You did a great job of pulling data for the marketing team. However, the marketing manager, who you helped, realized that they had made a mistake. It turns out that instead of just the query, the manager needs to create a new table in the company's analytics database. Furthermore, they need to make some changes to the data that is present in the **customers** table. It is your job to help the marketing manager with the table:

1. Open pgAdmin, connect to the **sqlda** database and open SQL query editor. Create a new table called **customers_nyc** that pulls all the rows from the **customers** table where the customer lives in New York City in the state of New York.

2. Delete all customers in postal code 10014 from the new table. Due to local laws, they will not be eligible for marketing.

3. Add a new text column called **event**.

4. Set the value of the event column to **thank-you party**.

   The following is the expected output:

customer_id bigint	title text		first_name text	last_name text		suffix text	email text		gender text	ip_address text		phone text
52	[null]		Giusto	Backe		[null]	gbacke1f@digg.com		M	26.56.68.189		212-959-91
162	[null]		Artair	Betchley		[null]	abetchley4h@dagondesign.com		M	108.147.128.250		[null]
374	[null]		Verge	Esel		[null]	veselad@vistaprint.com		M	58.238.20.156		917-653-23
406	[null]		Rozina	Jeal		[null]	rjealb9@howstuffworks.com		F	50.235.32.29		917-610-25
456	Rev		Cybil	Noke		[null]	cnokecn@jigsy.com		F	5.31.139.106		212-306-60
472	[null]		Rawley	Yegorov		[null]	ryegorovd3@google.es		M	183.199.243.74		212-560-12
496	[null]		Layton	Spolton		[null]	lspoltondr@free.fr		M	108.112.8.165		646-900-82
1028	[null]		Issy	Andrieux		[null]	iandrieuxsj@dell.com		F	199.50.5.37		212-206-78
1037	[null]		Magdalene	Veryard		[null]	mveryardss@behance.net		F	93.201.129.213		[null]

Figure 2.46: The customers_nyc table with event set to thank-you party

You tell the manager that you have completed these steps. He tells the marketing operations team, who then uses the data to launch a marketing campaign. The marketing manager then asks you to delete the **customers_nyc** table.

> **NOTE**
>
> To access the source code for this specific section, please refer to https://packt.link/xeMaT.

In this activity, you used different CRUD operations to modify a table as requested by the marketing manager. You will now come full circle to explore how SQL and analytics connect.

> **NOTE**
>
> The solution for this activity can be found on page 437.

SQL AND ANALYTICS

Throughout this chapter, you may have noticed the terms *SQL table* and *dataset* are interchangeable. More specifically, it should be clear that SQL tables can be thought of as datasets, rows can be considered as individual units of observation, and columns can be considered as features. If you view SQL tables in this way, you can see that SQL is a natural way to store datasets on a computer.

However, SQL can go further than just providing a convenient way to store datasets. Modern SQL implementations also provide tools for processing and analyzing data through various functions. Using SQL, you can clean data, transform data into more useful formats, and analyze a variety of statistical measures to discover interesting patterns. The rest of this book will be dedicated to understanding how SQL can be used for these purposes productively and efficiently.

SUMMARY

Data analytics can be enhanced by the power of relational databases. Relational databases are a mature and ubiquitous technology used for storing and querying structured data. Relational databases store data in the form of relations, also known as tables, which allow an excellent combination of performance, efficiency, and ease of use.

SQL is the language used to access relational databases. SQL supports many different data types, including numeric data, text data, and even data structures.

SQL can be used to perform all the tasks in the lifecycle of **Create**, **Read**, **Update**, and **Delete** (**CRUD**). SQL can be used to create and drop tables, as well as insert, delete, and update data elements. When querying data, SQL allows a user to pick which fields to pull, as well as how to filter the data. This data can also be ordered, and SQL allows as much or as little data as you need to be pulled.

Having reviewed the basics of data analytics and SQL, you will move on to the next chapter's discussion of how SQL can be used to perform the first step in data analytics: cleaning and transformation of data.

3

SQL FOR DATA PREPARATION

OVERVIEW

In this chapter, you will learn how to clean and prepare data for analysis using SQL techniques. You will learn how to combine multiple tables and queries into a dataset using joins, unions, and subqueries. You will also use functions to transform data. These will make the data conform to certain standards before you apply advanced data analysis techniques in future chapters. By the end of this chapter, you will be able to transform and clean data using SQL functions and remove duplicate data using the `DISTINCT` and `DISTINCT ON` commands.

INTRODUCTION

In the previous chapters, you learned the basics of data analysis and SQL. You learned how to use **CREATE, INSERT, SELECT, ALTER, UPDATE, DELETE**, and **DROP** SQL statements to apply **create, read, update, and delete (CRUD)** operations on a table. These techniques are the foundation for data analytics.

However, in the real world, as a data analyst, you usually do not handle the entire CRUD flow. To be more specific, you usually do not create datasets from scratch. You will receive data from outside sources. This data is usually in a form that would not fit your needs perfectly and you would need to perform some transform operations to make the data usable. One such operation is the creation of clean datasets from existing raw datasets. The raw data may be missing some information, contain information that is not in the format that fits your needs, or contains information that may not be accurate.

According to Forbes, it is estimated that almost 80% of the time spent by analytics professionals involves preparing data. Building models with unclean data harms analysis by leading to poor conclusions. SQL can help in this tedious but important task by providing efficient ways to build clean datasets.

This chapter will start by discussing how to assemble data using **JOIN** and **UNION**. Furthermore, you will use different functions, such as **CASE WHEN, COALESCE, NULLIF**, and **LEAST/GREATEST**, to clean data. You will then learn how to transform and remove duplicate data from queries using the **DISTINCT** command.

ASSEMBLING DATA

In *Chapter 2, The Basics of SQL for Analytics*, you learned how to perform operations with a single table. But what if you need data from two or more tables? In this section, you will assemble data in multiple tables using joins and unions.

CONNECTING TABLES USING JOIN

Most of the time, the data you are interested in is spread across multiple tables. A simple **SELECT** statement over one table will not be enough to get you what you need. Fortunately, SQL has methods for bringing related tables together using the **JOIN** keyword.

To illustrate, look at two tables in the **ZoomZoom** database—**dealerships** and **salespeople**.

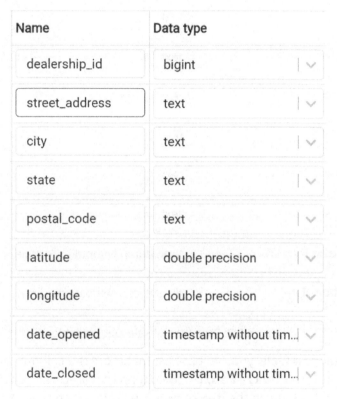

Figure 3.1: Structure of dealerships table

And the **salespeople** table looks like this:

Name	Data type
salesperson_id	bigint
dealership_id	bigint
title	text
first_name	text
last_name	text
suffix	text
username	text
gender	text
hire_date	timestamp without time zone
termination_date	timestamp without time zone

Figure 3.2: Structure of salespeople table

In the **salespeople** table, you can observe that there is a column called **dealership_id**. This **dealership_id** column is a direct reference to the **dealership_id** column in the **dealerships** table. When table A has a column that references the primary key of table B, the column is said to be a foreign key to table A. In this case, the **dealership_id** column in **salespeople** is a foreign key to the **dealerships** table.

> **NOTE**
>
> Foreign keys can also be added as a column constraint to a table to improve the integrity of the data by making sure that the foreign key never contains a value that cannot be found in the referenced table. This data property is known as **referential integrity**. The method of adding foreign key constraints can also help to improve performance in some databases. Foreign key constraints are not used in most analytical databases and are beyond the scope of this book. You can learn more about foreign key constraints in the official PostgreSQL documentation.

As these two tables are related, you can perform some interesting analyses with them. For instance, you may be interested in determining which salespeople work at a dealership in California. One way of retrieving this information is to first query which dealerships are in California. You can do this using the following query:

```
SELECT *
FROM dealerships
WHERE state='CA';
```

This query should give you the following results:

dealership_id bigint 🔒	state text 🔒
2	CA
5	CA

Figure 3.3: Dealerships in California

Now that you know that the only two dealerships in California have the IDs of **2** and **5**, respectively, you can then query the **salespeople** table, as follows:

```
SELECT *
FROM salespeople
WHERE dealership_id in (2, 5)
ORDER BY 1;
```

The following are the first nine rows of the output of the code:

salesperson_id 🔒 bigint	first_name 🔒 text	last_name 🔒 text
23	Beauregard	Peschke
51	Lanette	Gerriessen
57	Spense	Pithcock
61	Ludvig	Baynam
62	Carroll	Pudan
63	Adrianne	Otham
71	Georgianna	Bastian
75	Saundra	Shoebottom
108	Hale	Brigshaw

Figure 3.4: Salespeople in California

While this method gives you the results you want, it is tedious to perform two queries to get these results. What would make this process easier would be to somehow add the information from the **dealerships** table to the **salespeople** table and then filter for users in California. SQL provides such a tool with the **JOIN** clause. The **JOIN** clause is a SQL clause that allows a user to join one or more tables together based on distinct conditions.

TYPES OF JOINS

In this chapter, you will learn about three fundamental joins, which are illustrated in the following figure—inner joins, outer joins, and cross joins:

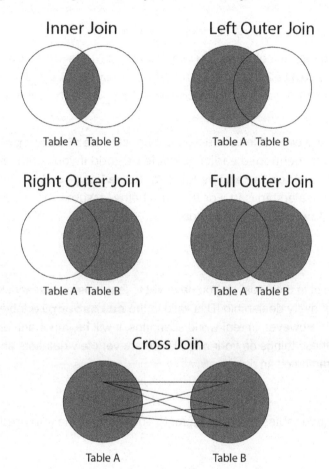

Figure 3.5: Major types of joins

INNER JOINS

An inner join connects rows in different tables, based on a condition known as the **join predicate**. In many cases, the join predicate is a logical condition of equality. Each row in the first table is compared against every other row in the second table. For row combinations that meet the inner join predicate, that row is returned in the query. Otherwise, the row combination is discarded.

Inner joins are usually written in the following form:

```
SELECT {columns}
FROM {table1}
INNER JOIN {table2}
    ON {table1}.{common_key_1}={table2}.{common_key_2};
```

Here, **{columns}** is the columns you want to get from the joined table, **{table1}** is the first table, **{table2}** is the second table, **{common_key_1}** is the column in **{table1}** you want to join on, and **{common_key_2}** is the column in **{table2}** to join on.

Now, go back to the two tables discussed previously—**dealerships** and **salespeople**. As mentioned earlier, it would be good if you could append the information from the **dealerships** table to the **salespeople** table knowing which state each dealership is in. For the time being, assume that all the salespeople IDs have a valid **dealership_id** value.

> **NOTE**
>
> At this point in the book, as you have yet to learn the necessary skills to verify that every dealership ID is valid in the **salespeople** table, so you assume it. However, in real-world scenarios, it will be important for you to validate these things on your own. There are very few datasets and systems that guarantee clean data.

You can join the two tables using an equal to condition in the join predicate, as follows:

```
SELECT *
FROM salespeople
INNER JOIN dealerships
    ON salespeople.dealership_id = dealerships.dealership_id
ORDER BY 1;
```

The following figure shows the first few rows of the output:

salesperson_id bigint	first_name text	last_name text
1	Electra	Elleyne
2	Montague	Alcoran
3	Ethyl	Sloss
4	Nester	Dugood
5	Cornall	Swanger
6	Ellary	Nend
7	Granville	Fidell
8	Lanie	Tisun
9	Lamar	Treleven

Figure 3.6: The salespeople table joined to the dealerships table

As you can see in the preceding output, the table is the result of joining the **salespeople** table to the **dealerships** table. Note that the first table listed in the query, **salespeople**, is on the left-hand side of the result, while the **dealerships** table is on the right-hand side. This left-right order will become very important in the next section when you learn about outer joins between tables. During an outer join, whether a table is on the left or right side can impact the output of the query. For an inner join, however, the order of tables is not important for join predicates that use an equal operation.

Now, look at the columns involved; **dealership_id** in the **salespeople** table matches **dealership_id** in the **dealerships** table. This shows how the join predicate is met. By running this **join** query, you have effectively created a new "super dataset" consisting of the two tables merged where the two **dealership_id** columns are equal.

You can now run a **SELECT** query over this "super dataset" in the same way as one large table using the clauses and keywords from *Chapter 2, The Basics of SQL for Analytics*. For example, going back to the multi-query issue to determine which sales query works in California, you can now address it with one easy query:

```
SELECT *
FROM salespeople
INNER JOIN dealerships
  ON salespeople.dealership_id = dealerships.dealership_id
WHERE dealerships.state = 'CA'
ORDER BY 1;
```

This gives you the following output, which displays the first few rows of the entire result set:

salesperson_id bigint	first_name text	last_name text	dealership_id bigint
23	Beauregard	Peschke	2
51	Lanette	Gerriessen	5
57	Spense	Pithcock	5
61	Ludvig	Baynam	5
62	Carroll	Pudan	2
63	Adrianne	Otham	2
71	Georgianna	Bastian	2
75	Saundra	Shoebottom	2
108	Hale	Brigshaw	2

Figure 3.7: Salespeople in California with one query

You will observe that the output in *Figure 3.6* and *Figure 3.7* is nearly identical, with the exception being that the table in *Figure 3.7* has the **dealerships** data appended as well. If you want to retrieve only the **salespeople** table portion of this, you can select the **salespeople** columns using the following star syntax:

```
SELECT salespeople.*
FROM salespeople
INNER JOIN dealerships
  ON dealerships.dealership_id = salespeople.dealership_id
WHERE dealerships.state = 'CA'
ORDER BY 1;
```

Here are the first few rows returned by this query:

salesperson_id bigint	dealership_id bigint	title text	first_name text	last_name text	suffix text	username text	gender text	hire_date timestamp without time	termination_date timestamp without time zone
23	2	[null]	Beauregard	Peschke	[null]	bpeschkem	Male	2021-05-09 00:00:00	[null]
51	5	[null]	Lanette	Gerriessen	[null]	lgerriessen1e	Female	2021-02-18 00:00:00	[null]
57	5	[null]	Spense	Pithcock	[null]	spithcock1k	Male	2020-08-11 00:00:00	[null]
61	5	[null]	Ludvig	Baynam	[null]	lbaynam1o	Male	2019-04-22 00:00:00	[null]
62	2	[null]	Carroll	Pudan	[null]	cpudan1p	Female	2019-01-12 00:00:00	[null]
63	2	[null]	Adrianne	Otham	[null]	aotham1q	Female	2017-08-16 00:00:00	[null]
71	2	[null]	Georgianna	Bastian	[null]	gbastian1y	Female	2021-08-19 00:00:00	[null]
75	2	[null]	Saundra	Shoebottom	[null]	sshoebottom22	Female	2020-11-12 00:00:00	[null]
108	2	[null]	Hale	Brigshaw	[null]	hbrigshaw2z	Male	2018-03-26 00:00:00	[null]

Figure 3.8: Salespeople in California with SELECT table alias

There is another shortcut that can help while writing statements with several **JOIN** clauses. You can alias table names to avoid typing the entire name of the table every time. Simply write the name of the alias after the first mention of the table after the **JOIN** clause, and you can save a decent amount of typing. For instance, for the preceding query, if you wanted to alias **salespeople** with **s** and **dealerships** with **d**, you could write the following statement:

```
SELECT s.*
FROM salespeople s
INNER JOIN dealerships d
  ON d.dealership_id = s.dealership_id
WHERE d.state = 'CA'
ORDER BY 1;
```

Alternatively, you could also put the **AS** keyword between the table name and alias to make the alias more explicit:

```
SELECT s.*
FROM salespeople AS s
INNER JOIN dealerships AS d
  ON d.dealership_id = s.dealership_id
WHERE d.state = 'CA'
ORDER BY 1;
```

Now that you have covered the basics of inner joins, it is time to discuss outer joins.

OUTER JOINS

As discussed, inner joins will only return rows from the two tables when the join predicate is met for both tables, that is, when both tables have rows that can satisfy the join predicate. Otherwise, no rows from either table are returned. It can happen that sometimes you want to return all rows from one of the tables, even if the other table does not have any row meeting the join predicate. In this case, since there is no row meeting the join predicate, the second table will return nothing but **NULL**. Outer join is a join type in which all rows from at least one table, if meeting the query **WHERE** condition, will be presented after the **JOIN** operation.

Outer joins can be classified into three categories: left outer joins, right outer joins, and full outer joins:

- Left outer join: **Left outer joins** are where the left table (that is, the table mentioned first in a join clause) will have every row returned. If a row from the other table (the right table) is not found, a row of **NULL** is returned from the right table. Left outer joins are performed by using the **LEFT OUTER JOIN** keywords, followed by a join predicate. This can also be written in short as **LEFT JOIN**.

  To show how left outer joins work, examine two tables: the **customers** table and the **emails** table. For the time being, assume that not every customer has been sent an email, and you want to mail all customers who have not received an email. You can use a left outer join to make that happen since the left side of the join is the **customers** table. To help manage the output, you will limit it to the first 1,000 rows. The following code snippet is utilized:

```
SELECT
    *
FROM
```

```
    customers c
LEFT OUTER JOIN
    emails e ON e.customer_id=c.customer_id
ORDER BY
    c.customer_id
LIMIT
    1000;
```

The following is the output of the preceding code:

customer_id bigint	first_name text	last_name text	customer_id bigint	email_id bigint
25	Jillie	Stoter	25	144199
25	Jillie	Stoter	25	370746
25	Jillie	Stoter	25	209822
26	Rhiamon	Wynes	26	324008
26	Rhiamon	Wynes	26	370747
27	Anson	Fellibrand	[null]	[null]
28	Gradey	Garrat	28	370748
28	Gradey	Garrat	28	324009
29	Ashia	Hyndman	29	245835
29	Ashia	Hyndman	29	282608
29	Ashia	Hyndman	29	9790

Figure 3.9: Customers left-joined to emails

When you look at the output of the query, you should see that entries from the **customers** table are present. However, for some of the rows, such as for **customer_id 27**, which can be seen in *Figure 3.9*, the columns belonging to the **emails** table are completely full of **NULL** values. This arrangement explains how the outer join is different from the inner join. If the inner join was used, the **customer_id 27** row would not show because there is no matching record in the **emails** table.

This query, however, is still useful because you can now use it to find people who have never received an email. Because those customers who were never sent an email have a null **customer_id** column in the values returned from **emails** table, you can find all these customers by checking the **customer_id** column in the **emails** table, as follows:

```sql
SELECT
    c.customer_id,
    c.title,
    c.first_name,
    c.last_name,
    c.suffix,
    c.email,
    e.email_id,
    e.email_subject,
    e.opened,
    e.clicked,
    e.bounced,
    e.sent_date,
    e.opened_date,
    e.clicked_date
FROM
  customers c
LEFT OUTER JOIN
  emails e ON c.customer_id = e.customer_id
WHERE
  e.customer_id IS NULL
ORDER BY
  c.customer_id
LIMIT
  1000;
```

The following is the output of the query:

customer_id bigint	first_name text	last_name text	customer_id bigint	email_id bigint
27	Anson	Fellibrand	[null]	[null]
32	Hamnet	Purselowe	[null]	[null]
70	Caty	Woolveridge	[null]	[null]
77	Donal	Lattey	[null]	[null]
112	Harcourt	Cripps	[null]	[null]
113	Giffy	Bennington	[null]	[null]
125	Bernard	Jirka	[null]	[null]
192	Selina	Hearl	[null]	[null]
199	Mercy	Martschik	[null]	[null]

Figure 3.10: Customers with no emails sent

As you can see, all entries are blank in the **email_id** column of the **emails** table, indicating that the customer of that row has not received any emails. You could simply grab the emails from this join to get all the customers who have not received an email.

- Right outer join: A **right outer join** is very similar to a left join, except the table on the "right" (the second listed table) will now have every row show up, and the "left" table will have **NULL** values if the **JOIN** condition is not met. To illustrate, let's "flip" the last query by right-joining the **emails** table to the **customers** table with the following query:

```
SELECT
    e.email_id,
    e.email_subject,
    e.opened,
    e.clicked,
    e.bounced,
    e.sent_date,
    e.opened_date,
e.clicked_date,
```

```
      c.customer_id,
      c.title,
      c.first_name,
      c.last_name,
      c.suffix,
c.email
FROM emails e
RIGHT OUTER JOIN customers c
  ON e.customer_id=c.customer_id
ORDER BY
  c.customer_id
LIMIT
  1000;
```

When you run this query, you will get something similar to the following result:

customer_id bigint	email_id bigint	customer_id bigint	first_name text	last_name text
25	174755	25	Jillie	Stoter
25	245834	25	Jillie	Stoter
25	370746	25	Jillie	Stoter
26	324008	26	Rhiamon	Wynes
26	370747	26	Rhiamon	Wynes
[null]	[null]	27	Anson	Fellibrand
28	324009	28	Gradey	Garrat
28	370748	28	Gradey	Garrat
29	245835	29	Ashia	Hyndman
29	67733	29	Ashia	Hyndman

Figure 3.11: Emails right-joined to the customers table

Notice that this output is similar to what was produced in *Figure 3.9*, except that the data from the **emails** table is now on the left-hand side, and the data from the **customers** table is on the right-hand side. Once again, **customer_id 27** has **NULL** for the email. This shows the symmetry between a right join and a left join.

- Full outer join: Finally, there is the **full outer join**. The full outer join will return all rows from the left and right tables, regardless of whether the join predicate is matched. For rows where the join predicate is met, the two rows are combined just like in an inner join. For rows where it is not met, each row from both tables will be selected as an individual row, with **NULL** filled in for the columns from the other table. The full outer join is invoked by using the **FULL OUTER JOIN** clause, followed by a join predicate. Here is the syntax of this join:

```
SELECT
  *
FROM
  emails e
FULL OUTER JOIN
  customers c
  ON e.customer_id=c.customer_id;
```

The following is the output of the code:

customer_id bigint	email_id bigint	customer_id bigint	first_name text	last_name text
575	175138	575	Hillie	Suatt
1074	175484	1074	Fonz	O'Loghlen
4229	177740	4229	Clarance	Iley
4359	177826	4359	Gerald	Ben-Aharon
8197	180518	8197	Barton	Gatley
3802	285737	3802	Forster	Ccomini
7759	289032	7759	Worthington	Borris
9566	290506	9566	Micaela	Shippey
13851	294066	13851	Anastassia	Sperling

Figure 3.12: Emails are full outer joined to the customers table

In this section, you learned how to implement three different types of outer joins. In the next section, you will learn about the cross join.

CROSS JOINS

Cross join is a join type that has no join predicate. That means every row from the "left" table will be matched to all the rows in the "right" table, regardless of whether they are related or not. It is also referred to as the Cartesian product. It is named "Cartesian" after the French mathematician René Descartes, who raised the idea of this type of operation. It can be invoked using a **CROSS JOIN** clause, followed by the name of the other table. To better understand this, take the example of the **products** table.

A common analysis is called market basket analysis, which studies the selling patterns between multiple products. For example, diapers are usually sold together with baby wipes. So, if you are running a two-month giveaway for diapers for marketing purposes and expect more customers to come to the diaper aisle or web page, you may want to place baby wipes there too. To perform market basket analysis, you want to know every possible combination of two products that you could create from a given set of products (such as the ones found in the **products** table) to create a two-month giveaway for marketing purposes. You can use a cross join to get the answer to the question using the following query:

```sql
SELECT
    P1.product_id, p1.model,
    P2.product_id, p2.model
FROM
    products p1
CROSS JOIN
    products p2;
```

The output of this query is as follows:

product_id bigint	model text		product_id bigint	model text
1	Lemon		1	Lemon
1	Lemon		2	Lemon Limited Edition
1	Lemon		3	Lemon
1	Lemon		5	Blade
1	Lemon		7	Bat
1	Lemon		8	Bat Limited Edition
1	Lemon		12	Lemon Zester
1	Lemon		4	Model Chi
1	Lemon		6	Model Sigma
1	Lemon		9	Model Epsilon
1	Lemon		10	Model Gamma

Figure 3.13: The cross join of a product to itself

In this case, you have joined every value of every field in one table to the same in another table. The result of the query has 144 rows, which is the equivalent of multiplying the 12 products by the same 12 products (12 * 12). You can also see that cross join does not require a join predicate. In other words, a cross join can simply be thought of as just an outer join with no conditions for joining.

In general, cross joins are not used much in practice as they can hamper the process if you are not careful. Cross joining two large tables can lead to the origination of hundreds of billions of rows, which can stall and crash a database. So, if you decide to use a cross join, ensure you take utmost care when using it.

So far, you have covered the basics of using joins to fuse tables for a custom analysis of data. You will practice this in the following exercise.

EXERCISE 3.01: USING JOINS TO ANALYZE A SALES DEALERSHIP

In this exercise, you will use joins to bring related tables together. For instance, the head of sales at your company would like a list of all customers who bought a car. To do the task, you need to create a query that will return all customer IDs, first names, last names, and valid phone numbers of customers who purchased a car.

> **NOTE**
>
> For all exercises in this book, you will be using **pgAdmin**. All the code files for the exercises and the activity in this chapter are also available on GitHub at https://packt.link/Y08W5.

To complete this exercise, perform the following steps:

1. Open **pgAdmin**, connect to the **sqlda** database, and open SQL query editor.

2. Use an inner join to bring the **sales**, **customers**, and **products** tables together, which returns data for customer IDs, first names, last names, and valid phone numbers:

```
SELECT
    c.customer_id, c.first_name,
    c.last_name, c.phone
FROM
    sales s
INNER JOIN
    customers c ON c.customer_id=s.customer_id
INNER JOIN
    products p ON p.product_id=s.product_id
WHERE
    p.product_type='automobile'
    AND c.phone IS NOT NULL;
```

You should get an output similar to the following:

customer_id bigint	first_name text	last_name text	phone text
46003	Anabelle	Southby	410-100-8687
19035	Belia	Turbat	202-781-5824
35824	Wyatan	Dickie	405-786-0858
13206	Stace	Tuison	810-769-8255
2958	Kirstyn	Draysay	208-534-6858
32636	Kile	Fishlee	937-207-1484
26730	Raina	Titterell	304-871-4445
23832	Harrietta	Leverette	803-298-1584
35844	Maura	Clyne	904-169-7028
43229	Field	Lopes	757-409-4658
6038	Carey	Swadling	727-426-1044

Figure 3.14: Customers who bought a car

You can see that running the query helped you to join the data from the **sales**, **customers**, and **products** tables and obtain a list of customers who bought a car and have a phone number.

> **NOTE**
>
> To access the source code for this specific section, please refer to https://packt.link/Y08W5.

In this exercise, using joins, you were able to bring together related tables easily and efficiently. Several times, you will also want to combine the result of your queries to form new queries so that you can build data analysis on top of existing analysis. You can now move forward to learn about methods for joining queries in a dataset.

SUBQUERIES

So far, you have been pulling data from tables. You may have observed that the results of all **SELECT** queries are two-dimensional relations that look like the tables in a relational database. Knowing this, you may wonder whether there is some way to use the relations produced by the **SELECT** queries instead of referencing an existing table in your database. The answer is "yes." You can simply take a query, insert it between a pair of parentheses, and give it an alias. This will help you to build an analysis on top of existing analysis, thus reducing errors and improving efficiency.

For example, if you wanted to find all the salespeople working in California and get the results the same as in *Figure 3.7*, you could write the query using the following alternative:

```
SELECT
   *
FROM
   salespeople
INNER JOIN (
   SELECT
      *
   FROM
      dealerships
   WHERE
      dealerships.state = 'CA'
   ) d
ON d.dealership_id = salespeople.dealership_id
ORDER BY
   1;
```

Here, instead of joining the two tables and filtering for rows with the state equal to **'CA'**, you first find the dealerships where the state equals **'CA'**, and then inner join the rows in that query to **salespeople**.

If a query only has one column, you can use a subquery with the **IN** keyword in a **WHERE** clause. For example, another way to extract the details from the **salespeople** table using the dealership ID for the state of California would be as follows:

```
SELECT
   *
FROM
   salespeople
```

```
WHERE dealership_id IN (
  SELECT dealership_id FROM dealerships
  WHERE dealerships.state = 'CA'
  )
ORDER BY
  1;
```

As illustrated in all of these examples, it is quite easy to write the same query using multiple techniques. In the next section, you will learn about unions.

UNIONS

Up till now, in this chapter, you have learned how to join data horizontally. You can use joins to add new columns horizontally. However, you may be interested in putting multiple queries together vertically, that is, by keeping the same number of columns but adding multiple rows. Please see this example for more clarity on this.

Suppose you wanted to visualize the addresses of dealerships and customers using Google Maps. To do this, you would need the addresses of both customers and dealerships. You could build a query with all customer addresses as follows:

```
SELECT
  street_address, city, state, postal_code
FROM
  customers
WHERE
  street_address IS NOT NULL;
```

You could also retrieve dealership addresses with the following query:

```
SELECT
  street_address, city, state, postal_code
FROM
  dealerships
WHERE
  street_address IS NOT NULL;
```

To reduce complexity, it would be nice if there were a way to assemble the two queries into one list with a single query. This is where the **UNION** keyword comes into play. You can use the two previous queries and create the following query:

```
(
SELECT
  street_address, city, state, postal_code
FROM
  customers
WHERE
  street_address IS NOT NULL
)
UNION
(
SELECT
  street_address, city, state, postal_code
FROM
  dealerships
WHERE
  street_address IS NOT NULL
)
ORDER BY
  1;
```

This produces the following output:

street_address text	city text	state text	postal_code text
0 1st Avenue	Madison	WI	53710
0 1st Plaza	Scranton	PA	18514
0 2nd Parkway	Maple Plain	MN	55572
0 2nd Pass	Richmond	VA	23213
0 2nd Point	Charleston	WV	25389
0 4th Plaza	New Orleans	LA	70124
0 4th Terrace	North Las Vegas	NV	89036
0 6th Center	Austin	TX	78732
0 6th Circle	Atlanta	GA	30392

Figure 3.15: Union of addresses

Please note that there are certain conditions that need to be kept in mind when using **UNION**. Firstly, **UNION** requires the subqueries to have the same number of columns and the same data types for the columns. If they do not, the query will fail to run. Secondly, **UNION** technically may not return all the rows from its subqueries. **UNION**, by default, removes all duplicate rows in the output. If you want to retain the duplicate rows, it is preferable to use the **UNION ALL** keyword. For example, if both of the previous queries return a row with address values such as '123 Main St', 'Madison', 'WI', '53710', the result of the **UNION** statement will only contain one record for this value set, but the result of the **UNION ALL** statement will include two records of the same value, one from each query.

In the next exercise, you will implement union operations.

EXERCISE 3.02: GENERATING AN ELITE CUSTOMER PARTY GUEST LIST USING UNION

In this exercise, you will assemble two queries using **UNION**. To help build marketing awareness for the new **Model Chi**, the marketing team would like to throw a party for some of ZoomZoom's wealthiest customers in Los Angeles, CA. To help facilitate the party, they would like you to make a guest list with ZoomZoom customers who live in Los Angeles, CA, as well as salespeople who work at the ZoomZoom dealership in Los Angeles, CA. The guest list should include details such as the first and last names and whether the guest is a customer or an employee.

To complete the task, execute the following:

1. Open **pgAdmin**, connect to the **sqlda** database, and open the SQL query editor.

   Write a query that will make a list of ZoomZoom customers and company employees who live in Los Angeles, CA. The guest list should contain first and last names and whether the guest is a customer or an employee:

```
(
SELECT
    first_name, last_name, 'Customer' as guest_type
FROM
    customers
WHERE
    city='Los Angeles'
    AND state='CA'
)
UNION
(
```

```
SELECT
  first_name, last_name,
  'Employee' as guest_type
FROM
  salespeople s
INNER JOIN
  dealerships d ON d.dealership_id=s.dealership_id
WHERE
  d.city='Los Angeles'
  AND d.state='CA'
);
```

You should get the following output:

first_name text	last_name text	guest_type text
Hyman	Gabbitus	Customer
Brandise	Yude	Customer
Barron	Dawney	Customer
Bob	Adamolli	Customer
Carroll	Pudan	Employee
Abbott	Poupard	Customer
Tonnie	Housecraft	Customer
Creight	Conkay	Customer
Cordi	Larmett	Customer
Demetre	Quarterman	Customer
Cordy	MacGinney	Customer

Figure 3.16: Customer and employee guest list in Los Angeles, CA

You can see the guest list of customers and employees from Los Angeles, CA, after running the **UNION** query.

2. To demonstrate the usage of **UNION ALL**, first run a simple query that combines the **products** table with all the rows:

```
SELECT * FROM products
UNION
SELECT * FROM products
ORDER BY 1;
```

You can see that the query returns 12 rows and there are no duplicated rows, just the same as the original **products** table. However, say you run the following query:

```
SELECT * FROM products
UNION ALL
SELECT * FROM products
ORDER BY 1;
```

You will see that the query returns 24 rows, in which each row is repeated twice. This is because the **UNION ALL** statement keeps the duplicated rows from both **products** tables.

> **NOTE**
>
> To access the source code for this specific section, please refer to
> https://packt.link/Y08W5.

In the exercise, you used the **UNION** keyword to combine rows from different queries effortlessly. In the next section, you will explore **common table expressions (CTEs)**.

COMMON TABLE EXPRESSIONS

CTEs are simply a different version of subqueries. CTEs establish temporary tables by using the **WITH** clause. To understand this clause better, look at the following query, which you used before to find California-based salespeople:

```
SELECT
  *
FROM
  salespeople

INNER JOIN (
  SELECT
```

```
      *
  FROM
    dealerships
  WHERE
    dealerships.state = 'CA'
  ) d
ON d.dealership_id = salespeople.dealership_id
ORDER BY
  1;
```

This could be written using CTEs, as follows:

```
WITH d as (
  SELECT
    *
  FROM
    dealerships
  WHERE
    dealerships.state = 'CA'
  )
SELECT
  *
FROM
  salespeople
INNER JOIN
  d ON d.dealership_id = salespeople.dealership_id
ORDER BY
  1;
```

The one advantage of CTEs is that they can be designed to be recursive. **Recursive CTEs** can reference themselves. Because of this feature, you can use them to solve problems that other queries cannot. However, recursive CTEs are beyond the scope of this book.

Now that you know several ways to join data across a database, look at how to transform the data from these outputs.

CLEANING DATA

Often, the raw data presented in a query output may not be in the desired form. You may want to remove values, substitute values, or map values to other values. To accomplish these tasks, SQL provides a wide variety of statements and functions. Functions are keywords that take in inputs (such as a column or a scalar value) and process those inputs into some sort of output. You will learn about some useful functions for data transformation and cleaning in the following sections.

THE CASE WHEN FUNCTION

CASE WHEN is a function that allows a query to map various values in a column to other values. The general format of a **CASE WHEN** statement is as follows:

```
CASE
   WHEN condition1 THEN value1
   WHEN condition2 THEN value2
   …
   WHEN conditionX THEN valueX
   ELSE else_value
END;
```

Here, **condition1** and **condition2**, through **conditionX**, are Boolean conditions; **value1** and **value2**, through **valueX**, are values to map to the Boolean conditions; and **else_value** is the value that is mapped if none of the Boolean conditions is met. For each row, the program starts at the top of the **CASE WHEN** statement and evaluates the first Boolean condition. The program then runs through each Boolean condition from the first one. For the first condition from the start of the statement that evaluates as **True**, the statement will return the value associated with that condition. If none of the statements evaluates as **True**, then the value associated with the **ELSE** statement will be returned.

For example, you want to return all rows for customers from the **customers** table. Additionally, you would like to add a column that labels a user as being an **Elite Customer** type if they live in postal code **33111**, or as a **Premium Customer** type if they live in postal code **33124**. Otherwise, it will mark the customer as a **Standard Customer** type. This column will be called **customer_type**. You can create this table by using a **CASE WHEN** statement, as follows:

```
SELECT
  CASE
    WHEN postal_code='33111' THEN 'Elite Customer'
    WHEN postal_code='33124' THEN 'Premium Customer'
```

```
    ELSE 'Standard Customer'
  END AS customer_type,
  *
FROM customers;
```

This query should give the following output:

customer_type 🔒 text	customer_id 🔒 bigint	first_name 🔒 text	last_name 🔒 text
Standard Customer	224	Tommy	Attenbrow
Standard Customer	225	Dari	Garbutt
Elite Customer	226	Veriee	Woodrough
Standard Customer	227	Lenci	Story
Standard Customer	228	Skipp	Collocott
Standard Customer	229	Lucio	Mallen
Standard Customer	230	Newton	Roydon
Standard Customer	231	Hayley	Raund
Standard Customer	232	Godwin	Plet
Standard Customer	233	Vilhelmina	Behnecke

Figure 3.17: The customer_type query

As you can see in the preceding table, there is a column called **customer_type** indicating the type of customer a user is. The **CASE WHEN** statement effectively mapped a postal code to a string describing the customer type. Using a **CASE WHEN** statement, you can map values in any way you please.

EXERCISE 3.03: USING THE CASE WHEN FUNCTION TO GET REGIONAL LISTS

The aim of this exercise is to create a query that will map various values in a column to other values. For instance, the head of sales has an idea to try and create specialized regional sales teams that will be able to sell scooters to customers in specific regions, as opposed to generic sales teams.

To make their idea a reality, the head of sales would like a list of all customers mapped to regions. For customers from the states of MA, NH, VT, ME, CT, or RI, they would like them labeled as **New England**. Customers from the states of GA, FL, MS, AL, LA, KY, VA, NC, SC, TN, VI, WV, or AR, they would like the customers labeled as **Southeast**. Customers from any other state should be labeled as **Other**.

To complete this exercise, perform the following steps:

1. Open **pgAdmin**, connect to the **sqlda** database, and open the SQL query editor.

2. Create a query that will produce a **customer_id** column and a column called **region**, with the states categorized as in the following scenario:

```sql
SELECT
  c.customer_id,
  CASE
    WHEN c.state in (
      'MA', 'NH', 'VT', 'ME',
      'CT', 'RI')
    THEN 'New England'
    WHEN c.state in (
      'GA', 'FL', 'MS',
      'AL', 'LA', 'KY', 'VA',
      'NC', 'SC', 'TN', 'VI',
      'WV', 'AR')
    THEN 'Southeast'
ELSE 'Other'
  END as region
FROM
  customers c
ORDER BY
  1;
```

This query will map a state to one of the regions based on whether the state is in the **CASE WHEN** condition listed for that line. You should get the following output:

customer_id 🔒 bigint	region 🔒 text
1	Other
2	Other
3	Southeast
4	Southeast
5	Southeast
6	Southeast
7	Southeast
8	New England
9	Other
10	Other
11	Other

Figure 3.18: The regional query output

In the preceding output, in the case of each customer, a region has been mapped based on the state where the customer resides.

> **NOTE**
>
> To access the source code for this specific section, please refer to https://packt.link/Y08W5.

In this exercise, you learned how to map various values in a column to other values using the **CASE WHEN** function. In the next section, you will learn about a useful function, **COALESCE**, which will help to replace the **NULL** values.

THE COALESCE FUNCTION

Another common requirement is to replace the **NULL** values with a standard value. This can be accomplished easily by means of the **COALESCE** function. **COALESCE** allows you to list any number of columns and scalar values, and, if the first value in the list is **NULL**, it will try to fill it in with the second value. The **COALESCE** function will keep continuing down the list of values until it hits a non-**NULL** value. If all values in the **COALESCE** function are **NULL**, then the function returns **NULL**.

To illustrate a simple usage of the **COALESCE** function, study the **customers** table. Some of the records do not have the value of the **phone** field populated:

first_name text	last_name text	phone text
Jarred	Bester	[null]
Ag	Smerdon	[null]
Giuditta	Eim	202-227-5491
Nichole	Rosle	614-146-7408
Chic	Bryning	512-939-4727
Jessee	Lytell	[null]
Tova	Simao	[null]
Huberto	Colerick	513-537-8523
Sherwynd	Lammert	[null]
Hayyim	Tuftin	281-129-7442
Morganica	Itzkin	415-568-8196

Figure 3.19: The COALESCE query

For instance, the marketing team would like a list of the first names, last names, and phone numbers of all customers for a survey. However, for customers with no phone number, they would like the table to instead write the value **NO PHONE**. You can accomplish this request with **COALESCE**:

```
SELECT
  first_name, last_name,
  COALESCE(phone, 'NO PHONE') as phone
FROM
```

```
    customers
ORDER BY
    1;
```

This query produces the following results:

first_name text	last_name text	phone text
Aaren	Whelpdale	607-761-2568
Aaren	Sadat	504-559-3464
Aaren	Norrey	NO PHONE
Aaren	Lamlin	414-937-4628
Aaren	Deeman	NO PHONE
Aarika	Emmanuel	NO PHONE
Aarika	Guerin	501-121-5841
Aarika	Chadwell	915-856-7492
Aarika	Danaher	904-175-3112

Figure 3.20: The COALESCE query

When dealing with creating default values and avoiding **NULL**, **COALESCE** will always be helpful.

THE NULLIF FUNCTION

NULLIF is used as the opposite of **COALESCE**. While **COALESCE** is used to convert **NULL** into a standard value, **NULLIF** is a two-value function and will return **NULL** if the first value equals the second value.

For example, the marketing department has created a new direct mail piece to send to the customer. One of the quirks of this new piece of advertising is that it cannot accept people who have titles (Mr, Dr, Mrs, and so on) longer than three letters. However, some records may have a title that is longer than three letters. If the system cannot accept them, they should be removed during the retrieval of results.

In the sample database, the only known title longer than three characters is **Honorable**. Therefore, they would like you to create a mailing list that is just all the rows with valid street addresses and to block out all titles with **NULL** that are spelled as **Honorable**. This could be done with the following query:

```
SELECT customer_id,
       NULLIF(title, 'Honorable') as title,
       first_name,
       last_name,
       suffix,
       email,
       gender,
       ip_address,
       phone,
       street_address,
       city,
       state,
       postal_code,
       latitude,
       longitude,
       date_added
FROM
  customers c
ORDER BY
  1;
```

This will remove all mentions of **Honorable** from the **title** column.

customer_id bigint	title text	first_name text	last_name text	suffix text	email text
1	[null]	Arlena	Riveles	[null]	ariveles0@stumbleupon.com
2	Dr	Ode	Stovin	[null]	ostovin1@npr.org
3	[null]	Braden	Jordan	[null]	bjordan2@geocities.com
4	[null]	Jessika	Nussen	[null]	jnussen3@salon.com
5	[null]	Lonnie	Rembaud	[null]	lrembaud4@discovery.com
6	[null]	Cortie	Locksley	[null]	clocksley5@weather.com
7	[null]	Wood	Kennham	[null]	wkennham6@sohu.com
8	[null]	Rutger	Humblestone	[null]	rhumblestone7@digg.com
9	[null]	Melantha	Tibb	[null]	mtibb8@bbb.org

Figure 3.21: The NULLIF query

Next, you will learn about other types of functions, such as the **LEAST** and **GREATEST** functions.

THE LEAST/GREATEST FUNCTIONS

Two functions that come in handy for data preparation are the **LEAST** and **GREATEST** functions. Each function takes any number of values and returns the least or the greatest of the values, respectively.

For example, if you use the **LEAST** function with two parameters, such as **600** and **900**, **600** will be returned as the value. It is the opposite of what the **GREATEST** function will return. The parameters can either be literal values or the values stored inside numeric fields.

The simple use of this variable would be to replace the value if it is too high or low. You can study an example closely to understand it better. For instance, the sales team may want to create a sales list where every scooter is $600 or less. You can create this using the following query:

```
SELECT
    product_id, model,
    year, product_type,
    LEAST(600.00, base_msrp) as base_msrp,
    production_start_date,
    production_end_date
FROM
    products
WHERE
    product_type='scooter'
ORDER BY
    1;
```

This query should give the following output:

product_id bigint	model text	year bigint	product_type text	base_msrp numeric	production_start_date timestamp without time zone	production_end_date timestamp without time zone
1	Lemon	2013	scooter	399.99	2012-10-28 00:00:00	2015-02-03 00:00:00
2	Lemon Limited Edition	2014	scooter	600.00	2013-08-30 00:00:00	2013-11-24 00:00:00
3	Lemon	2016	scooter	499.99	2015-12-27 00:00:00	2021-08-24 00:00:00
5	Blade	2017	scooter	600.00	2017-02-17 00:00:00	2017-09-23 00:00:00
7	Bat	2019	scooter	599.99	2019-06-07 00:00:00	[null]
8	Bat Limited Edition	2020	scooter	600.00	2019-10-13 00:00:00	[null]
12	Lemon Zester	2022	scooter	349.99	2021-10-01 00:00:00	[null]

Figure 3.22: Cheaper scooters

From the output, you can see that if **base_msrp** was lower than **600**, the SQL query will return the original **base_msrp**. But if **base_msrp** is higher than **600**, you will get **600** back. It is the lower value of **base_msrp** and **600** that the query returns, which is what the **LEAST()** function is supposed to do.

THE CASTING FUNCTION

Another useful data transformation is to change the data type of a column within a query. This is usually done to use a function only available to one data type, such as text, while working with a column that is in a different data type, such as numeric. To change the data type of a column, you simply need to use the **column::datatype** format, where **column** is the column name and **datatype** is the data type you want to change the column to.

For example, to change the year in the **products** table to a text column in a query, use the following query:

```
SELECT
    product_id,
    model,
    year::TEXT,
    product_type,
    base_msrp,
    production_start_date,
    production_end_date
FROM
    products;
```

This query produces the following output:

product_id bigint	model text	year text	product_type text	base_msrp numeric	production_start_date timestamp without time zone	production_end_date timestamp without time zone
1	Lemon	2013	scooter	399.99	2012-10-28 00:00:00	2015-02-03 00:00:00
2	Lemon Limited Edition	2014	scooter	799.99	2013-08-30 00:00:00	2013-11-24 00:00:00
3	Lemon	2016	scooter	499.99	2015-12-27 00:00:00	2021-08-24 00:00:00
5	Blade	2017	scooter	699.99	2017-02-17 00:00:00	2017-09-23 00:00:00
7	Bat	2019	scooter	599.99	2019-06-07 00:00:00	[null]
8	Bat Limited Edition	2020	scooter	699.99	2019-10-13 00:00:00	[null]
12	Lemon Zester	2022	scooter	349.99	2021-10-01 00:00:00	[null]
4	Model Chi	2017	automobile	115000.00	2017-02-17 00:00:00	2021-08-24 00:00:00

Figure 3.23: The year column as text

This will convert the **year** column to text. You can now apply text functions to this transformed column. Please note that not every data type can be cast to a specific data type. For instance, **datetime** cannot be cast to float types. Your SQL client will throw an error if you ever make an unexpected conversion.

TRANSFORMING DATA

Each dataset is unique along with each of the business use cases for the datasets. That means the processing and transforming of datasets are unique in their own way. However, there are some processing logics that you will frequently run into in the real world. You will learn some of these in the sections in this section.

THE DISTINCT AND DISTINCT ON FUNCTIONS

When looking through a dataset, you may be interested in determining the unique values in a column or group of columns. This is the primary use case of the **DISTINCT** keyword.

For example, if you wanted to know all the unique model years in the **products** table, you could use the following query:

```
SELECT DISTINCT year
FROM products
ORDER BY 1;
```

This should give the following result:

year bigint
2013
2014
2016
2017
2018
2019
2020
2022

Figure 3.24: Distinct model years

You can also use it with multiple columns to get all the distinct column combinations present. For example, to find all distinct years and what product types were released for those model years, you can simply use the following:

```
SELECT DISTINCT year, product_type
FROM products
ORDER BY 1, 2;
```

This should give the following output:

year bigint	product_type text
2013	scooter
2014	scooter
2016	scooter
2017	automobile
2017	scooter
2018	automobile
2019	scooter
2020	automobile
2020	scooter
2022	automobile
2022	scooter

Figure 3.25: Distinct model years and product types

Another keyword related to **DISTINCT** is **DISTINCT ON**. Now, **DISTINCT ON** allows you to ensure that only one row is returned, and one or more columns are always unique in the set. The general syntax of a **DISTINCT ON** query is as follows:

```
SELECT DISTINCT ON (distinct_column)
column_1,
column_2,
...
column_n
FROM table
ORDER BY order_column;
```

Here, **distinct_column** is the column(s) you want to be distinct in your query, **column_1** through **column_n** are the columns you want in the query, and **order_column** allows you to determine the first row that will be returned for a **DISTINCT ON** query if multiple columns have the same value for **distinct_column**.

For **order_column**, the first column mentioned should be **distinct_column**. If an **ORDER BY** clause is not specified, the first row will be decided randomly.

For example, you want to get a unique list of **salespeople** where each salesperson has a unique first name. In the case that two salespeople have the same first name, you will return the one that joined the company earlier. This query would look as follows:

```
SELECT DISTINCT ON (first_name)
  *
FROM
  salespeople
ORDER BY
  first_name, hire_date;
```

It should return this output:

salesperson_id bigint	dealership_id bigint	title text	first_name text	last_name text	suffix text	username text	gender text	hire_date timestamp without time	termination_date timestamp without time zone
139	18	[null]	Alexina	Coatswor...	[null]	acoatsworth3u	Female	2018-03-23 00:00:00	[null]
100	18	[null]	Alie	Bellfield	[null]	abellfield2r	Female	2020-08-07 00:00:00	[null]
287	7	[null]	Allayne	Billingham	[null]	abillingham7y	Male	2017-04-02 00:00:00	[null]
203	2	[null]	Amabelle	Bigby	[null]	abigby5m	Female	2019-10-07 00:00:00	[null]
176	19	[null]	Amble	Moulding	[null]	amoulding4v	Male	2020-11-23 00:00:00	[null]
109	9	[null]	Andrey	Haack	[null]	ahaack30	Male	2018-09-06 00:00:00	[null]
246	10	[null]	Annabell	Gilmore	[null]	agilmore6t	Female	2020-04-25 00:00:00	[null]
193	20	[null]	Any	Dellenbro...	[null]	adellenbrook5c	Male	2019-02-07 00:00:00	[null]
260	14	[null]	Aprilette	Bimson	[null]	abimson77	Female	2017-07-03 00:00:00	[null]
149	6	[null]	Arlen	Orridge	[null]	aorridge44	Female	2020-09-29 00:00:00	[null]
196	7	[null]	Arlinda	Vaissiere	[null]	avaissiere5f	Female	2018-04-30 00:00:00	[null]

Figure 3.26: DISTINCT ON first_name

This table now guarantees that every row has a distinct username. If there are multiple users with the same first name, then the user who was hired first by the company will be pulled by the query.

For example, if the **salespeople** table has multiple rows with the first name **Abby**, the row in *Figure 3.26* with the name of **Abby** (that is, the first row in the outputs) is for the first person employed at the company with the name **Abby**. Likewise, when you have two employees with the same first name, the query results will order them by the start date. For example, when two employees, **Andrey Haack** with the start date of **2016-01-10** and **Andrey Kures** with the start date of **2016-05-17**, exist in the database, **Andrey Haack** will be listed first, since his start date is earlier.

In the next section, you will go through an activity demonstrating how SQL can be used to make a dataset for a model.

ACTIVITY 3.01: BUILDING A SALES MODEL USING SQL TECHNIQUES

In this activity, you will clean and prepare the data for analysis using SQL techniques. The data science team wants to build a new model to help predict which customers are the best prospects for remarketing. A new data scientist has joined their team. It is your responsibility to help the new data scientist prepare and build a dataset to be used to train a model. Write a query to assemble a dataset. Here are the steps to perform:

1. Open **pgAdmin**, connect to the **sqlda** database, and open the SQL query editor.

2. Use **INNER JOIN** to join the **customers** table to the **sales** table.

3. Use **INNER JOIN** to join the **products** table to the **sales** table.

4. Use **LEFT JOIN** to join the **dealerships** table (right table) to the **sales** table (left table).

5. Return all columns of the **customers** table and the **products** table.

6. Return the **dealership_id** column from the **sales** table, but fill in **dealership_id** in **sales** with **-1** if it is **NULL**.

7. Add a column called **high_savings** that returns **1** if the sales amount was **500** less than **base_msrp** or lower. Otherwise, it returns **0**. Please make sure that you perform the query on a joined table.

Expected Output:

The following figure shows some of the rows from the output of this activity. You can see that a number of **dealership_id** are replaced with **-1** by the query, as they are indeed **NULL**. This is because internet sales do not go through a dealership and thus do not have a **dealership_id** value. Some of the rows also have their value in the **high_savings** column marked as **1**, indicating the sales amount is $500 or more below **base_msrp**. You can go through some rows, try to get the original data, and confirm the SQL is written properly:

sales_dealership double precision	high_savings integer	customer_id bigint	title text	first_name text	last_name text	suffix text
-1	0	2275	[null]	Chic	Bryning	[null]
-1	0	2275	[null]	Chic	Bryning	[null]
19	0	2552	[null]	Tova	Simao	[null]
-1	0	3050	[null]	Huberto	Colerick	[null]
1	0	3615	[null]	Hayyim	Tuftin	[null]
-1	0	4396	[null]	Morganica	Itzkin	[null]
-1	0	4610	[null]	Carroll	Pavy	[null]
19	0	4836	[null]	Rani	Quested	[null]
19	0	4836	[null]	Rani	Quested	[null]
-1	0	5090	[null]	Ingemar	Taye	[null]

Figure 3.27: Building a sales model query

You have now learned how SQL can be used to clean and organize data for analytical purposes.

> **NOTE**
>
> The solution for this activity can be found on page 440.

SUMMARY

SQL provides you with many tools for mixing and cleaning data. In this chapter, you first learned how to combine two or more tables. You started with the **JOIN** keyword, which fuses data from tables based on their common columns. There are several types of **JOIN**. Depending on whether you want to retain the data in a certain table or not, you can choose **INNER JOIN**, **LEFT OUTER JOIN**, **RIGHT OUTER JOIN**, **FULL OUTER JOIN**, or **CROSS JOIN**. You then learned how to use subqueries and CTEs to preserve and reuse the results of queries. You can also use **UNION** and **UNION ALL** to merge the results of two queries with the same structure into one result set.

After learning how to combine data from different datasets, you learned how to perform certain transformations on the data. You first started with the **CASE WHEN** function, which is a generic way to convert one expression into another based on custom-defined conditions. You then learned how to use the **COALESCE()** and **NULLIF()** functions to convert between **NULL** and non-**NULL** values. You also learned how to change the data type of an expression using casting functions, and finally, you learned about the **DISTINCT** and **DISTINCT ON** functions to get distinct lists of values.

Now that you know how to prepare a dataset, you will learn how to start making analytical insights in the next chapter, using aggregate functions.

4

AGGREGATE FUNCTIONS FOR DATA ANALYSIS

OVERVIEW

In this chapter, you will study the conceptual logic of aggregate functions, write SQL to execute these functions, and learn how to analyze data using them. You will also learn how to modify them using keywords such as **HAVING** and **GROUP BY**.

By the end of this chapter, you will be able to apply these functions to gain new insights into data and understand the properties of datasets, such as data quality.

INTRODUCTION

In the previous chapter, you learned how to use SQL to prepare datasets for analysis. Eventually, the purpose of data preparation is to make the data suitable for analysis so that you can make sense of it. Once the data has been prepared, the next step is to analyze it. Generally, data scientists and analytics professionals will try to understand the data by summarizing it and trying to find high-level patterns. SQL can help with this task primarily by using aggregate functions. These functions take multiple rows as input and return new information based on those input rows. To begin, you will learn about aggregate functions.

In this chapter, you will understand the fundamentals of aggregate functions through the following topics:

- Aggregate Functions

- Aggregate Functions with the **GROUP BY** Clause

- Aggregate Functions with the **HAVING** Clause

- Using Aggregates to Clean Data and Examine Data Quality

AGGREGATE FUNCTIONS

In addition to just seeing individual rows of data, it is also interesting to understand the properties of an entire column or table. For example, say you just received a sample dataset of a fictional company called ZoomZoom, which specializes in car and electronic scooter retailing. You are wondering about the number of customers that this ZoomZoom database contains. You could select all the data from the table and then see how many rows were pulled back, but it would be incredibly tedious to do so. Luckily, there are functions provided by SQL that can be used to perform this type of calculation on large groups of rows. These functions are called **aggregate functions**.

Aggregate functions take in one or more columns with multiple rows and return a number based on those columns. The following table provides a summary of the major aggregate functions that are used in SQL:

Function	Explanation
COUNT(columnX)	Counts the number of rows in columnX that have a non-NULL value.
COUNT(*)	Counts the number of rows in the output table.
MIN(columnX)	Returns the minimum value in columnX. For text columns, it returns the value that would appear first alphabetically.
MAX(columnX)	Returns the maximum value in columnX.
SUM(columnX)	Returns the sum of all values in columnX.
AVG(columnX)	Returns the average of all values in columnX.
STDDEV(columnX)	Returns the sample standard deviation of all values in columnX.
VAR(columnX)	Returns the sample variance of all values in columnX.
REGR_SLOPE(columnX, columnY)	Returns the slope of linear regression for columnX as the response variable and columnY as the predictor variable.
REGR_INTERCEPT(columnX, columnY)	Returns the intercept of linear regression for columnX as the response variable and columnY as the predictor variable.
CORR(columnX, columnY)	Calculates the Pearson correlation between columnX and columnY in the data.

Figure 4.1: Major aggregate functions

The most frequently used aggregate functions include **SUM()**, **AVG()**, **MIN()**, **MAX()**, **COUNT()**, and **STDDEV()**. You will also notice the **CORR()** function, which was discussed in *Chapter 1, Understanding and Describing Data*. SQL provides this function so that you do not need to calculate it manually.

Aggregate functions can help you to smoothly execute several tasks, such as the following:

- Aggregate functions can be used with the **WHERE** clause to calculate aggregate values for specific subsets of data. For example, if you want to know how many customers ZoomZoom has in California, you could use the following query:

```
SELECT
   COUNT(*)
FROM
   customers
WHERE
   state='CA';
```

This results in the following output:

Figure 4.2: Result of COUNT(*) with the WHERE clause

- You can do arithmetic with aggregate functions. In the following query, you can divide the count of rows in the **customers** table by 2:

```
SELECT
   COUNT(*)/2
FROM
   customers;
```

This query will return **25000**.

Figure 4.3: Result of function – constant calculation

- You can use aggregate functions with each other in mathematical ways. If you want to calculate the average value of a specific column, you can use the **AVG** function. For example, to calculate the average **Manufacturer's Suggested Retail Price (MSRP)** of products at ZoomZoom, you can use the **AVG (base_ msrp)** function in a query. In addition, you can also build the **AVG** function using **SUM** and **COUNT**, as follows:

```
SELECT
  SUM(base_msrp)/COUNT(*) AS avg_base_msrp
FROM
  Products;
```

You will get the following result:

avg_base_msrp
numeric

33358.327500000000

Figure 4.4: Result of function calculation

A frequently seen scenario is a calculation involving the **COUNT ()** function. For example, you can use the **COUNT** function to count the total number of ZoomZoom customers by counting the total rows in the **customers** table:

```
SELECT
  COUNT(customer_id)
FROM
  customers;
```

The **COUNT** function will return the number of rows without a **NULL** value in the column. Since the **customer_id** column is a primary key and cannot be **NULL**, the **COUNT** function will return the number of rows in the table. In this case, the query will return the following output:

count
bigint

50000

Figure 4.5: Result of the COUNT column

As shown here, the **COUNT** function works with a single column and counts how many non-**NULL** values it has. However, if the column has at least one **NULL** value, you will not be able to determine how many rows there are. To get a count of the number of rows in that situation, you could use the **COUNT** function with an asterisk in brackets, **(*)**, to get the total count of rows:

```
SELECT
    COUNT (*)
FROM
    customers;
```

This query will also return **50000**:

count bigint

50000

Figure 4.6: Result of COUNT(*) as compared to the COUNT column

One of the major themes you will find in data analytics is that analysis is fundamentally only useful when there is a strong variation in the data. A column where every value is exactly the same is not a particularly useful column. To identify this potential issue, it often makes sense to determine how many distinct values there are in a column. To measure the number of distinct values in a column, you can use the **COUNT DISTINCT** function. The structure of such a query would look as follows:

```
SELECT
    COUNT (DISTINCT {column1})
FROM
    {table1}
```

Here, **{column1}** is the column you want to count and **{table1}** is the table with the column.

For example, say you want to verify that your customers are based in all 50 states of the US, possibly with the addition of Washington D.C., which is technically a federal territory but is treated as a state in your system. For this, you need to know the number of unique states in the customer list. You can use **COUNT(DISTINCT expression)** to process the query:

```
SELECT
    COUNT(DISTINCT state)
FROM
    customers;
```

This query returns the following output:

Figure 4.7: Result of COUNT DISTINCT

This result shows that you do have a national customer base in all 50 states and Washington D.C.. You can also calculate the average number of customers per state using the following SQL:

```
SELECT
    COUNT(customer_id)::numeric / COUNT(DISTINCT state)
FROM
    customers;
```

This query returns the following output:

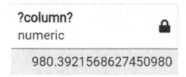

Figure 4.8: Result of COUNT division with casting

1. Note that in the preceding SQL, the count of customer ID is cast as numeric. The reason you must cast this as numeric is that the **COUNT ()** function always returns an integer. PostgreSQL treats integer division differently than float division in that it will ignore the decimal part of the result. For example, dividing 7 by 2 as integers in PostgreSQL will give you 3 instead of 3.5. In the preceding example, if you do not specify the casting, the SQL and its result will be as follows:

```
SELECT
   COUNT(customer_id)  / COUNT(DISTINCT state)
FROM
   customers;
```

You will get this output:

Figure 4.9: Result of COUNT division without casting

2. To get a more precise answer with a decimal part, you have to cast one of the numbers as a float. There is also an easier way to convert an integer into a float, which is to multiply it by 1.0. As 1.0 is a numeric value, its calculation with an integer value will result in a numeric value. For example, the following SQL will generate the same output as the SQL in the code block preceding *Figure 4.8*:

```
SELECT
   COUNT(customer_id) * 1.0 / COUNT(DISTINCT state)
FROM
   customers;
```

In the next section, you will work on an exercise to learn how to use aggregate functions as part of data analysis.

> **NOTE**
>
> For all the exercises in this book, you will be using pgAdmin 4, which you should have installed by following the instructions in the *Preface*. All the exercises and activities are also available on GitHub at https://packt.link/OU9zr.

EXERCISE 4.01: USING AGGREGATE FUNCTIONS TO ANALYZE DATA

In this exercise, you will analyze and calculate the price of a product using different aggregate functions. For instance, say you are curious about the data at your company and interested in understanding some of the basic statistics around ZoomZoom product prices. Now, you want to calculate the lowest price, highest price, average price, and standard deviation of the price for all the products the company has ever sold.

Perform the following steps to complete this exercise:

1. Open **pgAdmin**, connect to the **sqlda** database, and open SQL query editor.

2. Calculate the lowest price, highest price, average price, and standard deviation of the price using the **MIN**, **MAX**, **AVG**, and **STDDEV** aggregate functions, respectively, from the **products** table:

```
SELECT
  MIN(base_msrp),
  MAX(base_msrp),
  AVG(base_msrp),
  STDDEV(base_msrp)
FROM
  products;
```

The preceding code will produce an output similar to this:

min numeric	max numeric	avg numeric	stddev numeric
349.99	115000.00	33358.327500000000	44484.40866379

Figure 4.10: Statistics of the product price

From the preceding output, you can see that the minimum price is **349.99**, the maximum price is **115000.00**, the average price is **33358.32750**, and the standard deviation of the price is **44484.40866**.

> **NOTE**
>
> Your results may vary in comparison to the preceding output probably because your PostgreSQL instance may be configured to show a different number of decimal points in the output. The other reason for the difference in outputs could be that the data contained in the database has been modified from what it was when the original database was created from the dump file. However, the key objective here is to demonstrate how you can use the aggregate functions to analyze data.

In this exercise, you used aggregate functions to learn about the basic statistics of prices. Next, you will use aggregate functions with the **GROUP BY** clause.

> **NOTE**
>
> To access the source code for this specific section, please refer to
> https://packt.link/OU9zr.

AGGREGATE FUNCTIONS WITH THE GROUP BY CLAUSE

So far, you have used aggregate functions to calculate statistics for an entire column. However, most times you are interested in not only the aggregate values for a whole table but also the values for smaller groups in the table. To illustrate this, refer back to the **customers** table. You know that the total number of customers is 50,000. However, you might want to know how many customers there are in each state. But how can you calculate this?

You could determine how many states there are with the following query:

```
SELECT DISTINCT
  state
FROM
  customers;
```

You will see 50 distinct states, Washington D.C., and **NULL** returned as a result of the preceding query, totaling 52 rows. Once you have the list of states, you could then run the following query for each state:

```
SELECT
  COUNT(*)
FROM
  customers
WHERE
  state='{state}'
```

Although you can do this, it is incredibly tedious and can take a long time if there are many states. The **GROUP BY** clause provides a much more efficient solution.

THE GROUP BY CLAUSE

GROUP BY is a clause that divides the rows of a dataset into multiple groups based on some sort of key that is specified in the clause. An aggregate function is then applied to all the rows within a single group to produce a single number for that group. The **GROUP BY** key and the aggregate value for the group are then displayed in the SQL output. The following diagram illustrates this general process:

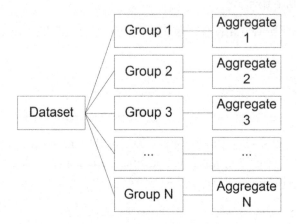

Figure 4.11: General GROUP BY computational model

In the preceding diagram, you can see that the dataset has multiple groups (**Group 1**, **Group 2**, ..., **Group N**). Here, the aggregate function is applied to all the rows in **Group 1** and generates the result **Aggregate 1**. Then, the aggregate function is applied to all the rows in **Group 2** and generates the result **Aggregate 2**, and so on.

The **GROUP BY** statements usually have the following structure:

```
SELECT
    {KEY},
    {AGGFUNC(column1)}
FROM
    {table1}
GROUP BY
    {KEY}
```

Here, **{KEY}** is a column or a function on a column that is used to create individual groups. For each value of **{KEY}**, a group is created. **{AGGFUNC(column1)}** is an aggregate function on a column that is calculated for all the rows within each group. **{table}** is the table or set of joined tables from which rows are separated into groups.

To illustrate this point, you can count the number of customers in each US state using a **GROUP BY** query:

```
SELECT
   state, COUNT(*)
FROM
   customers
GROUP BY
   state;
```

The computational model looks like this:

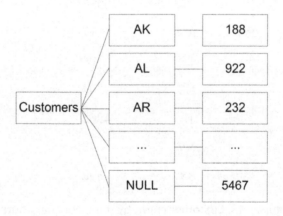

Figure 4.12: Customer count by the state computational model

Here, **AK**, **AL**, **AR**, and the other keys are abbreviations for US states. This grouping is a two-step process. In the first step, SQL will create groups based on the existing states, one group for each state, labeling the group with the state. SQL then will allocate customers into different groups based on their states. Once all the customers are allocated to their respective state groups, the execution goes into the second step. In this step, SQL will apply the aggregate function to each group and associate the result with the group label, which is **state** in this case. The output of the SQL will be a set of aggregate function results with its state label. You should get the following output, in which **state** is the label and **count** is the aggregate result:

state text	count bigint
KS	619
[null]	5467
CA	5038
NH	77
OR	386
ND	93
TX	4865
NV	643
KY	598

Figure 4.13: Customer count by the state query output

The **{KEY}** value for the **GROUP BY** operation can also be a function of column(s). The underlying example counts customers based on the year they were added to the database. Here, the year was the result of the **TO_CHAR** function on the **date_added** column:

```
SELECT
  TO_CHAR(date_added, 'YYYY'),
  COUNT(*)
FROM
  customers
```

```
GROUP BY
  TO_CHAR(date_added, 'YYYY')
ORDER BY
  1;
```

The result of this SQL is as follows:

to_char 🔒 text	count 🔒 bigint
2012	743
2013	5292
2014	5358
2015	5452
2016	5348
2017	5373
2018	5470
2019	5375
2020	5349

Figure 4.14: Customer count GROUP BY function

You can also use the column number to perform a **GROUP BY** operation:

```
SELECT
  state,
  COUNT(*)
FROM
  customers
GROUP BY
  1;
```

This SQL will return the same result as the previous one, which used the column name in the **GROUP BY** clause.

If you want to return the output in alphabetical order, simply use the following query:

```
SELECT
    state,
    COUNT(*)
FROM
    customers
GROUP BY
    state
ORDER BY
    state;
```

Alternatively, you can write the following with the column order number in **GROUP BY** and **ORDER BY** instead of column names:

```
SELECT
    state,
    COUNT(*)
FROM
    customers
GROUP BY
    1
ORDER BY
    1;
```

Either of these queries will give you the following result:

state text	count bigint
AK	188
AL	922
AR	232
AZ	931
CA	5038
CO	1042
CT	576
DC	1447
DE	149

Figure 4.15: Customer count by the state query output in alphabetical order

Often, though, you may be interested in ordering the aggregates themselves. You may want to know the number of customers in each state in increasing order so that you know which state has the least number of customers. You can then use this result to make a business decision, such as launching a new marketing campaign in the states where you don't have enough presence. This would require you to order the aggregates themselves. The aggregates can also be ordered using **ORDER BY**, as follows:

```
SELECT
    state,
    COUNT(*)
FROM
    customers
GROUP BY
    state
ORDER BY
    COUNT(*);
```

This query gives you the following output:

state text	count bigint
VT	16
WY	23
ME	25
RI	47
NH	77
ND	93
MT	122
SD	124
DE	149

Figure 4.16: Customer count by the state query output in increasing order

You may also want to count only a subset of the data, such as the total number of male customers in a particular state. To calculate the total number of male customers, you can use the following query:

```
SELECT
    state, COUNT(*)
FROM
    customers
WHERE
    gender='M'
GROUP BY
    state
ORDER BY
    State;
```

This gives you the following output:

state text	count bigint
AK	87
AL	489
AR	120
AZ	415
CA	2572
CO	526
CT	301
DC	713
DE	74

Figure 4.17: Male customer count by the state query output in alphabetical order

As shown here, grouping by one column can provide some great insight. You can get different aspects of the entire dataset, as well as any subset that you may think of. You can use these characteristics to construct a hypothesis and try to verify it. For example, you can identify the sales and the count of customers in each state, or better yet, the count of a specific subgroup of customers. From there, you can run a bivariate analysis, just like what you learned in *Chapter 1, Understanding and Describing Data*. If you can find a relationship between the sales amount and the particular group of customers, you may be able to figure out some way to reach out to more of these customers and thus increase the sales, or to figure out why other groups of customers are not as motivated.

In the next section, you will see that **GROUP BY** can be generalized to multiple columns to provide more granular insight.

MULTIPLE-COLUMN GROUP BY

While **GROUP BY** with one column is helpful, you can go even further and use **GROUP BY** on multiple columns. For instance, say you wanted to get a count of not just the number of customers ZoomZoom had in each state but also how many male and female customers it had in each state. You can find this using multiple **GROUP BY** columns, as follows:

```
SELECT
   state, gender, COUNT(*)
FROM
   customers
GROUP BY
   state, gender
ORDER BY
   state, gender;
```

This gives you the following result:

state text	gender text	count bigint
AK	F	101
AK	M	87
AL	F	433
AL	M	489
AR	F	112
AR	M	120
AZ	F	516
AZ	M	415
CA	F	2466

Figure 4.18: Customer count by the state and gender query outputs in alphabetical order

Any number of columns can be used in a **GROUP BY** operation in the same way as illustrated in the preceding example. In this case, SQL will create one group for each unique combination of column values, such as one group for **state=AK** and **gender=F**, another for **state=AK**, and **gender=M**, and so on, then calculate the aggregate function for each group and label the result with a value from all the grouping columns.

Now, test your understanding by implementing the **GROUP BY** clause in an exercise.

EXERCISE 4.02: CALCULATING THE COST BY PRODUCT TYPE USING GROUP BY

In this exercise, you will analyze and calculate the cost of products using aggregate functions and the **GROUP BY** clause. The marketing manager wants to know the minimum, maximum, average, and standard deviation of the price for each product type that ZoomZoom sells for a marketing campaign. Perform the following steps to complete this exercise:

1. Open **pgAdmin**, connect to the **sqlda** database, and open SQL query editor.

2. Calculate the lowest price, highest price, average price, and standard deviation of the price using the **MIN**, **MAX**, **AVG**, and **STDDEV** aggregate functions from the **products** table and use **GROUP BY** to check the price of all the different product types:

```
SELECT
    product_type,
    MIN(base_msrp),
    MAX(base_msrp),
    AVG(base_msrp),
    STDDEV(base_msrp)
FROM
    products
GROUP BY
    1
ORDER BY
    1;
```

You should get the following result:

product_type text	min numeric	max numeric	avg numeric	stddev numeric
automobile	35000.00	115000.00	79250.000000000000	30477.45068079
scooter	349.99	799.99	578.5614285714285714	167.971085947212

Figure 4.19: Basic price statistics by product type

From the preceding output, the marketing manager can check and compare the price of various products that ZoomZoom sells for the campaign.

> **NOTE**
>
> To access the source code for this specific section, please refer to https://packt.link/OU9zr.

In this exercise, you calculated the basic statistics by product type using aggregate functions and the **GROUP BY** clause. Next, you will learn how to implement grouping sets.

GROUPING SETS

It is very common to want to see the statistical characteristics of a dataset from several different perspectives. For instance, say you wanted to count the total number of customers you have in each state, while simultaneously, you also wanted the total number of male and female customers you have in each state. One way you could accomplish this is by using the **UNION ALL** keyword, which was discussed in *Chapter 2, The Basics of SQL for Analytics*:

```
(
  SELECT
    state,
    NULL as gender,
    COUNT (*)
  FROM
    customers
  GROUP BY
    1, 2
  ORDER BY
```

```
     1, 2
)
UNION ALL
(

   SELECT
     state,
     gender,
     COUNT(*)
   FROM
     customers
   GROUP BY
     1, 2
   ORDER BY
     1, 2
)
ORDER BY 1, 2;
```

This query produces the following result:

state text	gender text	count bigint
AK	F	101
AK	M	87
AK	[null]	188
AL	F	433
AL	M	489
AL	[null]	922
AR	F	112
AR	M	120
AR	[null]	232

Figure 4.20: Customer count by the state and gender query
outputs in alphabetical order

Fundamentally, what you are doing here is creating multiple sets of aggregation, one grouped by state and another grouped by state and gender, and then joining them together. Thus, this operation is called grouping sets, which means multiple sets are generated using GROUP BY. However, using **UNION ALL** is tedious and can involve writing lengthy queries. An alternative way to do this is to use the **GROUPING SETS** statement. This statement allows a user to create multiple sets of grouping for viewing, similar to the **UNION ALL** statement. For example, using the **GROUPING SETS** keyword, you could rewrite the previous **UNION ALL** query, like so:

```
SELECT
  state,
  gender,
  COUNT(*)
FROM
  customers
GROUP BY GROUPING SETS (
  (state),
  (state, gender)
)
ORDER BY
  1, 2;
```

This creates the same output as the previous **UNION ALL** query. Now, you will learn how ordered set aggregates work in the next section.

ORDERED SET AGGREGATES

Up until this point, none of the aggregates discussed depended on the order of the data. That is because none of the aggregate functions (**COUNT, SUM, AVG, MIN, MAX**, and so on) you have encountered so far was ordinal. You can order the data using **ORDER BY**, but this is not required to complete the calculation, nor will the order impact the result. However, there is a subset of aggregate statistics that depends on the order of the column to calculate. For instance, the median of a column is something that requires the order of the data to be specified. To calculate these use cases, SQL offers a series of functions called **ordered set aggregate** functions. The following table lists the main ordered set aggregate functions:

Function	Explanation
`mode()`	Returns the value that appears most often. In the case of a tie, it returns the first value in order.
`Percentile_cont(fraction)`	Returns a value corresponding to the specified fraction in the ordering, interpolating between adjacent input items if needed.
`Percentile_disc(fraction)`	Returns the first input value whose position in the ordering equals or exceeds the specified fraction.

Figure 4.21: Major ordered set aggregate functions

These functions are used in the following format:

```
SELECT
  {ordered_set_function} WITHIN GROUP (ORDER BY {order_column})
FROM {table};
```

Here, **{ordered_set_function}** is the ordered set aggregate function, **{order_column}** is the column to order results for the function by, and **{table}** is the table the column is in. For example, you can calculate the median price of the **products** table by using the following query:

```
SELECT
  PERCENTILE_CONT(0.5)
  WITHIN GROUP (ORDER BY base_msrp)
  AS median
FROM
  products;
```

The reason you use **0.5** is that the median is the 50th percentile, which is 0.5 as a fraction. This gives you the following result:

Figure 4.22: Result of an ordered set aggregate function

With ordered set aggregate functions, you now have the tools for calculating virtually any aggregate statistic of interest for a dataset. In the next section, you will learn how to use aggregates to deal with data quality.

AGGREGATE FUNCTIONS WITH THE HAVING CLAUSE

You learned about the **WHERE** clause in this chapter when you worked on **SELECT** statements, which select only certain rows meeting the condition from the original table for later queries. You also learned how to use aggregate functions with the **WHERE** clause in the previous section. Bear in mind that the **WHERE** clause will always be applied to the original dataset. This behavior is defined by the SQL **SELECT** statement syntax, regardless of whether there is a **GROUP BY** clause or not. Meanwhile, **GROUP BY** is a two-step process. In the first step, SQL selects rows from the original table or table set to form aggregate groups. In the second step, SQL calculates the aggregate function results. When you apply a **WHERE** clause, its conditions are applied to the original table or table set, which means it will always be applied in the first step. Sometimes, you are only interested in certain rows in the aggregate function result with certain characteristics, and only want to keep them in the query output and remove the rest. This can only happen after the aggregation has been completed and you get the results, thus it is part of the second step of **GROUP BY** processing. For example, when doing the customer counts, perhaps you are only interested in places that have at least 1,000 customers. Your first instinct may be to write something such as this:

```
SELECT
   state, COUNT(*)
FROM
   customers
WHERE
   COUNT(*)>=1000
GROUP BY
   state
ORDER BY
   state;
```

However, you will find that the query does not work and gives you the following error:

```
ERROR:  aggregate functions are not allowed in WHERE
LINE 3: WHERE COUNT(*)>=1000
              ^
SQL state: 42803
Character: 45
```

Figure 4.23: Error showing the query is not working

This is because **COUNT(*)** is calculated at the second step on the aggregated groups. Thus, this filter can only be applied to the aggregated groups, not the original dataset. So, using the **WHERE** clause on aggregate functions will produce an error. To use the filter on aggregate functions, you need to use a new clause: **HAVING**. The **HAVING** clause is similar to the **WHERE** clause, except it is specifically designed for **GROUP BY** queries. It applies the filter condition on the aggregated groups instead of the original dataset. The general structure of a **GROUP BY** operation with a **HAVING** statement is as follows:

```
SELECT
  {KEY},
  {AGGFUNC(column1)}
FROM
  {table1}
GROUP BY
  {KEY}
HAVING
  {OTHER_AGGFUNC(column2)_CONDITION}
```

Here, **{KEY}** is a column or a function on a column that is used to create individual groups, **{AGGFUNC(column1)}** is an aggregate function on a column that is calculated for all the rows within each group, **{table}** is the table or set of joined tables from which rows are separated into groups, and **{OTHER_AGGFUNC(column2)_CONDITION}** is a condition similar to what you would put in a **WHERE** clause involving an aggregate function. Now, test your understanding by implementing an exercise while using the **HAVING** clause.

EXERCISE 4.03: CALCULATING AND DISPLAYING DATA USING THE HAVING CLAUSE

In this exercise, you will calculate and display data using the **HAVING** clause. The sales manager of ZoomZoom wants to know the customer count for the states that have at least 1,000 customers who have purchased any product from ZoomZoom. Perform the following steps to help the manager to extract the data:

1. Open **pgAdmin**, connect to the **sqlda** database, and open SQL query editor.

2. Calculate the customer count by states with at least **1000** customers using the **HAVING** clause:

```
SELECT
    state, COUNT(*)
FROM
    customers
GROUP BY
    state
HAVING
    COUNT(*)>=1000
ORDER BY
    state;
```

This query will give you the following output:

| state | count |
text	bigint
CA	5038
CO	1042
DC	1447
FL	3748
GA	1251
IL	1094
NC	1070
NY	2395
OH	1656

Figure 4.24: Customer count by states with at least 1,000 customers

Here, you can see the states that have more than 1,000 ZoomZoom customers, with **CA** having **5038**, the highest number of customers, and **CO** having **1042**, the lowest number of customers.

> **NOTE**
>
> To access the source code for this specific section, please refer to https://packt.link/OU9zr.

In this exercise, you have used the **HAVING** clause to calculate and display data more efficiently.

USING AGGREGATES TO CLEAN DATA AND EXAMINE DATA QUALITY

In *Chapter 3*, *SQL for Data Preparation*, you learned how SQL can be used to clean data. While the techniques mentioned in that chapter do an excellent job of cleaning data, aggregates add a number of techniques that can make cleaning data even easier and more comprehensive. In this section, you will look at some of these techniques.

FINDING MISSING VALUES WITH GROUP BY

As mentioned in *Chapter 3*, *SQL for Data Preparation*, one of the biggest issues with cleaning data is dealing with missing values. You learned how to find missing values and how to resolve this issue. In this chapter, you will learn how to determine the extent of missing data in a dataset.

Using aggregates, identifying the amount of missing data can tell you not only which columns have missing data but also the usability of the columns when so much of the data is missing. Depending on the extent of missing data, you will have to determine whether it makes sense to delete rows with missing data, fill in missing values, or just delete columns if they do not have enough data to make definitive conclusions.

The easiest way to determine whether a column is missing values is to use a modified **CASE WHEN** statement, which provides flexible logic to check whether a condition is met, with the **SUM** and **COUNT** functions to determine what percentage of data is missing. The query looks as follows:

```
SELECT
    SUM(
CASE
    WHEN
```

```
        {column1} IS NULL
          OR
        {column1} IN ({missing_values})
          THEN 1
          ELSE 0
END
      )::FLOAT/COUNT(*)
FROM
    {table1}
```

Here, **{column1}** is the column that you want to check for missing values, **{missing_values}** is a comma-separated list of values that are considered missing, and **{table1}** is the table or subquery with the missing values.

Based on the results of this query, you may have to vary your strategy for dealing with missing data. If a very small percentage of your data is missing (<1%), then you might consider just filtering out or deleting the missing data from your analysis. If some of your data is missing (<20%), you may consider filling in your missing data with a typical value, such as the mean or the mode, to perform an accurate analysis. If more than 20% of your data is missing, you may have to remove the column from your data analysis, as there would not be enough data to make accurate conclusions based on the values in the column.

Now, work on an example and look at missing data in the **customers** table. Specifically, look at the missing data in the **state** column. Based on some prior knowledge, the business team has determined that if the **state** column in a row contains **NULL** or is an empty string (**' '**), this value is considered a missing value. You now need to determine the extent of missing values to see whether this **state** column is still useful. You will do so by dividing the number of records that have the missing value in the **state** column by the total number of the records:

```
SELECT
    SUM(
CASE
    WHEN state IS NULL OR state IN ('') THEN 1
        ELSE 0
END
      )::FLOAT/COUNT(*) AS missing_state
FROM
    customers;
```

This gives you the following output:

missing_state
double precision

0.10934

Figure 4.25: Result of NULL and missing value percentage calculation

As shown here, a little under 11% of the state data is missing. For analysis purposes, you may want to consider that these customers are from California, since **CA** is the most common state in the data. However, the far more accurate thing to do would be to find and fill in the missing data.

If you are only concerned about **NULL** values, and there is no need to check other missing values, you can also use a **COUNT ()** function, which counts from the column. Such a **COUNT ()** function will only count the non-**NULL** values. By dividing this value by the total count, you will get the percentage of non-**NULL** values. By subtracting non-NULL percentage from 100%, you will get the percentage of **NULL** values in the total count:

```
SELECT
  COUNT(state) * 1.0 / COUNT(*) AS non_null_state,
  1 - COUNT(state) * 1.0 / COUNT(*) AS null_state
FROM
  customers;
```

This gives you the following output of the percentages of non-**NULL** and **NULL** values displayed as fractions:

non_null_state numeric	null_state numeric
0.89066000000000000000	0.10934000000000000000

Figure 4.26: Result of NULL value percentage calculation

You can see that the `null_state` value here is the same as the `missing_state` value in the previous SQL. This shows that there is actually no value with an empty string (`' '`). All missing values are **NULL**.

MEASURING DATA UNIQUENESS WITH AGGREGATES

Another common task that you might want to perform is to determine whether every value in a column is unique. While in many cases this can be solved by setting a column with a **PRIMARY KEY** constraint, this may not always be possible. To solve this problem, you can write the following query:

```
SELECT
   COUNT (DISTINCT {column1})=COUNT(*)
FROM
   {table1}
```

Here, **{column1}** is the column you want to count and **{table1}** is the table with the column. If this query returns **True**, then the column has a unique value for every single row; otherwise, at least one of the values is repeated. If values are repeated in a column that you are expecting to be unique, there may be some issues with the data **Extract, Transform, and Load** (**ETL**) or there may be a join that has caused a row to be repeated.

As a simple example, verify that the **customer_id** column in **customers** is unique:

```
SELECT
   COUNT(DISTINCT customer_id)=COUNT(*) AS equal_ids
FROM
   customers;
```

This query gives you the following output, which shows that the values in the **customer_id** column are truly unique:

equal_ids boolean
true

Figure 4.27: Result of comparing COUNT DISTINCT versus COUNT(*)

Now that you have learned about the many ways to use aggregate queries, you will apply this to some sales data in the following activity.

ACTIVITY 4.01: ANALYZING SALES DATA USING AGGREGATE FUNCTIONS

In this activity, you will analyze data using aggregate functions. The CEO, COO, and CFO of ZoomZoom would like to gain some insight into the common statistical characteristics of sales now that the company feels they have a strong enough analytics team with your arrival. The task has been given to you, and your boss has politely let you know that this is the most important project the analytics team has worked on. Perform the following steps to complete this activity:

1. Open **pgAdmin**, connect to the **sqlda** database, and open SQL query editor.

2. Calculate the total number of unit sales the company has made.

3. Calculate the total sales amount in dollars for each state.

4. Identify the top five best dealerships in terms of the most units sold (ignore internet sales).

5. Calculate the average sales amount for each channel, as shown in the **sales** table, and look at the average sales amount, first by **channel** sales, then by **product_id**, and then both together.

   Expected Output:

channel text	product_id bigint	avg_sales_amount double precision
dealership	3	477.253737607644
dealership	4	109822.274881517
dealership	5	664.330132075472
dealership	6	62563.3763837638
dealership	7	573.744146637002
dealership	8	668.850500463391
dealership	9	33402.6845637584
dealership	10	81270.1121794872
dealership	11	91589.7435897436

Figure 4.28: Sales after the GROUPING SETS channel and product_id

6. Calculate the percentage of sales transactions that have a **NULL** dealership.

7. Calculate the percentage of internet sales the company has made for each year. Order the year in a timely fashion and you will get time series data. Does this time series suggest something?

Just by looking at the numbers, it does seem that the sales increase both in the internet channel and the non-internet channel, simultaneously. So, it is an overall increase in the whole ZoomZoom sales portfolio. At this point, as you have gained some insight into the common statistical characteristics of sales, you can get back to the sales manager and present your findings, work with the business team to dive deeper into possible reasons for this increase, and try to apply the findings to the company's sales strategy.

Using aggregates, you have unlocked patterns that will help your company to understand how to make more revenue and make the company better overall.

> **NOTE**
>
> The solution for this activity can be found on page 442.

SUMMARY

In this chapter, you learned how to calculate the statistical properties of a dataset using aggregate functions, such as the average, count, minimum, maximum, and standard deviation. Aggregate functions themselves are applied to a whole dataset. In order to use them to analyze the statistics of sub-datasets inside a larger dataset, you also learned about the **GROUP BY** clause of the **SELECT** statement, which divides a large dataset into smaller ones based on the keys you provided and applies aggregate functions to each of the groups.

To make the **GROUP BY** clause more useful, several additional properties were introduced, most importantly the **HAVING** clause. This **HAVING** clause is used to filter the values of aggregated groups. It is applied at the second stage of the **GROUP BY** clause execution and should be distinguished from the **WHERE** clause, which is applied to the original data table or table set and is applied at the first stage of the **GROUP BY** execution.

Now that you learned about aggregate functions and the **GROUP BY** clause, you are now able to proceed with using tools to examine data quality on a dataset level, instead of on a data entry level, like what you did in *Chapter 3, SQL for Data Preparation*. This includes checking the percentage of missing values and confirming the uniqueness of a column. You then practiced some of these skills in an activity.

So far, you have learned about two kinds of functions. The row-level functions that you learned about in *Chapter 3, SQL for Data Preparation*, such as **CASE**, **NULLIF**, and **COALESCE**, are applied to one data row and will generate one output value for each row in the raw data. The aggregate functions that you learned about in this chapter, such as **COUNT** and **SUM**, are applied to a dataset of many rows and will generate one output value for the entire dataset. The former can be used to analyze the characteristics of a data point, while the latter can be used to analyze the statistics of a dataset. There is one more kind of function, which studies the characteristics of a row in relation to other rows in the dataset. This function will generate one output for each row in a dataset and is called a window function. You will learn all about window functions in *Chapter 5, Window Functions for Data Analysis*.

5

WINDOW FUNCTIONS FOR DATA ANALYSIS

OVERVIEW

In this chapter, you will learn the conceptual logic of window functions, write SQL to execute these functions, and modify them using keywords such as **PARTITION BY** and **ORDER BY**.

By the end of this chapter, you will be able to apply these functions to gain new insights into data and understand the properties of datasets, such as ranking and percentiles.

INTRODUCTION

You have learned simple functions such as **CASE WHEN**, **COALESCE**, and **NULLIF** in *Chapter 3, SQL for Data Preparation*. These functions receive data from a single row and produce a result for this row. The result of these functions is only determined by the data value in the row and has nothing to do with the dataset it is in. You have also learned aggregate functions such as **SUM**, **AVG**, and **COUNT** in *Chapter 4, Aggregate Functions for Data Analysis*. These functions receive data from a dataset of multiple rows and produce a result for this dataset. Both types of functions are useful in different scenarios. For example, if you have the physical checkup results of all newborn babies in a country, such as weight and height, you can check each baby's health by checking these measurements to be within a given range using **CASE WHEN** function. You can also use aggregate functions to get the average and standard deviation of the weight and height of babies in this country. Both types of functions provide useful insights into the health and welfare of this country's babies.

Sometimes, you may also want to know the characteristics of a data point in regard to its position in the dataset. A typical example is a rank. Rank is determined by both the measurement itself and the dataset it is in. A baby's height and weight will likely have different ranks in the dataset for the whole country and in the dataset for the city. Within the same dataset, there also might be subgroups, which are also called **partitions**, that the rank is based on. For example, ranking in different states in the whole country from the same country-wide dataset requires dividing the dataset into multiple partitions, each corresponding to a state. Ranking is thus calculated inside each partition. Within the partition, the rows related to the calculation (that is, the number of rows that are before the current row, which determines the rank of the current row) are selected to calculate the result. These selected rows form a **window**. Essentially, what you want to achieve is that given a dataset, you want to get a result for each row. This result is defined based on the value of the row, the window on which it is applied, and the dataset itself. The function used to perform this type of calculation is called **window function**.

The following topics will be covered in this chapter:

- Window Functions

- Basics of Window Functions

- The **WINDOW** Keyword

- Statistics with Window Functions

- Window Frame

WINDOW FUNCTIONS

Continuing with the discussion on Window Functions, you want to find the earliest customers for ZoomZoom. In a more technical term, this means you want to rank every customer according to the date they became a customer, with the earliest customer being ranked 1, the second-earliest customer being ranked 2, and so on. You can get all the customers using the following query:

```
SELECT
  customer_id, first_name, last_name, date_added
FROM
  customers
ORDER BY
  date_added;
```

The result is:

customer_id bigint	first_name text	last_name text	date_added timestamp without time zone
30046	Nanete	Hassur	2012-11-09 00:00:00
35683	Betteanne	Rulf	2012-11-09 00:00:00
7486	Ciro	Ferencowicz	2012-11-09 00:00:00
12484	Lillis	Brayley	2012-11-09 00:00:00
2625	Binky	Dawtrey	2012-11-09 00:00:00
17099	Pearla	Halksworth	2012-11-09 00:00:00
18685	Ingram	Crossman	2012-11-09 00:00:00
6173	Danila	Gristwood	2012-11-09 00:00:00
13390	Danika	Lough	2012-11-09 00:00:00
30555	Stanwood	Stookes	2012-11-09 00:00:00

Figure 5.1: Customers ordered by date_added

You can order the customers from the earliest to the most recent, copy the output to an Excel spreadsheet, and assign a row number to each row so that you have the rank for each customer. But this is not automatic and is prone to errors. SQL provides several ways using which you can achieve it. Later in this chapter, you will learn how to assign numbers to ordered records by using the **RANK** window function. Here, you can first use an aggregate function to get the dates and order them that way:

```
SELECT
    date_added, COUNT(*)
FROM
    customers
GROUP BY
    date_added
ORDER BY
    date_added;
```

The following is the output of the preceding code:

date_added timestamp without time zone	count bigint
2010-03-15 00:00:00	11
2010-03-16 00:00:00	13
2010-03-17 00:00:00	12
2010-03-18 00:00:00	19
2010-03-19 00:00:00	23
2010-03-20 00:00:00	16
2010-03-21 00:00:00	20
2010-03-22 00:00:00	14
2010-03-23 00:00:00	11
2010-03-24 00:00:00	21
2010-03-25 00:00:00	15

Figure 5.2: Aggregate date-time ordering

This result gives the dates in a ranked order. With this result, you can calculate how many customers joined ZoomZoom before each customer, simply by adding up the counts from the days before the customer's joining date. However, this approach is still manual, requires extra calculation, and still does not directly provide rank information. This is where window functions come into play. Window functions can take multiple rows of data and process them, but still retain all the information in the rows. For things such as ranks, this is exactly what you need.

To better understand this, you will see what a windows function query looks like in the next section.

THE BASICS OF WINDOW FUNCTIONS

The following is the basic syntax of a window function:

```
SELECT {columns},
{window_func} OVER (PARTITION BY {partition_key} ORDER BY {order_key})
FROM table1;
```

Here, **{columns}** are the columns to retrieve from tables for the query, **{window_func}** is the window function you want to use, **table1** is the table or joined tables you want to pull data from, and the **OVER** keyword indicates where the window definition starts. The window definition in this basic syntax includes two parts, **{partition_key}** and **{order_key}**. The former is the column or columns you want to partition on (more on this later), and the latter is the column or columns you want to order by.

To illustrate this, look at an example. You might be saying to yourself that you do not know any window functions, but the truth is that all aggregate functions can be used as window functions. Now, use **COUNT(*)** in the following query:

```
SELECT
  customer_id,
  title,
  first_name,
  last_name,
  gender,
  COUNT(*) OVER () as total_customers
FROM
  customers
ORDER BY
  customer_id;
```

This results in the following output:

customer_id bigint	title text	first_name text	last_name text	gender text	total_customers bigint
1	[null]	Arlena	Riveles	F	50000
2	Dr	Ode	Stovin	M	50000
3	[null]	Braden	Jordan	M	50000
4	[null]	Jessika	Nussen	F	50000
5	[null]	Lonnie	Rembaud	F	50000
6	[null]	Cortie	Locksley	M	50000
7	[null]	Wood	Kennham	M	50000
8	[null]	Rutger	Humblestone	M	50000
9	[null]	Melantha	Tibb	F	50000
10	Ms	Barbara-anne	Gowlett	F	50000
11	Mrs	Urbano	Middlehurst	M	50000

Figure 5.3: Customers listed using the COUNT(*) window query

As shown in *Figure 5.3*, the query returns **title**, **first_name**, and **last_name**, just like a typical **SELECT** query. However, there is now a new column called **total_customers**. This column contains the count of users that would be created by the following query:

```
SELECT
    COUNT(*)
FROM
    customers;
```

The above query returns **50,000**. The query returned all of the rows, and the **COUNT(*)** in the query returns the **COUNT** as any normal aggregate function would.

Now, regarding the other parameters of the query, what happens if you add **OVER** clause to convert this **COUNT** into a window function, keeping the function as **COUNT** but defining the window using **PARTITION BY**, such as in the following query?

```
SELECT
    customer_id,
    title,
    first_name,
    last_name,
    gender,
```

```
  COUNT(*) OVER (PARTITION BY gender) as total_customers
FROM
  customers
ORDER BY
  customer_id;
```

The following is the output of the preceding code:

customer_id bigint	title text	first_name text	last_name text	gender text	total_customers bigint
1	[null]	Arlena	Riveles	F	25044
2	Dr	Ode	Stovin	M	24956
3	[null]	Braden	Jordan	M	24956
4	[null]	Jessika	Nussen	F	25044
5	[null]	Lonnie	Rembaud	F	25044
6	[null]	Cortie	Locksley	M	24956
7	[null]	Wood	Kennham	M	24956
8	[null]	Rutger	Humblestone	M	24956
9	[null]	Melantha	Tibb	F	25044
10	Ms	Barbara-anne	Gowlett	F	25044
11	Mrs	Urbano	Middlehurst	M	24956

Figure 5.4: Customers listed using COUNT(*) partitioned by the gender window query

Here, you can see that **total_customers** has now changed counts to one of two values, **24956** or **25044**. As you use the **PARTITION BY** clause over the **gender** column, SQL divides the dataset into multiple partitions based on the unique values of this column. Inside each partition, SQL calculates the total **COUNT**. For example, there are **24956** males, so the **COUNT** window function for the male partition returns **24596**, which you can confirm with the following query:

```
SELECT
  gender,
  COUNT(*)
FROM
  customers
GROUP BY
  1;
```

Now you see how the partition is defined and used with the **PARTITION BY** clause. For females, the count is equal to the female count, and for males, the count is equal to the male count. What happens now if you use **ORDER BY** instead in the **OVER** clause as follows?

```
SELECT
    customer_id, title,
    first_name, last_name, gender,
    COUNT(*) OVER (ORDER BY customer_id) as total_customers
FROM
    customers
ORDER BY
    customer_id;
```

The following is the output of the preceding code:

customer_id bigint	title text	first_name text	last_name text	gender text	total_customers bigint
1	[null]	Arlena	Riveles	F	1
2	Dr	Ode	Stovin	M	2
3	[null]	Braden	Jordan	M	3
4	[null]	Jessika	Nussen	F	4
5	[null]	Lonnie	Rembaud	F	5
6	[null]	Cortie	Locksley	M	6
7	[null]	Wood	Kennham	M	7
8	[null]	Rutger	Humblestone	M	8
9	[null]	Melantha	Tibb	F	9
10	Ms	Barbara-anne	Gowlett	F	10
11	Mrs	Urbano	Middlehurst	M	11

Figure 5.5: Customers listed using COUNT(*) ordered by the customer_id window query

You will notice something akin to a running count for the total customers. This is where the definition of 'window' in window function comes from. When you use this window function, since you did not specify a **PARTITION BY**, the full dataset is used for calculation. Within this dataset, when **ORDER BY** is not specified, it is assumed that there is only one window, which contains the entire dataset. However, when **ORDER BY** is specified, the rows in the dataset are ordered according to it. For each unique value in the order, SQL forms a value group, which contains all the rows containing this value. The query then creates a window for each value group. The window will contain all the rows in this value group and all rows that are ordered before this value group. An example is shown below:

customer_id bigint	title text	first_name text	last_name text	gender text	
1	[null]	Arlena	Riveles	F	Window for row 1
2	Dr	Ode	Stovin	M	Window for row 2
3	[null]	Braden	Jordan	M	Window for row 3

Figure 5.6: Windows for customers using COUNT(*) ordered
by the customer_id window query

Here, the dataset is ordered using **customer_id**, which happens to be the primary key. As such each row has a unique value and forms a value group. The first value group, without any row before it, forms its own window, which contains only the first row. The second value group's window will contain both itself and the row before it, which means the first and second row. Then the third value group's window will contain itself and the two rows before it, and so on and so forth. Every value group has its window. Once the windows are established, for every value group, the window function is calculated based on the window. In this example, this means **COUNT** is applied to every window. Thus, value group 1 (the first row) gets **1** as the result since its Window 1 contains one row, value group 2 (the second row) gets **2** since its Window 2 contains two rows, and so on and so forth. The results are applied to every row in this value group if the group contains multiple rows. Note that the window is used for calculation only. The results are assigned to rows in the value group, not assigned to the rows in the window.

What happens when you combine **PARTITION BY** and **ORDER BY**? Now, look at the following query:

```
SELECT
  customer_id,
  title,
  first_name,
  last_name,
  gender,
  COUNT(*) OVER (
PARTITION BY gender ORDER BY customer_id
  ) as total_customers
FROM
  customers
ORDER BY
  customer_id;
```

When you run the preceding query, you get the following result:

customer_id bigint	title text	first_name text	last_name text	gender text	total_customers bigint
1	[null]	Arlena	Riveles	F	1
2	Dr	Ode	Stovin	M	1
3	[null]	Braden	Jordan	M	2
4	[null]	Jessika	Nussen	F	2
5	[null]	Lonnie	Rembaud	F	3
6	[null]	Cortie	Locksley	M	3
7	[null]	Wood	Kennham	M	4
8	[null]	Rutger	Humblestone	M	5
9	[null]	Melantha	Tibb	F	4
10	Ms	Barbara-anne	Gowlett	F	5
11	Mrs	Urbano	Middlehurst	M	6

Figure 5.7: Customers listed using COUNT(*) partitioned
by gender ordered by the customer_id window query

Like the previous query, it appears to be some sort of rank. However, it seems to differ based on gender. In this particular SQL, the query divides the table into two subsets based on the column **PARTITION BY**. That is because the **PARTITION BY** clause, like **GROUP BY**, will first divide the dataset into groups (which is called partition here) based on the value in the **gender** column. Each partition is then used as a basis for doing a count, with each partition having its own set of value groups. These value groups are ordered inside the partition, windows are created based on the value groups and their orders, and the window function is applied to the values. The results are finally assigned to every row in the value groups.

This process is illustrated in *Figure 5.8*. This process produces the count you can see. The three keywords, **OVER()**, **PARTITION BY**, and **ORDER BY**, are the foundation of the power of window functions.

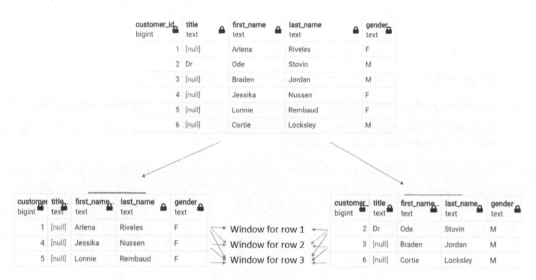

Figure 5.8: Windows for customers listed using COUNT(*) partitioned by gender and ordered by the customer_id window query

Now that you understand window functions, attempt applying them in the next exercise.

EXERCISE 5.01: ANALYZING CUSTOMER DATA FILL RATES OVER TIME

In this exercise, you will apply window functions to a dataset and analyze the data. For the last six months, ZoomZoom has been experimenting with various promotions to make their customers more engaged in the sale activity. One way to measure the level of engagement is to measure people's willingness to fill out all fields on the customer form, especially their address. To achieve this goal, the company would like a running total of how many users have filled in their street addresses over time. Write a query to produce these results.

> **NOTE**
>
> For all the exercises in this chapter, please use pgAdmin 4.

Perform the following steps to complete this exercise:

1. Open **pgAdmin**, connect to the **sqlda** database, and open SQL query editor.

2. Use window functions and write a query that will return customer information and how many people have filled out their street address. Also, order the list by date. The query will look as follows:

```
SELECT
  customer_id,
  street_address,
  date_added::DATE,
  COUNT(
    CASE
      WHEN street_address IS NOT NULL THEN customer_id
      ELSE NULL
    END
  ) OVER (ORDER BY date_added::DATE)
    as non_null_street_address,
  COUNT(*) OVER (ORDER BY date_added::DATE)
    as total_street_address
FROM
  customers
ORDER BY
  date_added;
```

You should get the following result:

customer_id bigint	street_address text	date_added date	null_street_address bigint	total_street_address bigint
17099	130 Marcy Crossing	2012-11-09	10	11
30046	13961 Steensland Trail	2012-11-09	10	11
6173	79865 Hagan Terrace	2012-11-09	10	11
12484	[null]	2012-11-09	10	11
30555	294 Quincy Hill	2012-11-09	10	11
18685	86 Michigan Junction	2012-11-09	10	11
7486	61 Village Crossing	2012-11-09	10	11
13390	38463 Forest Dale Way	2012-11-09	10	11
2625	0353 Iowa Road	2012-11-09	10	11
35683	1 Cordelia Crossing	2012-11-09	10	11

Figure 5.9: Street address filter ordered by the date_added window query

3. Write a query to see how the numbers of people filling out the street field change over time.

4. In *step 1*, you have already got every customer address ordered by the signup date. In *Figure 5.10*, the two columns following the signup date column are the number of non-**NULL** addresses and the number of all customer addresses for each rolling day, that is, a sum from the beginning of sales to the current day. As you learned in *Chapter 4, Aggregate Functions for Data Analysis*, by dividing the number of non-**NULL** addresses by the number of all customer addresses, you can get the percentage of customers with non-**NULL** street addresses and derive the percentage of customers with **NULL** street addresses. Tracking this number will provide an insight into the way customers interact with your sales force over time. Also, because both numbers of addresses are calculated for each rolling day, the percentage is also for each rolling day. This is an example of different window functions sharing the same window in the same query.

You can also rewrite the following query using a **WINDOW** clause to make the query simpler, which will be introduced in the next section.

rolling_average

```
1 WITH
2 daily_rolling_count as (
3   SELECT
4     customer_id,
5     street_address,
6     date_added::DATE,
7     COUNT(
8       CASE
9         WHEN street_address IS NOT NULL THEN customer_id
10          ELSE NULL
11        END
12      ) OVER (ORDER BY date_added::DATE)
13        as non_null_street_address,
14      COUNT(*) OVER (ORDER BY date_added::DATE)
15        as total_street_address
```

You can find the complete code here: https://packt.link/iMJ6d

The result is:

date_added date	non_null_street_address bigint	total_street_address bigint	null_address_percentage numeric
2012-11-09	10	11	0.09090909090909090909
2012-11-10	22	24	0.08333333333333333333
2012-11-11	33	36	0.08333333333333333333
2012-11-12	50	55	0.09090909090909090909
2012-11-13	71	78	0.08974358974358974359
2012-11-14	86	94	0.08510638297872340426
2012-11-15	105	114	0.07894736842105263158
2012-11-16	118	128	0.07812500000000000000
2012-11-17	128	139	0.07913669064748201439

Figure 5.10: Percent of NULL Addresses per day

This result will give you the list of the rolling percentage of **NULL** street address in each day. You can then provide the full dataset to data analytics and visualization software such as Excel to study the general trend of the data, discover patterns of change, and raise suggestions on how to increase the engagement of customers to the company management.

> **NOTE**
>
> To access the source code for this specific section, please refer to https://packt.link/fAhGN.

In this exercise, you have learned how to use window functions to analyze data. In the next section, you will understand how to use the **WINDOW** keyword in your queries.

THE WINDOW KEYWORD

Now that you understand the basics of window functions, it is time to introduce a syntax that will make it easier to write them. In many scenarios, your analysis involves running multiple functions against the same window so that you can compare them side by side, and you are very likely running them within the same query. For example, when you are doing some gender-based analysis, you may be interested in calculating a running total number of customers as well as the running total number of customers with a title, using the same partition that is based on gender. You will result in writing the following query:

```
SELECT
  customer_id,
  title,
  first_name,
  last_name,
  gender,
  COUNT(*) OVER (
    PARTITION BY gender ORDER BY customer_id
  ) as total_customers,
  SUM(CASE WHEN title IS NOT NULL THEN 1 ELSE 0 END) OVER (
    PARTITION BY gender ORDER BY customer_id
  ) as total_customers_title
FROM customers
ORDER BY customer_id;
```

The following is the output of the preceding code:

customer_id 🔒 bigint	title 🔒 text	first_name 🔒 text	last_name 🔒 text	gender 🔒 text	total_customers 🔒 bigint	total_customers_title 🔒 bigint
1	[null]	Arlena	Riveles	F	1	0
2	Dr	Ode	Stovin	M	1	1
3	[null]	Braden	Jordan	M	2	1
4	[null]	Jessika	Nussen	F	2	0
5	[null]	Lonnie	Rembaud	F	3	0
6	[null]	Cortie	Locksley	M	3	1
7	[null]	Wood	Kennham	M	4	1
8	[null]	Rutger	Humblestone	M	5	1
9	[null]	Melantha	Tibb	F	4	0
10	Ms	Barbara-anne	Gowlett	F	5	1

Figure 5.11: Running total of customers overall with the title by gender window query

> **NOTE**
>
> Here, the queried dataset incorrectly applies the label "gender" in place of "sex." The data for "gender" can be assumed as "sex" for this section. "Gender" must not be considered in the context of range of identities or with reference to any social and cultural differences.

Although the query gives you the result, it can be tedious to write—especially the **OVER** clause as it is the same for the two functions. Fortunately, you can simplify this by using the **WINDOW** clause to define a generic window for multiple functions in the same query. The **WINDOW** clause facilitates the aliasing of a window.

You can simplify the preceding query by writing it as follows:

```
SELECT
  customer_id,
  title,
  first_name,
  last_name,
  gender,
  COUNT(*) OVER w as total_customers,
  SUM(
    CASE
```

```
        WHEN title IS NOT NULL THEN 1
        ELSE 0
    END
  ) OVER w as total_customers_title
FROM
  customers
WINDOW w AS (
  PARTITION BY gender ORDER BY customer_id
)
ORDER BY customer_id;
```

This query should give you the same result you can see in the preceding screenshot. However, you did not have to write a long **PARTITION BY** and **ORDER BY** query for each window function. Instead, you simply made an alias with the defined **WINDOW w**.

STATISTICS WITH WINDOW FUNCTIONS

Now that you understand how window functions work, you can start using them to calculate useful statistics, such as ranks, percentiles, and rolling statistics.

In the following table, you have summarized a variety of statistical functions that are useful. It is also important to emphasize again that all aggregate functions can also be used as window functions (**AVG**, **SUM**, **COUNT**, and so on):

Name	Description
ROW_NUMBER	Number the current row within its partition starting from 1.
DENSE_RANK	Rank the current row within its partition without gaps.
RANK	Rank the current row within its partition with gaps.
LAG	Return a value evaluated at the row that is at a specified physical offset row before the current row within the partition.
LEAD	Return a value evaluated at the row that is offset rows after the current row within the partition.
NTILE	Divide rows in a partition as equally as possible and assign each row an integer starting from 1 to the argument value.

Figure 5.12: Statistical window functions

Normally, a call to any of these functions inside a SQL statement would be followed by the **OVER** keyword. This keyword will then be followed by more keywords like **PARTITION BY** and **ORDER BY**, either of which may be optional, depending on which function you are using.

For example, the **ROW_NUMBER()** function will look like this:

```
ROW_NUMBER() OVER(
    PARTITION BY column_1, column_2
    ORDER BY column_3, column_4
)
```

You will practice how to use these statistical functions in the next exercise.

EXERCISE 5.02: RANK ORDER OF HIRING

In this exercise, you will use statistical window functions to understand a dataset. ZoomZoom would like to have a marketing campaign for their most tenured customers in different states. ZoomZoom wants you to write a query that will rank the customers according to their joining date (**date_added**) for each state. Perform the following steps to complete this exercise:

1. Open **pgAdmin**, connect to the **sqlda** database, and open SQL query editor.

2. Calculate a rank for every customer, with a rank of 1 going to the first **date_added**, 2 to the second one, and so on, using the **RANK()** function:

```
SELECT
    customer_id,
    first_name,
    last_name,
    state,
    date_added::DATE,
    RANK() OVER (
        PARTITION BY state ORDER BY date_added
    ) AS cust_rank
FROM
    customers
ORDER BY
    state, cust_rank;
```

The following is the output of the preceding code:

customer_id 🔒 bigint	first_name 🔒 text	last_name 🔒 text	state 🔒 text	date_added 🔒 date	cust_rank 🔒 bigint
10732	Dael	Persent	AK	2012-11-12	1
35117	Jourdain	Burnyeat	AK	2012-11-15	2
6500	Eugenia	Iacobacci	AK	2012-11-22	3
12603	Carce	Hubber	AK	2012-11-23	4
33836	Martie	Drinnan	AK	2012-12-23	5
18621	Pammi	Manby	AK	2013-01-05	6
45170	Dunstan	Gooddie	AK	2013-01-19	7
35168	Tracey	Ramstead	AK	2013-01-20	8
42141	Carlin	Hammant	AK	2013-02-24	9
14407	Cleopatra	Ferneyhou...	AK	2013-03-11	10

Figure 5.13: Salespeople rank-ordered by tenure

Here, you can see every customer with their information and rank in the **cust_rank** column based on their joining date for each state.

> **NOTE**
>
> To access the source code for this specific section, please refer to https://packt.link/fAhGN.

In this exercise, you used the **RANK()** function to rank the data in a dataset in a certain order. In the next section, you will learn how to use the window frame.

> **NOTE**
>
> One question regarding **RANK()** is the handling of tied values. **RANK()** is defined as the rank of rows, not the rank of values. For example, if the first two rows have a tie, the third row will get **3** from the **RANK()** function. **DENSE_RANK()** could also be used just as easily as **RANK()**, but it is defined as the rank of values, not the rank of rows. In the example above, the value of **DENSE_RANK()** for the third row will be **2** instead of **3**, as the third row contains the 2nd value in the list of values.

WINDOW FRAME

As mentioned in the earlier sections discussing the basics of window functions, by default, a window is set for each value group to encompass all the rows from the first to the current row in the partition, as shown in *Figure 5.6*. However, this is the default and can be adjusted using the **window frame** clause. A window function query using the window frame clause would look as follows:

```
SELECT
  {columns},
  {window_func} OVER (
    PARTITION BY {partition_key}
    ORDER BY {order_key}
    {rangeorrows} BETWEEN {frame_start} AND {frame_end}
  )
FROM
  {table1};
```

Here, **{columns}** are the columns to retrieve from tables for the query, **{window_func}** is the window function you want to use, **{partition_key}** is the column or columns you want to partition on, **{order_key}** is the column or columns you want to order by, **{rangeorrows}** is either the **RANGE** keyword or the **ROWS** keyword, **{frame_start}** is a keyword indicating where to start the window frame, **{frame_end}** is a keyword indicating where to end the window frame, and **{table1}** is the table or joined tables you want to pull data from.

One point to consider is the values that **{frame_start}** and **{frame_end}** can take. To give further details, **{frame_start}** and **{frame_end}** can be one of the following values:

- **UNBOUNDED PRECEDING**: A keyword that, when used for **{frame_start}**, refers to the first record of the partition.

- **{offset} PRECEDING**: A keyword referring to **{offset}** (an integer) rows or ranges before the current row.

- **CURRENT ROW**: Refers to the current row.

- **{offset} FOLLOWING**: A keyword referring to **{offset}** (an integer) rows or ranges after the current row.

- **UNBOUNDED FOLLOWING**: A keyword that, when used for **{frame_end}**, refers to the last record of the partition.

By adjusting the window, various useful statistics can be calculated. One such useful statistic is the **rolling average**. The rolling average is simply the average for a statistic in a given time window. For instance, you want to calculate the seven-day rolling average of sales over time for ZoomZoom. You will need to get the daily sales first by running a **SUM … GROUP BY sales_transaction_date**. This will provide you with a list of daily sales, each row being a day with sales. When you order this list of rows by date, the six preceding rows plus the current row will provide you with a window of seven rolling days. Taking an **AVG** over these seven rows will give you the seven-day rolling average of the given day.

This calculation can be accomplished with the following query:

`rolling_average`

```
1 WITH
2  daily_sales as (
3   SELECT
4     sales_transaction_date::DATE,
5     SUM(sales_amount) as total_sales
6   FROM sales
7   GROUP BY 1
8 ),
9 moving_average_calculation_7 AS (
10    SELECT
11     sales_transaction_date,
12    total_sales,
13    AVG(total_sales) OVER (
14      ORDER BY sales_transaction_date
15      ROWS BETWEEN 6 PRECEDING and CURRENT ROW
```

You can find the complete code here: https://packt.link/4RmVy

The following is the output of the preceding code:

sales_transaction_date 🔒 date	sales_moving_average_7 🔒 double precision
2012-11-04	[null]
2012-11-06	[null]
2012-11-09	[null]
2012-11-11	[null]
2012-11-12	[null]
2012-11-13	[null]
2012-11-15	394.2758571428571
2012-11-17	399.99000000000007
2012-11-18	399.99000000000007
2012-11-19	399.99000000000007

Figure 5.14: The seven-day moving average of sales

A natural question when considering N-day moving window is how to handle the first N-1 days in the ordered column. In the previous query, the first six rows are defined as null using a **CASE** statement because in this scenario the seven-day moving average is only defined if there are seven days' worth of information. Without the **CASE** statement, the window calculation will calculate values for the first seven days using the first few days. For these days, the seven-day moving average is the average of whatever days are in the window. For example, the seven-day moving average for the second day is the average of the first day and second day, and the seven-day moving average for the sixth day is the average of the first six days. Both this approach of calculation and the **NULL** approach can make sense in their respective situations. It is up to the data analyst to determine which one makes more sense to a particular question.

Another point of difference to consider is the difference between using a **RANGE** or **ROW** in a frame clause. In the previous example, you used **ROW** as the daily sales contain one row per day. **ROW** refers to actual rows and will take the rows before and after the current row to calculate values. **RANGE** refers to the values of the **{frame_ start}** and **{frame_end}** in the **{order key}** column. It differs from **ROW** when two rows have the same values based on the **ORDER BY** clause used in the window. If there are multiple rows having the same value as the value designated in **{frame_ start}** or **{frame_end}**, all these rows will be added to the window frame when **RANGE** is specified.

In the following exercise, you will use a rolling window to calculate statistics with ordered data.

EXERCISE 5.03: TEAM LUNCH MOTIVATION

In this activity, you will use a window frame to find some important information in your data. To help improve sales performance, the sales team has decided to buy lunch for all salespeople at the company every time they beat the figure for the best daily total earnings achieved over the last 30 days. Write a query that produces the total sales in dollars for a given day and the target the salespeople must beat for that day, starting from January 1, 2019. Perform the following steps to complete this exercise:

1. Open **pgAdmin**, connect to the **sqlda** database, and open SQL query editor.

2. Calculate the total sales for a given day and the target using the following query:

`Exercise5.03.sql`

```
1 WITH
2 daily_sales as (
3   SELECT
4     sales_transaction_date::DATE,
5     SUM(sales_amount) as total_sales
6   FROM
7     sales
8   GROUP BY
9     1
10 ),
11 sales_stats_30 AS (
12   SELECT
13     sales_transaction_date,
14     total_sales,
15     MAX(total_sales) OVER (
```

You can find the complete code here: https://packt.link/7HmGh

You should get the following results:

sales_transaction_date 🔒 date	total_sales 🔒 double precision	max_sales_30 🔒 double precision
2019-01-01	6249.874999999999	546899.892
2019-01-02	119599.90800000001	546899.892
2019-01-03	71799.87400000001	546899.892
2019-01-04	130649.87600000003	546899.892
2019-01-05	6649.866999999999	546899.892
2019-01-06	73049.84900000002	546899.892
2019-01-07	122049.85900000001	546899.892
2019-01-08	197749.84399999998	546899.892
2019-01-09	5399.891999999999	546899.892
2019-01-10	252899.862	546899.892
2019-01-11	164349.86299999995	546899.892

Figure 5.15: Best sales over the last 30 days

Notice the use of a window frame from **30 PRECEDING** to **1 PRECEDING**. By using **1 PRECEDING**, you are removing the current row from the calculation. The result is a 30-day rolling max in the 30 days before the current day.

3. Now you will calculate the total sales each day and compare it with that day's target, which is the 30-day moving average you just calculated in the previous step. The total sales in each day have already been calculated in the SQL above in the first common table expression and are later referenced in the main query. So, you can write the following SQL:

Exercise5.03.sql

```
1 WITH
2 daily_sales as (
3   SELECT
4     sales_transaction_date::DATE,
5     SUM(sales_amount) as total_sales
6   FROM sales
7   GROUP BY 1
8 ),
9 sales_stats_30 AS (
10   SELECT
11     sales_transaction_date,
12     total_sales,
13     MAX(total_sales) OVER (
14       ORDER BY sales_transaction_date
15       ROWS BETWEEN 30 PRECEDING and 1 PRECEDING
```

You can find the complete code here: https://packt.link/7HmGh

sales_transaction_date date	total_sales double precision	max_sales_30 double precision
2019-02-01	405149.90299999993	357099.81599999993
2019-02-03	514299.7639999999	405149.90299999993
2019-03-10	574449.8389999999	484599.8279999999
2019-07-12	356129.78899999993	304959.828
2019-08-31	338629.905	245659.883
2019-10-22	268354.902	237889.84599999993
2019-10-27	470234.8829999999	268354.902
2019-12-27	393599.76699999993	344879.814
2019-12-28	657459.8209999999	393599.76699999993
2020-02-08	740254.7989999998	387994.82
2020-05-06	411539.79899999994	374689.79099999997

Figure 5.16: Max Daily Sales Moving-30 Day

> **NOTE**
>
> To access the source code for this specific section, please refer to https://packt.link/fAhGN.

As you can see, window frames make calculating moving statistics simple, and even kind of fun. Now, you will conclude this chapter with an activity that will test your ability to use window functions.

ACTIVITY 5.01: ANALYZING SALES USING WINDOW FRAMES AND WINDOW FUNCTIONS

In this activity, you will use window functions and window frames in various ways to gain insight into sales data. It is the beginning of the year, and time to plan the selling strategy for the new year at ZoomZoom. The sales team wants to see how the company has performed overall, as well as how individual days have performed over the year. To achieve this, ZoomZoom's head of Sales would like you to run an analysis for them. Perform the following steps to complete this activity:

1. Open **pgAdmin**, connect to the **sqlda** database, and open SQL query editor.

2. Calculate the total sales amount by day for all the days in the year 2021 (that is, before the date January 1, 2022).

3. Calculate the rolling 30-day average for the daily total sales amount.

4. Calculate which decile each date would be in compared to other days based on their daily 30-day rolling sales amount.

Expected Output:

sales_transaction_date date	sales_amount double precision	moving_avg double precision	decile integer
2021-01-02	248239.73599999998	320739.70100000006	1
2021-01-12	164189.76699999996	313294.72081818176	1
2021-01-11	432599.66599999997	301364.2263	1
2021-01-13	12829.790999999997	300869.30799999996	1
2021-01-10	307994.72699999984	300627.50399999996	1
2021-01-06	90089.649	298480.7152	1
2021-02-06	50389.734999999986	293352.5650333333	1
2021-01-05	331084.6939999999	290329.7205	1
2021-02-02	161009.56200000003	288809.9029333333	1
2021-02-03	275539.70199999993	287062.8974	1
2021-01-08	183449.789	286991.85057142854	1

Figure 5.17: Deciles for dealership sales amount

In this activity, you used window functions to get the sales trend of your entire year and utilized this sales trend to identify the days that ZoomZoom is doing well or less ideal.

> **NOTE**
>
> The solution for this activity can be found on page 449.

SUMMARY

In this chapter, you learned about the window functions, which generate output for a row based on its position inside the dataset or subgroups within the dataset. This is different from the simple functions you learned in *Chapter 3*, *SQL for Data Preparation*, that generates an output for a row regardless of the characteristics of the dataset, and different from the aggregate functions you learned in *Chapter 4*, *Aggregate Functions for Data Analysis*, that generates an output for all rows in a dataset or subgroups in the dataset.

You learned some of the most common window functions including **COUNT**, **SUM**, and **RANK**. You also learned how to construct a basic window using **OVER**. The output of window function depends on the current row's position in the dataset or subgroups within the dataset, which is called **partition**, as well as the collection of rows required by the calculation, which is called **window**. As such there are several keywords that may impact how the calculation is done, such as **PARTITION BY**, **ORDER BY,** and window frame keywords. The **PARTITION BY** clause determines the partition, the **ORDER BY** clause determines the position of the row within the partition, and the window frame keywords determine the range and size of the window. You then learned how to use window functions to get analytical insights. For example, by defining window frame over a daily summary such as daily sales, you can create rolling statistics, and gain useful insights into the time trend of the sales.

At this point, you have learned all the fundamental statements of SQL. You have learned how to handle the full CRUD lifecycle using SQL, how to put tables together using **JOIN** and **UNION**, and you have learned how to use different types of functions to obtain the desired results. In *Chapter 6*, *Importing and Exporting Data*, you will look at how to import and export data to utilize SQL with other programs. You will use the **COPY** command to upload data to your database in bulk. You will also use Excel to process data from your database and then simplify your code using python.

6

IMPORTING AND EXPORTING DATA

OVERVIEW

In this chapter, you will learn techniques that will help you move data between your database and analytics tools. You will start by learning about the `psql` tool, which will enable you to quickly query data from a database. With `psql`, you can also leverage the `COPY` command, which allows the efficient importing and exporting of data. With these simple tools, you will be able to interact with the database and efficiently move data back and forth. Further, you will process and analyze data using Python. You will also explore Python libraries such as `SQLAlchemy` and `pandas'` advanced functionality for interacting with your database in Python.

INTRODUCTION

To extract insights from your database, you need data. While many companies store and update data within a central database, there are scenarios in which you will need more data than is currently in your database. For example, you are working on an ambitious project to revamp a website whose performance has progressively degraded over the past nine years. The first step in solving such a problem is to do a root cause analysis of it. The central database houses daily logs of the site's page load times along with other details. You will need to retrieve this data, clean it up, and filter out the entries where the page load times were over a certain threshold. You will need to share this information with a team of engineers and developers who will categorize these outliers, attributing the poor load times to a server issue, badly written code, network failure, or poor caching, among other things. You will then need to do an analysis of the categorized data and update the database to include the "fault categories" as provided to you by the developers who do not have access to the database. For all this, you will first need to retrieve the data and store it in an Excel file that can be shared with the developers.

Not only will you want to upload data to your database for further analysis, but if you are doing advanced analytics, there will also be situations wherein you will need to download data from your database (for example, if you want to carry out a form of statistical analysis that is unavailable in SQL). For this reason, you will also learn about the process of extracting data from a database. This will allow you to use other software to analyze your data. You will look at how you can integrate your workflows with a specific programming language that is frequently used for analytics: Python. It is powerful because it is easy to use, allows advanced functionality, is open source, and has large communities supporting it due to its popularity. You will examine how large datasets can be passed between your programming language and your databases efficiently so that you can have workflows that take advantage of the analytics software tools that are available.

In this chapter, you will learn how to efficiently upload data to a centralized database for further analysis. You will start by looking at the bulk uploading and downloading functionality in the PostgreSQL **COPY** command as well as the command-line client, **psql**, and how to run the **COPY** command locally using the **\COPY** command from **psql**. To use the **\COPY** command, you will also gain an understanding of the concept of view, which by itself is a very important tool in any RDBMS. You will then move on to studying how to handle data using Python. You will learn how to integrate Python with PostgreSQL, how to use SQL from Python scripts, and how to use Python libraries to achieve various analyses.

First, start by exploring the workings of the **COPY** command.

THE COPY COMMAND

At this point, you are probably familiar with the **SELECT** statement (covered in *Chapter 2, The Basics of SQL for Analytics)*, which allows you to retrieve data from a database. While this command is useful for small datasets that can be scanned quickly, you will often want to save a large dataset to a file. By saving these datasets to files, you can further process or analyze the data locally using Excel or Python. To retrieve these large datasets, you can use the PostgreSQL **COPY** command, which efficiently transfers data from a database to a file, or from a file to a database. This **COPY** command must be executed when connected to the PostgreSQL database using a SQL client, such as the PostgreSQL **psql** command. In the next section, you will learn how to use the **psql** command, then you will learn how to copy data with it.

RUNNING THE PSQL COMMAND

You have been using the **pgAdmin** frontend client to access your PostgreSQL database, and you have briefly used the **psql** tool in the *Preface* when you set up your PostgreSQL environment. But you might not be aware that **psql** was one of the first PostgreSQL clients. This interface is still in use today. It enables users to run PostgreSQL scripts that can interact with the database server within the local computing environment.

The syntax of the **psql** command is as follows:

```
psql -h <host> -p <port> -d <database> -U <username>
```

In this command, you pass in flags that provide the information needed to make the database connection. In this case, you have the following:

- **-h** is the flag for the hostname. The string that comes after it (separated by a space) should be the hostname for your database, which can be an IP address, a domain name, or **localhost** if it is run on the local machine.

- **-p** is the flag for the database port. Usually, this is **5432** for PostgreSQL databases.

- **-d** is the flag for the database name. The string that comes after it should be the database name. In this book, you will always use the **sqlda** database.

- **-U** is the flag for the username. It is succeeded by the username. In this book, you will use the PostgreSQL super username, which is **postgres**.

Applying the syntax to the environment you set up for this book, that is, to locally connect to the **sqlda** database that is on your local system as the postgres user, you can use this command:

```
psql -h localhost -p 5432 -d sqlda -U postgres
```

You will be prompted to enter your password, which is the password you entered for the superuser when you installed PostgreSQL on your computer. After that, the cursor will change to **sqlda=#**, where **sqlda** is the current database that you are running in.

You can also simply run the **psql** command without the parameters. It will prompt you for all the information mentioned above. Once it has been entered, you will be provided with the same **sqlda=#** command interface as shown below.

SQL Shell (psql)

```
Server [localhost]:
Database [postgres]: sqlda
Port [5432]:
Username [postgres]:
Password for user postgres:
psql (14.2)
WARNING: Console code page (437) differs from Windows code page (1252)
         8-bit characters might not work correctly. See psql reference
         page "Notes for Windows users" for details.
Type "help" for help.

sqlda=#
```

Figure 6.1: Logging into psql

You are now inside **psql** and can execute SQL just like you can in **pgAdmin**. For example, you can execute the following query:

```
SELECT
  product_id
FROM
  products
LIMIT
  5;
```

The result is as follows:

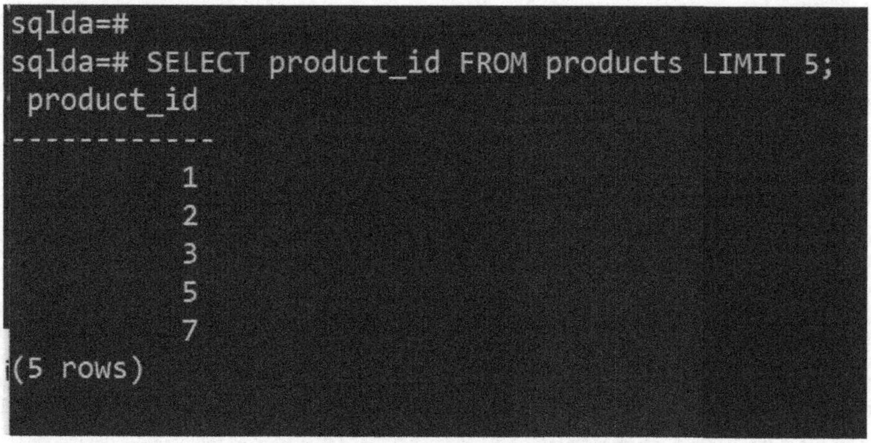

```
sqlda=#
sqlda=# SELECT product_id FROM products LIMIT 5;
 product_id
------------
          1
          2
          3
          5
          7
(5 rows)
```

Figure 6.2: Running SQL in psql

THE COPY STATEMENT

The **COPY** statement retrieves data from your database and dumps it into the file format that you choose. For example, consider the following statement:

```
COPY (
  SELECT
    customer_id,
    first_name,
    last_name
  FROM
    customers
  LIMIT
    5
)
TO STDOUT
WITH CSV HEADER;
```

The following is the output of the code:

```
customer_id,first_name,last_name
716,Jarred,Bester
1228,Ag,Smerdon
1876,Giuditta,Eim
1991,Nichole,Rosle
2275,Chic,Bryning
sqlda=#
```

Figure 6.3: Using COPY to print the results to STDOUT in CSV file format

This statement returns five rows from the **customers** table, with each record on a new line, and each value separated by a comma, in a typical **.csv** file format. The header is also included at the top.

Because the target of the **COPY** command is specified as **STDOUT**, the results will only be copied into the command-line interface and not into a file. Here is a breakdown of this command and the parameters that were passed in:

- **COPY** is simply the command used to transfer data to a file format.

- **(SELECT customer_id, first_name, last_name FROM customers LIMIT 5)** is the query that you want to copy the result from.

- **TO STDOUT** indicates that the results should be printed to the standard output rather than being saved to a file on the hard drive. Standard output is the common term for displaying output in a command-line terminal environment, which is often shortened to STDOUT.

- **WITH** is an optional keyword used to separate the parameters that you will use in the database-to-file transfer. Within **WITH**, you can specify multiple parameters, such as the following:

  - **CSV** indicates that you will use the **CSV** file format. You could have also specified **BINARY** or left this out altogether and received the output in text format.

- **HEADER** indicates that you want the header printed as well.

> **NOTE**
>
> You can learn more about the parameters available for the **COPY** command in the PostgreSQL documentation: https://www.postgresql.org/docs/current/sql-copy.html.

While the **STDOUT** option is useful, often, you will want to save data to a file. The **COPY** command offers the functionality to do this, but data is saved locally on the PostgreSQL server. You must specify the full file path (relative file paths are not permitted). If you have your PostgreSQL database running on your computer, you can test this out using the following command in **psql**:

```
COPY (
  SELECT *
  FROM customers
  LIMIT 5
)
TO 'c:\Users\Public\my_file.csv'
WITH CSV HEADER;
```

The output will be the following:

Figure 6.4: Output of the COPY statement

You will find that the file has now been saved in **CSV** format at the location you specified in the command.

Note that this example is executed in a PostgreSQL server that is hosted on a Windows machine. So, the full file path is in Windows file path format. If you are running the command on any other operating system, you need to adjust the file path accordingly. Also, you must use a folder that you have permission to work on. Otherwise, you will receive a permission error. For example, on a windows system, you may be restricted on which folder you can write to. In this chapter, all the files will be placed into the **c:\Users\Public** folder because the Windows system usually allows users to read/write in this folder, so it can be used for your exercise if you cannot find a better folder.

> **NOTE**
>
> The value in single quotes that follows the **To** keyword is the absolute path to the output file. The format of the path will depend on the operating system you are using. On Linux and Mac, the directory separator would be a forward-slash (/) character, and the root of the main drive would be /. On windows, however, the directory separator would be a back-slash (\) character and the path would start with the drive letter.

\COPY WITH PSQL

The **COPY** command, as stated above, runs on the PostgreSQL server. The PostgreSQL server in this book is installed on your local machine. So, your local machine is the server, and the **COPY** command will save the file to your local paths. However, in a real-world setup, servers are highly protected. Users usually do not have access to the file system of the server machines and need to download the files to their local machines.

The terminal **psql** allows the **COPY** command to be called remotely using the **psql**-specific **\COPY** instruction, which is similar in syntax to the **COPY** command but saves the file to the local machine. Once you have connected to your database using **psql**, you can test out the **\COPY** instruction by using the following command:

```
\COPY (SELECT * FROM customers LIMIT 5) TO 'c:\Users\Public\my_file.csv'
WITH CSV HEADER;
```

The following is the output of the code:

```
COPY 5
```

Here is a breakdown of this command and the parameters that were passed in:

- **\COPY** invokes the PostgreSQL **COPY** command to output the data.

- **(SELECT * FROM customers LIMIT 5)** is the query that you want to copy the result from.

- **TO 'c:\Users\Public\my_file.csv'** indicates that **psql** should save the output from standard output into **c:\Users\Public\my_file.csv**. Note that the **\COPY** command allows both absolute paths and relative paths. However, as there are many possible setups, this chapter will only use the absolute path, **c:\Users\Public**, for data files.

- The **WITH CSV HEADER** parameters operate in the same way as before.

You can also look at **my_file.csv**, which you can open with the text editor of your choice, such as Notepad:

```
my_file.csv - Notepad                                         —    □    ×
File  Edit  Format  View  Help
customer_id,title,first_name,last_name,suffix,email,gender,ip_address,phone,st
reet_address,city,state,postal_code,latitude,longitude,date_added
716,,Jarred,Bester,,jbesterjv@nih.gov,M,216.51.110.28,,,,,,,,,2018-09-19
00:00:00
1228,,Ag,Smerdon,,asmerdony3@house.gov,F,117.161.100.72,,,,,,,,,2021-12-23
00:00:00
1876,,Giuditta,Eim,,geim1g3@typepad.com,F,222.23.231.134,202-227-
5491,,,,,,,,2014-03-13 00:00:00
1991,,Nichole,Rosle,,nrosle1ja@ning.com,M,37.231.217.159,614-146-
7408,,,,,,,,2015-04-24 00:00:00
2275,,Chic,Bryning,,cbryning1r6@pcworld.com,M,117.177.14.194,512-939-
4727,,,,,,,,2016-11-05 00:00:00
```

Figure 6.5: The CSV file that you created using your \COPY command

It is worth noting here that while you can split the text of the **COPY** command into multiple lines, the **\COPY** command does not allow the query to contain multiple lines. A simple way to leverage multiline queries is to create a view containing your data before the **\COPY** command and drop the view after your **\COPY** command has finished. You will learn how to create a view in the next section.

CREATING TEMPORARY VIEWS

In many cases, you will find a certain query particularly helpful and would like to keep the definition so that you can use it later. In previous chapters, you have learned about the usage of subqueries as well as common table expressions. As useful as they are, subqueries and common table expressions are only effective within a single SQL query. You cannot refer to them outside their main query. To save a query definition for future usage, PostgreSQL allows you to create a view, which is a named **SELECT** query that you can reference later.

You can create a **VIEW** command called **customers_sample** using the following syntax:

```
CREATE TEMP VIEW customers_sample AS (
  SELECT
    *
  FROM
    customers
  LIMIT
    12
);
```

PostgreSQL will give you the following message, letting you know that the view has been created successfully:

Figure 6.6: Output of the CREATE VIEW statement

In this example, the SQL statement of this query is stored in a temporary view, which can be referenced in a similar way to the syntax used to reference a table. For example, look at the following query:

```
SELECT
  COUNT(1)
FROM
  customers_sample;
```

This would output **12**.

A view is a named SQL query and does not save any data. Instead, every time the view is referenced in a query, SQL replaces the view name with the query defined in the view, similar to handling a subquery. Views are saved in the schema until explicitly dropped. However, you can also add a **TEMP** keyword to instruct SQL to remove the view automatically once you are logged out of the server.

You can also manually delete the view using a simple command:

```
DROP VIEW customers_sample;
```

The output will be as follows:

```
DROP VIEW
```

For example, consider these commands:

```
CREATE TEMP VIEW customers_sample AS (
  SELECT
    *
  FROM
    customers
  LIMIT
    5
);


\COPY (SELECT * FROM customers_sample) TO 'c:\Users\Public\my_file.csv'
WITH CSV HEADER

DROP VIEW customers_sample;
```

The output of this would be identical to the output in the first export example. While you can perform this action either way, for readability, you will use the latter format in this book for longer queries.

CONFIGURING COPY AND \COPY

There are several options that you can use to configure the **COPY** and
\COPY commands:

- **FORMAT**: `format_name` can be used to specify the format. The options for `format_name` are **csv**, **text**, or **binary**. Alternatively, you can simply specify **CSV** or **BINARY** without the **FORMAT** keyword, or not specify the format at all and let the output default to a text file format.

- **DELIMITER**: `delimiter_character` can be used to specify the delimiter character for CSV or text files (for example **,** for CSV files, or **|** for pipe-separated files).

- **NULL**: `null_string` can be used to specify how **NULL** values should be represented (for example, whether blanks represent **NULL** values or **NULL** if that is how missing values should be represented in the data).

- **HEADER**: This specifies that the header should be output.

- **QUOTE**: `quote_character` can be used to specify how fields with special characters (for example, a comma in a text value within a CSV file) can be wrapped in quotes so that they are ignored by **COPY**.

- **ESCAPE**: `escape_character` specifies the character that can be used to escape the following character.

- **ENCODING**: `encoding_name` allows the specification of the encoding, which is particularly useful when you are dealing with foreign languages that contain special characters or user input.

For example, running from **psql**, the following would create a pipe-separated file, with a header, with empty (0 lengths) strings to represent a missing (**NULL**) value, and the double quote (**"**) character to represent the quote character:

```
\COPY customers TO 'c:\Users\Public\my_file.csv' WITH CSV HEADER DELIMITER
'|' NULL '' QUOTE '"'
```

The following is the output of the code:

```
COPY 50000
```

In the next section, you will learn how to use the **COPY** and **\COPY** commands to upload large amounts of data to a database.

USING COPY AND \COPY TO BULK UPLOAD DATA TO YOUR DATABASE

The **COPY** and **\COPY** commands can be used to efficiently download data, but they can also be used to upload data. The **COPY** and **\COPY** commands are far more efficient at uploading data than an **INSERT** statement. There are a few reasons for this:

- When using **COPY**, there is only one push of a data block, which occurs after all the rows have been properly allocated.

- There is less communication between the database and the client, so there is less network latency.

- PostgreSQL includes optimizations for **COPY** that would not be available through **INSERT**.

Here is an example of using the **\COPY** command to copy rows into a table from a file. First, run the following SQL to create a new table for **\COPY** command testing:

```
CREATE TABLE customers_csv AS (
    SELECT * FROM customers LIMIT 1
);
```

Then, run the following **\COPY** command to test its data loading functionality:

```
\COPY customers_csv FROM 'c:\Users\Public\my_file.csv' CSV HEADER
DELIMITER '|'
```

This outputs the following:

```
COPY 50000
```

Here is a breakdown of this command and the parameters that were passed in:

- **\COPY** is invoking the PostgreSQL **COPY** command to load the data into the database.

- **customers_csv** is the name of the table that you want to append to.

- **FROM 'c:\Users\Public\my_file.csv** specifies that you are uploading records from **c:\Users\Public\my_ file.csv**. The **FROM** keyword specifies that you are uploading records, as opposed to the **TO** keyword, which you use to download records.

- The **WITH CSV HEADER** parameters operate the same as before.

- **DELIMITER '|'** specifies what the delimiter is in the file. For a CSV file, this is assumed to be a comma, so you do not need this parameter. However, for readability, it might be useful to explicitly define this parameter, if for no other reason than to remind yourself how the file has been formatted.

> **NOTE**
>
> While **COPY** and **\COPY** are great for exporting data to other tools, there is additional functionality in PostgreSQL for exporting a database backup.
>
> For these maintenance tasks, you can use **pg_dump** for a specific table and **pg_dumpall** for an entire database or schema. These commands even let you save data in a compressed (**tar**) format, which saves space. Unfortunately, the output format from these commands is typically SQL, and it cannot be readily consumed outside of PostgreSQL. Therefore, it does not help you with importing or exporting data to and from other analytics tools, such as Python.

Since you have now learned how to import and export data, you will implement an exercise to export data to a file and process it in Excel.

> **NOTE**
>
> For the exercises and activities in this chapter, you will need to be able to access your database with **psql**. Here is the GitHub link to access the files of this chapter: https://packt.link/tcTFc.

EXERCISE 6.01: EXPORTING DATA TO A FILE FOR FURTHER PROCESSING IN EXCEL

The ZoomZoom executive committee is busy scouting for new locations to open their next dealership. Since the presentation needs to be made in PowerPoint, you can use Microsoft Excel to generate a bar chart of customer numbers per city based on the `.csv` file. Then, you can simply copy that chart to your slide. As a data analyst, you will be helping them make this decision by presenting the data in `.csv` file format about the cities that have the highest number of customers. The data will need to be retrieved from the **customers** table of the **sqlda** database. The **psql** and **\COPY** commands you learned about will come in handy. This analysis will help the ZoomZoom executive committee to decide where they might want to open the next dealership.

1. Open the command line to implement this exercise (such as CMD for Windows or Terminal for Mac) and connect to the **sqlda** database using the **psql** command.

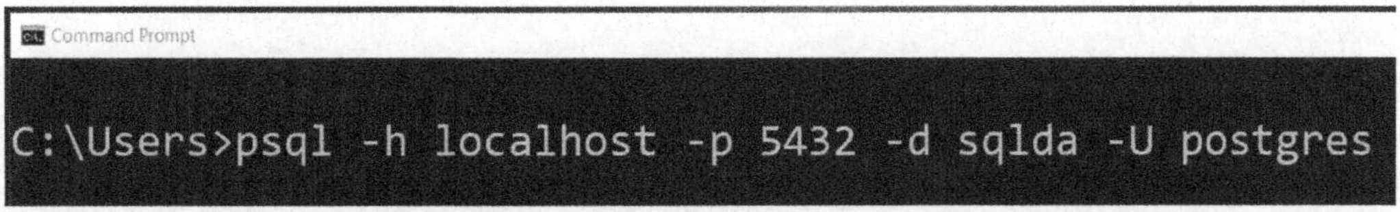

Figure 6.7: Running psql from the command line with parameters

Once this command is executed, the command terminal will look like this:

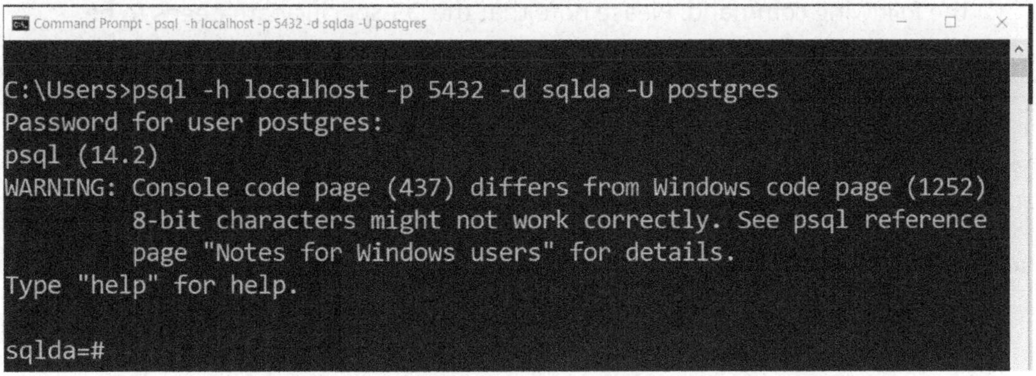

Figure 6.8: The psql interface after being launched from the command line

2. Create the **top_cities** view. The view will be defined as **SELECT city, count(1) AS number_of_customers** ..., which gives you the number of customers for each city. Because you add the **LIMIT 10** statement, you only grab the top 10 cities, as ordered by the second column (the number of customers). You also filter out the customers without a city:

```
CREATE TEMP VIEW top_cities AS (
  SELECT
    city,
    count(1) AS number_of_customers
  FROM
    customers
  WHERE
    city IS NOT NULL
  GROUP BY
    1
  ORDER BY
    2 DESC
  LIMIT
    10
);
```

3. Copy the **top_cities** view from your **ZoomZoom** database to a local file in **.csv** format. You do this by utilizing the temporary view you just created using the following command. Please note that the OS-specific path needs to be prepended to the **top_cities.csv** filename to specify the location to save the file. Here, in a windows environment, you will use **c:\Users\Public** as the folder:

```
\COPY (SELECT * FROM top_cities) TO 'c:\Users\Public\top_cities.csv'
WITH CSV HEADER DELIMITER ','
```

4. Drop the view:

```
DROP VIEW top_cities;
```

Here is a breakdown of these statements:

CREATE TEMP VIEW top_cities AS (...) indicates that you are creating a new temporary view.

\COPY ... copies data from this view to the **top_cities.csv** file on your local computer.

DROP VIEW top_cities; deletes the view because you no longer need it.

If you open the **top_cities.csv** text file, you should see the following output:

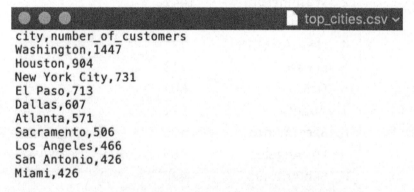

```
                                          📄 top_cities.csv ⌄
city,number_of_customers
Washington,1447
Houston,904
New York City,731
El Paso,713
Dallas,607
Atlanta,571
Sacramento,506
Los Angeles,466
San Antonio,426
Miami,426
```

Figure 6.9: Output from the \COPY command

> **NOTE**
>
> Here, the output file is **top_cities.csv**. You will be using this file in the upcoming exercises in this chapter.

Now that you have the output from your database in **CSV** file format, you can open it with a spreadsheet program, such as Excel.

5. Using Microsoft Excel or your favorite spreadsheet software or text editor, open the **top_cities.csv** file:

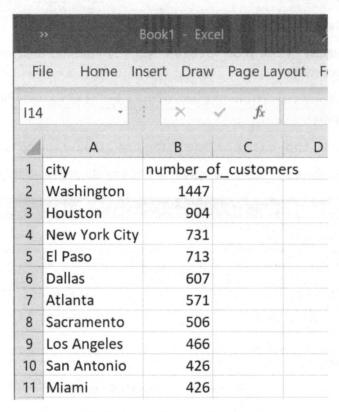

Figure 6.10: The top_cities.csv file open in Excel

6. Next, select all the data, which in this case is from cell A1 to cell B11:

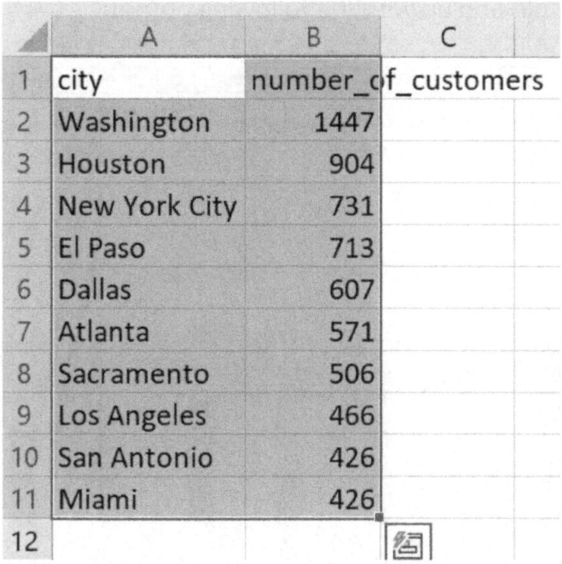

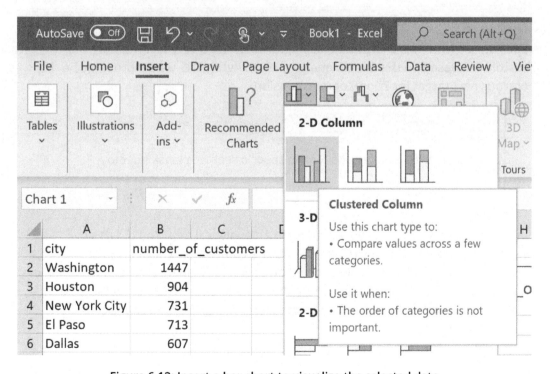

Figure 6.11: Select the entire dataset by clicking and dragging from cell A1 to cell B11

7. Next, in the top menu, go to **Insert** and then click on the bar chart icon (▯▯▾) to create a **2-D Column** chart:

Figure 6.12: Insert a bar chart to visualize the selected data

8. Finally, you should end up with the following output:

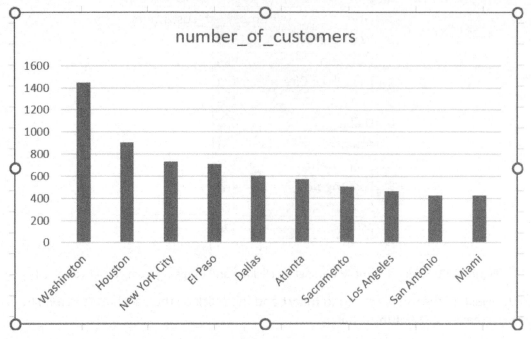

Figure 6.13: The final output from your visualization

You can see from this chart that Washington D.C. has a very high number of customers. Based on this simple analysis, Washington D.C. would probably be the obvious next target for ZoomZoom expansion.

> **NOTE**
>
> To access the source code for this specific section, please refer to https://packt.link/tcTFc.

In this exercise, you leveraged your data in an analytical tool. You did this by exporting the data using **psql** and the **\COPY** command to perform data visualization in Excel. This analysis could be useful for helping an executive to make a data-driven decision regarding where they should open their next retail location. Next, you will look at how you can use advanced programmatic analytical tools to leverage your data.

USING PYTHON WITH YOUR DATABASE

While SQL has a breadth of functionality, many data scientists and data analysts are starting to use Python too. This is because Python is a high-level language that can be easily used to process data. While the functionality of SQL covers most of the daily needs of data scientists, Python is growing fast and has generally become one of the most important data analytics tools in recent polls. A lot of Python's functionality is also fast, in part because so much of it is written in C, a low-level programming language.

The other large advantage that Python has is that it is versatile. While SQL is generally only used in the data science and statistical analysis communities, Python can be used to do anything from statistical analysis to building a web application. As a result, the developer community is much larger for Python. A larger developer community is a big advantage because there is better community support (for example, on Stack Overflow), and more Python packages and modules are being developed every day. The last major benefit of Python is that as it is a general programming language, it can be easier to deploy Python code to a production environment, and certain controls (such as Python namespaces) make Python less susceptible to errors. As a result of these advantages, it might be useful to learn Python as a data scientist.

GETTING STARTED WITH PYTHON

You have been running SQL against the PostgreSQL server and obtaining results via client software such as **pgAdmin** and psql throughout this book. PostgreSQL DBMS, as well as other relational DBMSs, allows for many ways of client connection. You can run your SQL through any of these connection methods and retrieve data in the same way as with **pgAdmin** and **psql**. When you use Python for data analytics, you will use a specific Python library called **psycopg2**. This library, when called from a Python runtime environment, will connect to the PostgreSQL server and handle traffic between your Python script and the database server. In its simplest form, once you connect to the PostgreSQL server using **psycopg2**, you can submit SQL to the database using Python scripts, the same way that you would with **psql**.

While there are many ways to get access to Python, the Anaconda distribution of Python makes it particularly easy to obtain and install Python and other analytical tools, as it comes with many commonly used analytics packages preinstalled alongside a great package manager. For that reason, you will be using the Anaconda distribution in this book.

You can take the following steps to get set up using the Anaconda distribution and to connect to Postgres:

1. Download and install Anaconda: https://www.anaconda.com/distribution/. During the installation, make sure that the **Add Anaconda to PATH** option is selected.

2. Once you have gone through the installation steps, open the Anaconda Prompt for Mac/Windows. Type **python** into the command line and check that you can access the Python interpreter, which should look like this:

Anaconda Prompt (Anaconda3) - python

```
(base) C:\Users\Dell>python
Python 3.9.7 (default, Sep 16 2021, 16:59:28) [MSC v.1916 64 bit (AMD64)] :: Anaconda, Inc. on win32
Type "help", "copyright", "credits" or "license" for more information.
>>>
```

Figure 6.14: The Python interpreter is now available and ready for input

> **NOTE**
>
> If you get an error, it may be because you need to specify your Python path. You can enter **quit()** to exit.
>
> Additionally, as you can see from the screenshot, the python version used in this book is 3.9.7. At the time that this book is in writing, there is a known issue in Anaconda that **psycopg2** is not compatible with certain python version 3.9.12 or newer. If you run into any issue with **psycopg2** importing, please reinstall your python using version 3.9.7.

3. Next, download and install the PostgreSQL database client for Python, **psycopg2**, using the Anaconda package manager. Open Anaconda Navigator for Mac/Windows. In the left panel, choose the **Environments** tab. Then, in the first drop-down box of the right panel, choose **All**.

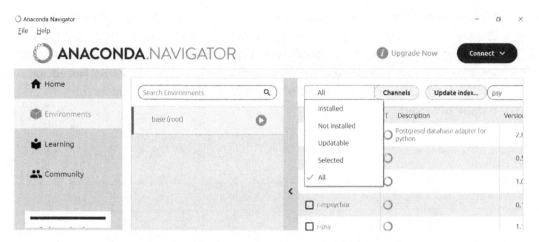

Figure 6.15: Checking the psycopg2 installation status

Type **psy** in the search box. You will see a list of libraries, including **psycopg2**. If it is not installed yet (that is, the box in front of it is not checked), check the box and click on the **Apply** button in the bottom-right corner. Follow the instructions for installation.

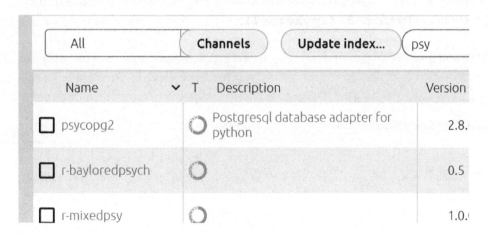

Figure 6.16: Installation checkbox for psycopg2

4. You can use Python in notebook form in your web browser. This is useful for displaying visualizations and running exploratory analyses. In this chapter, you are going to use Jupyter Notebook, which was installed as part of the Anaconda installation. From the **Home** tab of Anaconda Navigator, find Jupyter Notebook and click on **Launch**. You should see something like this pop up in your default browser:

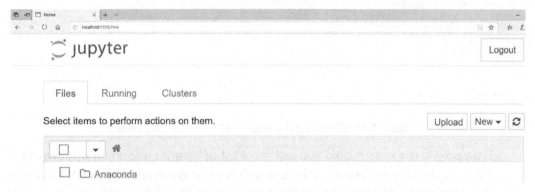

Figure 6.17: The Jupyter Notebook pop-up screen in your browser

5. Next, you will create a new notebook by clicking the **New** drop-down button and choosing **Python 3 (ipykernel)**:

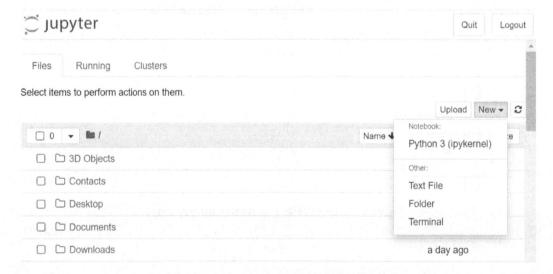

Figure 6.18: Opening a new Python 3 Jupyter notebook

You now have a notebook. Each notebook consists of multiple cells. Each cell contains some Python statements that will be executed together as one step.

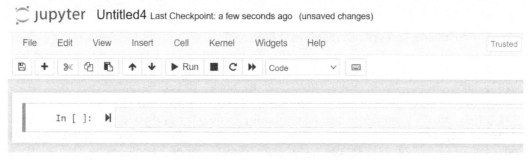

Figure 6.19: A new Jupyter notebook

6. Start writing the following Python script to import **psycopg2** into your Python runtime by typing it in the cell and clicking on the **Run** button above:

```
import psycopg2
```

7. As you finish running one cell, a new cell is created. Type the following code in the new cell and click on the **Run** button. This statement establishes the connection from your Python program (which is a client) to the database server specified in the parameters:

```
conn = psycopg2.connect(
        host="localhost",
        user="postgres",
        password="my_password",
        dbname="sqlda",
        port=5432
    )
```

8. Type the following script in the new cell that is automatically generated and click **Run**. This code creates a Python cursor that can send SQL statements to the database server and retrieve results:

```
cur = conn.cursor()
```

9. Now you can execute a sample SQL statement from the cursor by using its **execute()** method:

```
cur.execute("SELECT * FROM customers LIMIT 5")
```

10. Finally, you can retrieve the result and display it:

```
records = cur.fetchall()
print(records)
```

The following screenshot displays the output:

```
[(716, None, 'Jarred', 'Bester', None, 'jbesterjv@nih.gov', 'M', '216.51.110
.28', None, None, None, None, None, None, None, datetime.datetime(2018, 9, 1
9, 0, 0)), (1228, None, 'Ag', 'Smerdon', None, 'asmerdony3@house.gov', 'F',
'117.161.100.72', None, None, None, None, None, None, None, datetime.datetim
e(2021, 12, 23, 0, 0)), (1876, None, 'Giuditta', 'Eim', None, 'geim1g3@typep
ad.com', 'F', '222.23.231.134', '202-227-5491', None, None, None, None, None
, None, datetime.datetime(2014, 3, 13, 0, 0)), (1991, None, 'Nichole', 'Rosl
e', None, 'nrosle1ja@ning.com', 'M', '37.231.217.159', '614-146-7408', None,
 None, None, None, None, None, None, datetime.datetime(2015, 4, 24, 0, 0)), (2275,
 None, 'Chic', 'Bryning', None, 'cbryning1r6@pcworld.com', 'M', '117.177.14.
194', '512-939-4727', None, None, None, None, None, None, datetime.datetime(
2016, 11, 5, 0, 0))]
```

Figure 6.20: The output from your database connection in Python

You may wonder how this is different from running the same SQL from **pgAdmin**. After all, while you were able to connect to the database and read the data, several steps were required, and the syntax was a little bit more complex than for some of the other approaches you have tried. The power of Python in data analytics, as well as other programming languages, lies in the fact that inside a Python program, you can directly process the data, which is generally faster and has more functionalities. In the next section, you will learn how to use some of the other packages in Python to facilitate interfacing with the database.

IMPROVING POSTGRESQL ACCESS IN PYTHON WITH SQLALCHEMY AND PANDAS

While **psycopg2** is a powerful database client for accessing PostgreSQL from Python, it is just a connector. It does nothing more than passing the SQL and the resulting data between your program and the database server. There are more things in Python that can help the data analytics process. You can enhance the code by using a couple of other packages—namely, **pandas** and **SQLAlchemy**. First, you will learn about **SQLAlchemy**, a Python SQL toolkit that maps representations of objects to database tables. You will get familiar with the **SQLAlchemy** database engine and some of the advantages that it offers. This will enable you to access a database seamlessly without worrying about connections and Python objects. Next, you will learn about **pandas**—a Python package that can perform data manipulation and facilitate data analysis.

The **pandas** package will help you represent your data table structure (called a DataFrame) in memory. pandas also has high-level APIs that will enable you to read data from a database in just a few lines of code.

While both packages are powerful, it is worth noting that they still use the **psycopg2** package to connect to the database and execute queries. The big advantage that these packages provide is that they abstract some of the complexities of connecting to the database. By abstracting these complexities, you can connect to the database without worrying that you might forget to close a connection or remove a Python object such as a cursor.

WHAT IS SQLALCHEMY?

SQLAlchemy is a Python SQL toolkit and **Object-Relational Mapper (ORM)** that maps representations of objects to database tables. An ORM builds up mappings between SQL tables and programming language objects; in this case, Python objects. For example, in the following figure, there is a **customer** table in the database. The Python ORM will thus create a class called **customer** and keep the content in the object synchronized with the data in the table. For each row in the **customer** table, a **customer** object will be created inside the Python runtime. When there are changes (inserts, updates, and/or deletes), the ORM can initialize a sync and make the two sides consistent.

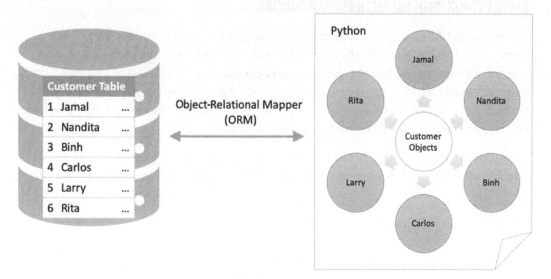

Figure 6.21: An ORM maps rows in a database to objects in memory

While the **SQLAlchemy ORM** offers many great functionalities, its key benefit is the **Engine** object. A **SQLAlchemy Engine** object contains information about the type of database (in your case, PostgreSQL) and a connection pool. The connection pool allows multiple connections to the database that operate simultaneously. The connection pool is also beneficial because it does not create a connection until a query is sent to be executed. Because these connections are not formed until the query is executed, the **Engine** object is said to exhibit lazy initialization. The term "lazy" is used to indicate that nothing happens (the connection is not formed) until a request is made. This is advantageous because it minimizes the time it takes for Python to establish and maintain the connection and reduces the load on the database.

Another advantage of the **SQLAlchemy Engine** object is that it automatically commits changes to the database due to **CREATE TABLE**, **UPDATE**, **INSERT**, and other statements that modify a database. This will help the data in the database and the data in Python to be synchronized all the time.

In your case, you will want to use it because it provides a robust **Engine** object to access databases. If the connection is dropped, the **SQLAlchemy Engine** object can instantiate that connection because it has a connection pool. It also provides a nice interface that works well with other packages (such as **pandas**).

USING PYTHON WITH SQLALCHEMY AND PANDAS

Normally, **SQLAlchemy** and **pandas** come together with Anaconda. When you install Anaconda on your machine, you have already set them up. However, if you are not sure about the installation, you can open Anaconda Navigator and go to the **Environments** tab. From there, you can verify the installed packages and install them if they are not there. From the same location, you can also install the packages referenced later in this book, such as **matplotlib**, if necessary.

Now, open Anaconda Navigator if you have not done so. Launch Jupyter Notebook and create a new notebook. Enter the following **import** statements in the first cell:

```
from sqlalchemy import create_engine
import pandas as pd
```

You will notice that you are importing two packages here. The first is the **create_ engine** module within the **sqlalchemy** package, and the second is **pandas**, which you rename to **pd** following the standard convention (and it has fewer characters). Using these two packages, you will be able to read and write data to and from your database and visualize the output.

Hit the **run** button or press *Shift + Enter* to run these commands. A new active cell should pop up:

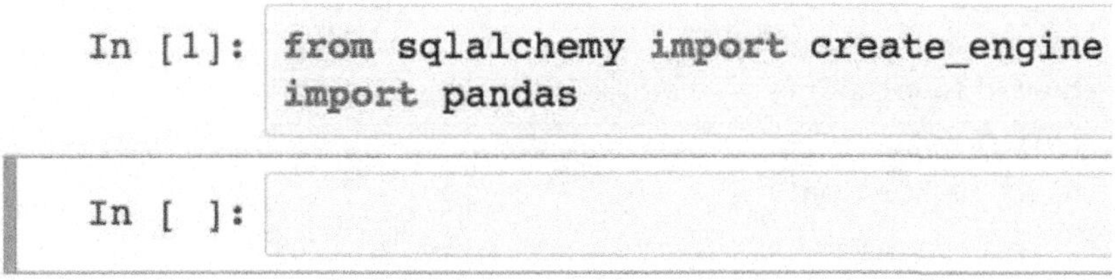

```
In [1]:  from sqlalchemy import create_engine
         import pandas

In [ ]:
```

Figure 6.22: Running your first cell in the Jupyter notebook

Next, you will configure your notebook to display plots and visualizations inline. You can do this with the following command:

```
%matplotlib inline
```

This tells the **matplotlib** package (which is a dependency of **pandas**) to create plots and visualizations inline in your notebook. Hit *Shift + Enter* again to jump to the next cell.

In the new cell, you will define your connection string:

```
cnxn_string = (
    "postgresql+psycopg2://{username}:{pswd}@{host}:{port}/{database}"
)
print(cnxn_string)
```

Press *Shift + Enter* again, and you should now see this connection string was printed. This is a generic connection string for **psycopg2**. You need to fill in your parameters to create the database **Engine** object. You can replace the parameters using the parameters that are specific to your connection. The particular parameters corresponding to the setup of this book are as follows:

```
engine = create_engine(
    cnxn_string.format(
        username="postgres",
        pswd="your_password",
        host="localhost",
        port=5432,
        database="sqlda"
    )
)
```

In this command, you run **create_engine** to create your database **Engine** object. You pass in your connection string and you format it for your specific database connection by filling in the placeholders for **{username}**, **{pswd}**, **{host}**, **{port}**, and **{database}**. The host is either an IP address, domain name, or the word **localhost** if the database is hosted locally. Make sure you update the password to match your setup.

Because **SQLAlchemy** is lazy, you will not know whether your database connection was successful until you try to send a command. You can test whether this database **Engine** object works by running the following command and hitting *Shift + Enter*:

```
engine.execute("SELECT * FROM customers LIMIT 2;").fetchall()
```

You should see something like this:

```
In [2]:   ▶| engine.execute("SELECT * FROM customers LIMIT 2;").fetchall()

Out[2]:  [(716, None, 'Jarred', 'Bester', None, 'jbesterjv@nih.gov', 'M', '21
          6.51.110.28', None, None, None, None, None, None, None, datetime.dat
          etime(2018, 9, 19, 0, 0)),
           (1228, None, 'Ag', 'Smerdon', None, 'asmerdony3@house.gov', 'F', '1
          17.161.100.72', None, None, None, None, None, None, None, datetime.d
          atetime(2021, 12, 23, 0, 0))]
```

Figure 6.23: Executing a query within Python

The output of this command is a Python list containing rows from your database as tuples. While you have successfully read data from your database, you will probably find it more practical to read your data into a **pandas** DataFrame in the next section.

READING AND WRITING TO A DATABASE WITH PANDAS

Python comes with great data structures, including lists, dictionaries, and tuples. While these are useful, your data can often be represented in table form, with rows and columns, similar to how you would store data in your database. For these purposes, the **DataFrame** object in **pandas** can be particularly useful. In addition to providing powerful data structures, **pandas** also offers the following:

- Functionality to read data directly from a database

- Data visualization

- Data analysis tools

If you continue from where you left off with your Jupyter notebook, you can use the SQLAlchemy **Engine** object to read data into a **pandas** DataFrame:

```
customers_data = pd.read_sql_table('customers', engine)
```

You have now stored your entire **customers** table as a **pandas** DataFrame in the **customers_data** variable. The **pandas read_sql_table** function requires two parameters: the name of a table and the connectable database (in this case, the **SQLAlchemy Engine** object). Alternatively, you can use the **read_sql_query** function, which takes a query string instead of a table name.

Here is an example of what your notebook might look like at this point:

```
In [1]: from sqlalchemy import create_engine
        import pandas as pd
        % matplotlib inline

In [2]: cnxn_string = ("postgresql+psycopg2://{username}:{pswd}"
                       "@{host}:{port}/{database}")
        print(cnxn_string)

        postgresql+psycopg2://{username}:{pswd}@{host}:{port}/{database}

In [3]: engine = create_engine(cnxn_string.format(
            username="                ",
            pswd="                      ",
            host="                                          ",
            port=5432,
            database="        "))

In [4]: engine.execute("SELECT * FROM customers LIMIT 2;").fetchall()

Out[4]: [(1, None, 'Arlena', 'Riveles', None, 'ariveles0@stumbleupon.com', 'F', '98.36.172.246', None, None, None, None, None
         , None, None, datetime.datetime(2017, 4, 23, 0, 0)),
          (2, 'Dr', 'Ode', 'Stovin', None, 'ostovin1@npr.org', 'M', '16.97.59.186', '314-534-4361', '2573 Fordem Parkway', 'Sa
         int Louis', 'MO', '63116', 38.5814, -90.2625, datetime.datetime(2014, 10, 2, 0, 0))]

In [5]: customers_data = pd.read_sql_table('customers', engine)

In [ ]: |
```

Figure 6.24: The entirety of your Jupyter notebook

Now that you know how to read data from the database, you can start to do some basic analysis and visualization. In essence, a **pandas** DataFrame is a relational table with enhanced information. You can apply similar operations in SQL on the DataFrames, such as querying, inserting, filtering, and deleting. For example, the **head()** method returns the first few (default of 5) rows of the DataFrame, much like the **LIMIT** clause in SQL. Then, in addition, you can also perform many more operations, such as pivoting, multi-column search and replacement, and semi-structured data parsing, which are not possible or are very difficult to achieve using SQL. For example, the **min()**/**max()** methods will return the minimum/maximum values of every column, without the need to specify the column name. The full functionalities of **pandas** are beyond the scope of this book, but will demonstrate some basic ones in the coming exercises.

WRITING DATA TO THE DATABASE USING PYTHON

There will always be scenarios in which you will want to use Python to write data back to the database. Luckily for you, **pandas** and **SQLAlchemy** make this a relatively easy task.

If you have your data in a **pandas** DataFrame, you can write data back to the database using the **pandas to_sql (...)** function, which requires two parameters: the name of the table to write to and the connection. Best of all, the **to_sql (...)** function can also create the target table for you by inferring column types using a DataFrame's data types. In the coming exercise, *Exercise 6.02, Reading, Visualizing, and Saving Data in Python* you will test out this functionality using the **top_cities_data** DataFrame that you created in *Step 8*.

Now, implement an exercise to read, visualize, and save data using Python.

EXERCISE 6.02: READING, VISUALIZING, AND SAVING DATA IN PYTHON

In the previous exercise, you executed a SQL query to get a list of the cities that have the highest number of customers. Then you dumped the result into a **CSV** file using the **COPY** command and sent the file to the business department. Upon receiving the file, they created a visualization on top of the **CSV** file in Excel and copied and pasted the visualization into a Microsoft PowerPoint slide file for presentation.

Looking at this process, you can see that there is still a lot of manual work and coordination between different applications. The whole process involves three applications: psql, Excel, and PowerPoint. There is a **.csv** file passing between psql and Excel, and there are copy and paste activities between Excel and PowerPoint.

In this exercise, you will analyze the same demographic information of customers by their city to better understand the target audience by reading data from the database output and visualizing the results using Python with Jupyter notebooks, SQLAlchemy, and **pandas**. You will run the SQL inside Python, retrieve data in a **pandas** DataFrame, and create a visualization inside Jupyter Notebook.

All this is automated and there are no other applications involved. There will not be a need to pass files and clipboards between applications. The following steps are involved:

1. Open Anaconda Navigator and launch Jupyter Notebook. Create a new notebook.

2. Run the following code in the first cell. The code imports required libraries into the Python runtime:

```
from sqlalchemy import create_engine
import pandas as pd
```

3. The second cell sets up the **matplotlib** environment for drawing. **Matplotlib** is a Python library that is widely used for data visualization, that is, drawing charts based on data. It comes together with **pandas** and should have already been installed in your environment. Running this command allows **matplotlib** to output the visualization directly to Jupyter Notebook:

```
%matplotlib inline
```

4. The third cell establishes a connection to the database server. You will need to adjust this code based on your server's setup:

```
cnxn_string = (
    "postgresql+psycopg2://{username}:{pswd}@{host}:{port}/
{database}"
)

engine = create_engine(
    cnxn_string.format(
        username="postgres",
        pswd="my_password",
        host="localhost",
        port=5432,
        database="sqlda"
    )
)
```

5. Enter the following query surrounded by triple quotes (triple quotes allow strings that span multiple lines in Python):

```
query = """
  SELECT
    city,
    COUNT(1) AS number_of_customers,
    COUNT(NULLIF(gender, 'M')) AS female,
    COUNT(NULLIF(gender, 'F')) AS male
  FROM
    customers
  WHERE
    city IS NOT NULL
  GROUP BY
    1
  ORDER BY
    2 DESC
  LIMIT
    10
"""
```

For each city, this query calculates the count of customers and calculates the count for each gender. It also removes customers with missing city information and aggregates your customer data by the first column (the city). In addition to this, it sorts the data by the second column (the count of customers) from largest to smallest (descending). Then, it limits the output to the top 10 (that is, the 10 cities with the highest number of customers).

6. Read the query result into a **pandas** DataFrame with the following command and execute the cells using *Shift + Enter*:

```
top_cities_data = pd.read_sql_query(query, engine)
```

The **pandas read_sql_query** method will run a SQL query against the database server that the engine points to and return the result in a **pandas** DataFrame. Here, **top_cities_data** is the DataFrame that **pandas** returned. View the data of **top_cities_data** by entering this name in a new cell and simply hitting *Shift + Enter*. Just as with the Python interpreter, Jupyter Notebook will display the output value:

In [6]: ▶ `top_cities_data`

Out[6]:

	city	number_of_customers	female	male
0	Washington	1447	734	713
1	Houston	904	446	458
2	New York City	731	369	362
3	El Paso	713	369	344
4	Dallas	607	309	298
5	Atlanta	571	292	279
6	Sacramento	506	244	262
7	Los Angeles	466	241	225
8	San Antonio	426	207	219
9	Miami	426	195	231

Figure 6.25: Storing the result of a query as a pandas DataFrame

You will notice that **pandas** also numbers the rows by default. In **pandas**, this is called an index.

7. Now, plot the number of men and women in each of the top 10 cities. To view the stats for each city separately, you can use a simple bar plot:

```
ax = top_cities_data.plot.bar(
    'city',
    y=['female', 'male'],
    title='Number of Customers by Gender and City'
)
```

The **plot()** method of the **pandas** DataFrame will draw a chart in the notebook. The chart type depends on the submethod that the **plot()** method uses. The **bar()** method will draw a bar chart. You can also choose other visualization types such as a pie chart (**pie()**), line chart (**line()**), and scatter plot (**scatter()**). Here is a screenshot of what your resulting output notebook should look like:

Figure 6.26: Data visualization in the Jupyter notebook

The results show that there is no significant difference in the gender of your customers in the cities that you are considering expanding into.

8. Now, use the following command to save the DataFrame into a database table:

```
top_cities_data.to_sql(
    'top_cities_data',
    engine,
    index=False,
    if_exists='replace'
)
```

In addition to the two required parameters, you added two optional parameters to this function. The **index** parameter specifies whether you want the index to be a column in your database table as well (a value of **False** means that you will not include it), and the **if_exists** parameter allows you to specify how to handle a scenario in which there is already a table with the same name in the database. In this case, you want to drop that table and replace it with the new data, so you use the **'replace'** option. In general, you should exercise caution when using the **'replace'** option as you can inadvertently lose your existing data.

9. You can utilize the data using SQL as it is currently saved in the database. You can query this data from any database client, including **pgAdmin**. For example, in the following SQL, you examine the relationship between the number of customers and the sales:

```
SELECT
    t.city,
    t.number_of_customers,
    SUM(s.sales_amount)
FROM
    sales s
JOIN
    customers c
    ON s.customer_id = c.customer_id
JOIN
```

```
    top_cities_data t
    ON c.city = t.city
GROUP BY
    1, 2
ORDER BY
    2 DESC;
```

The following is the output of the code:

city text	number_of_customers bigint	sum double precision
Washington	1447	7211615.17500016
Houston	904	4012994.146000084
New York City	731	4844309.108000096
El Paso	713	3915465.7800000175
Dallas	607	3016611.1790000196
Atlanta	571	3075851.129000037
Sacramento	506	3421386.767000016
Los Angeles	466	2840496.7450000183
Miami	426	2012762.256999997
San Antonio	426	3256747.3140000138

Figure 6.27: Data created in Python that has now been imported into your database

NOTE

To access the source code for this specific section, please refer to
https://packt.link/tcTFc.

In this exercise, you were able to read data from your database programmatically and perform data visualization on the result.

While the **to_sql()** functionality is simple and works as intended, it uses **insert** statements to send data to the database. For a small table of 10 rows, this is fine; however, for larger tables, the **psql \COPY** command is going to be much faster. Next, you will look at how you can write data (such as results from statistical analysis) back to the database using **COPY**.

IMPROVING PYTHON WRITE SPEED WITH COPY

You can use the **COPY** command in conjunction with Python, **SQLAlchemy**, and **pandas** to deliver the same speed that you get with the **COPY** command in psql. For instance, say you define the following function:

```
import csv
from io import StringIO

def psql_insert_COPY(table, conn, keys, data_iter):
    # gets a DBAPI connection that can provide a cursor
    dbapi_conn = conn.connection
    with dbapi_conn.cursor() as cur:
        s_buf = StringIO()
        writer = csv.writer(s_buf)
        writer.writerows(data_iter)
        s_buf.seek(0)

        columns = ', '.join('"{}"'.format(k) for k in keys)
        if table.schema:
            table_name = '{}.{}'.format(table.schema, table.name)
        else:
            table_name = table.name

        sql = 'COPY {} ({}) FROM STDIN WITH CSV'.format(table_name, columns)
        cur.COPY_expert(sql=sql, file=s_buf)
```

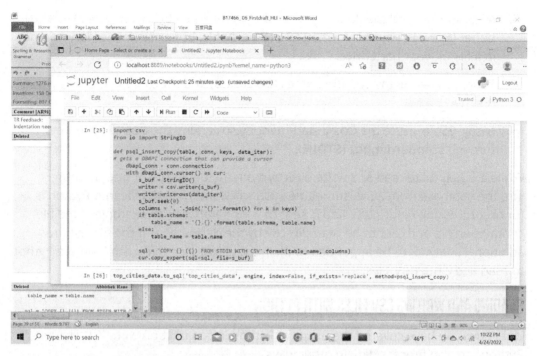

Figure 6.28: Python code for importing data using COPY

You can then leverage the **method** parameter in **to_sql**, as shown here:

```
top_cities_data.to_sql(
    'top_cities_data',
    engine,
    index=False,
    if_exists='replace',
    method=psql_insert_COPY
)
```

The **psql_insert_COPY** function defined here can be used without modifications to any of your PostgreSQL imports from **pandas**. Here is a breakdown of what this code does:

1. After performing some necessary imports, you begin by defining the function using the **def** keyword followed by the function name (**psql_insert_COPY**) and the parameters (**table**, **conn**, **keys**, and **data_iter**).

2. Next, you establish a connection (**dbapi_conn**) and a cursor (**cur**) that you can use for execution.

3. Next, you write all the data in your rows (represented by **data_iter**) to a string buffer (**s_buf**), which is formatted like a **CSV** file, but exists in memory and not in a file on your hard drive.

4. Then, you define the column names (**columns**) and the table name (**table_name**).

5. Lastly, you execute the **COPY** statement by streaming the **CSV** file contents through **standard input (STDIN)**.

While it is helpful to read and write directly from the database, or import data into the database from a file, sometimes you will want to read a file into Python for preprocessing before the data is sent to your database (for example, if the file contains errors and cannot be read directly by the database or if the file requires additional analytics to be appended to it). In these instances, you can leverage Python to read and write **CSV** files.

READING AND WRITING CSV FILES WITH PYTHON

Until now, you have covered the usage of Python in conjunction with SQL. However, Python can also process data in other ways.

In addition to reading and writing data to your database, you can use Python to read and write data from your local file system. The commands for reading and writing **CSV** files with **pandas** are very similar to those used for reading and writing from your database:

- For writing, **pandas.DataFrame.to_csv(file_path, index=False)** would write the DataFrame to your local file system using the supplied **file_path** parameter. **DataFrame** is a property of **pandas** that temporarily stores data. The **to_csv()** method of DataFrame has the following parameters: **file_path**, which is a string representing the path to the output file in a format specific to the OS, and **index**, which, if set to **true**, will write row numbers into the output data.

- For reading, **pandas.read_csv(file_path, dtype={})** would return a DataFrame representation of the data supplied in the CSV file located at the **file_path**.

When reading a **CSV** file, **pandas** will infer the correct data type based on the values in the file. For example, if the column contains only integer numbers, it will create the column with an **int64** data type.

Similarly, it can infer whether a column contains floats, timestamps, or strings. **pandas** can also infer whether there is a header for the file, and generally, this functionality works well. If there is a column that is not read incorrectly (for example, a five-digit US zip code might be read in as an integer causing the leading zeros to fall off, meaning "07123" would become "7123" without the leading zeros), you can specify the column type directly using the **dtype** parameter. For example, if you have a **zip_code** column in your dataset, you could specify that it is a string using **dtype={'zip_code': str}**.

> **NOTE**
>
> There are many ways in which a .csv file might be formatted. While pandas can generally infer the correct header and data types, many parameters are provided to customize the reading and writing of a .csv file for your needs.

Using the **top_cities_data** dataset in your notebook, you can test out this functionality:

```
top_cities_data.to_csv(
    'c:\\Users\\Public\\top_cities_analysis.csv',
    index=False
)


my_data = pd.read_csv(
    'c:\\Users\\Public\\top_cities_analysis.csv'
)


my_data
```

my_data now contains the data that you wrote to a **CSV** file and then read back in. You do not need to specify the optional **dtype** parameter in this case because your columns could be inferred correctly using **pandas**. You should see an identical copy of the data that is in **top_cities_data**:

	city	number_of_customers	female	male
0	Washington	1447	734	713
1	Houston	904	446	458
2	New York City	731	369	362
3	El Paso	713	369	344

Figure 6.29: Checking that you can write and read CSV files in pandas

In this example, you were able to read and write a **CSV** file from Python using data you queried from your database. With these skills, you can now import and export data between a file and your database, between Python and your database, and between Python and a file.

BEST PRACTICES FOR IMPORTING AND EXPORTING DATA

At this point, you have seen several different methods for reading and writing data between your computer and your database. Each method has its own use case and purpose. Generally, there are going to be two key factors that should guide your decision-making process:

- You should try to access the database with the same tool that you will use to analyze the data. As you add more steps to get your data from the database to your analytics tool, you increase the ways in which new errors can arise. When you cannot access the database using the same tool that you will use to process the data, you should use psql to read and write **CSV** files to your database.

- When writing data, you can save time by using the **COPY** or **\COPY** commands.

GOING PASSWORDLESS

In addition to everything mentioned so far, it is also a good idea to set up a **.pgpass** file. A **.pgpass** file specifies the parameters that you use to connect to your database, including your password. All of the programmatic methods of accessing the database discussed in this chapter (using either **psql** or Python) will allow you to skip the **password** parameter if your **.pgpass** file contains the password for the matching hostname, database, and username. This not only saves you time but also increases the security of your database because you can freely share your code without having to worry about passwords embedded in the code.

On Unix-based systems and macOS, you can create the **.pgpass** file in your home directory. On Windows, you can create the file in **%APPDATA%\postgresql\pgpass.conf**. **%APPDATA%** is a Windows system value that points to the current application data folder. You can get the actual value of it by opening Windows Explorer, typing the exact word **%APPDATA%**, into the address bar and hitting *Enter*. The folder you are in is the folder this **%APPDATA%** value points to. The **.pgpass** file should contain one line for every database connection that you want to store, and it should follow this format (customized for your database parameters):

```
hostname:port:database:username:password
```

For your setup, the entry should be as follows (with the password properly set):

```
localhost:5432:sqlda:postgres:my_password
```

For Unix and Mac users, you will need to change the permissions on the file using the following command on the command line (in Terminal):

```
chmod 0600 ~/.pgpass
```

For Windows users, it is assumed that you have secured the permissions of the file so that other users cannot access it.

Once you have created the file, you can test that it works by calling **psql** as follows in the terminal:

```
psql -h localhost -p 5432 -d sqlda -U postgres
```

As you can see, there is no prompt for the password. `psql` directly gets into the command interface.

```
C:\Users\Dell>psql -h localhost -p 5432 -d sqlda -U postgres
psql (14.2)
WARNING: Console code page (437) differs from Windows code page
         8-bit characters might not work correctly. See psql ref
         page "Notes for Windows users" for details.
Type "help" for help.

sqlda=#
```

Figure 6.30: Passwordless login to psql from the command line

Since the `.pgpass` file was created successfully, you will not be prompted for your password.

With this, you can now connect to your database without typing the password, which both speeds up your development and mitigates the risk that you will accidentally share a password.

In the following activity, you will use everything you have learned from this chapter to see how you can discover sales trends by importing new datasets.

ACTIVITY 6.01: USING AN EXTERNAL DATASET TO DISCOVER SALES TRENDS

In this activity, you are going to use the United States Census data on public transportation usage by zip code to see whether the level of use of public transportation shows any correlation to ZoomZoom sales in a given location. This will allow you to practice the following skills:

- Importing and exporting data to and from your database

- Interacting with your database programmatically (for example, using Python in conjunction with SQLAlchemy and **pandas**)

> **NOTE**
>
> Before you begin, you will need to download the public transportation statistics by zip code dataset from GitHub: https://packt.link/NdMNL.

This dataset contains three columns:

- **zip_code**: This is the five-digit United States postal code that is used to identify a region.

- **public_transportation_pct**: This is the percentage of the population in a postal code that has been identified as using public transportation to commute to work.

- **public_transportation_population**: This is the raw number of people in a zip code that use public transportation to commute to work.

Perform the following steps to complete this activity:

1. Copy the data from the public transportation dataset to the ZoomZoom customer database by importing this data into a new table in the ZoomZoom database.

2. Find the maximum and minimum values of **public_transportation_pct** in this data. Values less than 0 will most likely be missing data.

3. Calculate the average sales amounts for customers that live in high public transportation usage regions (over 10%) as well as low public transportation usage regions (less than, or equal to, 10%).

4. Read the data into **pandas** and plot a histogram of the distribution (Hint: you can use **my_data.plot.hist(y='public_transportation_pct')** to plot a histogram if you read the data into a **my_data pandas** DataFrame).

5. Using **pandas**, test using the **to_sql** function with and without the **method=psql_insert_COPY** parameter. How do the speeds compare? (Hint: in a Jupyter notebook, you can add **%time** in front of your command to see how long it takes to execute the code.)

6. Group customers based on their zip code public transportation usage rounded to the nearest 10% and look at the average number of transactions per customer. Export this data to Excel and create a scatterplot to better understand the relationship between public transportation usage and sales.

7. Based on this analysis, determine what recommendations you would have for the executive team at ZoomZoom when considering expansion opportunities.

> **NOTE**
>
> To access the source code for this specific section, please refer to https://packt.link/tcTFc.

> **NOTE**
>
> The solution for this activity can be found on page 453.

SUMMARY

In this chapter, you learned how to interface your database with other analytical tools for further analysis and visualization. While SQL is powerful, there will still be those odd analyses that need to be undertaken in other systems. To solve this problem, SQL allows you to transfer data in and out of the database for whatever tasks you may require.

Initially, we looked at how you can use the psql command-line tool to query a database. From there, we were able to explore the **COPY** command and the psql-specific **\COPY** command, which enabled you to import and export data to and from the database in bulk. Next, you looked at programmatically accessing the database using analytical software such as Python. From there, you were able to explore some of the advanced functionality in Python, including **SQLAlchemy** and **pandas**, which enabled you to perform data manipulation and visualization using a programming language.

In the next chapter, you will examine data structures that can be used to store complex relationships in data. You will learn how to mine insights from text data, as well as looking at the **JSON** and array data types so that you can make full use of all the information that is available.

7

ANALYTICS USING COMPLEX DATA TYPES

OVERVIEW

This chapter covers how to make the most of your data by analyzing complex and alternative data types. While data is typically thought of as numbers, in the real world, it frequently exists in other formats: text, dates and times, and latitude and longitude. In addition to these specialty data types, other data types provide the context regarding sequential or non-predeterministic attributes. The goal of this chapter is to show how you can use SQL and analytics techniques to produce insights from these other data types.

By the end of this chapter, you will be able to perform descriptive analytics on time series data using `datetime`. You will use geospatial data to identify relationships, then extract insights from complex data types (that is, arrays, JSON, and JSONB) and perform text analytics.

INTRODUCTION

In this book, you have learned a lot about SQL's processing power over numbers and strings. The majority of data analytics tasks are indeed analyzing numbers and strings. However, in the real world, data is often found in various other formats, such as words, locations, dates, and, sometimes, complex data structures. This data, although presented as numbers and strings, has its own domain of operation and computation instead of simple arithmetic. For example, adding one day to January 31, 2022, will result in February 1, 2022, not January 32, 2022.

In this chapter, you will look at these data types and examine how you can use this data in your analysis:

- Date and time

- Geospatial

- **JSON**

- **ARRAY**

- Text

By the end of the chapter, you will have broadened your analysis capabilities so that you can leverage just about any type of data available to you.

DATE AND TIME DATA TYPES FOR ANALYSIS

You may be familiar with dates and times, but do you know how these quantitative measures are represented? They are represented using numbers, but not a single number. Instead, they are measured with a set of numbers, with one number each for year, month, day, hour, minute, second, and millisecond.

This is a complex representation, comprising several different components. For example, knowing the current minute without knowing the current hour does not serve any purpose. Additionally, there are complex ways of interacting with dates and times; for example, different points in time can be subtracted from one another. The current time can be represented differently depending on where you are in the world.

As a result of these intricacies, you need to take special care when working with this type of data. In fact, PostgreSQL, like most databases, offers special data types that can represent these types of values. You will start by examining the **DATE** type.

THE DATE DATA TYPE

Dates can be easily represented using strings or numbers (for example, both **January 1, 2022** and **01/01/2022** clearly represent a specific date), but dates are a special form of data as they represent a quantitative value that does not always follow the simple numerical sequence. Adding 1 week to the current date means adding 7 days, for example. A given date has different properties that you might want to use in your analysis—for instance, the year or the day of the week that the date represents. Working with dates is also necessary for time series analysis, which is one of the most common types of analysis that come up. The SQL standard includes the **DATE** data type, and PostgreSQL offers great functionality for interacting with this data type.

The most common concern about the **DATE** data type is the display format. Different regions use different formats to represent the same date. For example, the date **January 14, 2022** is written as **01/14/2022** in some countries but **14/01/2022** in others. You can set your database to display dates in the format that you are most familiar with. PostgreSQL uses the **DateStyle** parameter to configure these settings. To view your current settings, you can use the following command:

```
SHOW DateStyle;
```

The following is the output of the preceding query in a system where both the PostgreSQL server and the pgAdmin client are installed on the same Windows server whose system locale is set to the United States:

```
DateStyle
-----------
ISO, MDY
(1 row)
```

The first output specifies the **International Organization Standardization (ISO)** output format, which displays the date as *Year-Month-Day*, and the second output parameter specifies the ordering for input or output. In this case, since both the server and client are using a United States locale, *Month/Day/Year* is used as the display style. If your PostgreSQL server or client is installed on an operating system with a different system locale than the one mentioned here, the result of the previous command may be different. For example, if you wanted to set it to the European format of *Day, Month, Year*, you would set **DateStyle** to **'GERMAN, DMY'**. You can configure the output for your database using the following command:

```
SET DateStyle='GERMAN, DMY';
```

For this chapter, you will use the ISO display format (*Year-Month-Day*) and the *Month/Day/Year* input format. You can configure this format by using the preceding command.

Now, start by testing out the **DATE** format:

```
SELECT '1/8/2022'::DATE;
```

The following is the output of the query:

```
date
------------
 2022-01-08
(1 row)
```

As you can see, when you input a string, **1/8/2022**, using the *Month/Day/Year* format, PostgreSQL understands that this is January 8, 2022 (and not August 1, 2022). It displays the date using the ISO format specified previously, in the form of YYYY-MM-DD.

Similarly, you could use the following formats with dashes and periods to separate the date components, with the same result:

```
SELECT '1-8-2022'::DATE;
```

The following is the output of the query:

```
date
------------
 2022-01-08
(1 row)
```

In addition to displaying dates that are input as strings, you can display the current date by simply using the **current_date** keyword in PostgreSQL:

```
SELECT current_date;
```

The following is the output of the query:

```
current_date
--------------
 2022-06-05
(1 row)
```

The **DATE** data type is useful. The natural extension of it is the data type representing the time, such as 10 a.m. or 2 p.m., in a day. The interesting fact is that when people talk about time, they usually refer to the combination of a day and a time. Simply referring to a time is not enough to determine the exact moment that something happens. For example, "the class starts at 6 p.m." very likely implies that the class starts at 6 p.m. every Monday for this semester. To avoid any confusion, the SQL standard offers the **TIMESTAMP** data type, which represents a date and a time, down to a microsecond, for example, **2022-06-05 13:47:44.472096**.

You can see the current timestamp using the **NOW()** function, and you can specify your time zone using **AT TIME ZONE '<time zone>'**. Here is an example of the **NOW()** function with the Eastern Standard time zone specified:

```
SELECT NOW() AT TIME ZONE 'EST';
```

The following is the output of the query:

```
timezone
---------------------------
 2022-06-05 13:47:44.472096
(1 row)
```

You can also use the **TIMESTAMP** data type without the time zone specified. You can get the current time zone with the **NOW()** function:

```
SELECT NOW();
```

The following is the output of the query. The **-04** at the end of the string indicates the output time zone:

```
now
-------------------------------
 2022-06-05 13:47:44.472096-04
(1 row)
```

> **NOTE**
>
> In general, it is recommended that you use the timestamp with the time zone specified. If you do not specify the time zone, the value of the timestamp could be questionable (for example, the time could be represented in the time zone where the company is located, in **Coordinated Universal Time** (**UTC**) time, or the customer's time zone).

The **DATE** and **TIMESTAMP** data types are helpful not only because they display dates in a readable format, but also because they store these values using fewer bytes than the equivalent string representation (a **DATE** type value requires only 4 bytes, while the equivalent text representation might be 8 bytes for an eight-character representation such as **'20160101'**). Additionally, PostgreSQL provides special functionalities to manipulate and transform dates. This is particularly useful for data analytics.

TRANSFORMING DATE DATA TYPES

Often, you will want to decompose your dates into their component parts. For example, while daily sales are important, you may also be interested in the summary for each year and month, so that you can review the monthly trend of your sales. You may see from this trend which month is your bestselling one so that you can prepare your inventory in advance. To do this, you can use **EXTRACT(component FROM date)**. Here is an example:

```
SELECT
    current_date,
    EXTRACT(year FROM current_date) AS year,
    EXTRACT(month FROM current_date) AS month,
    EXTRACT(day FROM current_date) AS day;
```

The following is the output of the code:

```
current_date | year | month | day
-------------+------+-------+-----
2022-06-05   | 2022 |     6 | 5
(1 row)
```

Similarly, you can abbreviate these components as **y**, **mon**, and **d**, and PostgreSQL will understand what you want:

```
SELECT
    current_date,
    EXTRACT(y FROM current_date) AS year,
    EXTRACT(mon FROM current_date) AS month,
    EXTRACT(d FROM current_date) AS day;
```

The following is the output of the code:

```
current_date | year | month | day
--------------+------+-------+-----
2022-06-05   | 2022 |   6 | 5
(1 row)
```

In addition to the year, month, and day, you will sometimes want additional components, such as day of the week, week of the year, or quarter. You can extract these date parts as follows:

```
SELECT
    current_date,
    EXTRACT(dow FROM current_date) AS day_of_week,
    EXTRACT(week FROM current_date) AS week_of_year,
    EXTRACT(quarter FROM current_date) AS quarter;
```

The following is the output of the code:

```
current_date | day_of_week | week | quarter
--------------+-------------+------+---------
2022-06-05   |          0 |  23 |       2
(1 row)
```

> **NOTE**
>
> **EXTRACT** always outputs a number; so, in this case, `day_of_week` starts at 0 (Sunday) and goes up to 6 (Saturday). Instead of `dow`, you can use `isodow`, which starts at 1 (Monday) and goes up to 7 (Sunday).

In addition to extracting date parts from a date, you may want to simply truncate your date or timestamp. For example, say you want to view the year and month summary for sales, but you only have the date in the sales table. To aggregate the sales for year/month, you need to remove the day and timestamp from the date and get the year+month output. This can be done using many functions, such as **DATE_TRUNC()**, **DATE_PART()**, or **EXTRACT()**, each with a slightly different syntax and purpose. In the following example, you will use the **TO_CHAR()** function, which extracts the designated parts of a date and organizes them into one string, because it offers maximum flexibility over what information you can get and how you want to present it:

```
SELECT NOW(), TO_CHAR(NOW(), 'yyyymm') AS yearmonth;
```

The following is the output of the code:

```
        now         |      yearmonth
----------------------------+------------------------
 2022-06-05 19:40:08.691618+00 | 202206
```

The date part extraction functions such as **TO_CHAR()** and **EXTRACT()** are particularly useful for **GROUP BY** statements. For example, you can use it to group sales by year and month and get the monthly sales for the whole year:

```
SELECT
  TO_CHAR(sales_transaction_date, 'yyyymm') AS yearmonth,
  SUM(sales_amount) AS total_quarterly_sales
FROM
  sales
GROUP BY
  1
ORDER BY
  1 DESC;
```

The result is as follows:

month text	total_quarterly_sales double precision
202201	5706307.722000058
202112	5455222.157000077
202111	4280693.541000046
202110	3318119.411000051
202109	3509884.9920000336
202108	3937509.896000073
202107	5485778.13700009
202106	5065843.292000066
202105	6948262.514000091

Figure 7.1: Monthly sales using TO_CHAR

INTERVALS

In addition to representing dates, you can also represent fixed time intervals using the **INTERVAL** data type. This data type is useful if you want to analyze how long something takes. For example, when customers receive a promotional email, they may not open it immediately. The interval between the date the email is received and the date the email is opened can indicate how attractive the email is to the customers. If you want to know how long it takes a customer to open an email after receiving it, you need to calculate the interval between those two dates.

Here is an example:

```
SELECT INTERVAL '5 days';
```

The following is the output of the code:

```
interval
----------
 5 days
(1 row)
```

Intervals are useful for measuring the difference between two timestamps by subtracting these two timestamps. They can also be used to add to/subtract from a timestamp to get a new timestamp. For example, if you want to measure the length of February, you can calculate the interval between the first day of February and the first day of March:

```
SELECT TIMESTAMP '2022-03-01 00:00:00' - TIMESTAMP '2022-02-01
00:00:00' AS days_in_feb;
```

The following is the output of the code:

```
days_in_feb
-------------
 28 days
(1 row)
```

Alternatively, intervals can be used to add the number of days to a timestamp to get a new timestamp, such as "what is the date 7 days from now?":

```
SELECT TIMESTAMP '2022-06-05 00:00:00' + INTERVAL '7 days' AS new_date;
```

The following is the output of the code:

```
new_date
----------------------
 2022-06-12 00:00:00
(1 row)
```

While intervals offer a precise method for doing timestamp arithmetic, the **DATE** format can be used with integers to accomplish a similar result. In the following example, you simply add 7 (an integer) to the date to calculate the new date:

```
SELECT DATE '2022-06-05' + 7 AS new_date;
```

The following is the output of the code:

```
new_date
------------
 2022-06-12
(1 row)
```

Similarly, you can subtract two dates and get an integer result:

```
SELECT DATE '2022-03-01' - DATE '2022-02-01' AS days_in_feb;
```

The following is the output of the code:

```
days_in_feb
-------------
28
(1 row)
```

While the **DATE** data type offers ease of use, the timestamp with the **TIME ZONE** data type offers precision. If you need your date/time field to be precisely the same as the time at which the action occurred, you should use the timestamp with the time zone. If not, you can use the **DATE** field.

> **NOTE**
>
> All the exercises and activity code for this chapter can also be found on GitHub: http://packt.link/LpoE0.

EXERCISE 7.01: ANALYTICS WITH TIME SERIES DATA

ZoomZoom has ramped up its efforts to recruit more customers during the year 2021, hoping that it can sell more vehicles as the number of new customers grows. In this exercise, you will perform a basic analysis using time series data to gain insight into whether the sales were affected by the number of new customers. While it makes sense to have a day-by-day comparison, daily sales/recruitments can fluctuate significantly. It is generally recommended to start from a longer time span, such as monthly sales/recruitment, and break down the numbers once you find any patterns.

Perform the following steps to complete the exercise:

1. First, look at the number of monthly sales. You can use the following aggregate query with the **TO_CHAR** method:

```
SELECT
  TO_CHAR(sales_transaction_date, 'yyyymm') AS month_date,
  COUNT(1) AS number_of_sales
FROM
  sales
WHERE
  EXTRACT(year FROM sales_transaction_date) = 2021
GROUP BY
  1
ORDER BY
  1;
```

After running this SQL, you will get the following result:

month_date 🔒 text	number_of_sales 🔒 bigint
202101	989
202102	929
202103	1111
202104	994
202105	887
202106	765
202107	788
202108	593
202109	585
202110	634
202111	736
202112	893

Figure 7.2: Monthly number of sales

2. Run another query to get the number of new customers joining each month:

```
SELECT
  TO_CHAR(date_added, 'yyyymm') AS month_date,
  COUNT(1) AS number_of_new_customers
FROM
  customers
WHERE
  EXTRACT(year FROM date_added) = 2021
GROUP BY
  1
ORDER BY
  1;
```

The following is the output of the preceding query:

month_date text	number_of_new_customers bigint
202101	466
202102	439
202103	455
202104	433
202105	463
202106	439
202107	482
202108	467
202109	421
202110	447
202111	474
202112	507

Figure 7.3: Number of new customer sign-ups every month

You can probably see that the flow of new potential customers is fairly steady and hovers around 400-500 new customer sign-ups every month, while the number of sales (as queried in step 1) varies considerably. So, it looks like the effort of signing up new customers may not be directly related to the sales amount.

> **NOTE**
>
> To access the source code for this specific section, please refer to http://packt.link/LpoE0.

In this exercise, you used a PostgreSQL function to extract year and month parts from a date and used the extracted information to aggregate sales data and customer recruitment data to form a time series for comparison. In the next section, you will learn about another data type that has its own domain of operations, geospatial data.

PERFORMING GEOSPATIAL ANALYSIS IN POSTGRESQL

In addition to looking at time series data to better understand trends, you can also use geospatial information (such as city, country, or latitude and longitude) to better understand your customers. For example, governments use geospatial analysis to better understand regional economic differences, while a ride-sharing platform might use geospatial data to find the closest driver for a customer.

You can represent a geospatial location using latitude and longitude coordinates, and this will be the fundamental building block for you to begin geospatial analysis.

LATITUDE AND LONGITUDE

Locations are often thought about in terms of the address—the city, state, country, or postal code that is assigned to the location that you are interested in. This is usually from an analytics perspective. For example, you can look at the sales volume in the ZoomZoom sales table by city and come up with meaningful results about which cities are performing well.

Often, you need to understand geospatial relationships numerically to understand the distances between two points or relationships that vary based on where you are on a map. After all, if you live on the border between two cities, it is unlikely that your spending behavior will suddenly change if you walk across into the other city.

Latitude and longitude allow you to look at the location in a continuous context. This allows you to analyze the numeric relationships between location and other factors (for example, sales). Latitude and longitude also enable you to look at the distances between two locations.

Latitude tells you how far north or south a point is. A point at +90° latitude is at the North Pole, while a point at 0° latitude is at the equator, and a point at -90° is at the South Pole. On a map, lines of constant latitude run east and west.

Longitude tells you how far east or west a point is. On a map, lines of constant longitude run north and south. Greenwich, England, is the point of 0° longitude. Points can be defined using longitude as west (-) or east (+) of this point and values range from -180° west to +180° east. These values are equivalent because they both point to the vertical line that runs through the Pacific Ocean, which is halfway around the world from Greenwich, England.

REPRESENTING LATITUDE AND LONGITUDE IN POSTGRESQL

In PostgreSQL, you can represent latitude and longitude using two floating-point numbers. In fact, this is how latitude and longitude are represented in the ZoomZoom **Customers** table:

```
SELECT
    latitude,
    longitude
FROM
    customers
WHERE
    latitude IS NOT NULL
LIMIT
    10;
```

Here is the output of the preceding query:

31.6948	-106.3
30.6589	-88.178
40.0086	-76.5972
38.4142	-81.7582
47.1441	-122.4434
36.3551	-119.301
38.8318	-77.2888
39.5645	-75.597
38.5814	-90.2625
30.6143	-87.2758

Figure 7.4: The latitudes and longitudes of ZoomZoom customers

Here, you can see that all the latitudes are positive because the United States is north of the equator. All the longitudes are negative because the United States is west of Greenwich, England. You can also notice that some customers do not have latitude and longitude values filled in, because their location is unknown.

While these values can give you the exact location of a customer, you cannot do much with that information, because distance calculations require trigonometry and make simplifying assumptions that the earth is perfectly round.

Thankfully, PostgreSQL has the tools to solve this problem. You can calculate distances in PostgreSQL using two packages, **earthdistance** and **cube**. You can install these two packages by running the following two commands in **pgAdmin**:

```
CREATE EXTENSION cube;
CREATE EXTENSION earthdistance;
```

These two extensions only need to be installed once by running the two preceding commands. The **earthdistance** module depends on the **cube** module so you must install the **cube** module first. Once you install the **earthdistance** module, you can define a **POINT** data type:

```
SELECT
    POINT(longitude, latitude)
FROM
    customers
WHERE
    longitude IS NOT NULL
LIMIT
    10;
```

Here is the output of the preceding query:

(-72.5783,42.0999)
(-82.3932,34.8001)
(-106.3,31.6948)
(-85.0707,41.0938)
(-93.7665,44.8055)
(-118.2987,33.7866)
(-122.5485,47.1591)
(-77.0146,38.8933)
(-89.4528,43.073)
(-83.0114,39.969)

Figure 7.5: Customer latitude and longitude represented as points in PostgreSQL

> **NOTE**
>
> A **POINT** data type is defined as a combination of two numbers enclosed with parenthesis, with the first number being longitude and the second being latitude, such as (**−90, 38**). This is contrary to the convention of latitude followed by longitude. The rationale behind this is that longitude more closely represents points along an x axis, latitude more closely represents points on the y axis, and in mathematics, graphical points are usually noted by their x coordinate followed by their y coordinate.

The **earthdistance** module also allows you to calculate the distance between points in miles:

```
SELECT
 point(-90, 38) <@> point(-91, 37) AS distance_in_miles;
```

Here is the output of the preceding query:

```
distance_in_miles
--------------------
  88.1949338379752
(1 row)
```

In this example, you defined two points, (**38° N**, **90° W**) and (**37° N**, **91° W**), and were able to calculate the distance between these points using the **<@>** operator. This operator calculates the distance in miles (in this case, these two points are **88.2** miles apart).

In the next exercise, you will see how you can use these distance calculations in a practical business context.

EXERCISE 7.02: GEOSPATIAL ANALYSIS

In this exercise, you will identify the closest dealership for each customer. ZoomZoom marketers are trying to increase customer engagement by helping customers find their nearest dealership. The product team is also interested to know what the typical distance is between each customer and their closest dealership.

Follow these steps to implement the exercise:

1. Create a table with the longitude and latitude points for every customer:

```
CREATE TEMP TABLE customer_points AS (
  SELECT
    customer_id,
point(longitude, latitude) AS lng_lat_point
  FROM
customers
  WHERE
longitude IS NOT NULL
  AND
    latitude IS NOT NULL
);
```

2. Create a similar table for every dealership:

```
CREATE TEMP TABLE dealership_points AS (
  SELECT
    dealership_id,
    point(longitude, latitude) AS lng_lat_point
```

```
FROM
    dealerships
);
```

3. Cross-join these tables to calculate the distance from each customer to each dealership (in miles):

```
CREATE TEMP TABLE customer_dealership_distance AS (
  SELECT
    customer_id,
    dealership_id,
    c.lng_lat_point <@> d.lng_lat_point AS distance
  FROM
    customer_points c
  CROSS JOIN
    dealership_points d
);
```

4. Finally, for each customer ID, you select the dealership with the shortest distance. So far, you have got the location for customers and dealerships and obtained distances from each customer to each dealership. The next task is to find the customer-dealership combination that has the shortest distance for the customer using a **DISTINCT ON** clause. As discussed in *Chapter 6*, *Importing and Exporting Data*, the **DISTINCT ON** clause guarantees only the first record for each unique value of the column in parentheses. In this case, you will get one record for every **customer_id** value, and because this is sorted by distance to dealerships, you will get the dealership that has the shortest distance:

```
CREATE TEMP TABLE closest_dealerships AS (
  SELECT DISTINCT ON (customer_id)
    customer_id,
    dealership_id,
    distance
  FROM customer_dealership_distance
  ORDER BY customer_id, distance
);
```

5. Now that you have the data to fulfill the marketing team's request, you can calculate the typical distance from each customer to their closest dealership. You have learned that there are two common ways to represent the typical value of a dataset, mean and median. You will get both using the following query:

```
SELECT
  AVG(distance) AS avg_dist,
  PERCENTILE_DISC(0.5)
    WITHIN GROUP (ORDER BY distance) AS median_dist
FROM
  closest_dealerships;
```

Here is the output of the preceding query:

avg_dist double precision 🔒	median_dist double precision 🔒
146.77826608034164	91.23958293233487

Figure 7.6: The average and median distances between customers and their closest dealership

The result is that the average distance is about **147** miles away, but the median distance is about **91** miles.

There is a clear difference between the mean and median. As you learned in *Chapter 1*, *Understanding and Describing Data*, both are important indicators of central tendency, which represents the most typical value of the dataset. But why are these two typical values for the same dataset so different? What does this tell you about the data? In *Chapter 1*, *Understanding and Describing Data*, you learned that the mean is more sensitive to outliers. There are apparently some customers whose distance to the closest dealership is much greater than most customers. As such, the mean is significantly larger than the median. Generally, it is a good idea to calculate both the mean and median of a variable. If there is a significant difference in the values of the mean and the median, then the dataset may have outliers. You need to identify these outliers for further analysis.

As you identify the issue with this dataset, a question is whether these outliers are caused by data quality issues or not. As you identify which customers are outliers, you review their residential data source to confirm that their registered address is truly their most up-to-date residential address, not the address they lived at 10 years ago. Once identified, you will use the techniques you learned in previous chapters to update the information and rerun the analysis, thus forming a loop of data cleansing and improvement. This is a very common and useful workflow in the data analytics field. It will also help improve the quality of operational data and reduce unnecessary waste and mistakes by the operation team.

But what if the data is correct? How will this information be useful to the business? Always remember that the purpose of data analytics is to provide insight into the business. Now that you know some customers live further from dealerships than most customers, what decisions can you make based on this knowledge? Do you consider the existence of these customers to indicate the need for more dealerships in their area? These observations and analyses are exactly what the management team expects the data analysts to do and should be discussed with the management team.

> **NOTE**
>
> To access the source code for this specific section, please refer to http://packt.link/LpoE0.

In this section, you have learned that the calculation of geospatial data requires two particular packages, together with a specific data type, **POINT**. In this exercise, you identified the closest dealership for each customer by creating the **POINT** value for each customer and each dealership, calculating the distance between each customer and every possible dealership using the distance calculation function between points, identifying the closest dealership for each customer using the **DISTINCT ON** clause, and finding the average and median distances to a dealership for your customers. You were also introduced to some further discussion on what the result data may bring you, both from a data cleansing perspective and a data analysis perspective. The result of this analysis could provide management with a fresh idea to expand the business.

USING ARRAY DATA TYPES IN POSTGRESQL

While the PostgreSQL data types that you have explored so far allow you to store many different types of data, occasionally you will want to store a series of values in a table. For example, you might want to store a list of the products that a customer has purchased or the employee ID numbers associated with a specific dealership. For this scenario, PostgreSQL offers the **ARRAY** data type, which allows you to store a list of values.

STARTING WITH ARRAYS

PostgreSQL arrays allow you to store multiple values in a field in a table. For example, consider the following first record in the **customers** table:

```
customer_id        | 1
title              | NULL
first_name         | Arlena
last_name          | Riveles
suffix             | NULL
email              | ariveles0@stumbleupon.com
gender             | F
ip_address         | 98.36.172.246
phone              | NULL
street_address     | NULL
city               | NULL
state              | NULL
postal_code        | NULL
latitude           | NULL
longitude          | NULL
date_added         | 2019-12-19 00:00:00
```

Each field contains exactly one value (the **NULL** value is still a value); however, there are some attributes that might contain multiple values with an unspecified length. For instance, say you wanted to have a **purchased_products** field. This could contain zero or more values within the field. Imagine the customer purchased the **Lemon** and **Bat Limited Edition** scooters. You could represent that as follows:

```
purchased_products | {Lemon,"Bat Limited Edition"}
```

You can define an array in a variety of ways. One of the ways to get started is simply by creating an array using the following command:

```
SELECT
  ARRAY['Lemon', 'Bat Limited Edition'] AS example_purchased_products;
```

The following is the output of the code:

```
example_purchased_products
--------------------------------

 {Lemon,"Bat Limited Edition"}
```

PostgreSQL knows that the **Lemon** and **Bat Limited Edition** values are of the **TEXT** data type, so it creates a **TEXT** array to store these values.

While you can create an array for any data type, the array is limited to values for that data type only. So, you could not have an integer value followed by a text value or vice versa (this would produce an error).

You can also create arrays using the **ARRAY_AGG** aggregate function. This aggregate function will create an array of all the values in the group. This is useful when you want to have a consolidated list of sub-attributes for each value in a parent attribute. For example, the following query aggregates all the vehicles for each product type:

```
SELECT
  product_type, ARRAY_AGG(DISTINCT model) AS models
FROM
  products
GROUP BY
  1;
```

The following is the output of the preceding query, in which all the models of **automobile** form an array that corresponds to the automobile product type, and all the models of **scooter** form an array that corresponds to the scooter product type:

automobile	{"Model Chi","Model Epsilon","Model Gamma","Model Sigma"}
scooter	{Bat,"Bat Limited Edition",Blade,Lemon,"Lemon Limited Edition","Lemon Zester"}

Figure 7.7: Output of the ARRAY_AGG function

You can also specify how to order the elements by including an **ORDER BY** statement in the **ARRAY_AGG** function, as in the following example:

```
SELECT
  product_type,
  ARRAY_AGG(model ORDER BY year) AS models
FROM
  products
GROUP BY
  1;
```

This is the output:

| automobile | {"Model Chi","Model Sigma","Model Epsilon","Model Gamma","Model Chi"} |
| scooter | {Lemon,"Lemon Limited Edition",Lemon,Blade,Bat,"Bat Limited Edition","Lemon Zester"} |

Figure 7.8: Output of the ARRAY_AGG function with ORDER BY

But there might be situations where you would want to reverse this operation. This can be done by using the **UNNEST** function, which creates one row for every value in the array:

```
SELECT UNNEST(ARRAY[123, 456, 789]) AS example_ids;
```

Here is the output of the preceding query:

```
example_ids
-------------
123
456
789
(3 rows)
```

You can also create an array by splitting a string value using the **STRING_TO_ARRAY** function. A common scenario is that when you use external transaction systems, many systems these days will generate text outputs containing all the information in one string. You will need to break the string into multiple parts and parse each part accordingly. Here is an example:

```
SELECT STRING_TO_ARRAY('hello there how are you?', ' ');
```

In this example, the sentence is split using the second string (' '), and you end up with the following result:

```
string_to_array
-------------------------
{hello,there,how,are,you?}
(1 row)
```

Similarly, you can run the reverse operation and concatenate an array of strings into a single string:

```
SELECT
  ARRAY_TO_STRING(
    ARRAY['Lemon', 'Bat Limited Edition'], ', '
  ) AS example_purchased_products;
```

In this example, you can join the individual string with the second string using ' , ':

```
example_purchased_products
-------------------------
Lemon, Bat Limited Edition
```

There are other functions that allow you to interact with arrays. Here are a few examples of the additional array functionalities that PostgreSQL provides:

Desired Operation	Postgres Function Example	Example Output
Concatenate two arrays	ARRAY_CAT(ARRAY[1, 2],ARRAY[3,4]) or ARRAY[1, 2] | | ARRAY[3, 4]	{1, 2, 3, 4}
Append a value to an array	ARRAY_APPEND(ARRAY[1, 2], 3) or ARRAY[1, 2] | | 3	{1, 2, 3}
Check whether a value is contained in an array	3 = ANY(ARRAY[1, 21)	f
Check whether two arrays overlap	ARRAY[1, 2, 3] && ARRAY[3, 4]	t
Check whether an array contains another array	ARRAY[1, 2, 3] @> ARRAY[2, 1]	t

Figure 7.9: Examples of additional array functionality

In *Exercise 7.03, Analyzing Sequences Using Arrays*, you will apply these operators and array functionality to capture sequences of marketing touchpoints.

EXERCISE 7.03: ANALYZING SEQUENCES USING ARRAYS

In this exercise, you will use arrays to analyze sequences. ZoomZoom sends emails to customers in series. For example, before the December holiday season, they will send out an email providing a product catalog of all the things they sell. During the season, they will send out updates on what product is selling well and what discounts are provided. After the season, they will send out thank you emails and offer further products and discounts. The marketing team wants you to identify the three most common email sequences. You will help them to better understand how different these sequences are by looking at whether these sequences are supersets of one another:

1. First, create a table that represents the email sequence for every customer:

```
CREATE TEMP TABLE customer_email_sequences AS (
  SELECT
    customer_id,
    ARRAY_AGG(
      email_subject ORDER BY sent_date
    ) AS email_sequence
  FROM
emails
  GROUP BY
    1
);
```

2. Next, identify the three most common email sequences. Given that you already have the email sequences, you can do this by using **ORDER BY** with **LIMIT 3**. As the **ORDER BY** clause is based on the occurrence of email sequences, the **SELECT** statement will yield the sequences with the most frequent ones first. Then with the **LIMIT 3** clause, the statement will return only the top 3 sequences:

```
CREATE TEMP TABLE top_email_sequences AS (
  SELECT
    email_sequence,
    COUNT(1) AS occurrences
  FROM
    customer_email_sequences
  GROUP BY
    1
  ORDER BY
```

```
      2 DESC
   LIMIT
      3
);

SELECT
   email_sequence
FROM
   top_email_sequences;
```

The code will generate three rows. They are too long to display inside one figure so only the first one is shown below:

{"The 2013 Lemon Scooter is Here","Shocking Holiday Savings On Electric Scooters","A Brand New Scooter...and Car","We cut you a deal: 20%% off a Blade","Zoom Zoom Black Friday Sale","An Electric Car for a New Age","Tis' the Season for Savings","Like a Bat out of Heaven","25% off all EVs. It's a Christmas Miracle!","We Really Outdid Ourselves this Year","Black Friday. Green Cars.","Save the Planet with some Holiday Savings.","A New Year, And Some New EVs"}

Figure 7.10: The first result from email sequences

3. Lastly, you would want to check which of these arrays is a superset of the other arrays. It is possible that some customers joined later than others, so they only received a part of the email sequence. You need to identify these sub-sequences as a part of the complete email sequence. The only issue is that the email sequence fields are very long and are not intuitive to read through with human eyes. To help with this, it is helpful to give your rows a numeric ID for identification:

```
ALTER TABLE
   top_email_sequences
ADD COLUMN
   id SERIAL PRIMARY KEY;
```

4. Next, you can cross-join the table to itself, and use the @> operator to check whether an array containing an email sequence contains another email sequence:

```
SELECT
   super_email_seq.id AS superset_id,
   sub_email_seq.id AS subset_id
FROM
   top_email_sequences AS super_email_seq
```

```
CROSS JOIN
   top_email_sequences AS sub_email_seq
WHERE
   super_email_seq.email_sequence @> sub_email_seq.email_sequence
AND
   super_email_seq.id != sub_email_seq.id;
```

The following is the output of the code:

1	2
1	3
3	2

Figure 7.11: These results indicate the top email sequences that are supersets of each other

From this, you can gather that the top email sequence contains the second and third most common email sequences, while the third most common email sequence is a superset of the second most common sequence. This type of analysis is generally helpful when looking at what customer touchpoints might lead someone to make a purchase or not. For example, some customers joining late may not have received the first email, the holiday season product catalog. But if a similar percentage of these customers and the customers who have received the first email made a purchase after receiving the holiday season discount email, you may reasonably suspect that the holiday season discount email is the main reason for purchase, not the product catalog. This is also known as **attribution modeling**.

> **NOTE**
>
> To access the source code for this specific section, please refer to http://packt.link/LpoE0.

While arrays are great for lists of values and sequences, the JSON data type can enable you to manage data in key-value pairs, which you will explore in detail in the next section.

USING JSON DATA TYPES IN POSTGRESQL

While arrays can be useful for storing a list of values in a single field, sometimes your data structures can be complex. You might want to store multiple values of different types in a single field, and you might want data to be keyed with labels rather than stored sequentially. These are common issues with log-level data, as well as alternative data. For example, a healthcare patient database may contain a field called prescription, which contains all the prescriptions of a patient. Some patients may not have any prescriptions, thus this field may be empty. Other patients may have multiple prescriptions, and each patient's prescription may be different from the others. One patient may have a hypertension drug of 10mg per day. Another may have an insomnia drug of two pills per night. Yet another patient may have both. It is very hard to store these in a predefined format, so they are usually stored as key-value pairs using the JSON format.

JavaScript Object Notation (JSON) is an open standard text format for storing data of varying complexity. It can be used to represent just about anything, such as the healthcare patient information you saw previously. This is different from the **ARRAY** data type, which can store multiple values. The values must be of the same type. A database table has column names, whereas JSON data has keys. You can use JSON to represent a record from your **customers** table easily by storing column names as keys and row values as values. The **row_to_json** function transforms rows to JSON:

```
SELECT row_to_json(c) FROM customers c limit 1;
```

Here is the output of the preceding query:

```
{"customer_id":716,"title":null,"first_name":"Jarred"
 ,"last_name":"Bester","suffix":null,"email"
 :"jbesterjv@nih.gov","gender":"M","ip_address":"216.51
 .110.28","phone":null,"street_address":null,"city":null
 ,"state":null,"postal_code":null,"latitude":null
 ,"longitude":null,"date_added":"2018-09-19T00:00:00"}
```

Figure 7.12: A row converted to JSON

This is a little hard to read, but you can add the **pretty_bool** flag to generate a readable version. In the following query, the second parameter of the **row_to_json** function is the **pretty_bool** flag and it is set to **TRUE**:

```
SELECT row_to_json(c, TRUE) FROM customers c limit 1;
```

Here is the output of the preceding query:

```
{"customer_id":716,
 "title":null,
 "first_name":"Jarred",
 "last_name":"Bester",
 "suffix":null,
 "email":"jbesterjv@nih.gov",
 "gender":"M",
 "ip_address":"216.51.110.28",
 "phone":null,
 "street_address":null,
 "city":null,
 "state":null,
 "postal_code":null,
 "latitude":null,
 "longitude":null,
 "date_added":"2018-09-19T00:00:00"}
```

Figure 7.13: JSON output from row_to_json

As you can see, once you reformat the JSON output from the query, **row_to_json** presents a simple, readable, text representation of your row. The JSON structure contains keys and values. In this example, the keys are simply the column names, and the values come from the row values. JSON values can either be numeric values (integers or floats), Boolean values (**True** or **False**), text values (wrapped with double quotation marks), or simply **NULL**.

JSON can also include nested data structures. For example, consider a hypothetical scenario in which you want to include purchased products in the table as well. Say that there are two purchased products, **Lemon** and **Bat Limited Edition**. You could write your JSON document this way:

```
{
  "customer_id":1,
  "example_purchased_products":["Lemon", "Bat Limited Edition"]
}
```

Or you could take this example one step further, adding the complete sales records of these two products to this customer's record:

```
{
    "customer_id": 7,
    "sales": [
        {
            "product_id": 7,
            "sales_amount": 599.99,
            "sales_transaction_date": "2019-04-25T04:00:30"
        },
        {
            "product_id": 1,
            "sales_amount": 399.99,
            "sales_transaction_date": "2011-08-08T08:55:56"
        },
        {
            "product_id": 6,
            "sales_amount": 65500,
            "sales_transaction_date": "2016-09-04T12:43:12"
        }
    ],
}
```

In this example, you have a JSON object with two keys: **customer_id** and **sales**. As you can see, the **sales** key points to a JSON array of values, but each value is another JSON object representing one sale. JSON objects that exist within a JSON object are referred to as **nested JSON**. In this case, you have represented all the sales transactions for a customer using a nested array that contains nested JSON objects for each sale.

While JSON is a universal format for storing data, it is inefficient because everything is stored as one long text string. To retrieve a value associated with a key, you would need to first parse the text, and this has a relatively high computational cost associated with it. If you just have a few JSON objects, this performance overhead might not be a big deal. However, it might become a burden if you are trying to perform a JSON operation on a large dataset, such as selecting the JSON object with **"customer_id": 7** from millions of other JSON objects in your database.

In the next section, you will learn about JSONB, a binary JSON format that is optimized for PostgreSQL. This data type allows you to avoid a lot of the parsing overhead associated with a standard JSON text string.

JSONB: PRE-PARSED JSON

As you saw previously, JSON is stored and transferred as a text string. For the computer to understand what key it contains and what value corresponds to each key, the computer must break up the string into key-value pairs. This will increase the time and resources required to handle JSON data. PostgreSQL provides a data type called JSONB, which is JSON but stored in pre-parsed format. Upon receiving a JSON string for a JSONB column, PostgreSQL will decompose the string into binary format. This is advantageous as there is a significant performance improvement when querying the keys or values in a JSONB field. This is because the keys and values do not need to be parsed; they have already been extracted and stored in an accessible binary format.

> **NOTE**
>
> JSONB differs from JSON in a few other ways as well. First, in JSONB, you cannot have more than one key with the same name. Second, the key order is not preserved. Third, semantically insignificant details, such as whitespace, are not preserved.

ACCESSING DATA FROM A JSON OR JSONB FIELD

JSON keys can be used to access the associated value using the -> operator. Here is an example:

```
SELECT
  '{
    "a": 1,
     "b": 2,
     "c": 3
  }'::JSON -> 'b' AS data;
```

In this example, you have a three-key JSON value, and you are trying to access the value for the **b** key. The output is a single output: **2**. This is because the **-> 'b'** operation gets the value for the **b** key from the preceding JSON format, **{"a": 1, "b": 2, "c": 3}**.

PostgreSQL also allows more complex operations to access the nested JSON format by using the **#>** operator. Look at the following example:

```
SELECT
  '{
    "a": 1,
    "b": [
        {"d": 4},
        {"d": 6},
        {"d": 4}
    ],
    "c": 3
  }'::JSON #> ARRAY['b', '1', 'd'] AS data;
```

On the right side of the **#>** operator, a text array defines the path to access the desired value. Its operation can be broken down into three steps:

1. Select the **'b'** value, which is a list of nested JSON objects.

2. Select the element in the array denoted by **'1'**, which is a nested JSON object **{"d": 6}**. Note that with the suffix **'1'**, the second element is returned because array indexes start at 0.

3. Select the value associated with the **'d'** key, and the output is **6**.

These functions work with JSON or JSONB fields (keep in mind that they will run much faster on JSONB fields). JSONB, however, also enables additional functionality. For example, you want to filter rows based on a key-value pair, such as filtering on the **customer_id** field inside the sales transaction record of the JSON format. You could use the **@>** operator, which checks whether the JSONB object on the left contains the key value on the right. Here is an example:

```
SELECT
  *
FROM
  customer_sales
WHERE
  customer_json @> '{"customer_id":20}'::JSONB;
```

The preceding query outputs the corresponding JSONB record:

```
{"email": "ihughillj@nationalgeographic.com", "phone": null, "sales":
[], "last_name": "Hughill", "date_added": "2012-08-08T00:00:00", "first_
name":"Itch", "customer_id": 20}
```

With JSONB, you can also make your output more readable using the **jsonb_ pretty** function:

```
SELECT JSONB_PRETTY(customer_json) FROM customer_sales WHERE customer_
json @> '{"customer_id":20}'::JSONB;
```

Here is the output of the preceding query:

```
{
    "email": "ihughillj@nationalgeographic.com",
    "phone": null,
    "sales": [
    ],
    "last_name": "Hughill",
    "date_added": "2012-08-08T00:00:00",
    "first_name": "Itch",
    "customer_id": 20
}
```

Figure 7.14: Output from the JSONB_PRETTY function

One issue with JSON format is that it is not accepted by all the data processing software on the market. To make use of this software, you will need to break JSON into a relational dataset, which means the result must be a two-dimensional table with two columns. One column contains the key and the other contains the value. You can also select just the keys from the JSONB field, and unnest them into multiple rows using the **JSONB_OBJECT_KEYS** function. Using this function, you can also extract the value associated with each key from the original JSONB field using the **->** operator. Here is an example:

```
SELECT
   JSONB_OBJECT_KEYS(customer_json) AS keys,
   customer_json -> JSONB_OBJECT_KEYS(customer_json) AS values
FROM
   customer_sales
WHERE
   customer_json @> '{"customer_id":20}'::JSONB
;
```

The following is the output of the preceding query:

email	"ihughillj@nationalgeographic.com"
phone	null
sales	[]
last_name	"Hughill"
date_added	"2012-08-08T00:00:00"
first_name	"Itch"
customer_id	20

Figure 7.15: Key-value pairs exploded into multiple rows using
the JSONB_OBJECT_KEYS function

LEVERAGING THE JSON PATH LANGUAGE FOR JSONB FIELDS

In addition to the previous functions (such as **JSONB_OBJECT_KEYS**) and operators
(such as **->**), PostgreSQL also offers a special JSON path language that can be
leveraged to query data within a JSONB field. The first of these functions can check
whether a path exists in your JSON object:

```
SELECT
  jsonb_path_exists(customer_json, '$.sales[0]')
FROM
  customer_sales
LIMIT
  3;
```

The following is the output of the document:

```
jsnob_path_exists
-----------------

t
t
t
(3 rows)
```

The **jsonb_path_exists** function has two required parameters: the JSONB value and the JSON path. The JSON path expression uses the JSON path language. Within this JSON path language, **$** represents the root of the JSON value, and the **.key** notation is used to access the value for a given key. In this case, you can access the sales element directly under root using **$.sales**. The **[0]** value represents that you want the first value contained in the **sales** array. Alternatively, you could have specified **[*]** to represent all elements in the **sales** array. This query simply goes through the JSON value in each row, checks whether the JSON value contains a sales field under its root or not, and returns a Boolean value of **true** or **false** based on the result.

You can also add additional filters to this query. For example, you might want to check whether there are any sales with a **sale_amount** value of over $400. You can do this by adding a **filter** expression, which makes SQL return **TRUE** only for the rows containing the path, as well as meeting the filter criteria:

```
SELECT
    jsonb_path_exists(
        customer_json,
        '$.sales[*].sales_amount ? (@ > 400)'
    )
FROM
    customer_sales
LIMIT
    3;
```

The following is the output of the document:

```
jsnob_path_exists
------------------
t
f
f
(3 rows)
```

In this altered query, you added another element to the path, **.sales_amount**, which gets the sale amount for each sale in the **sales** array. You also added a filter expression using the **?** operator. In this case, the **? (@ > 400)** filter expression indicates that you only get **true** for values greater than 400.

In addition to checking whether a JSON path exists (with or without additional filter criteria), you can also query the result:

```
SELECT
  jsonb_path_query(customer_json, '$.sales[0].sales_amount')
FROM
  customer_sales
LIMIT
  3;
```

The following is the output of the document:

```
jsnob_path_query
-----------------
479.992
314.991
319.992
(3 rows)
```

In this case, the **jsonb_path_query** function grabs the first sale using the positional index, **[0]**, and grabs the value associated with the **sales_amount** key. Similar to **UNNEST**, the **jsonb_path_query** function will expand a result with more than one match to multiple rows:

```
SELECT
  jsonb_path_query('{"test":[1, 2, 3]}', '$.test[*]')
;
```

The following is the output of the code:

```
jsnob_path_query
-----------------
1
2
3
(3 rows)
```

> **NOTE**
>
> If a path does not exist that meets the filter criteria (if any), **jsonb_path_query** will remove that entire row from the output. This is a bit counterintuitive because, normally, row filtering can only happen due to expressions evaluated in the **WHERE** clause, so this functionality can produce unexpected results.

But what if you want to grab the array of sales amounts in cases where there are multiple sales or no sales? In the following examples, you might want to instead use **jsonb_path_query_array**. In the following example, you return the entire array of sales amounts that are greater than $400:

```
SELECT
  jsonb_path_query_array(
    customer_json,
    '$.sales[*].sales_amount ? (@ > 400)'
  )
FROM
  customer_sales
LIMIT
  3;
```

The following is the output of the code:

```
jsnob_path_query_array
-----------------
[479.992]
[]
[]
(3 rows)
```

In this case, the first record contains the **$.sales[*].sales_amount** path, and has one sale over the threshold, so the **jsonb_path_query_array** function returns the sales value array. The second and third rows had sales in the **$.sales[*].sales_amount** path but none of the values are over the threshold. So, the **jsonb_path_query_array** function returns the **NULL** array for both rows.

CREATING AND MODIFYING DATA IN A JSONB FIELD

You can also add and remove elements from JSONB. For example, to add a new key-value pair, **"c": 2**, you can do the following:

```
select jsonb_insert('{"a":1,"b":"foo"}', ARRAY['c'], '2');
```

Here is the output of the preceding query:

```
{"a": 1, "b": "foo", "c": 2}
```

If you wanted to insert values into a nested JSON object, you could do that too:

```
select jsonb_insert('{"a":1,"b":"foo", "c":[1, 2, 3, 4]}', ARRAY['c',
'1'], '10');
```

This would return the following output:

```
{"a": 1, "b": "foo", "c": [1, 10, 2, 3, 4]}
```

In this example, **ARRAY[c, 1]** represents the path where the new value should be inserted. In this case, it first grabs the **c** key and the corresponding array value, then inserts the value (**10**) at position **1**.

To remove a key, you can simply subtract the key that you want to remove. Here is an example:

```
SELECT '{"a": 1, "b": 2}'::JSONB - 'b';
```

In this case, you have a JSON object with two keys: **a** and **b**. When you subtract **b**, you are left with just the **a** key and its associated value:

```
{"a": 1}
```

So far in this section, you have learned the definition of JSON, how to use JSON data in PostgreSQL, the benefits of the JSONB data type, and how to explore and process JSONB data using specific functions. In addition to the methodologies described here, you might want to search through multiple layers of nested objects. You will practice these skills in the following exercise.

EXERCISE 7.04: SEARCHING THROUGH JSONB

In this exercise, you will identify the values using data stored as JSONB. Many source systems today will send the transaction information to downstream systems such as data analytics software in the format of a JSON string. You will need to properly identify values from JSON strings before many of the downstream systems can utilize the content. Suppose you want to identify all customers who purchased a Blade scooter; you can do this using data stored as JSONB. Complete the exercise by implementing the following steps:

1. In this step, you will explode each sale into its own row using the **JSONB_ ARRAY_ELEMENTS** function:

```
CREATE TEMP TABLE customer_sales_single_sale_json AS (
  SELECT
    customer_json,
    JSONB_ARRAY_ELEMENTS(customer_json -> 'sales') AS sale_json
```

```
    FROM
      customer_sales
    LIMIT
      10
);
```

2. Filter this output and grab the records where **product_name** is **'Blade'**:

```
SELECT DISTINCT
   customer_json
FROM
   customer_sales_single_sale_json
WHERE
   sale_json ->> 'product_name' = 'Blade';
```

The **->>** operator is similar to the **->** operator, except it returns text output rather than JSONB output. This outputs the following result:

```
{"email": "nespinaye@51.la","phone": "818-658-6748","sales"
: [{"product_id": 5,"product_name": "Blade","sales_amount":
559.992,"sales_transaction_date": "2014-07-19T06:33:44"}],
"last_name": "Espinay","date_added": "2014-07-05T00:00:00",
"first_name": "Nichols","customer_id": 15}
```

Figure 7.16: Records where product_name is Blade

3. Use the **JSONB_PRETTY()** function to format the output and make the result easier to read:

```
SELECT DISTINCT
   JSONB_PRETTY(customer_json)
FROM
   customer_sales_single_sale_json
WHERE
   sale_json ->> 'product_name' = 'Blade';
```

Here is the output of the preceding query:

```
{
    "email": "nespinaye@51.la",
    "phone": "818-658-6748",
    "sales": [
        {
            "product_id": 5,
            "product_name": "Blade",
            "sales_amount": 559.992,
            "sales_transaction_date": "2014-07-19T06:33:44"
        }
    ],
    "last_name": "Espinay",
    "date_added": "2014-07-05T00:00:00",
    "first_name": "Nichols",
    "customer_id": 15
}
```

Figure 7.17: Format the output using JSONB_PRETTY()

You can now easily read the formatted result after using the **JSONB_PRETTY ()** function.

4. Perform this same action with the JSON path expressions:

```
CREATE TEMP TABLE blade_customer_sales AS (
  SELECT
    jsonb_path_query(
      customer_json,
      '$ ? (@.sales[*].product_name == "Blade")'
    ) AS customer_json
  FROM
    customer_sales
);


SELECT
  JSONB_PRETTY(customer_json)
FROM
  blade_customer_sales;
```

5. Finally, count the number of customers who purchased a Blade:

```
SELECT
    COUNT(1)
FROM
    blade_customer_sales;
```

The following is the output of the code:

```
Count
------
986
(1 row)
```

In this exercise, you identified the values using data stored as JSONB. You used **NB_PRETTY()** and **JSONB_ARRAY_ELEMENTS()** to complete this exercise.

> **NOTE**
>
> To access the source code for this specific section, please refer to http://packt.link/LpoE0.

As you learned in *Chapter 1, Understanding and Describing Data*, data can be categorized as structured, semi-structured, and unstructured. Relational datasets are the most common type of structured data, and JSON is one of the most common types of semi-structured data, which allows you to store complex information using text. You will also often run into data that is stored in an unstructured format, such as free speech text. Lots of effort has been put into unstructured text analysis. While it can be difficult to decode these text fields if there is no predefined structure, you can often produce meaningful insights from these fields. In the following section, you will look at various techniques for interacting with text fields, and then examine how you can produce analytics-based insights from pure text.

TEXT ANALYTICS USING POSTGRESQL

In addition to performing analytics using complex data structures within PostgreSQL, you can also make use of the non-numeric data available. Often, the text contains valuable insights. For instance, you can imagine a salesperson keeping notes on prospective clients, such as "Very promising interaction, the customer is looking to make a purchase tomorrow," is valuable data, as does this note: "The customer is uninterested. They no longer have a need for the product." While this text can be valuable for someone to manually read, it can also be valuable in the analysis. Keywords in these statements, such as "promising," "purchase," "tomorrow," "uninterested," and "no," can be extracted using the right techniques to try to identify top prospects in an automated fashion.

Any block of text can have keywords that can be extracted to uncover trends or make predictions—for example, in customer reviews, email communications, or sales notes. In many circumstances, text data might be the most relevant data available, and you need to use it to create meaningful insights.

In this section, you will look at how you can use some PostgreSQL functionality to extract keywords that will help you to identify trends. You will also leverage text search capabilities in PostgreSQL to enable rapid searching.

TOKENIZING TEXT

While large blocks of text (for example, sentences and paragraphs) can provide useful information to convey to a human reader, there are few analytical solutions that can draw insights from unprocessed text. In almost all these cases, it is helpful to parse text into individual words.

Often, the text is broken down into component tokens, where each token is a sequence of characters that are grouped together to form a semantic unit. Usually, each token is simply a word in the sentence, although in certain cases (such as the word "can't"), your parsing engine might parse two tokens: "can" and "not."

> **NOTE**
>
> Even cutting-edge **Natural Language Processing** (**NLP**) techniques usually involve tokenization before the text can be processed. NLP can be useful to run an analysis that requires a deeper understanding of the text.

Words and tokens are useful because they can be matched across documents in your data. This allows you to draw high-level conclusions at the aggregate level. For example, if you have a dataset containing sales notes, and parse out the "interested" token, you can hypothesize that sales notes containing "interested" are associated with customers who are more likely to make a purchase. So, when a new customer comes and makes an initial request, if you see the word "interested" in the note, you may want to pay more attention to this request, which has a higher potential of realizing a sale.

PostgreSQL has functionality that makes tokenization easy. You can start by using the **STRING_TO_ARRAY** function, which splits a string into an array using a delimiter, for example, a space:

```
SELECT STRING_TO_ARRAY('Danny and Matt are friends.', ' ');
```

The following is the output of the preceding query:

```
{Danny,and,Matt,are,friends.}
```

In this example, the sentence **'Danny and Matt are friends.'** is split using the space character.

In this example, the output includes punctuation, which might be better removed. You can remove punctuation by using the **REGEXP_REPLACE** function. This function accepts four arguments: the text you want to modify, the text pattern that you want to replace, the text that should replace it, and any additional flags (most commonly, you will add the **g** flag, specifying that the replacement should happen globally, or as many times as the pattern is encountered). You can remove the period using a pattern that matches the punctuation defined in the \ ! @#$%^&* () - = _+ , . <>/?| [] string and replace it with space or an empty string:

```
SELECT
  REGEXP_REPLACE(
    'Danny and Matt are friends.',
    '[!,.?-]',
    ' ',
    'g'
  );
```

The following is the output of the preceding query:

```
Danny and Matt are friends
```

As you can see, the punctuation has been removed.

PostgreSQL also includes stemming functionality, which is useful for identifying the root stem of the token. **Stem** refers to the base word of a term. For example, the tokens "run," "ran," and "running" contain the same stem, "run," and are not that different in terms of their meaning. The **TS_LEXIZE** function can help you standardize your text by returning the stem of the word, as demonstrated in the following example:

```
SELECT TS_LEXIZE('english_stem', 'running');
```

The preceding code returns the following:

```
{run}
```

You can use these techniques to identify tokens in text. You will learn how to apply them in the next exercise.

EXERCISE 7.05: PERFORMING TEXT ANALYTICS

You probably have visited some e-commerce websites that, after a purchase, ask you to leave some feedback. From a technical perspective, this feedback is free-form text containing different words. If you can systematically extract some information, you can help the business team to improve its process and enhance the user experience.

You have similar data in your ZoomZoom database. In this exercise, you want to quantitatively identify keywords that correspond with higher-than-average ratings or lower-than-average ratings using text analytics. In your ZoomZoom database, you have access to some customer survey feedback, along with ratings for how likely the customer is to refer their friends to ZoomZoom. These keywords will allow you to identify key strengths and weaknesses for the executive team to consider in the future. You can follow these steps to complete the exercise:

1. Query the data from the customer survey table to gain some familiarity with the dataset. This will help you to understand the columns in the table and the data inside those columns:

```
SELECT * FROM customer_survey limit 5;
```

The following is the output of the preceding query:

rating integer	feedback text
9	I highly recommend the lemon scooter. It's so fast
10	I really enjoyed the sale - I was able to get the Bat for a 20% discount
4	Overall, the experience was ok. I don't think that the customer service rep was really understanding the issue.
9	The model epsilon has been a fantastic ride - one of the best cars I have ever driven.
9	I've been riding the scooter around town. It's been good in urban areas.

Figure 7.18: Example customer survey responses in your database

You can see that you have access to two columns, a numeric rating between 1 and 10 and the **feedback** column in text format.

2. Tokenize the text by parsing it out into individual words and their associated ratings. This will provide you with the tokens in this text and their frequency of appearance. They in turn will provide the foundation for contextual analysis. You can do this using the **STRING_TO_ARRAY** and **UNNEST** array transformations:

```
SELECT
  UNNEST(STRING_TO_ARRAY(feedback, ' ')) AS word,
  rating
FROM
  customer_survey
LIMIT
  10;
```

The following is the output of the preceding query:

I	9
highly	9
recommend	9
the	9
lemon	9
scooter.	9
It's	9
so	9
fast	9
I	10

Figure 7.19: Transformed text output

As you can see from the output in *Figure 7.19*, there are still some issues with these tokens that can prevent you from using them in contextual analysis. For example, you see punctuation such as in **It's** and capitalization such as in **I** and **It's**. There are also words that do not provide any meaning, such as **the** and **so**, which are called stop words. You need to remove the stop words and punctuation, convert the capitalization, and remove forms and tenses to get tokens into their stems. This process is called **standardization**, which will be carried out in *Step 3*.

3. Standardize the text using the **TS_LEXIZE** function and the English stemmer, **'english_stem'**. You will then remove characters that are not letters in the original text using **REGEXP_REPLACE**. Adding these functions together with the original query will output the following:

```
SELECT
    (
    TS_LEXIZE(
        'english_stem',
        UNNEST(
          STRING_TO_ARRAY(
            REGEXP_REPLACE(feedback, '[^a-zA-Z]+', ' ', 'g'),
```

```
        ' '
        )
      )
    )
  )[1] AS token,
  rating
FROM
  customer_survey
LIMIT
  10;
```

The following is the output of the code:

[null]	9
high	9
recommend	9
[null]	9
lemon	9
scooter	9
[null]	9
[null]	9
[null]	9
fast	9

Figure 7.20: Output from TS_LEXIZE and REGEX_REPLACE

NOTE

When you apply these standardization transformations, the outputs are called **tokens** rather than words. Tokens refer to each linguistic unit.

Now, you have the key tokens and their associated ratings. Note that the output of the standardization operation produces **NULL** values for the tokens that have been removed, so you will need to filter out those rating pairs.

4. Find the average rating associated with each token using a **GROUP BY** clause:

```
SELECT
  (
    TS_LEXIZE(
      'english_stem',
      UNNEST(
        STRING_TO_ARRAY(
          REGEXP_REPLACE(feedback, '[^a-zA-Z]+', ' ', 'g'),
          ' '
        )
      )
    )
  )[1] AS token,
  AVG(rating) AS avg_rating
FROM
  customer_survey
GROUP BY
  1
HAVING
  COUNT(1) >= 3
ORDER BY
  2
;
```

In this query, you group by the first expression in the **SELECT** statement where you perform the tokenization. You can now take the average rating associated with each token. This is to make sure that you only take tokens with more than a couple of occurrences so that you can filter out the noise. In this case, due to the small sample size of feedback responses, you only require that the token occurs three or more times (**HAVING COUNT(1) >= 3**). Finally, you order the results by the second expression—the average score. The result is shown here:

pop	2.0000000000000000
batteri	2.3333333333333333
servic	2.3333333333333333
custom	2.3333333333333333
issu	2.5000000000000000
long	2.6666666666666667
ship	2.6666666666666667
email	3.5000000000000000
help	4.0000000000000000
one	4.3333333333333333

Figure 7.21: Average ratings associated with text tokens

At one end of the spectrum, you see quite a few results that are negative: **pop** probably refers to popping tires, and **batteri** probably refers to issues with battery life. On the positive side, you gather that customers respond favorably to **discount**, **sale**, and **dealership**.

5. Verify the assumptions by filtering survey responses that contain these tokens using an **ILIKE** expression. The **ILIKE** expression allows you to match text that contains a pattern. In this example, you are trying to find text that contains the text **pop**, and the operation is case-insensitive. By wrapping this in % symbols, you are specifying that the text can contain any number of characters on the left or right. This is done as follows:

```
SELECT
  *
FROM
  customer_survey
```

```
WHERE
    feedback ILIKE '%pop%';
```

The query returns three relevant survey responses:

1	On my second trip one of the tires popped. I would have really expected it to get repaired under the warranty.
3	I was riding to work and one my wheels popped! It was going to cost $200 to fix it - what a scam!
2	I popped a wheel, and can't seem to fix it.

Figure 7.22: Filtering survey responses using ILIKE

> **NOTE**
>
> To access the source code for this specific section, please refer to
> http://packt.link/LpoE0.

Upon receiving the results of your analysis, you can report the key issues to your product team to review. You can also report the high-level findings that the customers like discounts and the feedback have been positive following the introduction of dealerships.

> **NOTE**
>
> **ILIKE** is similar to another SQL expression: **LIKE**. The **ILIKE** expression is case-insensitive, and the **LIKE** expression is case-sensitive, so typically, it will make sense to use **ILIKE**. In situations where performance is critical, **LIKE** might be slightly faster.

PERFORMING TEXT SEARCH

While you can perform text analytics using aggregations, it might be helpful to instead query your database for relevant posts, similar to how you might query a search engine.

While you can do this using an **ILIKE** expression in your **WHERE** clause, this is not terribly fast or extensible. For example, what if you wanted to search the text for multiple keywords, correct searches with misspellings, or handle scenarios where one of the words might be missing altogether?

For these situations, you can use the text search functionality in PostgreSQL.

This functionality scales up to millions of documents when it is fully optimized.

> **NOTE**
>
> **Documents** represent the individual records in a search database. Each document represents the entity that you want to search for. For example, on a personal website, this might be a blog post that includes the title, author, and article for one entry. For a survey, it might include the survey responses or perhaps the survey response combined with the survey question. A document can span multiple fields or even multiple tables.

You can start with the **to_tsvector** function, which will perform a similar function to the **TS_LEXIZE** function, but instead of producing a token from a word like the **TS_LEXIZE** function, this **to_tsvector** function will tokenize the entire document. The output data type from this operation is a **tsvector** data type, which is specialized and specifically designed for text search operations. Here is an example:

```
SELECT
  feedback,
  to_tsvector('english', feedback) AS tsvectorized_feedback
FROM
  customer_survey
LIMIT
  1;
```

The query produces the following result:

feedback text	🔒	tsvectorized_feedback tsvector	🔒
I highly recommend the lemon scooter. It's so fast		'fast':10 'high':2 'lemon':5 'recommend':3 'scooter':6	

Figure 7.23: The tsvector tokenized representation of the original feedback

In this case, the feedback, **I highly recommend the lemon scooter. It's so fast** was converted into a tokenized vector: **'fast':10 'high':2 'lemon':5 'recommend':3 'scooter':6**. Like the **TS_LEXIZE** function, less meaningful "stop words" were removed, such as **I, the, It's**, and **so**. Other words, such as **highly**, were stemmed from their root (**high**). Word order was not preserved. The **to_tsvector** function can also take in JSON or JSONB syntax and tokenize the values (no keys) as a **tsvector** object.

Now that you have broken down the text using the **tsvector** data type with meaningful tokens and their frequency, you will use a **tsquery** data type to perform a search on **tsvector**. The **tsquery** data type defines a search query in the form of a useful data type that PostgreSQL can use to search. For example, suppose you want to construct a search query with the **lemon scooter** keywords. You can write it as follows:

```
SELECT to_tsquery('english', 'lemon & scooter');
```

Or, if you do not want to specify the Boolean syntax, you can write this:

```
SELECT plainto_tsquery('english', 'lemon scooter');
```

Both queries produce the same result:

```
plainto_tsquery
-----------------
'lemon' & 'scooter'
(1 row)
```

> **NOTE**
>
> **to_tsquery** accepts Boolean syntax, such as **|** for **or** and **&** for **and**. It also accepts **!** for **not**.

You can also use Boolean operators to concatenate **tsquery** objects. For example, the **&&** operator will produce a query that requires the left query and the right query, while the **||** operator will produce a query that matches either the left or the right **tsquery** object:

```
SELECT
  plainto_tsquery('english', 'lemon')
  &&
  plainto_tsquery('english', 'bat')
  ||
  plainto_tsquery('english', 'chi');
```

This produces the following result:

```
'lemon' & 'bat' | 'chi'
```

You can query a **tsvector** object using a **tsquery** object using the @@ operator.

A **tsquery** data type is often used together with the **tsvector** data type for patterned search. For example, you can search all customer feedback for **lemon scooter**:

```
SELECT
  *
FROM
  customer_survey
WHERE
  to_tsvector('english', feedback)
    @@ plainto_tsquery('english', 'lemon scooter');
```

This returns the following three results:

9	I highly recommend the lemon scooter. It's so fast
8	The lemon scooter has been incredible! I love it!
6	The lemon scooter was a little too fast for me. I will be returning this item.

Figure 7.24: Search query output using the PostgreSQL search functionality

So far in this section, you have learned how to handle text strings, how to tokenize and standardize them, and how to search the tokens inside the strings. In the next section, you will learn how to optimize text search on PostgreSQL.

OPTIMIZING TEXT SEARCH ON POSTGRESQL

While the PostgreSQL search syntax in the previous example is quite straightforward, it needs to convert all text documents into a **tsvector** object every time a new search is performed. Additionally, the search engine needs to check every document to see whether any content in the document matches the query terms. This process can be tedious. You can improve this in two steps:

1. Store the **tsvector** objects so that they do not need to be recomputed.

2. Store the tokens and their associated documents in a **Generalized Inverted Index (GIN)**. This is a specific format of PostgreSQL storage that can help you store indexes of complex data such as **tsvector**, similar to how an index in the back of a book has words or phrases and their associated page numbers so that you do not have to check each document to see where it matches.

To do these two things, you will need to precompute and store the **tsvector** objects for each document, then create a GIN based on **tsvector**.

To precompute the **tsvector** objects, use a materialized view. A **materialized view** is defined as a named query, similar to a view. But unlike a regular view, where the results are queried every time, the results for a materialized view are stored as if it is a table.

Because a materialized view stores the results in a stored table, it can get out of sync with the underlying tables that it queries. It might be prudent to refresh it, such as dropping the materialized view and recreating it before usage. You can create a materialized view of your survey results using the following query:

```
DROP MATERIALIZED VIEW IF EXISTS customer_survey_search;


CREATE MATERIALIZED VIEW customer_survey_search AS (
  SELECT
    rating,
    feedback,
    to_tsvector('english', feedback)
      ||
      to_tsvector('english', rating::text) AS searchable
  FROM
    customer_survey
);
```

You can see that your **searchable** column is composed of two columns: the **rating** and **feedback** columns. There are many scenarios where you will want to search on multiple fields, and you can easily concatenate multiple **tsvector** objects together with the **||** operator.

You can test that the view worked by querying a row:

```
SELECT * FROM customer_survey_search LIMIT 1;
```

The query produces the following output:

rating integer	feedback text	searchable tsvector
9	I highly recommend the lemon scooter. It's so fast	'9':11 'fast':10 'high':2 'lemon':5 'recommend':3 'scooter':6

Figure 7.25: A record from your materialized view with tsvector

In addition to dropping and recreating, you can also use the following syntax to refresh the view (for example, after an insert or update):

```
REFRESH MATERIALIZED VIEW customer_survey_search;
```

This will recompute the view concurrently while the old copy of the view remains available and unlocked.

Next, you will add the **GIN** index with the following syntax, which will help improve the performance by storing some key information in an organized manner:

```
CREATE INDEX
   idx_customer_survey_search_searchable
ON
   customer_survey_search
USING GIN(searchable);
```

With these two operations (creating the materialized view and creating the GIN index), you can now easily query your feedback table using search terms:

```
SELECT
   rating,
   feedback
FROM
   customer_survey_search
WHERE
   searchable @@ plainto_tsquery('dealership');
```

The following is the output of the preceding query:

8	I really appreciated having a dealership so close to me - it made the transaction much easier!
9	The sales people at the dealership were so nice and helpful!
10	The millburn dealership is the best! Those folks are great!

Figure 7.26: Output from the materialized view optimized for search

While the query time improvement might be small or non-existent for a small table of 32 rows, these operations greatly improve the speed for large tables (for example, with millions of rows), and enable users to quickly search their database in a matter of seconds.

In the following activity, you will put these ideas into practice by creating a searchable sales database that will allow you to leverage text queries to find the information that you need.

ACTIVITY 7.01: SALES SEARCH AND ANALYSIS

In this activity, you will set up a search materialized view and answer some business questions using what you have learned in the previous sections. The head of sales at ZoomZoom has identified a problem: there is no easy way for the sales team to search for a customer. You volunteered to create a proof-of-concept internal search engine that will make all customers searchable by their contact information and the products that they have purchased in the past.

Perform the following steps to complete the activity:

1. Use the **customer_sales** table and create a searchable materialized view with one record per customer. This view should be keyed off the **customer_id** column and searchable on everything related to that customer: name, email address, phone number, and purchased products. It is acceptable to include other fields as well.

2. A salesperson asks you whether you can use your new search prototype to find a customer by the name of Danny who purchased the Bat scooter. Query your new searchable view using the **Danny Bat** keywords. How many rows did you get?

3. The sales team wants to know how common it is for someone to buy a scooter and automobile combination. To do that, join the **products** table to get all distinct pairs of scooters and automobiles.

4. You can assume that limited-edition releases can be grouped together with their standard model counterpart (for example, **Bat** and **Bat Limited Edition** can be considered the same scooter). Simply filter out **Bat Limited Edition** from the product pairs.

5. Using the results from the cross join, create a query that counts how many customers were found to match each of the product pairs.

Here is the expected output:

```
                   query                     | count
---------------------------------------------+-------
        'lemon' & 'model' & 'sigma'          |  340
        'lemon' & 'model' & 'chi'           |  331
        'bat' & 'model' & 'epsilon'         |  241
        'bat' & 'model' & 'sigma'           |  226
        'bat' & 'model' & 'chi'             |  221
        'lemon' & 'model' & 'epsilon'       |  217
        'bat' & 'model' & 'gamma'           |  153
        'lemon' & 'model' & 'gamma'         |  133
   'lemon' & 'zester' & 'model' & 'chi'     |   28
   'lemon' & 'zester' & 'model' & 'epsilon' |   22
        'blade' & 'model' & 'chi'           |   21
   'lemon' & 'zester' & 'model' & 'sigma'   |   17
        'blade' & 'model' & 'sigma'         |   12
   'lemon' & 'zester' & 'model' & 'gamma'   |   11
        'blade' & 'model' & 'epsilon'       |    4
        'blade' & 'model' & 'gamma'         |    4
(16 rows)
```

Figure 7.27: Customer counts for each scooter and automobile combination

> **NOTE**
>
> To access the source code for the specific section, please refer to http://packt.link/LpoE0.

> **NOTE**
>
> The solution for this activity can be found on page 463.

In this activity, you searched and analyzed the data using the materialized view. Then, you learned about the use of SQL keywords such as **DISTINCT** and **JOIN** to transform the query. Lastly, you learned how to query your database using **tsquery** objects to get the final output.

SUMMARY

In this chapter, you covered special data types, including date and time, geospatial, complex data structures, and text data types. For date and time data types, you explored how to manipulate time series data, extract components, and represent the information in practical ways that would allow you to build analysis. For geospatial data types, you learned how to convert latitude and longitude into **POINT** data types that allow you to calculate distances between locations.

For complex data types, you explored several powerful data types: arrays, JSON, and JSONB. For these data types, you learned how to create these values, as well as how to write complex queries to navigate their structure.

Finally, you learned that text data can be useful in analytics—first in running an analysis on keywords, and also in the context of text search, which can be a valuable analytical tool.

As your datasets grow larger and larger, these complex analyses become slower and slower. In *Chapter 8*, *Performant SQL*, you will take an in-depth look at how you can begin to optimize these queries using an explanation and analysis of the query plan, as well as additional tools, such as indexes, that can speed up your queries.

8

PERFORMANT SQL

OVERVIEW

In this chapter, you will learn how to optimize a database to allow queries to be executed with fewer resources. First, you will look at how a database engine performs basic queries by developing your understanding of sequential scans. After that, you will look at optimizing **SELECT** queries by creating indexes on database tables, which improve performance. You will also learn about tools and techniques for terminating inefficient queries that are consuming your database resources. After all this, you will explore advanced functionalities by creating custom functions for special computations and examine how to apply custom constraints to your database by using triggers.

INTRODUCTION

In *Chapter 7, Analytics Using Complex Data Types*, you learned the necessary skills to effectively analyze data within a SQL database. In this chapter, you will turn your attention to the efficiency of this analysis, investigating how you can increase the performance of SQL queries. Efficiency and performance are key components of data analytics. Without considering these factors, physical constraints, such as time and processing power, can significantly affect the outcome of an analysis.

In this chapter, you will first learn the different ways PostgreSQL performs query planning, in which the PostgreSQL database evaluates the SQL statement and underlying physical implementation and decides how to execute this SQL. You will learn the most basic way of retrieving data, which is scanning by sequence. You will then learn the concept of an index and the two most common indexes in PostgreSQL, the B-tree index and the hash index. From there, you will learn how to kill long-running queries to free up resources and allow other queries to run.

After covering these topics, you will be introduced to functions and triggers. You will learn the definition of functions and the commands to manipulate them. You will also learn the concept of a trigger, a special type of function triggered by an event.

THE IMPORTANCE OF HIGHLY EFFICIENT SQL

To understand why performance is so important, consider the following scenarios.

You are performing **post hoc analysis** (that is, analysis after the fact or event). You have completed a study and collected a large dataset of individual observations of various factors or features. One such example is described within your ZoomZoom database, which analyzes the sales data for each customer.

With the data collection process, you want to analyze the data for patterns and insights as specified by your problem statement. If your dataset is sufficiently large, you could quickly encounter issues if you do not optimize the queries first; the most common issue would simply be the time taken to execute the queries. While this does not sound like a significant issue, unnecessarily long processing times can cause the following problems:

- **Reduction in the depth of the completed analysis**: As each query takes a long time, the practicalities of project schedules may limit the number of queries. So, the depth and complexity of the analysis may be limited.

- **Limiting the selection of data for analysis**: By artificially reducing the dataset using subsampling, you may be able to complete the analysis in a reasonable time but would have to sacrifice the number of observations being used. This may, in turn, lead to bias being accidentally included in the analysis.

- **Increase in project cost**: The need to use many more resources simultaneously to complete the analysis in a reasonable time would increase the project cost.

Similarly, another potential issue with suboptimal queries is an increase in the required system memory and compute power. This can result in either of the following two scenarios:

- Failure of the analysis due to insufficient resources

- Significant increase in the cost of the project to recruit the required resources

These days, analysis or queries are increasingly becoming a part of a larger service or product. For instance, when an analysis is being completed as a component of a bidding website that sets the pricing based on previous transactions, database queries may need to be completed in real-time, or at least near real-time. In such cases, optimization and efficiency are key for the product to be a success.

Another such example is a GPS navigation system that incorporates the state of traffic as reported by other users. For such a system to be effective and provide up-to-date navigation information, the database must be analyzed at a rate that keeps up with the speed of the car and the progress of the journey. Any delays in the analysis that would prevent the navigation from being updated in response to traffic would significantly impact the application's commercial viability.

After looking at this example, you can see that efficiency is not only important in an effective and thorough post hoc analysis but also critical when incorporating data analysis as a component of a separate product or service.

While it is certainly not the job of a data scientist or data analyst to ensure that the production process and the database are working at optimal efficiency, it is critical that the queries of the underlying analysis are as effective as possible. If you do not have an efficient and current database in the first place, further refinements will not help to improve the performance of the analysis. In the next section, you will learn the methods for increasing the performance of scans for information throughout a database.

DATABASE SCANNING METHODS

You have learned that all database operations are carried out by **database management systems** (**DBMSs**) such as PostgreSQL. Typically, the DBMS will run these operations in a server's memory, which stores the data to be processed. The problem with this approach is that memory storage is not large enough for modern databases, which are frequently in a scale of gigabytes, if not terabytes. Data in the majority of modern databases is saved on hard disks and uploaded into memory when it is used in a database operation. Yet again, a DBMS can only upload a small part of the database into memory. Whenever it figures that it needs a certain dataset, it must go to the hard disk to retrieve the unit of storage (which is called a hard disk block) that has the required data in it. The process that the PostgreSQL server uses to search through a database is known as scanning.

SQL-compliant databases, such as PostgreSQL, provide several different methods for scanning, searching, and selecting data. The right scan method to use is dependent on the use case and the state of the database at the time of scanning. How many records are in the database? Which fields are you interested in? How many records do you expect to be returned? How often do you need to execute the query? These are just some of the questions that you may want to ask when selecting the most appropriate scanning method.

Throughout this section, you will understand some of the search methods available, how they are used within SQL to execute scans, and several scenarios where they should or should not be used.

These topics will be organized into these sections:

- Query Planning

- Index Scanning

- Effective Index Use

- Killing Queries

- Functions and Triggers

QUERY PLANNING

Before investigating the different methods of executing queries, it is useful to understand how the PostgreSQL server makes various decisions about the types of queries to be used. SQL-compliant databases possess a powerful tool known as a **Query Planner**, which implements a set of features within the server to analyze a request and decide how to execute the statement. The Query Planner optimizes different variables within the request with the aim of reducing the overall execution time.

> **NOTE**
>
> These variables are described in greater detail in the PostgreSQL documentation (https://www.postgresql.org/docs/current/runtime-config-query.html) and include parameters that correspond to the cost of sequential page fetches, CPU operations, and cache size.

Interpreting the planner is critical if you want to achieve high performance from a database. Doing so allows you to modify the contents and structure of queries to optimize performance. Unfortunately, query planning can require some practice to be comfortable with interpreting the output. Even the PostgreSQL official documentation notes that plan reading is an art that deserves significant attention. In this chapter, you will not see the details of how a Query Planner implements its analysis since there are core technical details involved. However, it is important to understand how to interpret the plan reported by the Query Planner. You will start with a simple plan and then work your way through more complicated queries and query plans. In the following exercise, you will learn about the **EXPLAIN** command, which displays the plan for a query before it is executed. When you use the **EXPLAIN** command in combination with a SQL statement, the SQL interpreter will not execute the statement, but rather return the steps that are going to be executed (a query plan) by the interpreter to return the desired results.

An example of using the **EXPLAIN** command is shown in the following exercise.

> **NOTE**
>
> You have learned how to use the PostgreSQL psql tool and pgAdmin. Query Planner outputs its plan in pure text format. To better display and analyze the output of Query Planner, you will use psql in this chapter because it can display text in a clearer format, but some screenshots that are easier to read in graphic format will be generated using pgAdmin.
>
> For all exercises and activities in this chapter, please note that query analysis metrics will vary depending on system configuration. Thus, you may get outputs that may vary from those presented in the exercises and activities. The key point is that the outputs provided in this chapter demonstrate the working of the principles.
>
> All the exercises and activities in this chapter are also available on GitHub at https://packt.link/PDtJk.

EXERCISE 8.01: INTERPRETING THE QUERY PLANNER

In this exercise, you will interpret a query plan of the **emails** table of the **sqlda** database using the **EXPLAIN** command. Then, you will employ a more involved query, searching for dates between two specific values in the **clicked_date** field.

Follow these steps to complete the exercise:

1. Open the default command-line interface (CMD or Terminal) and connect to the **sqlda** database:

```
C:\> psql -h localhost -p 5432 -d sqlda -U postgres
```

Upon successful connection, you will be presented with the interface to the PostgreSQL database:

```
Type "help" for help
sqlda=#
```

2. Enter the following command to get the query plan of the **emails** table:

```
EXPLAIN SELECT * FROM emails;
```

Information similar to the following will then be presented:

```
Seq Scan on emails   (cost=0.00..9605.58 rows=418158 width=79)
```

This information is returned by the Query Planner; while this is the simplest example possible, there is quite a bit to unpack in the planner information. There is a lot of information returned in a query plan and being able to comprehend the output is vital in tuning the performance of your database queries.

So, look through the output step by step. The first aspect of the plan that is provided is the type of scan executed by the query:

```
Seq Scan on emails   (cost=0.00..9605.58 rows=418158 width=79)
```

Extracting data using this **SELECT** command directly from the database executes a sequential scan, where the database server traverses through each record in the database and compares each record to the criteria in the sequential scan, returning those records that match the criteria, if there is a **WHERE** clause.

A **sequential scan** is the easiest to understand and is guaranteed to work in every scenario. In some circumstances, the sequential scan is not the fastest or most efficient option; however, it will always produce the correct result. This is essentially a brute-force scan and, thus, can always be called upon to execute a search. In certain situations, a sequential scan is the most efficient method and will be automatically selected by the PostgreSQL server. This is particularly the case if any of the following is true:

- The table is quite small.

- The field used in searching contains many duplicates.

- The planner determines that the sequential scan would be equally or more efficient for the given criteria compared to any other scan.

You will cover more of the scan types later in the chapter, but **Seq Scan**, or sequential scan, is a simple yet robust type of query.

Following the **Seq Scan** keyword and the table of its target are a series of measurements. The first measurement reported by the planner, as shown here, is the startup cost:

```
Seq Scan on emails   (cost=0.00..9605.58 rows=418158 width=79)
```

The startup cost is the time expended before the scan starts. This time may be required to first sort the data or complete other preprocessing applications. It is also important to note that the time measured is reported in cost units as opposed to seconds or milliseconds. Often, the cost units are an indication of the number of disk requests or page fetches made, rather than this being a measure in absolute terms. The reported cost is typically more useful as a means of comparing the performance of various queries, rather than as an absolute measure of time.

The next number in the sequence indicates the total cost of executing the query if all available rows are retrieved:

```
Seq Scan on emails   (cost=0.00..9605.58 rows=418158 width=79)
```

There are some circumstances in which not all the available rows may be retrieved, but you will learn about that in the *Index Scanning* section of this chapter.

The next figure in the plan indicates the total number of rows that are available to be returned if the plan is completely executed:

```
Seq Scan on emails   (cost=0.00..9605.58 rows=418158 width=79)
```

The final figure, as suggested by its name, indicates the width of each row in bytes:

```
Seq Scan on emails   (cost=0.00..9605.58 rows=418158 width=79)
```

> **NOTE**
>
> When executing the **EXPLAIN** command, PostgreSQL does not actually implement the query or return the values. It does, however, return a description, along with the processing costs involved in executing each stage of the plan.

3. Query plan the **emails** table and set the limit to **5**. This will give you an insight into how PostgreSQL adjusts its execution plan when the SQL changes. Enter the following statement in the PostgreSQL interpreter:

```
EXPLAIN SELECT * FROM emails LIMIT 5;
```

This repeats the previous statement, but the result is limited to the first five records. This query will produce the following output from the planner:

```
Limit  (cost=0.00..0.11 rows=5 width=79)
  ->  Seq Scan on emails   (cost=0.00..9605.58 rows=418158 width=79)
```

Referring to the preceding output, you can see that there are two individual rows in the plan. This indicates that the plan is composed of two separate steps, with the lower line of the plan being executed first. This lower line is a repeat of what is shown in *step 2*. The upper line of the plan is the component that limits the result to only **5** rows. The **Limit** process is an additional cost of the query; however, it is quite insignificant compared to the lower-level plan, which retrieves approximately **418158** rows at a cost of **9605.58** page requests. The **Limit** stage only returns **5** rows at a cost of **0.11** page requests.

> **NOTE**
>
> The overall estimated cost of a request comprises the time taken to retrieve the information from the disk and the number of rows that need to be scanned. The internal parameters **seq_page_cost** and **cpu_tuple_cost** define the cost of the corresponding operations within the tablespace for the database. While not recommended at this stage, these two variables can be changed to modify the steps prepared by the planner.
>
> For more information, refer to the PostgreSQL documentation: https://www.postgresql.org/docs/current/runtime-config-query.html.

4. Now, employ a more involved query, searching for dates between two specific values in the **clicked_date** column. Enter the following statement into the PostgreSQL interpreter:

```
EXPLAIN
SELECT *
FROM emails
WHERE clicked_date BETWEEN '2011-01-01' and '2011-02-01';
```

This will produce a query plan similar to this:

```
Gather  (cost=1000.00..9037.59 rows=1 width=79)
  Workers Planned: 2
  ->  Parallel Seq Scan on emails   (cost=0.00..8037.49 rows=1
      width=79)
```

```
Filter: ((clicked_date >= '2011-01-01 00:00:00'::timestamp
        without time zone) AND (clicked_date <= '2011-02-01
        00:00:00'::timestamp without time zone))
```

The first aspect of this query plan to note is that it comprises a few different steps. The lower-level query is similar to the previous query in that it executes a sequential scan. However, rather than limiting the output, you are filtering it based on the timestamp strings provided.

Here, the sequential scan is to be completed in parallel, as indicated by the **Parallel Seq Scan**. PostgreSQL also indicates that it will use two workers to execute this scan. Whether PostgreSQL will use a parallel scan or not depends on the setup of the server, as well as the power of the computer hardware. If PostgreSQL server feels that parallel scan is too complex for the hardware or server to handle, it may choose regular sequential scan, like what you saw in the steps above.

In this example, PostgreSQL believes that parallel scan can provide better performance and decides to utilize two workers for it. Each individual sequence scan should return approximately 54 rows, taking a cost of **8037.49** to complete. The upper level of the plan is a **Gather** state, which is executed at the start of the query. You can see here for the first time that the upfront costs are non-zero (**1000**) and a total of **9037.59**, including the gather and search steps.

> **NOTE**
>
> To access the source code for this specific section, please refer to https://packt.link/PDtJk.

In this exercise, you worked with the Query Planner and the output of the **EXPLAIN** command. These relatively simple queries highlighted several features of the SQL Query Planner as well as the detailed information that is provided by it. It will serve you well in your data science endeavors with a good understanding of the Query Planner and the rich information returned. Just remember that this understanding will come with time and practice. Next, you will practice this skill in an activity.

ACTIVITY 8.01: QUERY PLANNING

In this activity, you will query the plan for reading and interpreting the information returned by the planner. For instance, say you are still dealing with the ZoomZoom dataset in the **sqlda** database of customer records and your finance team would like to implement a system to regularly generate a report of customer activity in a specific geographical region. To ensure that your report can be run in a timely manner, you need an estimate of how long the SQL queries will take. You will use the **EXPLAIN** command to find out how long some of the report queries will take:

1.   Open PostgreSQL with **psql** and connect to the **sqlda** database.

2.   Use the **EXPLAIN** command to return the query plan to select all available records within the **customers** table.

3.   Read the output of the plan and determine the total query cost, the setup cost, the number of rows to be returned, and the width of each row.

4.   Repeat the query from *step 2* of this activity, this time limiting the number of returned records to **15**. Review the updated query plan and compare its output against the output of the previous step, paying special attention to how many steps are involved in the query plan and what the cost of the limiting step is.

5.   Update the SQL to select all rows where customers live within a latitude of **30** and **40** degrees. Generate the query plan. Compare the total plan cost as well as the number of rows returned by the query to the numbers from previous steps.

Expected output:

```
Seq Scan on customers   (cost=0.00..1785.00 rows=26369 width=140)
   Filter: ((latitude >= '30'::double precision) AND (latitude <=
'40'::double precision))
```

In this activity, you practiced reading the plans returned by the Query Planner. As discussed at the very beginning of this section, plan reading requires substantial practice to master. This activity began this process, and it is strongly recommended that you frequently use the **EXPLAIN** command to improve your plan reading.

You will continue to practice reading query plans throughout this chapter as you look at different scan types and the methods and their use to improve performance. In the next section, you will learn how to improve the performance of your queries using index scans.

> **NOTE**
>
> The solution for this activity can be found on page 468.

INDEX SCANNING

Index scans improve the performance of your database queries. Index scans differ from sequential scans in that index scans execute a preprocessing step before the search of database records can occur.

The simplest way to think of an index scan is just like the index of a text or reference book. When creating a non-fiction book, a publisher parses through the contents of the book and writes the page numbers corresponding with each alphabetically sorted topic. Just as the publisher goes to the initial effort of creating an index for the reader's reference, you can create a similar index within the PostgreSQL database.

This index within the database creates a prepared and organized set or a subset of references to the data under specified conditions. When a query is executed and an index is present that contains information relevant to the query, the planner may elect to use the data that was preprocessed and prearranged within the index. Without using an index, the database needs to repeatedly scan through all records, checking each record for the information of interest. Even if all the desired information is at the start of the database, without indexing, the search will still scan through all available records. Clearly, this would take a significantly longer time than necessary.

There are several different indexing strategies that PostgreSQL can use to create more efficient searches, including **B-trees**, **hash indexes**, **generalized inverted indexes (GINs)**, and **generalized search trees (GiSTs)**. Each of these different index types has its own strengths and weaknesses and is therefore used in different situations. One of the most frequently used indexes is the B-tree, which is the default indexing strategy used by PostgreSQL and is available in almost all database software. You will first spend some time investigating the B-tree index, looking at what makes it useful, as well as some of its limitations.

THE B-TREE INDEX

The B-tree index is a type of extended binary search tree and is characterized by the fact that it is a self-balancing structure, maintaining its own data structure for efficient searching. A generic B-tree structure can be found in *Figure 8.1*, in which you can see that each node in the tree has no more than two elements (thus providing balance) and that each node has at most three children. These traits are common among B-trees, where each node is limited to **n** components, thus forcing the split into **n+1** child nodes. The branches of the trees terminate at leaf nodes, which, by definition, have no children:

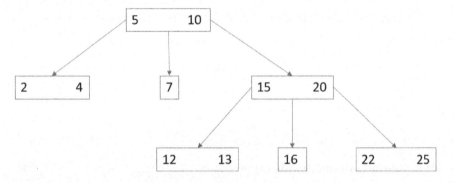

Figure 8.1: Generic B-tree

Using the preceding figure as an example, say you were looking for the number **13** in the B-tree index. You would start at the first node and select whether the number was less than **5** or greater than **10**. This would lead you down the right-hand branch of the tree, where you would again choose between less than **15** and greater than **20**. You would then select less than **15** and arrive at the location of **13** in the index.

You can immediately see that this operation would be much faster than looking through all available values. You can also see that for performance, the tree must be balanced to allow for an easy path for traversal. Additionally, there must be sufficient information to allow splitting because if you had a tree index with only a few possible values to split on and many samples, you would simply divide the data into a few groups.

Considering B-trees in the context of database searching, you would notice that you require a condition to divide the information (or split) with and need sufficient information for a meaningful split. You do not need to worry about the logic of following the tree, as that will be managed by the database itself and can vary depending on the conditions for searching. Even so, it is important for you to understand the strengths and weaknesses of the method to allow you to make appropriate choices when creating the index for optimal performance.

To create an index for a set of data, you use the following syntax:

```
CREATE INDEX <index name> ON <table name>(table column);
```

You can also add additional conditions and constraints to make the index more selective:

```
CREATE INDEX <index name> ON <table name>(table column) WHERE
[condition];
```

You can also specify the type of index:

```
CREATE INDEX <index name> ON <table name> USING TYPE(table column)
```

PostgreSQL supports multiple index types, such as B-tree, hash, and GiST. For example, say you execute the following query to create a B-tree type index on a column:

```
CREATE INDEX ix_customers ON customers USING BTREE(customer_id);
```

This outputs the following message:

```
CREATE INDEX
```

This indicates that the index was created successfully.

In the next exercise, you will start with a simple plan and work your way through more complicated queries and query plans, using index scans.

EXERCISE 8.02: CREATING AN INDEX SCAN

In this exercise, you will create a number of different index scans and investigate the performance characteristics of each of the scans.

Continuing with the scenario from *Activity 8.01*, *Query Planning*, say you had completed your report service but wanted to make the queries faster. You will try to improve this performance using indexing and index scans. You will recall that you are using a table of customer information that includes contact details such as name, email address, phone number, and address information, as well as the latitude and longitude details of their address. Follow these steps to complete this activity:

1. Open PostgreSQL and connect to the **sqlda** database:

```
C:\> psql -h localhost -p 5432 -d sqlda -U postgres
```

Upon successful connection, you will be presented with the interface to the PostgreSQL database:

```
Type "help" for help
sqlda=#
```

2. Starting with the **customers** database, use the **EXPLAIN** command to determine the cost of the query and the number of rows returned in selecting all the entries with a **state** value of **FO**:

```
EXPLAIN SELECT * FROM customers WHERE state='FO';
```

The output of the preceding code will be similar to the following. Please note that the actual numbers may vary but the structure will be similar:

```
Seq Scan on customers   (cost=0.00..1660.00 rows=1 width=140)
   Filter: (state = 'FO'::text)
```

Note that there is only **1** row returned and that the setup cost is **0**, but the total query cost is **1660**.

3. Determine how many unique **state** values there are using the **EXPLAIN** command:

```
EXPLAIN SELECT DISTINCT state FROM customers;
```

The output is similar to the following:

```
HashAggregate  (cost=1660.00..1660.51 rows=51 width=3)
  Group Key: state
  ->  Seq Scan on customers  (cost=0.00..1535.00 rows=50000 width=3)
```

So, there are **51** unique values within the **state** column.

4. Create an index called **ix_state** using the **state** column of **customers**:

```
CREATE INDEX ix_state ON customers(state);
```

5. Rerun the **EXPLAIN** statement from *step 2*:

```
EXPLAIN SELECT * FROM customers WHERE state='FO';
```

The output of the preceding code is similar to this:

```
Index Scan using ix_state on customers  (cost=0.29..8.31 rows=1
width=140)
  Index Cond: (state = 'FO'::text)
```

Notice that an index scan is being used with the index you created in *step 4*. You can also see that you have a non-zero setup cost (**0.29**), but the total cost is much reduced from the previous **1660** to only **8.31**. This shows the power of the index scan.

Now, consider a slightly different example, looking at the time it takes to return a search on the **gender** column.

6. Use the **EXPLAIN** command to return the query plan for a search for all records of males within the database:

```
EXPLAIN SELECT * FROM customers WHERE gender='M';
```

The output is as follows:

```
Seq Scan on customers  (cost=0.00..1660.00 rows=24957 width=140)
  Filter: (gender = 'M'::text)
```

As there is no index on the **gender** column, and the existing index on the **state** column is not relevant, PostgreSQL will still use a sequential scan for this statement.

7. Create an index called **ix_gender** using the **gender** column of **customers**:

```
CREATE INDEX ix_gender ON customers(gender);
```

8. Confirm the presence of the index using **\d**, which lists all the columns and indexes for the particular table:

```
\d customers;
```

Scrolling to the bottom, you can see the indexes using the **ix_prefix**, as well as the column from the table used to create the index:

```
                            Table "public.customers"
      Column     |             Type            | Collation | Nullable |
Default
-----------------+-----------------------------+-----------+----------+--
-------
 customer_id     | bigint                      |           |          |
 title           | text                        |           |          |
 first_name      | text                        |           |          |
 last_name       | text                        |           |          |
 suffix          | text                        |           |          |
 email           | text                        |           |          |
 gender          | text                        |           |          |
 ip_address      | text                        |           |          |
 phone           | text                        |           |          |
 street_address  | text                        |           |          |
 city            | text                        |           |          |
 state           | text                        |           |          |
 postal_code     | text                        |           |          |
 latitude        | double precision            |           |          |
 longitude       | double precision            |           |          |
 date_added      | timestamp without time zone |           |          |
Indexes:
    "ix_customers_customer_id" btree (customer_id)
    "ix_gender" btree (gender)
    "ix_state" btree (state)
```

9. Rerun the **EXPLAIN** statement from *step 6*:

```
EXPLAIN SELECT * FROM customers WHERE gender='M';
```

The following is the output of the preceding code:

```
Bitmap Heap Scan on customers   (cost=285.71..1632.67 rows=24957
width=140)
  Recheck Cond: (gender = 'M'::text)
   ->  Bitmap Index Scan on ix_gender   (cost=0.00..279.47 rows=24957
width=0)
        Index Cond: (gender = 'M'::text)
```

Notice that the query cost has not changed much, despite the use of the **index** scan. This is because there is insufficient information to create a useful tree within the **gender** column. There are only two possible values, **M** and **F**. The gender index essentially splits the information in two: one branch for males and the other for females. The index has not split the data into branches of the tree well enough to gain any benefit. The planner still needs to scan through at least half of the data, and so it is not worth the overhead of the index.

10. Use **EXPLAIN** to return the query plan, searching for latitudes less than **38** degrees and greater than **30** degrees:

```
EXPLAIN SELECT * FROM customers WHERE (latitude < 38) AND (latitude >
30);
```

The following is the output of the preceding code:

```
Seq Scan on customers   (cost=0.00..1785.00 rows=17944 width=140)
   Filter: ((latitude < '38'::double precision) AND (latitude >
'30'::double precision))
```

Notice that the query is using a sequential scan with a filter because there is no index set on the filter condition, so PostgreSQL has to scan the entire table row by row. The initial sequential scan returns **17944** before the filter and costs **1785** with **0** startup costs.

11. Now create an index on the filtered column so that PostgreSQL has some prior knowledge on how data is stored based on latitude. Create an index called **ix_latitude** using the **latitude** column of **customers**:

```
CREATE INDEX ix_latitude ON customers(latitude);
```

12. Rerun the query of *step 10* and observe the output of the plan:

```
Bitmap Heap Scan on customers   (cost=384.22..1688.38 rows=17944
width=140)
   Recheck Cond: ((latitude < '38'::double precision) AND (latitude >
'30'::double precision))
   ->  Bitmap Index Scan on ix_latitude  (cost=0.00..379.73 rows=17944
width=0)
         Index Cond: ((latitude < '38'::double precision) AND
(latitude > '30'::double precision))
```

You can see that this plan is more involved than the previous plan, with a bitmap heap scan and a bitmap index scan being used. A bitmap scan is a frequently used scanning method in PostgreSQL, in which PostgreSQL determines the exact way of index processing. It is closely related to the physical implementation of database storage. As such, explaining the exact details of a bitmap scan is out of the scope of this book.

Now you can get some more information by adding the **ANALYZE** command to **EXPLAIN**.

13. Use **EXPLAIN ANALYZE** to query plan the content of the **customers** table with latitude values between **30** and **38**:

```
EXPLAIN ANALYZE SELECT * FROM customers WHERE (latitude < 38) AND
(latitude > 30);
```

The following output will be displayed:

```
Bitmap Heap Scan on customers   (cost=384.22..1688.38 rows=17944
width=140) (actual time=53.413..57.385 rows=17896 loops=1)
   Recheck Cond: ((latitude < '38'::double precision) AND (latitude >
'30'::double precision))
   Heap Blocks: exact=1033
   ->  Bitmap Index Scan on ix_latitude  (cost=0.00..379.73 rows=17944
width=0) (actual time=53.195..53.195 rows=17896 loops=1)
         Index Cond: ((latitude < '38'::double precision) AND
(latitude > '30'::double precision))
Planning Time: 0.169 ms
Execution Time: 57.981 ms
```

From the last two rows, you can see that there is **0.169 ms** of planning time and **57.981 ms** of execution time, with the index scan taking almost the same amount of time to execute as the bitmap heat scan takes to start.

14. Create another index for **latitude** between **30** and **38** on the **customers** table:

```
CREATE INDEX ix_latitude_less ON customers(latitude) WHERE (latitude
< 38) and (latitude > 30);
```

15. Re-execute the query in *step 10* and compare the query plans:

```
Bitmap Heap Scan on customers  (cost=298.25..1602.41 rows=17944
width=140) (actual time=2.316..7.222 rows=17896 loops=1)
  Recheck Cond: ((latitude < '38'::double precision) AND (latitude >
'30'::double precision))
  Heap Blocks: exact=1033
  ->  Bitmap Index Scan on ix_latitude_less  (cost=0.00..293.77
rows=17944 width=0) (actual time=2.165..2.165 rows=17896 loops=1)
Planning Time: 0.293 ms
Execution Time: 7.905 ms
```

When you use a generic column index that includes all the elements in the column, the planning time was **0.169 ms** and the execution time was **57.981 ms**. With a more targeted index that only includes a part of the values in the column, the numbers were **0.293 ms** and **7.905 ms**, respectively. Using this more targeted index, you were able to shave **50.076 ms** off the execution time at the cost of an additional **0.124 ms** of planning time.

> **NOTE**
>
> To access the source code for this specific section, please refer to https://packt.link/PDtJk.

Thus far, you can improve the performance of your query as indexes have made the searching process more efficient. You may have had to pay an upfront cost to create the index, but once created, repeat queries can be executed more quickly. Next, you will practice index scanning in an activity.

ACTIVITY 8.02: IMPLEMENTING INDEX SCANS

In this activity, you will determine whether index scans can be used to reduce query time. After creating your customer reporting system for the marketing department in *Activity 8.01*, *Query Planning*, you have received another request to allow records to be identified by their IP address or the associated customer names. You know that there are a lot of different IP addresses, and you need performant searches. Plan out the queries required to search for records by IP address as well as for certain customers with the suffix **Jr** in their name.

Here are the steps to follow:

1. Use the **EXPLAIN** and **ANALYZE** commands to profile the query plan to search for all records with an IP address of **18.131.58.65**. How long does the query take to plan and execute?

2. Create a generic index based on the IP address column.

3. Rerun the query in *step 1*. How long does the query take to plan and execute?

4. Create a more detailed index based on the IP address column with the condition that the IP address is **18.131.58.65**.

5. Rerun the query in *step 1*. How long does the query take to plan and execute? What are the differences between each of these queries?

6. Use the **EXPLAIN ANALYZE** commands to profile the query plan to search for all records with a suffix of **Jr**. How long does the query take to plan and execute?

7. Create a generic index based on the suffix address column.

8. Rerun the query of *step 6*. How long does the query take to plan and execute?

    Expected output:

    ```
    Bitmap Heap Scan on customers   (cost=5.07..302.60 rows=100 width=140)
    (actual time=0.072..0.170 rows=102 loops=1)
      Recheck Cond: (suffix = 'Jr'::text)

      Heap Blocks: exact=98

      ->  Bitmap Index Scan on ix_suffix   (cost=0.00..5.04 rows=100
    width=0) (actual time=0.056..0.056 rows=102 loops=1)
            Index Cond: (suffix = 'Jr'::text)
    Planning Time: 0.676 ms
    Execution Time: 0.212 ms
    ```

Thus, you can improve the performance of your query as indexes have made the searching process more efficient. You will learn how the hash index works in the next section.

> **NOTE**
>
> The solution for this activity can be found on page 469.

THE HASH INDEX

The final indexing type you will cover is the hash index. The hash index has only recently gained stability as a feature within PostgreSQL, with previous versions issuing warnings that the feature is unsafe and reporting that the method is typically not as performant as B-tree indexes. At the time of writing, the hash index feature is relatively limited in the comparative statements it can run, with equality (=) being the only one available.

So, given that the feature is only just stable and somewhat limited in options for use, why would anyone use it? Well, hash indices can describe large datasets (in the order of tens of thousands of rows or more) using very little data, allowing more of the data to be kept in memory and reducing search times for some queries. This is particularly important for databases that are at least several gigabytes in size.

A hash index is an indexing method that utilizes a hash function to achieve its performance benefits. A hash function is a mathematical function that takes data or a series of data and returns a unique series of alphanumeric characters depending upon what information was provided and the unique hash code used.

For instance, say you had a customer named *Josephine Marquez*. You could pass this information to a hash function, which could produce a hash result such as *01f38e*. Suppose you also had records for Josephine's husband, Julio; the corresponding hash for Julio could be *43eb38a*. A hash map uses a key-value pair relationship to find data.

You will use the values of a hash function to provide the key, using the data contained in the corresponding row of the database as the value. As long as the key is unique to the value, you can quickly access the information you require. This method can also reduce the overall size of the index in memory if only the corresponding hashes are stored, thereby dramatically reducing the search time for a query.

Similar to the syntax for creating a B-tree index, a hash index can be created using the following syntax:

```
CREATE INDEX <index name> ON <table name> USING HASH(table column)
```

The following example shows how to create a hash index on the **gender** columns in the **customers** table:

```
CREATE INDEX ix_gender ON customers USING HASH(gender);
```

If there is already an index with the same name existing in the database, you can use a **DROP INDEX <index_name>** command to drop and recreate it. In the previous section, it was mentioned that the Query Planner can ignore the indices created if it deems them to not be significantly faster or more appropriate for the existing query. As the hash scan is somewhat limited in use, it may not be uncommon for a different search to ignore the indices. Now, you will perform an exercise to implement the hash index. This will also show you the difference in performance between different index types.

EXERCISE 8.03: GENERATING SEVERAL HASH INDEXES TO INVESTIGATE PERFORMANCE

In this exercise, you will generate several hash indexes and investigate the potential performance increases that can be gained from using them. You will start the exercise by rerunning some of the queries of previous exercises and comparing the execution times:

1. Drop all existing indexes using the **DROP INDEX** command for each of the indexes that you have created previously (**ix_gender**, **ix_state**, and **ix_latitude_less**); otherwise, you will run into an issue with the following steps:

```
DROP INDEX <index name>;
```

2. Use **EXPLAIN** and **ANALYZE** on the **customers** table where the gender is male, but without using a hash index:

```
EXPLAIN ANALYZE SELECT * FROM customers WHERE gender='M';
```

An output similar to this will be displayed:

```
Seq Scan on customers  (cost=0.00..1660.00 rows=24957 width=140)
(actual time=0.168..130.498 rows=24956 loops=1)
  Filter: (gender = 'M'::text)
  Rows Removed by Filter: 25044
Planning Time: 0.217 ms
Execution Time: 12.833 ms
```

From the output, you can see that the estimated planning time is **0.217 ms** and the execution time is **12.833 ms**. Note that you may not have the same time with this query plan, and the plan may not always produce the same values. The key here is to compare the values with the values when PostgreSQL uses an index for execution, not the absolute values.

3. Create a B-tree index on the **gender** column and repeat the query to determine the performance using the default index:

```
CREATE INDEX ix_gender ON customers USING btree(gender);
```

The following is the output of the preceding code:

```
Bitmap Heap Scan on customers   (cost=285.71..1632.67 rows=24957
width=140) (actual time=1.002..7.162 rows=24956 loops=1)
   Recheck Cond: (gender = 'M'::text)
   Heap Blocks: exact=1035
      ->  Bitmap Index Scan on ix_gender   (cost=0.00..279.47 rows=24957
width=0) (actual time=0.875..0.875 rows=24956 loops=1)
         Index Cond: (gender = 'M'::text)
Planning Time: 0.173 ms
Execution Time: 8.303 ms
```

From the output, you can decipher that the Query Planner has selected the B-tree index, but the costs of the scans do not differ much, although the planning and execution time estimates have been modified. This is because there are only two values in the column. Thus the selectivity of this index is not high.

4. Repeat the following query at least five times manually and observe the time estimates after each execution:

```
EXPLAIN ANALYZE SELECT * FROM customers WHERE gender='M';
```

The results of the five individual queries should be similar to the one shown previously, just that the planning and execution times differ for each separate execution of the query.

5. You created a B-tree index called **ix_gender** in *step 3*. Now drop the index so that you can create another index with the same name using **HASH** in the next step:

```
DROP INDEX ix_gender;
```

6. Create a hash index on the **gender** column so that you can compare the hash index with the B-tree index:

```
CREATE INDEX ix_gender ON customers USING HASH(gender);
```

7. Repeat the query from *step 4* to see the execution time:

```
EXPLAIN ANALYZE SELECT * FROM customers WHERE gender='M';
```

The following output will be displayed:

```
Seq Scan on customers  (cost=0.00..1660.00 rows=24957 width=140)
(actual time=0.029..14.028 rows=24956 loops=1)
  Filter: (gender = 'M'::text)
  Rows Removed by Filter: 25044
Planning Time: 0.981 ms
Execution Time: 14.979 ms
```

PostgreSQL determined that there was no benefit to using the hash index on the **gender** column. So the index was not used by the planner. This is because the **gender** column could have only two possible values and the selectivity is very low.

8. Use the **EXPLAIN ANALYZE** command to profile the performance of the query that selects all customers where the state is **FO**:

```
EXPLAIN ANALYZE SELECT * FROM customers WHERE state='FO';
```

The following output will be displayed:

```
Seq Scan on customers  (cost=0.00..1660.00 rows=1 width=140) (actual
time=13.321..13.321 rows=0 loops=1)
  Filter: (state = 'FO'::text)
  Rows Removed by Filter: 50000
Planning Time: 0.118 ms
Execution Time: 13.338 ms
```

9. Create a B-tree index on the **state** column of the **customers** table and repeat the query profiling:

```
CREATE INDEX ix_state ON customers USING BTREE(state);
EXPLAIN ANALYZE SELECT * FROM customers WHERE state='FO';
```

The following is the output of the preceding code:

```
Index Scan using ix_state on customers   (cost=0.29..8.31 rows=1
width=140) (actual time=0.045..0.045 rows=0 loops=1)
   Index Cond: (state = 'FO'::text)
Planning Time: 0.404 ms
Execution Time: 0.069 ms
```

Here, you can see a significant performance increase due to the B-tree index with a slight setup cost. How does the index scan perform? Since the execution time has dropped from **13.338 ms** to **0.069 ms**, it is reasonable to accept that the planning cost has increased by approximately 300%, from **0.118 ms** to **0.404 ms**.

10. Similar to what you just did to the index on the **gender** column, create a hash index for the **state** column and compare the performance. Drop the **ix_state** B-tree index and create a hash index:

```
DROP INDEX ix_state;
CREATE INDEX ix_state ON customers USING HASH(state);
```

11. Use **EXPLAIN** and **ANALYZE** to profile the performance of the hash scan:

```
EXPLAIN ANALYZE SELECT * FROM customers WHERE state='FO';
```

The following is the output of the preceding code:

```
Index Scan using ix_state on customers   (cost=0.00..8.02 rows=1
width=140) (actual time=0.032..0.032 rows=0 loops=1)
   Index Cond: (state = 'FO'::text)
Planning Time: 0.359 ms
Execution Time: 0.054 ms
```

You can see that, for this specific query, a hash index is particularly effective, reducing both the planning/setup time and cost of the B-tree index, as well as reducing the execution time to less than **1 ms** from **13.338 ms**.

> **NOTE**
>
> To access the source code for this specific section, please refer to
> https://packt.link/PDtJk.

In this exercise, you used hash indexes to find the effectiveness of a particular query. You saw how the execution time goes down when using a hash index in a query. You will practice this skill in the coming activity.

ACTIVITY 8.03: IMPLEMENTING HASH INDEXES

In this activity, you will investigate the use of hash indexes to improve performance using the **emails** table from the **sqlda** database. Here is the scenario. You have received another request from the marketing department. This time, they would like you to analyze the performance of an email marketing campaign.

Given that the success rate of email campaigns is low, different emails are sent to multiple customers at a time. Use the **EXPLAIN** and **ANALYZE** commands to determine the planning time and cost, as well as the execution time and cost, of selecting all rows where the email subject is **Shocking Holiday Savings On Electric Scooters**:

1. Use the **EXPLAIN** and **ANALYZE** commands to determine the planning time and cost, as well as the execution time and cost, of selecting all rows where the email subject is **Shocking Holiday Savings On Electric Scooters**.

2. Create a hash scan on the **email_subject** column.

3. Repeat *step 1*. Compare the output of the Query Planner without the hash index to the output with the hash index.

4. Create a hash scan on the **customer_id** column.

5. Use **EXPLAIN** and **ANALYZE** to estimate how long it would take to select all rows with a **customer_id** value greater than **100**. Also, determine the type of scan used and why.

   Expected output:

```
Seq Scan on emails   (cost=0.00..10650.98 rows=417346 width=79)
(actual time=0.067..105.158 rows=417315 loops=1)
  Filter: (customer_id > 100)
  Rows Removed by Filter: 843
Planning Time: 0.548 ms
Execution Time: 117.899 ms
```

In this activity, a sequential scan was used in this query rather than the hash scan created due to the current limitations of hash scan usage. Explaining the exact nature of this limitation is beyond the scope of this book. At the time of writing, the use of the hash scan is limited to equality comparisons, which involve searching for values equal to a given value.

> **NOTE**
>
> The solution for this activity can be found on page 471.

EFFECTIVE INDEX USE

So far in this chapter, you have looked at different scanning methods and the use of both B-trees and hash scans as a means of reducing query times. You have also seen different examples of where an index was created for a field or condition and was explicitly not selected by the Query Planner when executing the query as it was deemed a more inefficient choice.

In this section, you will spend some time learning about the appropriate use of indexes to reduce query times since, while indexes may seem like an obvious choice for increasing query performance, this is not always the case.

Consider the following situations:

- **The field you have used for your index is frequently changing**: In this situation, where you are frequently inserting or deleting rows in a table, the index that you have created may quickly become inefficient as it was constructed for data that is either no longer relevant or has since had a change in value.

  Consider the index at the back of this book. If you moved the order of the chapters around, the index would no longer be valid and would need to be revised. In such a situation, you may need to periodically re-index the data to ensure the references to the data are up to date.

  In SQL, you can rebuild the data indices by using the `REINDEX` command, which leads to a scenario where you will need to consider the cost, means, and strategy of frequent re-indexing versus other performance considerations, such as the query benefits introduced by the index, the size of the database, or even whether changes to the database structure could avoid the problem altogether.

- **The index is out of date and the existing references are either invalid or there are segments of data without an index, preventing the use of the index by the Query Planner**: In general, PostgreSQL will automatically update indexes as the underlying table changes. But there are extremely rare cases when the update may not function properly. In such a situation, the index is so old that it cannot be used and thus needs to be updated.

- **You are frequently looking for records containing the same search criteria within a specific field**: In *Exercise 8.02*, *Creating an Index Scan*, you considered an example similar to this when looking for customers within a database whose records contained latitude values of less than **38** and greater than **30**, using `SELECT * FROM customers WHERE (latitude < 38) and (latitude > 30)`.

  In this example, it may be more efficient to create a partial index using a subset of data, like this: `CREATE INDEX ix_latitude_less ON customers(latitude) WHERE (latitude < 38) and (latitude > 30)`. In this way, the index is only created using the data you are interested in, and is thereby smaller in size, quicker to scan, and easier to maintain, and can also be used in more complex queries.

- **The database is not particularly large**: In such a situation, the overhead of creating and using the index may simply not be worth it. Sequential scans, particularly those using data already in RAM, are quite fast, and if you create an index on a small dataset, there is no guarantee that the Query Planner will use it or get any significant benefit from using it.

So far, all the query plans in this chapter have only dealt with single-table queries. As you can imagine, when the query contains more tables, its query plan will become more complex. This is especially true when you try to join two or more tables because at this point, you are not only picking data from the hard disk but also trying to match data (with a join key) in one table to the data in another. The interpretation and understanding of these plans are no doubt very important but are way beyond the scope of this book. If you are interested in learning more about this topic, you should get yourself familiar with single-table query plans first, then seek further studies on the official PostgreSQL website.

In the next section, you will learn how to speed up normal query execution by terminating long-running queries.

KILLING QUERIES

Sometimes, you have a lot of data or perhaps insufficient hardware resources, and a query just runs for a very long time. In such a situation, you may need to stop the query—perhaps so you can implement an alternative query to get the information you need, but without the delayed response. In this section, you are going to investigate how you can stop hanging or, at least, extremely long-running queries using a secondary PostgreSQL interpreter. The following are some of the commands that you will use to kill queries:

- **pg_sleep** is a command that allows you to tell the SQL interpreter to essentially do nothing for a specified period as defined by the input to the function in seconds.

- The **pg_cancel_backend** command causes the interpreter to end the query specified by the process ID (**PID**). The process will be terminated cleanly, allowing for appropriate resource cleanup. Clean termination should also be the first preference as it reduces the possibility of data corruption and damage to the database.

- The **pg_terminate_background** command stops an existing process but, as opposed to **pg_cancel_background**, forces the process to terminate without cleaning up any resources being used by the query. The query is immediately terminated, and data corruption may occur as a result.

To invoke these commands, you need the command to be evaluated, and one common method is to use a simple **select** statement, such as the following:

```
SELECT pg_terminate_background(<PID>);
```

PID is the process ID of the query you would like to terminate. Assuming this runs successfully, it would output the following:

```
pg_terminate_backend
----------------------
 t
(1 row)
```

Now that you have learned how to kill a query in both a clean and a forced manner, you will step through an exercise to kill a long-running query.

EXERCISE 8.04: CANCELING A LONG-RUNNING QUERY

In this exercise, you will cancel a long-running query to save time when you are stuck at query execution. You have been lucky enough to receive a large data store and you decide to run what you originally thought was a simple enough query to get some basic descriptive statistics of the data. For some reason, however, the query is taking an extremely long time and you are not even sure that it is running.

You decide it is time to cancel the query, which means you would like to send a stop signal to the query but allow it sufficient time to clean up its resources gracefully. As there may be a wide variety of hardware available to you and the data required to induce a long-running query could be quite a lot to download, you will simulate a long-running query using the **pg_sleep** command.

For this exercise, you will require two separate SQL interpreter sessions running in separate windows, as shown in the following steps:

1. Launch two separate interpreters by running **psql sqlda**:

```
C:\> psql -U postgres sqlda
```

2. In the first terminal, execute the **sleep** command with a parameter of **1000** seconds:

```
SELECT pg_sleep(1000);
```

After pressing *Enter*, you should notice that the cursor of the interpreter does not return. Instead, this window seems to be hanging, without responding to any keyboard or mouse inputs.

3. In the second terminal, select the **pid** and **query** columns from the **pg_stat_activity** table where **state** is **active**:

```
SELECT pid, query FROM pg_stat_activity WHERE state = 'active';
```

The following is the output of the preceding code:

```
 pid  |                            query
------+-----------------------------------------------------------------
---
 6452 | SELECT pid, query FROM pg_stat_activity WHERE state =
'active';
 6336 | SELECT pg_sleep(1000);
(2 rows)
```

4. In the second terminal, pass the PID of the **pg_sleep** query to the **pg_cancel_backend** command to terminate the **pg_sleep** query with a graceful cleanup. Note that the PID (**6336**) might be different in your environment, so use whatever PID you got from the previous step:

```
SELECT pg_cancel_backend(6336);
```

The following is the output of the preceding code:

```
pg_cancel_backend
-----------------------
t
(1 row)
```

5. Observe the first terminal and notice that the **sleep** command is no longer executing, as indicated by the return message:

```
ERROR:   canceling statement due to user request
```

The above output shows an error as the query was canceled after the user's request.

> **NOTE**
>
> To access the source code for this specific section, please refer to https://packt.link/PDtJk.

In this exercise, you learned how to cancel a query that is taking a long time to execute. In the next section, you will learn how to use functions and triggers in your SQL queries and analyze data.

FUNCTIONS AND TRIGGERS

So far in this chapter, you have discovered how to quantify query performance via the Query Planner. In this section, you will construct reusable queries and statements via functions, as well as automatic function execution via trigger callbacks. The combination of these two SQL features can be used to not only run queries or re-index tables as data is added to, updated in, or removed from the database but also run hypothesis tests and track their results throughout the life of the database.

FUNCTION DEFINITIONS

As in almost all other programming or scripting languages, functions in SQL are contained sections of code that provide a lot of benefits, such as efficient code reuse and simplified troubleshooting processes. You can use functions to repeat or modify statements or queries without re-entering the statement each time or searching for its use throughout longer code segments. One of the most powerful aspects of functions is that they allow you to break code into smaller, testable chunks. As the popular computer science expression goes, "If the code is not tested, it cannot be trusted."

So, how do you define functions in SQL? There is a relatively straightforward syntax, with the SQL syntax keywords:

```
CREATE FUNCTION some_function_name (function_arguments)
RETURNS return_type AS $return_name$
DECLARE return_name return_type;
BEGIN
 <function statements>;
RETURN <some_value>;
END; $return_name$
LANGUAGE PLPGSQL;
```

The following is a short explanation of the functions used in the preceding code:

- **some_function_name** is the name issued to the function and is used to call the function at later stages.

- **function_arguments** is an optional list of function arguments. This could be empty, without any arguments provided, if you do not need any additional information to be provided to the function. To provide additional information, you can use either a list of different data types as the arguments (such as integer and numeric data types) or a list of arguments with parameter names (such as the **min_val** integer and the **max_val** numeric data type).

- **return_type** is the data type being returned from the function.

- **DECLARE return_name return_type** statement is only required if **return_name** is provided, and a variable is to be returned from the function. **return_name** is the name of the variable to be returned (optional). If **return_name** is not required, this line can be omitted from the function definition.

- **function_statements** are the SQL statements to be executed within the function.

- **some_value** is the data to be returned from the function.

- **PLPGSQL** specifies the language to be used in the function. PostgreSQL allows you to use other languages; however, their use in this context lies beyond the scope of this book.

For example, you can create a simple function to add three numbers, as follows:

```
CREATE FUNCTION add_three(a integer, b integer, c integer)
RETURNS integer AS $$
BEGIN
    RETURN a + b + c;
END;
$$ LANGUAGE PLPGSQL;
```

You can then call it in your queries, as follows:

```
SELECT add_three(1, 2, 3);
```

The following is the output of the code:

```
add_three
-----------
        6
(1 row)
```

Now, you will implement an exercise to create a function without arguments.

> **NOTE**
>
> The complete PostgreSQL documentation for functions can be found at https://www.postgresql.org/docs/current/extend.html.

EXERCISE 8.05: CREATING FUNCTIONS WITHOUT ARGUMENTS

In this exercise, you will create the most basic function—one that simply returns a constant value—so you can build up a familiarity with the syntax. You will construct your first SQL function that does not take any arguments as additional information. This function may be used to repeat SQL query statements that provide basic statistics about the data within the tables of the **sqlda** database. These are the steps to follow:

1. Connect to the **sqlda** database via **psql**.

2. Create a function called **fixed_val** that does not accept any arguments and returns an integer. This is a multiline process. Enter the following line first:

```
CREATE FUNCTION fixed_val()
RETURNS integer AS $$
```

    This line starts the function declaration for **fixed_val**, and you can see that there are no arguments to the function, as indicated by the open/closed brackets, **()**, nor any returned variables.

3. Enter the **BEGIN** keyword (notice that as you are not returning a variable, the line containing the **DECLARE** statement has been omitted):

```
BEGIN
```

4. You want to return the value **1** from this function, so enter the **RETURN 1** statement:

```
RETURN 1;
```

5. End the function definition:

```
END; $$
```

6. Add the **LANGUAGE** statement, as shown in the following function definition:

```
LANGUAGE PLPGSQL;
```

    This will complete the function definition.

7. Now that the function is defined, you can use it. As with almost all other SQL statements you have completed to date, you simply use the **SELECT** command:

```
SELECT * FROM fixed_val();
```

This will display the following output:

```
fixed_val
---------
1
(1 row)
```

Notice that the function is called using the open and closed brackets in the **SELECT** statement.

8. Use **EXPLAIN** and **ANALYZE** in combination with this statement to characterize the performance of the function:

```
EXPLAIN ANALYZE SELECT * FROM fixed_val();
```

Here is the output of the preceding code:

```
Function Scan on fixed_val  (cost=0.25..0.26 rows=1 width=4) (actual
time=19.138..19.139 rows=1 loops=1)
Planning Time: 0.143 ms
Execution Time: 20.774 ms
```

Notice that the three rows being referenced in the preceding output refer not to the result of **SELECT * FROM fixed_val();** but rather to the result of the Query Planner. Looking at the first line of the information returned by the Query Planner, you can see that only one row of information is returned from the **SELECT** statement.

9. So far, you have seen how to create a simple function, but simply returning a fixed value is not particularly useful. You will now create a function that determines the number of samples in the **sales** table. Create a function called **num_samples** that does not take any arguments but returns an integer called **total** that represents the number of samples in the **sales** table:

```
CREATE FUNCTION num_samples() RETURNS integer AS $total$
```

10. You want to return a variable called **total**, and thus you need to declare it. Declare the **total** variable as an integer:

```
DECLARE total integer;
```

11. Enter the **BEGIN** keyword:

```
BEGIN
```

12. Enter the statement that determines the number of samples in the table and assigns the result to the **total** variable:

```
SELECT COUNT(*) INTO total FROM sales;
```

13. Return the value for **total**:

```
RETURN total;
```

14. End the function with the variable name:

```
END; $total$
```

15. Add the **LANGUAGE** statement, as shown in the following function definition:

```
LANGUAGE PLPGSQL;
```

This will complete the function definition, and upon successful creation, the **CREATE_FUNCTION** statement will be shown.

16. Use the function to determine how many rows or samples there are in the **sales** table:

```
SELECT num_samples();
```

Here is the output of the preceding code:

```
num_samples
---------
37711
(1 row)
```

You can see that by using the **SELECT** statement in combination with your SQL function, there are **37711** records in the **sales** database.

> **NOTE**
>
> To access the source code for this specific section, please refer to https://packt.link/PDtJk.

In this exercise, you have created your first user-defined SQL function and discovered how to create and return information from variables within the function.

In the following activity, you will create a new function that can be called in your queries.

ACTIVITY 8.04: DEFINING A LARGEST SALE VALUE FUNCTION

In this activity, you will create a user-defined function so you can calculate the value of the largest sale in a single function call. You will reinforce your knowledge of functions as you create a function that determines the value of the largest sale in a database. At this stage, your marketing department is starting to make a lot of data analysis requests, and you need to be more efficient in fulfilling them, as they are currently just taking too long.

Perform the following steps:

1. Connect to the **sqlda** database.

2. Create a function called **max_sale** that does not take any input arguments but returns a numeric value called **big_sale**.

3. Declare the **big_sale** variable and begin the function.

4. Insert the value of the largest sale into the **big_sale** variable.

5. Return the value for **big_sale**.

6. End the function with the **LANGUAGE** statement.

7. Call the function to find out what the value of the largest sale in the database is.

    Expected output:

    ```
    Max
    -------
    115000
    (1 row)
    ```

In this activity, you created a user-defined function to calculate the largest sale amount from a single function call using the **MAX** function. Next, you will create a function that takes arguments.

> **NOTE**
>
> The solution for this activity can be found on page 473.

EXERCISE 8.06: CREATING FUNCTIONS WITH ARGUMENTS

In this exercise, you will create a single function that will allow you to calculate information from multiple tables. Create a function that determines the average value from the sales **amount** column with respect to the value of the corresponding channel. After creating your previous user-defined function to determine the biggest sale in the database, you have observed a significant increase in the efficiency with which you fulfill your marketing department's requests.

Perform the following steps to complete the exercise:

1. Connect to the **sqlda** database.

2. Create a function called **avg_sales** that takes a text argument input, **channel_type**, and returns a numeric output:

```
CREATE FUNCTION avg_sales(channel_type TEXT)
RETURNS numeric AS $channel_avg$
```

3. Declare the numeric **channel_avg** variable and begin the function:

```
DECLARE channel_avg numeric;
BEGIN
```

4. Determine the average **sales_amount** only when the channel value is equal to **channel_type**:

```
SELECT
  AVG(sales_amount)
INTO
  channel_avg
FROM
  sales
WHERE
  channel=channel_type;
```

5. Return **channel_avg**:

```
RETURN channel_avg;
```

6. End the function and specify the **LANGUAGE** statement:

```
END; $channel_avg$
LANGUAGE PLPGSQL;
```

7. Determine the average sales amount for the **internet** channel:

```
SELECT avg_sales('internet');
```

Here is the output of the preceding code:

```
avg_sales
----------------
6413.11540412024
(1 row)
```

8. Now do the same for the **dealership** channel:

```
SELECT avg_sales('dealership');
```

Here is the output of the preceding code:

```
avg_sales
----------------
7939.33132075954
(1 row)
```

This output shows the average value for sales for a dealership, which is **7939.331**.

> **NOTE**
>
> To access the source code for this specific section, please refer to
> https://packt.link/PDtJk.

In this exercise, you were introduced to using function arguments to further modify the behavior of functions and the outputs they return. Next, you will learn about the **\df** and **\sf** commands.

THE \DF AND \SF COMMANDS

You can use the **\df** command in PostgreSQL to get a list of the functions available in memory, including the variables and data types passed as arguments. The following are the first few rows of this command:

```
                                        List of functions
  Schema |            Name        | Result data type |          Argument data
types                 | Type
--------+--------------------+------------------+------------------------
------------------+------
  public | cube               | cube             | cube, double precision
  | func
  public | cube               | cube             | cube, double precision,
double precision   | func
  public | cube               | cube             | double precision
  | func
  public | cube               | cube             | double precision,
double precision       | func
```

The **\sf function_name** command in PostgreSQL can be used to review the function definition for already-defined functions. For example, in the preceding section, you created a function called **max_sale**. In this case, say you execute the following query:

```
\sf max_sale
```

The output will show the definition of that function, as follows:

```
CREATE OR REPLACE FUNCTION public.max_sale()
 RETURNS integer
 LANGUAGE plpgsql
AS $function$
DECLARE big_sale numeric;
BEGIN
SELECT MAX(sales_amount) INTO big_sale FROM sales;
RETURN big_sale;
END; $function$
```

Now that you have walked through several exercises to create functions with and without arguments, you can apply your knowledge to real-world problems. In the following activity, you will practice creating functions that take arguments.

ACTIVITY 8.05: CREATING FUNCTIONS WITH ARGUMENTS

In this activity, your goal is to create a function with arguments and compute the output. You will construct a function that computes the average sales amount for transaction sales within a specific date range. Each date is to be provided to the function as a text string. These are the steps to follow:

1. Create the function definition for a function called **avg_sales_window** that returns a numeric value and takes two **DATE** values to specify the from and to dates in the form **YYYY-MM-DD**.

2. Declare the return variable as a numeric data type and begin the function.

3. Select the average sales amount as the return variable where the sales transaction date is within the specified date.

4. Return the function variable, end the function, and specify the **LANGUAGE** statement.

5. Use the function to determine the average sales value for transactions between 2020-04-12 and 2021-04-12.

    Expected output:

    ```
    avg_sales_window
    ----------------
    7663.13305937025
    (1 row)
    ```

In this activity, you constructed a function that computes the average sales amount for transaction sales within a specific date range from the database.

> **NOTE**
>
> The solution for this activity can be found on page 474.

In the next section, you will learn how to create and run triggers to automate database processes. You will also perform an exercise and activity using triggers.

TRIGGERS

Triggers, known as events or callbacks in other programming languages, are useful features that, as the name suggests, trigger the execution of SQL statements or functions in response to a specific event. Triggers can be initiated when one of the following happens:

- A row is inserted into a table.

- A field within a row is updated.

- A row within a table is deleted.

- A table is truncated; that is, all rows are quickly removed from a table.

The timing of the trigger can also be specified to occur:

- Before an insert, update, delete, or truncate operation

- After an insert, update, delete, or truncate operation

- Instead of an insert, update, delete, or truncate operation

Depending upon the context and the purpose of the database, triggers can have a wide variety of different use cases and applications. For example, in a production environment where a database is being used to store business information and make process decisions (such as for a ride-sharing application or an e-commerce store), triggers can be used before any operation to create access logs to the database. These logs can then be used to determine who has accessed or modified the data within the database. Alternatively, triggers could be used to remap database operations to a different database or table using the **INSTEAD OF** trigger.

In the context of a data analysis application, triggers can be used to either create datasets of specific features in real-time (such as for determining the average of data over time or a sample-to-sample difference), test hypotheses concerning the data, or flag outliers being inserted or modified in a dataset.

Given that triggers are used frequently to execute SQL statements in response to events or actions, you can also see why functions are often written specifically for or paired with triggers. Self-contained, repeatable function blocks can be used for both trialing/debugging the logic within the function as well as inserting the actual code within the trigger. So, how do you create a trigger? Similar to the case of function definitions, there is a standard syntax; again, they are SQL keywords:

```
CREATE TRIGGER some_trigger_name
{ BEFORE | AFTER | INSTEAD OF }
{ INSERT | DELETE | UPDATE | TRUNCATE }
ON table_name
FOR EACH { ROW | STATEMENT }
EXECUTE PROCEDURE function_name ( function_arguments)
```

Looking at this generic trigger definition, you can see that there are a few individual components:

- You need to provide a name for the trigger in place of **some_trigger_name**.

- You need to select when the trigger is going to occur, either **BEFORE**, **AFTER**, or **INSTEAD OF** an event.

- You need to select what type of event you want to trigger on, either **INSERT**, **DELETE**, **UPDATE**, or **TRUNCATE**.

- You need to provide the table you want to monitor for events in **table_name**.

- The **FOR EACH** statement is used to specify how the trigger is to be fired. You can fire the trigger for each row that is within the scope of the trigger, or just once per statement despite the number of rows being inserted into the table.

- Finally, you just need to provide **function_name** and any relevant/required **function_arguments** to provide the functionality that you want to use on each trigger.

Look at the following example, in which you want to add a check that prevents the system from accidentally creating a sale for an amount less than half of the base MSRP. Before you can create a trigger, you need to define a trigger function:

```
CREATE OR REPLACE FUNCTION check_sale_amt_vs_msrp()
RETURNS TRIGGER AS $$
DECLARE min_allowed_price numeric;
BEGIN
  SELECT
    base_msrp * 0.5
```

```
  INTO
    min_allowed_price
  FROM
    products
  WHERE
    product_id = NEW.product_id;
  IF NEW.sales_amount < min_allowed_price THEN
    RAISE EXCEPTION 'Sales amount cannot be less than half of MSRP';
  END IF;
  RETURN NEW;
END;
$$ LANGUAGE PLPGSQL;
```

Next, you need to create the trigger that will run if a record is added or updated:

```
CREATE TRIGGER sales_product_sales_amount_msrp
AFTER INSERT OR UPDATE
ON sales
FOR EACH ROW
EXECUTE PROCEDURE check_sale_amt_vs_msrp();
```

You can test that this works by testing an insertion into the sales table that does not meet the minimum sales amount criteria:

```
INSERT INTO sales (
  SELECT
    customer_id,
    product_id,
    sales_transaction_date,
    sales_amount/3.0,
    channel,
    dealership_id
  FROM
    sales
  LIMIT
    1
);
```

This gives the following output:

```
ERROR:  Sales amount cannot be less than half of MSRP
CONTEXT:  PL/pgSQL function check_sale_amt_vs_msrp() line 6 at RAISE
```

Now, implement an exercise to create triggers for updating fields.

> **NOTE**
>
> There are a number of different options available for SQL triggers that lie
> outside the scope of this book. For the complete trigger documentation, you
> can refer to https://www.postgresql.org/docs/current/sql-createtrigger.html.

EXERCISE 8.07: CREATING TRIGGERS TO UPDATE FIELDS

In this exercise, you will introduce two new tables into the **sqlda** database, one
called **new_products** and another called **order_info**. The **new_products**
table contains some product information together with their inventory, and the
order_info table contains the orders placed on different products.

For this exercise, you will create a trigger that updates the inventory (also called
stock) value within the **new_products** table for a product each time that an order is
inserted into a new **order_info** table. As orders are placed and items are bought,
the triggers will be fired, and the quantity of available stock will be updated. Using
such a trigger, you can update your analysis in real-time as end users interact with
the database. These triggers will remove the need for you to run the analysis for the
marketing department manually; instead, they will generate the results for you.

Here are the steps to perform:

1. Create the required tables in the **sqlda** database using the following queries:

```
CREATE TABLE order_info (
    order_id integer,
    customer_id integer,
    product_code text,
    qty integer
);
INSERT INTO order_info VALUES (1618, 3, 'GROG1', 12);
INSERT INTO order_info VALUES (1619, 2, 'POULET3', 3);
INSERT INTO order_info VALUES (1620, 4, 'MON123', 1);
INSERT INTO order_info VALUES (1621, 4, 'MON636', 3);
INSERT INTO order_info VALUES (1622, 5, 'MON666', 1);

CREATE TABLE new_products (
    product_code text,
```

```
    name text,
    stock integer
);
INSERT INTO new_products VALUES
('MON636', 'Red Herring', 99);
INSERT INTO new_products VALUES
('MON666', 'Murray"s Arm', 0);
INSERT INTO new_products VALUES
('GROG1', 'Grog', 65);
INSERT INTO new_products VALUES
('POULET3', 'El Pollo Diablo', 2);
INSERT INTO new_products VALUES
('MON123', 'Rubber Chicken + Pulley', 7);
```

2. Create the required functions in the **sqlda** database using the **Functions. sql** code in the *Exercise 8.07* folder, which can be found in the accompanying source code. It is also available on GitHub: https://packt.link/PDtJk.

   You will need to open up a query tool such as pgAdmin and connect to the **sqlda** database. Copy and paste the content of the **Functions.sql** file into the query tool and run the statements. There are three functions in this **Functions.sql** file that you will use, which are as follows:

   - The **get_stock** function takes a product code as a **TEXT** input and returns the currently available stock for the specific product code.

   - The **insert_order** function is used to add a new order to the **order_info** table and takes **customer_id INTEGER**, **product_code TEXT**, and **qty INTEGER** as inputs; it will return the **order_id** instance generated for the new record.

   - The **update_stock** function will extract the information from the most recent order and update the corresponding stock information from the **products** table for the corresponding **product_code**.

3. Get a list of the functions using the **\df** command after loading the function definitions. This will display the following output:

```
                        List of functions
  Schema |    Name     |  Result data type  |  Argument data types  | Type
 --------+-------------+--------------------+-----------------------+------
  public | get_stock   | integer            |  text                 | func
 (1 row)
```

4. First, look at the current state of the **new_products** table:

```
SELECT * FROM new_products;
```

Here is the output of the preceding code:

```
product_code |           name           | stock
-------------+--------------------------+-------
 MON636      | Red Herring              |    99
 MON666      | Murray"s Arm             |     0
 GROG1       | Grog                     |    65
 POULET3     | El Pollo Diablo          |     2
 MON123      | Rubber Chicken + Pulley  |     7
(5 rows)
```

For the **order_info** table, you can write the following query:

```
SELECT * FROM order_info;
```

Here is the output of the preceding code:

```
order_id | customer_id | product_code | qty
---------+-------------+--------------+----
    1618 |           3 | GROG1        |  12
    1619 |           2 | POULET3      |   3
    1620 |           4 | MON123       |   1
    1621 |           4 | MON636       |   3
    1622 |           5 | MON666       |   1
(5 rows)
```

5. Insert a new order using the **insert_order** function with **customer_id 4**, **product_code MON636**, and **qty 10**:

```
SELECT insert_order(4, 'MON636', 10);
```

Here is the output of the preceding code:

```
insert_order
------------
1623
(1 row)
```

6. Review the entries for the **order_info** table:

```
SELECT * FROM order_info;
```

This will display the following output:

```
order_id | customer_id | product_code | qty
---------+-------------+--------------+-----
    1618 |           3 | GROG1        |  12
    1619 |           2 | POULET3      |   3
    1620 |           4 | MON123       |   1
    1621 |           4 | MON636       |   3
    1622 |           5 | MON666       |   1
    1623 |           4 | MON636       |  10
(6 rows)
```

Notice the additional row with **order_id 1623**.

7. Update the **new_products** table to account for the newly sold 10 red herrings using the **update_stock** function:

```
SELECT update_stock();
```

Here is the output of the preceding code:

```
update_stock
------------
89
(1 row)
```

This function call will determine how many red herrings are left in the inventory (after the sale of the 10 additional herrings) and will update the table accordingly.

8. Review the **new_products** table and notice the updated stock value for **Red Herring**:

```
SELECT * FROM new_products;
```

Here is the output of the preceding code:

```
product_code |           name            | stock
-------------+---------------------------+-------
 MON666      | Murray"s Arm              |    0
 GROG1       | Grog                      |   65
 POULET3     | El Pollo Diablo           |    2
 MON123      | Rubber Chicken + Pulley   |    7
 MON636      | Red Herring               |   89
(5 rows)
```

Updating the stock values manually will quickly become tedious. Create a trigger to do this automatically whenever a new order is placed.

9. Delete (**DROP**) the previous **update_stock** function. Before you can create a trigger, you must first adjust the **update_stock** function to return a trigger, which has the benefit of allowing for some simplified code:

```
DROP FUNCTION update_stock;
```

10. Create a new **update_stock** function that returns a trigger. Note that the function definition is also contained within the **Functions.sql** file for reference or direct loading into the database:

```
CREATE FUNCTION update_stock()
RETURNS TRIGGER AS $stock_trigger$
DECLARE stock_qty integer;
BEGIN
  stock_qty := get_stock(NEW.product_code) - NEW.qty;
  UPDATE
    new_products
  SET
    stock=stock_qty
  WHERE
    product_code=NEW.product_code;
  RETURN NEW;
END; $stock_trigger$
LANGUAGE PLPGSQL;
```

Note that in this function definition, you are using the **NEW** keyword followed by the dot operator (`.`) and the **product_code** (**NEW.product_code**) and **qty** (**NEW.qty**) field names from the **order_info** table. The **NEW** keyword refers to the record that was recently inserted, updated, or deleted and provides a reference to the information within the record.

In this exercise, you want the trigger to fire after the record is inserted into **order_info** and thus the **NEW** reference will contain this information. So, you can use the **get_stock** function with **NEW.product_code** to get the currently available stock for the record and simply subtract the **NEW.qty** value from the order record.

11. Finally, create the trigger. You want the trigger to occur after an **INSERT** operation on the **order_info** table. For each row, you want to execute the newly modified **update_stock** function to update the stock values in the product table:

```
CREATE TRIGGER update_trigger
AFTER INSERT ON order_info
FOR EACH ROW
EXECUTE PROCEDURE update_stock();
```

12. Now that you have created a new trigger, test it. Call the **insert_order** function to insert a new record into the **order_info** table:

```
SELECT insert_order(4, 'MON123', 2);
```

Here is the output of the preceding code:

```
insert_order
------------
1624
(1 row)
```

13. Look at the records from the **order_info** table:

```
SELECT * FROM order_info;
```

This will display the following output:

```
order_id | customer_id | product_code | qty
---------+-------------+--------------+-----
    1618 |           3 | GROG1        |  12
    1619 |           2 | POULET3      |   3
    1620 |           4 | MON123       |   1
    1621 |           4 | MON636       |   3
    1622 |           5 | MON666       |   1
    1623 |           4 | MON636       |  10
    1624 |           4 | MON123       |   2
(7 rows)
```

14. Look at the records for the **new_products** table:

```
SELECT * FROM new_products;
```

Here is the output of the preceding code:

```
product_code |           name           | stock
-------------+--------------------------+-------
 MON666      | Murray"s Arm             |     0
 GROG1       | Grog                     |    65
 POULET3     | El Pollo Diablo          |     2
 MON636      | Red Herring              |    89
 MON123      | Rubber Chicken + Pulley  |     5
(5 rows)
```

Our trigger worked. You can see that the available stock for **Rubber Chicken + Pulley MON123** has been reduced from **7** to **5**, in accordance with the quantity of the inserted order.

> **NOTE**
>
> To access the source code for this specific section, please refer to https://packt.link/PDtJk.

In this exercise, you have successfully constructed a trigger to execute a secondary function following the insertion of a new record into the database. In the next activity, you will create a trigger to keep track of the data.

ACTIVITY 8.06: CREATING A TRIGGER TO TRACK AVERAGE PURCHASES

Our goal here is to create a trigger for keeping track of the data that is updated. Say you are working as a data scientist for ZoomZoom. The business is looking at trying a few different strategies to increase the number of items in each sale. To simplify your analysis, you decide to add a simple trigger that, for each new order, computes the average quantity in all the orders and puts the result in a new table along with the corresponding **order_id**. Here are the steps to follow:

1. Connect to the **sqlda** database.

2. Create a new table called **avg_qty_log** that is composed of an **order_id integer** field and an **avg_qty numeric** field.

3. Create a function called **avg_qty** that does not take any arguments but returns a trigger. The function computes the average value for all order quantities (**order_info.qty**) and inserts the average value, along with the most recent **order_id**, into **avg_qty**.

4. Create a trigger called **avg_trigger** that calls the **avg_qty** function after each row is inserted into the **order_info** table.

5. Insert some new rows into the **order_info** table with quantities of **6**, **7**, and **8**.

6. Look at the entries in **avg_qty_log**. Is the average quantity of each order increasing?

   Expected output:

```
order_id |      avg_qty
---------+--------------------
    1625 | 4.7500000000000000
    1626 | 5.0000000000000000
    1627 | 5.3000000000000000
(3 rows)
```

In this activity, you created a trigger for continuously keeping track of the data that is updated in the database.

> **NOTE**
>
> The solution for this activity can be found on page 475.

SUMMARY

In this chapter, you have covered a wide variety of topics designed to help you understand and improve the performance of your SQL queries. The chapter began with a thorough discussion of the Query Planner, (including the **EXPLAIN** and **ANALYZE** statements) as well as various indexing methods. You discussed different compromises and considerations that can be made to reduce the time needed to execute queries. You considered several scenarios where indexing methods would be of benefit and others where the Query Planner may disregard the index, thus reducing the efficiency of the query. You then moved on to learn how to kill long-running queries. You also covered an in-depth look at functions and automatic function calls using triggers and learned about the **\df** and **\sf** commands.

In the next chapter, you will combine all the topics you have covered thus far in a final case study, applying your SQL knowledge and the scientific method in general, as you solve a real-world problem.

9

USING SQL TO UNCOVER THE TRUTH: A CASE STUDY

OVERVIEW

By the end of this chapter, you will be able to solve real-world problems outside of those described within this book by using the scientific method and critical thinking. You will be able to analyze your data and convert it into actionable tasks and information. To accomplish these goals, you will examine an extensive and detailed real-world case study of sales data. This case study will not only demonstrate the processes used in SQL analysis to find solutions for actual problems but will also provide you with confidence and experience in solving such problems.

INTRODUCTION

Throughout *SQL for Data Analytics, Third Edition*, you have learned a range of new skills (including basic descriptive statistics, SQL commands, and importing and exporting data in PostgreSQL) as well as more advanced methods to optimize and automate SQL (such as functions and triggers). In this final chapter of this workshop, you will combine these new skills with the scientific method and critical thinking to solve a real-world problem and determine the cause of an unexpected drop in sales.

This chapter provides a case study and will help you build your confidence in applying your new SQL skillset to your own problem domains. To solve the problem presented in this case study, you will use the complete range of your newly developed skills, from using basic SQL searches to filtering out the available information to aggregating and joining multiple sets of information and using windowing methods to group the data in a logical manner. By completing case studies such as this, you will refine one of the key tools in your data analysis toolkit, that is, SQL, to provide a boost to your data science career.

CASE STUDY

Throughout this chapter, you will work on a case study. The new ZoomZoom **Bat** Scooter is now available for sale exclusively through its website. Sales are looking good, but suddenly, preorders start plunging by 20% after a couple of weeks. What is going on? As the best data analyst at ZoomZoom, you have been assigned to figure this out.

THE SCIENTIFIC METHOD

In this case study, you will be following the scientific method to solve the problem. Here, you will test guesses (or hypotheses) using objectively collected data. The scientific method can be decomposed into the following key steps:

1. Define the question to answer, which in this case is what caused the drop in sales of the **Bat** Scooter after approximately 2 weeks.

2. Perform complete background research to gather sufficient information to propose an initial hypothesis for the event or phenomenon.

3. Construct a hypothesis to explain the event or answer the question.

4. Define and execute an objective experiment to test the hypothesis. In an ideal scenario, all aspects of the experiment should be controlled and fixed, except for the phenomenon that is being tested under the hypothesis.

5. Analyze the data that was collected during the experiment.

6. Report the results of the analysis, which will hopefully explain why there was a drop in the sale of **Bat** Scooters.

> **NOTE**
>
> In this chapter, you are completing a post hoc analysis of the data; that is, the event has happened, and all the available data has been collected. Post hoc data analysis is particularly useful when events have been recorded that cannot be repeated or when certain external factors cannot be controlled.

You can perform your analysis with the post hoc analysis data. You will also extract information to support or refute your hypothesis. You will, however, be unable to definitively confirm or reject the hypothesis without practical experimentation. The question that will be the subject of this chapter and that you need to answer is this: why did the sales of the ZoomZoom **Bat** Scooter drop by approximately 20% after about 2 weeks?

So, to make the process easier, you will first start with the basic SQL skills for data collection and processing.

EXERCISE 9.01: PRELIMINARY DATA COLLECTION USING SQL TECHNIQUES

In this exercise, you will collect preliminary data using SQL techniques. You have been told that the preorders for the ZoomZoom **Bat** Scooter were good, but the orders suddenly dropped by 20%. The goal of this exercise is to answer some core questions about **Bat** Scooter production, such as the following:

- When did production start?

- How much was the **Bat** Scooter selling for?

- How does the **Bat** Scooter compare with other types of scooters in terms of price?

Perform the following steps to complete this exercise:

1. Load the **sqlda** database using psql.

2. List the **model**, **base_msrp** (**MSRP** stands for **manufacturer's suggested retail price**), and **production_start_date** fields within the product table for product types matching **scooter**:

```
SELECT
    model, base_msrp, production_start_date
FROM
    Products
WHERE
    product_type='scooter'
ORDER BY
    base_msrp;
```

The following table shows the details of all the products with the **scooter** product type:

```
            model          | base_msrp | production_start_date
---------------------------+-----------+----------------------
 Lemon Zester              |    349.99 | 2021-10-01 00:00:00
 Lemon                     |    399.99 | 2012-10-28 00:00:00
 Lemon                     |    499.99 | 2015-12-27 00:00:00
 Bat                       |    599.99 | 2019-06-07 00:00:00
 Blade                     |    699.99 | 2017-02-17 00:00:00
 Bat Limited Edition       |    699.99 | 2019-10-13 00:00:00
 Lemon Limited Edition     |    799.99 | 2013-08-30 00:00:00
(7 rows)
```

Looking at the results from the search, you can see two scooter products with **Bat** in the name: **Bat** and **Bat Limited Edition**. The **Bat** Scooter started production on **2019-06-07** (date format: *YYYY-MM-DD*), with a suggested retail price of $599.99, and the **Bat Limited Edition** Scooter started production approximately 4 months later, on **2019-10-13**, with a price of $699.99.

Looking at the product information, you can see that the **Bat** Scooter's price looks different from the others as it is the only scooter with a suggested retail price of $599.99. There are others at $699.99 and above, or $499.99 and below. But **Bat** Scooter sits right in between.

Similarly, if you consider the production start date in isolation, the original **Bat** Scooter is again unique as it is the only scooter starting production in the second quarter, and one of only two in the first half of the year. All other scooters start production in the second half of the year, with only the Blade Scooter starting production in February.

Now that you have a basic understanding of the products, you would like to see how they perform in the market. To use the sales information in conjunction with the product information available, you also need to get the product ID for each of the scooters.

3. Extract the model names and product IDs for the scooters available within the database. You will need this information to reconcile the product information with the available sales information:

```
SELECT
   model, product_id
FROM
   Products
WHERE
   product_type='scooter';
```

The preceding query yields the product IDs shown in the following table:

```
         model          | product_id
------------------------+------------
  Lemon                 |      1
  Lemon Limited Edition |      2
  Lemon                 |      3
  Blade                 |      5
  Bat                   |      7
  Bat Limited Edition   |      8
  Lemon Zester          |     12
(7 rows)
```

4. In the following steps, you will go through a series of queries for analysis. In the real world, these analytics will involve a lot of research and experimentation and a lot of back and forth to find the proper SQL statements. As such, it is a good habit to save query results that you feel may be helpful, either as a view or directly into a table. In this step, you will insert the results of the preceding query into a new table called **product_names** and then select the newly inserted content:

```
SELECT
    model, product_id
INTO
    product_names
FROM
    Products
WHERE
    product_type='scooter';


SELECT
    *
FROM
    product_names;
```

Inspect the contents of the **product_names** table, as shown here:

```
          model         | product_id
------------------------+------------
    Lemon               |          1
    Lemon Limited Edition |        2
    Lemon               |          3
    Blade               |          5
    Bat                 |          7
    Bat Limited Edition |          8
    Lemon Zester        |         12
(7 rows)
```

> **NOTE**
>
> To access the source code for this specific section, please refer to https://packt.link/b3wRQ.

By completing this preliminary data collection step, you have obtained the information that is required to collect sales data on the **Bat** Scooter, as well as other scooter products for comparison. While *Exercise 9.01: Preliminary Data Collection Using SQL Techniques* involved using the simplest SQL commands, it has already yielded some useful information and should not be underestimated.

In *Exercise 9.02: Extracting the Sales Information*, you will try to extract the sales information related to the reduction in sales of the **Bat** Scooter.

EXERCISE 9.02: EXTRACTING THE SALES INFORMATION

In this exercise, you will use a combination of simple **SELECT** statements as well as aggregate and window functions to examine the sales data. You can use the preliminary information at hand to extract the **Bat** Scooter sales records and understand what is going on. You have a table, **product_names**, that contains both the model names and product IDs. You will need to combine this information with the sales records and extract only those for the **Bat** Scooter:

1. Load the **sqlda** database with psql.

2. To get yourself familiarized with the table, list the available fields in the **sqlda** database:

```
\d sales
```

The preceding query yields the following fields that are present in the database:

```
                            Table "public.sales"
            Column             |            Type             | Collation |
 Nullable | Default
-------------------------------+-----------------------------+-----------+--
--------+----------
  customer_id                  | bigint                      |           |
  product_id                   | bigint                      |           |
  sales_transaction_date       | timestamp without time zone |           |
  sales_amount                 | double precision            |           |
  channel                      | text                        |           |
  dealership_id                | double precision            |           |
```

In this result, you can see references to customer and product IDs, as well as the transaction date, sales information, the sales channel, and the dealership ID.

3. Use an inner join on the **product_id** columns of both the **product_names** table and the **sales** table. From the result of the inner join, select **model**, **customer_id**, **sales_transaction_date**, **sales_amount**, **channel**, and **dealership_id**, and store the values in a separate table called **product_sales**:

```sql
SELECT
  model,
  customer_id,
  sales_transaction_date::DATE as sales_date,
  sales_amount,
  channel,
  dealership_id
INTO
  products_sales
FROM
  Sales
INNER JOIN
  product_names
ON
  sales.product_id=product_names.product_id;
```

4. Note that the **sales_transaction_date** column is cast from **TIMESTAMP** data type to a **DATE** column **sales_date**. Since you need to determine the sales drop in terms of days, there is no need to keep the data about time. The date would suffice.

5. If you get an error, please drop the **products_sales** table using the following **DROP** query and rerun the code:

```sql
DROP TABLE IF EXISTS products_sales;
```

> **NOTE**
>
> Throughout this chapter, you will be storing the results of queries and calculations in separate tables as this will allow you to look at the results of the individual steps in the analysis. In a commercial/production setting, you would only store the end result in a separate table, depending on the context of the problem being solved.

6. Look at the first five rows of this new table by using the following query:

```
SELECT
    *
FROM
    products_sales
LIMIT
    5;
```

The following table lists the top five customers who made a purchase. It shows the sale amount and the transaction details, such as the date and time:

```
 model | customer_id | sales_date | sales_amount | channel  |
dealership_id
-------+-------------+------------+--------------+----------+--------
-------
 Lemon |       42104 | 2015-01-12 |      319.992 | internet |
 Lemon |       41604 | 2014-11-25 |       399.99 | internet |
 Lemon |       41575 | 2013-02-06 |      319.992 | internet |
 Lemon |       41531 | 2013-05-04 |       399.99 | internet |
 Lemon |       41443 | 2014-01-18 |       399.99 | internet |
(5 rows)
```

7. Select all the information from the **product_sales** table that is available for the **Bat** Scooter and order the sales information by **sales_date** in ascending order. By ordering the data in this way, you can look at the first few days of the sales records in detail:

```
SELECT
    *
FROM
    products_sales
WHERE
    model='Bat'
ORDER BY
    sales_date;
```

The preceding query generates the following output:

```
model | customer_id | sales_date | sales_amount |  channel   |
dealership_id
-------+-------------+------------+--------------+------------+------
----------
 Bat   |   42213 | 2019-06-07 |  599.99 | internet   |
 Bat   |   45868 | 2019-06-07 |  599.99 | internet   |
 Bat   |   11678 | 2019-06-07 |  599.99 | internet   |
 Bat   |    4319 | 2019-06-07 |  599.99 | internet   |
 Bat   |   31307 | 2019-06-07 |  599.99 | internet   |
 Bat   |   40250 | 2019-06-07 |  599.99 | dealership |  4
 Bat   |   35497 | 2019-06-07 |  599.99 | dealership |  2
 Bat   |   24125 | 2019-06-07 |  599.99 | dealership |  1
 Bat   |    4553 | 2019-06-07 |  599.99 | dealership | 11
 Bat   |    6322 | 2019-06-08 |  599.99 | internet   |
 Bat   |   45880 | 2019-06-08 |  599.99 | dealership |  7
 Bat   |   47790 | 2019-06-08 |  599.99 | dealership | 20
 Bat   |   43477 | 2019-06-08 |  599.99 | internet   |
 Bat   |    6342 | 2019-06-08 |  599.99 | internet   |
 Bat   |   46653 | 2019-06-08 |  599.99 | dealership |  6
 Bat   |   48809 | 2019-06-09 |  599.99 | internet   |
 Bat   |   49856 | 2019-06-09 |  599.99 | dealership | 10
 Bat   |   39653 | 2019-06-09 |  599.99 | dealership |  7
 Bat   |   49226 | 2019-06-09 | 539.991 | internet   |
 Bat   |   43013 | 2019-06-09 |  599.99 | dealership | 16
 Bat   |   42625 | 2019-06-09 |  599.99 | internet   |
 Bat   |   45256 | 2019-06-09 | 539.991 | dealership |  7
 Bat   |   23679 | 2019-06-09 | 539.991 | internet   |
 Bat   |    9045 | 2019-06-09 |  599.99 | dealership | 19
 Bat   |   18602 | 2019-06-09 |  599.99 | internet   |
 Bat   |   14298 | 2019-06-10 |  599.99 | internet   |
 Bat   |   21305 | 2019-06-10 |  599.99 | dealership | 19
-- More --
```

8. As you can see, there is one line stating **-- More --**, which means there are more rows in the result set than what is displayed by psql. To find out how many rows are returned in the result set, you will count the number of records available by using the following query:

```
SELECT
    COUNT(model)
FROM
    products_sales
WHERE
    model='Bat';
```

The model count for the **Bat** model is as follows:

```
count
---------
7328
(1 row)
```

So, you have **7328** sales, beginning on **2019-06-07**. Check the date of the final sales record by performing *step 8*.

9. Determine the last sale date for the **Bat** Scooter by selecting the maximum (using the **MAX** function) for **sales_date**:

```
SELECT
    MAX(sales_date)
FROM
    products_sales
WHERE
    model='Bat';
```

The last sale date is as follows:

```
max
----------------------
2022-01-25
```

The last sale in the database occurred on **2022-01-25**.

10. Now that you know the number of rows, as well as the starting and ending dates of the sales result for the **Bat** Scooter, you can focus on analyzing its sales pattern. You will collect the daily sales volume for the **Bat** Scooter and place it in a new table called **bat_sales** to confirm the information provided by the sales team stating that sales dropped by 20% after the first 2 weeks:

```
SELECT
  *
INTO
  bat_sales
FROM
  products_sales
WHERE
  model='Bat'
ORDER BY
  sales_date;
```

11. Now, display the first five records of **bat_sales** ordered by **sales_date**:

```
SELECT
  *
FROM
  bat_sales
ORDER BY
  sales_date
LIMIT
  5;
```

The following is the output of the preceding code:

```
model | customer_id | sales_date | sales_amount | channel  |
dealership_id
-------+-------------+------------+--------------+----------+--------
-------
 Bat   |       45868 | 2019-06-07 |       599.99 | internet |
 Bat   |       11678 | 2019-06-07 |       599.99 | internet |
 Bat   |        4319 | 2019-06-07 |       599.99 | internet |
 Bat   |       31307 | 2019-06-07 |       599.99 | internet |
 Bat   |       42213 | 2019-06-07 |       599.99 | internet |
(5 rows)
```

12. Now that you have the individual sales information, you will need to start looking at the daily sales as this exercise is aimed at researching daily sales patterns. Create a new table (**bat_sales_daily**) containing the sales transaction dates and a daily count of total sales:

```
SELECT
    sales_date,
    COUNT(sales_date)
INTO
    bat_sales_daily
FROM
    bat_sales
GROUP BY
    sales_date
ORDER BY
    sales_date;
```

13. Now that you know the daily number of sales, the next few steps will help you determine/confirm whether there has been a drop in sales. Examine the first **22** records (a little over 3 weeks), as sales were reported to have dropped after approximately the first 2 weeks:

```
SELECT
    *
FROM
    bat_sales_daily
ORDER BY
    sales_date
LIMIT
    22;
```

This will display the following output:

```
sales_date | count
------------+-------
 2019-06-07 |    9
 2019-06-08 |    6
 2019-06-09 |   10
 2019-06-10 |   10
 2019-06-11 |    5
 2019-06-12 |   10
 2019-06-13 |   14
```

```
2019-06-14 |      9
2019-06-15 |     11
2019-06-16 |     12
2019-06-17 |     10
2019-06-18 |      6
2019-06-19 |      2
2019-06-20 |      5
2019-06-21 |      6
2019-06-22 |      9
2019-06-23 |      2
2019-06-24 |      4
2019-06-25 |      7
2019-06-26 |      5
2019-06-27 |      5
2019-06-28 |      3
(22 rows)
```

You can see a drop in sales after **2019-06-17**, since there are 7 days in the first 11 rows that record double-digit sales and none over the next 11 days.

> **NOTE**
>
> To access the source code for this specific section, please refer to
> https://packt.link/b3wRQ.

At this stage, you can confirm that there has been a drop in sales, although you are yet to precisely quantify the extent of the reduction or the reason for the drop in sales. Well, you will discover the extent of the reduction in the next activity.

ACTIVITY 9.01: QUANTIFYING THE SALES DROP

In this activity, you will use your knowledge of the windowing methods that you learned about in *Chapter 4, Aggregate Functions for Data Analysis*, and *Chapter 5, Window Functions for Data Analysis*. In *Exercise 9.02, Extracting the Sales Information*, you identified the occurrence of the sales drop as being approximately 10 days after launch. Here, you will try to quantify the drop in sales for the **Bat** Scooter.

Perform the following steps to complete this activity:

1. Load the **sqlda** database with psql.

2. Using the **OVER** and **ORDER BY** statements, compute the daily cumulative sum of sales. This provides you with a discrete count of sales over a period of time on a daily basis. Insert the results into a new table called **bat_sales_growth**.

3. Compute a seven-day **lag** of the **sum** column, and then insert all the columns of **bat_sales_daily** and the new **lag** column into a new table, **bat_sales_daily_delay**. This **lag** column indicates the sales amount a week prior to the given record, allowing you to compare sales with the previous week.

4. Inspect the first 15 rows of **bat_sales_growth**.

5. Compute the sales growth as a percentage, comparing the current sales volume to that of a week prior. Insert the resulting table into a new table called **bat_sales_delay_vol**.

6. Compare the first 22 values of the **bat_sales_delay_vol** table to ascertain a sales drop.

   The expected output is as follows:

sales_date	count	sum	lag	volume
2019-06-07	9	9		
2019-06-08	6	15		
2019-06-09	10	25		
2019-06-10	10	35		
2019-06-11	5	40		
2019-06-12	10	50		
2019-06-13	14	64		
2019-06-14	9	73	9	7.1111111111111111
2019-06-15	11	84	15	4.6000000000000000
2019-06-16	12	96	25	2.8400000000000000
2019-06-17	10	106	35	2.0285714285714286
2019-06-18	6	112	40	1.8000000000000000
2019-06-19	2	114	50	1.2800000000000000
2019-06-20	5	119	64	0.8593750000000000000
2019-06-21	6	125	73	0.7123287671232876123
2019-06-22	9	134	84	0.5952380952380952810
2019-06-23	2	136	96	0.4166666666666666667
2019-06-24	4	140	106	0.3207547169811320754

```
2019-06-25 |      7 | 147 | 112 | 0.31250000000000000000
2019-06-26 |      5 | 152 | 114 | 0.33333333333333333333
2019-06-27 |      5 | 157 | 119 | 0.31932773109243697479
2019-06-28 |      3 | 160 | 125 | 0.28000000000000000000
(22 rows)
```

> **NOTE**
>
> The solution for this activity can be found on page 477.

EXERCISE 9.03: LAUNCH TIMING ANALYSIS

In this exercise, you will try to identify the causes of a sales drop. Now that you have confirmed the presence of the sales growth drop, you will try to explain the cause of the event. You will test the hypothesis that the timing of the scooter launch is the reason for the reduction in sales. Remember from *Exercise 9.01*, *Preliminary Data Collection Using SQL Techniques*, that the ZoomZoom **Bat** Scooter launched on **2019-06-07**. Perform the following steps to complete this exercise:

1. Load the **sqlda** database from psql.

2. Examine the other products in the database. To determine whether the launch date is the reason for the sales drop, you need to compare the ZoomZoom **Bat** Scooter to other scooter products according to the launch date. Execute the following query to check the launch dates:

```
SELECT * FROM products;
```

The result shows the launch dates for all the products:

```
product_id |            model          | year | product_type | base_msrp
| production_start_date | production_end_date
------------+---------------------------+------+--------------+----------
-+-----------------------+---------------------
          1 | Lemon                     | 2013 | scooter      |     399.99
| 2012-10-28 00:00:00   | 2015-02-03 00:00:00
          2 | Lemon Limited Edition     | 2014 | scooter      |     799.99
| 2013-08-30 00:00:00   | 2013-11-24 00:00:00
          3 | Lemon                     | 2016 | scooter      |     499.99
| 2015-12-27 00:00:00   | 2021-08-24 00:00:00
          5 | Blade                     | 2017 | scooter      |     699.99
| 2017-02-17 00:00:00   | 2017-09-23 00:00:00
          7 | Bat                       | 2019 | scooter      |     599.99
| 2019-06-07 00:00:00   |
          8 | Bat Limited Edition       | 2020 | scooter      |     699.99
| 2019-10-13 00:00:00   |
```

```
        12 | Lemon Zester           | 2022 | scooter    |    349.99
| 2021-10-01 00:00:00   |
         4 | Model Chi              | 2017 | automobile | 115000.00
| 2017-02-17 00:00:00   | 2021-08-24 00:00:00
         6 | Model Sigma            | 2018 | automobile |  65500.00
| 2017-12-10 00:00:00   | 2021-05-28 00:00:00
         9 | Model Epsilon          | 2020 | automobile |  35000.00
| 2019-10-13 00:00:00   |
        10 | Model Gamma            | 2020 | automobile |  85750.00
| 2019-10-13 00:00:00   |
        11 | Model Chi              | 2022 | automobile |  95000.00
| 2021-10-01 00:00:00   |
(12 rows)
```

All the other products were launched outside of the second quarter, unlike the **Bat** Scooter, which was launched in June.

3. List all the scooters from the **products** table, since you are only interested in comparing scooters:

```
SELECT
  *
FROM
  products
WHERE
  product_type='scooter';
```

The result shows all the information for products with the product type of **scooter**:

```
 product_id |          model          | year | product_type | base_msrp
 | production_start_date | production_end_date
------------+-------------------------+------+--------------+-----------
-+-----------------------+----------------------
          1 | Lemon                   | 2013 | scooter      |    399.99
| 2012-10-28 00:00:00   | 2015-02-03 00:00:00
          2 | Lemon Limited Edition   | 2014 | scooter      |    799.99
| 2013-08-30 00:00:00   | 2013-11-24 00:00:00
          3 | Lemon                   | 2016 | scooter      |    499.99
| 2015-12-27 00:00:00   | 2021-08-24 00:00:00
          5 | Blade                   | 2017 | scooter      |    699.99
| 2017-02-17 00:00:00   | 2017-09-23 00:00:00
          7 | Bat                     | 2019 | scooter      |    599.99
| 2019-06-07 00:00:00   |
          8 | Bat Limited Edition     | 2020 | scooter      |    699.99
| 2019-10-13 00:00:00   |
         12 | Lemon Zester            | 2022 | scooter      |    349.99
| 2021-10-01 00:00:00   |
(7 rows)
```

To test the hypothesis that the time of year had an impact on sales performance, you require a scooter model to use as the control or reference group. In an ideal world, you could launch the ZoomZoom **Bat** Scooter in a different location or region, but just at a different time, and then compare the two. However, this is not possible here.

Instead, you will choose a similar scooter that was launched at a different time. There are different options in the product database, each with its own similarities and differences from the experimental group (ZoomZoom **Bat** Scooter). You could choose the **Bat Limited Edition** Scooter as the control group and use it for comparison. As you can see from the preceding query result, it is slightly more expensive, but it was launched only 4 months after the **Bat** Scooter.

Looking at its name, the **Bat Limited Edition** Scooter seems to share most features with ZoomZoom **Bat** Scooter except for a few extra features because it is limited edition.

4. Select the first five rows of the **sales** database:

```
SELECT * FROM sales LIMIT 5;
```

The sales information for the first five customers is as follows:

```
 customer_id | product_id | sales_transaction_date | sales_amount |
channel  | dealership_id
--------------+------------+------------------------+--------------+--
---------+---------------
       27275 |          7 | 2021-03-16 08:40:24    |              |     539.991 |
internet |
        2017 |          7 | 2019-12-27 07:36:20    |              |     599.99 |
internet |
        7213 |          7 | 2021-12-04 18:43:30    |              |     479.992 |
internet |
       13194 |          7 | 2019-10-26 12:16:05    |              |     539.991 |
internet |
       34454 |          7 | 2020-01-03 04:11:06    |              |     479.992 |
internet |
(5 rows)
```

5. Select the **model** and **sales_transaction_date** columns from both the products and sales tables for the **Bat Limited Edition** Scooter. Store the results in a table, **bat_ltd_sales**, ordered by the **sales_transaction_date** column, from the earliest date to the latest:

```
SELECT
  products.model,
```

```
  sales.sales_transaction_date
INTO
  bat_ltd_sales
FROM
  sales
INNER JOIN
  products
ON
  sales.product_id=products.product_id
WHERE
  sales.product_id=8
ORDER BY
  sales.sales_transaction_date;
```

Here is the output:

```
SELECT 5803
```

6. Select the first five lines of **bat_ltd_sales** using the following query:

```
SELECT * FROM bat_ltd_sales LIMIT 5;
```

The following table shows the transaction details for the first five entries of **Bat Limited Edition**:

```
        model        | sales_transaction_date
---------------------+-------------------------
 Bat Limited Edition | 2019-10-13 01:49:02
 Bat Limited Edition | 2019-10-13 09:42:37
 Bat Limited Edition | 2019-10-13 10:48:31
 Bat Limited Edition | 2019-10-13 12:22:41
 Bat Limited Edition | 2019-10-13 13:51:34
(5 rows)
```

7. Calculate the total number of sales for **Bat Limited Edition**. You can check this by using the **COUNT** function:

```
SELECT COUNT(model) FROM bat_ltd_sales;
```

Here is the total sales count:

```
Count
---------
5803
(1 row)
```

This is compared to the original **Bat** Scooter, which sold 7,328 units.

8. Check the transaction details of the last Bat Limited Edition sale. You can check this by using the **MAX** function:

```
SELECT MAX(sales_transaction_date) FROM bat_ltd_sales;
```

The transaction details of the last **Bat Limited Edition** product are as follows:

```
max
--------------------
2022-01-25  15:08:03
```

9. Adjust the table to cast the transaction date column as a date, discarding the time information as you are only interested in the date of the sale, not the date and time of the sale. To do this, write the following query:

```
ALTER TABLE
    bat_ltd_sales
ALTER COLUMN
    sales_transaction_date TYPE date;
```

10. Again, select the first five records of **bat_ltd_sales** to check that the type of the **sales_transaction_date** column is changed to date:

```
SELECT
    *
FROM
    bat_ltd_sales
LIMIT
    5;
```

The following table shows the first five records of **bat_ltd_sales**:

```
        model        | sales_transaction_date
---------------------+------------------------
 Bat Limited Edition | 2019-10-13
 Bat Limited Edition | 2019-10-13
 Bat Limited Edition | 2019-10-13
 Bat Limited Edition | 2019-10-13
 Bat Limited Edition | 2019-10-13
(5 rows)
```

11. Similar to the standard **Bat** Scooter, create a count of sales of the **Bat Limited Edition** Scooter sale on a daily basis. Insert the results into the **bat_ltd_sales_count** table by using the following query:

```
SELECT
    sales_transaction_date,
    count(sales_transaction_date)
INTO
    bat_ltd_sales_count
FROM
    bat_ltd_sales
GROUP BY
    sales_transaction_date
ORDER BY
    sales_transaction_date;
```

12. List the sales count of all the **Bat Limited** products using the following query:

```
SELECT
    *
FROM
    bat_ltd_sales_count
ORDER BY
    sales_transaction_date;
```

The sales count contains many rows. Here are the first 17 rows:

```
 sales_transaction_date | count
------------------------+-------
 2019-10-13             |     6
 2019-10-14             |     2
 2019-10-15             |     1
 2019-10-16             |     4
 2019-10-17             |     5
 2019-10-18             |     6
 2019-10-19             |     5
 2019-10-20             |     4
 2019-10-21             |     6
 2019-10-22             |     2
 2019-10-23             |     2
 2019-10-24             |     2
 2019-10-25             |     4
```

```
2019-10-26              |    4
2019-10-27              |    5
2019-10-28              |    1
2019-10-29              |    3
```

13. Compute the cumulative sum of the daily sales figures and insert the resulting table into **bat_ltd_sales_growth**:

```
SELECT
  *,
  sum(count) OVER (ORDER BY sales_transaction_date)
INTO
  bat_ltd_sales_growth
FROM
  bat_ltd_sales_count;
```

14. Select the first 22 days of sales records from **bat_ltd_sales_growth**:

```
SELECT
  *
FROM
  bat_ltd_sales_growth
ORDER BY
  sales_transaction_date
LIMIT
  22;
```

The following table displays the first 22 records of sales growth:

```
sales_transaction_date | count | sum
-----------------------+-------+-----
2019-10-13              |    6 |    6
2019-10-14              |    2 |    8
2019-10-15              |    1 |    9
2019-10-16              |    4 |   13
2019-10-17              |    5 |   18
2019-10-18              |    6 |   24
2019-10-19              |    5 |   29
2019-10-20              |    4 |   33
2019-10-21              |    6 |   39
2019-10-22              |    2 |   41
2019-10-23              |    2 |   43
2019-10-24              |    2 |   45
```

```
2019-10-25                |    4 |    49
2019-10-26                |    4 |    53
2019-10-27                |    5 |    58
2019-10-28                |    1 |    59
2019-10-29                |    3 |    62
2019-10-30                |    8 |    70
2019-10-31                |    4 |    74
2019-11-01                |    7 |    81
2019-11-02                |    7 |    88
2019-11-03                |    8 |    96
(22 rows)
```

15. Compare this sales record with the one for the original **Bat** Scooter sales using the following code. The table is from *Activity 9.01, Quantifying the Sales Drop*:

```
SELECT
  *
FROM
  bat_sales_growth
ORDER BY
  sales_date
LIMIT
  22;
```

The following table shows the sales details for the first 22 records of the **bat_sales_growth** table:

```
sales_date | count | sum
-------------+--------+-----
2019-06-07 |    9 |    9
2019-06-08 |    6 |   15
2019-06-09 |   10 |   25
2019-06-10 |   10 |   35
2019-06-11 |    5 |   40
2019-06-12 |   10 |   50
2019-06-13 |   14 |   64
2019-06-14 |    9 |   73
2019-06-15 |   11 |   84
2019-06-16 |   12 |   96
2019-06-17 |   10 |  106
2019-06-18 |    6 |  112
2019-06-19 |    2 |  114
```

```
2019-06-20 |      5 | 119
2019-06-21 |      6 | 125
2019-06-22 |      9 | 134
2019-06-23 |      2 | 136
2019-06-24 |      4 | 140
2019-06-25 |      7 | 147
2019-06-26 |      5 | 152
2019-06-27 |      5 | 157
2019-06-28 |      3 | 160
(22 rows)
```

As you can see from the preceding numbers, sales of the **Bat Limited Edition** scooter did not reach double digits during the first 22 days, nor did the daily volume of sales fluctuate as much. In keeping with the overall sales figure, the Limited Edition scooters sold 64 fewer units over the first 22 days.

16. Compute the seven-day **lag** function for the **sum** column and insert the results into the **bat_ltd_sales_delay** table:

```
SELECT
  *,
  lag(sum , 7) OVER (ORDER BY sales_transaction_date)
INTO
  bat_ltd_sales_delay
FROM
  bat_ltd_sales_growth;
```

17. Compute the sales growth for **bat_ltd_sales_delay** in a similar manner that you did in *Activity 9.01*, *Quantifying the Sales Drop*. Label the column for the results of this calculation **volume** and store the resulting table in **bat_ltd_ sales_vol**:

```
SELECT
  *,
  (sum-lag)/lag AS volume
INTO
  bat_ltd_sales_vol
FROM
  bat_ltd_sales_delay;
```

18. Look at the first 22 records of sales in **bat_ltd_sales_vol**:

```
SELECT
  *
FROM
  bat_ltd_sales_vol
ORDER BY
  Sales_transaction_date
LIMIT
  22;
```

The sales volume can be seen as follows:

```
sales_transaction_date | count | sum | lag |       volume
-----------------------+-------+-----+-----+--------------------
 2019-10-13            |     6 |   6 |     |
 2019-10-14            |     2 |   8 |     |
 2019-10-15            |     1 |   9 |     |
 2019-10-16            |     4 |  13 |     |
 2019-10-17            |     5 |  18 |     |
 2019-10-18            |     6 |  24 |     |
 2019-10-19            |     5 |  29 |     |
 2019-10-20            |     4 |  33 |   6 | 4.5000000000000000
 2019-10-21            |     6 |  39 |   8 | 3.8750000000000000
 2019-10-22            |     2 |  41 |   9 | 3.5555555555555556
 2019-10-23            |     2 |  43 |  13 | 2.3076923076923077
 2019-10-24            |     2 |  45 |  18 | 1.5000000000000000
 2019-10-25            |     4 |  49 |  24 | 1.0416666666666667
 2019-10-26            |     4 |  53 |  29 | 0.8275862068965517
 2019-10-27            |     5 |  58 |  33 | 0.7575757575757575
 2019-10-28            |     1 |  59 |  39 | 0.5128205128205128
 2019-10-29            |     3 |  62 |  41 | 0.5121951219512195
 2019-10-30            |     8 |  70 |  43 | 0.6279069767441860
 2019-10-31            |     4 |  74 |  45 | 0.6444444444444444
 2019-11-01            |     7 |  81 |  49 | 0.6530612244897959
 2019-11-02            |     7 |  88 |  53 | 0.6603773584905660
 2019-11-03            |     8 |  96 |  58 | 0.6551724137931034
(22 rows)
```

Looking at the **volume** column, you can see that the sales growth is more consistent than for the original **Bat** Scooter. The growth within the first week is less than that of the original model, but it is sustained over a longer period. After 22 days of sales, the sales growth of the Limited Edition scooter is 65% compared to the previous week, as compared with the 28% growth you identified in *Activity 9.01, Quantifying the Sales Drop*.

> **NOTE**
>
> To access the source code for this specific section, please refer to https://packt.link/b3wRQ.

At this stage, you have collected data from two similar products that were launched at different periods and found some differences in the trajectory of the sales growth over the first 3 weeks of sales. In a professional setting, you may also consider employing more sophisticated statistical comparison methods, such as tests for differences in mean, variance, or survival analysis. These methods lie outside the scope of this book; therefore, you will only use simple comparison in this chapter.

While you can see that there is a difference in sales between the two **Bat** Scooters, you cannot rule out the fact that the sales differences can be attributed to the difference in the sales price of the two scooters. The Limited Edition scooter is $100 more expensive. In the next activity, you will compare the sales of the **Bat** Scooter to the 2016 **Lemon**, which is $100 cheaper, was launched 3 years prior, is no longer in production, and started production in the first half of the calendar year.

ACTIVITY 9.02: ANALYZING THE DIFFERENCE IN THE SALES PRICE HYPOTHESIS

In this activity, you are going to investigate the hypothesis that the reduction in sales growth can be attributed to the price point of the **Bat** Scooter. Previously in this chapter, you considered the impact of the launch date. However, there could be another factor—the sales price included. If you consider the product list of scooters in *Exercise 9.01, Preliminary Data Collection Using SQL Techniques*, and exclude the **Bat** Scooter, you can see that there are two price categories: $699.99 and above or $499.99 and below. The **Bat** Scooter sits exactly between these two groups; perhaps the reduction in sales growth can be attributed to the different pricing models.

In this activity, you will test this hypothesis by comparing Bat sales to the 2016 **Lemon**, whose production started on **2015-12-27**:

```
          model           | base_msrp | production_start_date
--------------------------+-----------+------------------------
 Lemon Zester             |    349.99 | 2021-10-01 00:00:00
 Lemon                    |    399.99 | 2012-10-28 00:00:00
 Lemon                    |    499.99 | 2015-12-27 00:00:00
 Bat                      |    599.99 | 2019-06-07 00:00:00
 Blade                    |    699.99 | 2017-02-17 00:00:00
 Bat Limited Edition      |    699.99 | 2019-10-13 00:00:00
 Lemon Limited Edition    |    799.99 | 2013-08-30 00:00:00
(7 rows)
```

Perform the following steps to complete this activity:

1. Load the **sqlda** database from psql.

2. Select the **sales_transaction_date** column for 2016 **Lemon** model sales and insert the column into a table called **lemon_sales**.

3. Count the sales records available for the 2016 **Lemon** model.

4. Display the latest **sales_transaction_date** column.

5. Convert the **sales_transaction_date** column into a **date** type.

6. Count the number of sales per day within the **lemon_sales** table and insert the data into a table called **lemon_sales_count**.

7. Calculate the cumulative sum of sales and insert the corresponding table into a new table labeled **lemon_sales_sum**.

8. Compute the seven-day **lag** function on the **sum** column and save the result to **lemon_sales_delay**.

9. Calculate the growth rate using the data from **lemon_sales_delay** and store the resulting table in **lemon_sales_growth**.

10. Inspect the first 22 records of the **lemon_sales_growth** table by examining the **volume** data.

The expected output is as follows:

```
sales_transaction_date | count | sum | lag |        volume
-----------------------+-------+-----+-----+----------------------
     2015-12-27         |    6  |   6 |     |
     2015-12-28         |    8  |  14 |     |
     2015-12-29         |    4  |  18 |     |
     2015-12-30         |    9  |  27 |     |
     2015-12-31         |    9  |  36 |     |
     2016-01-01         |    6  |  42 |     |
     2016-01-02         |    8  |  50 |     |
     2016-01-03         |    6  |  56 |   6 |    8.3333333333333333
     2016-01-04         |    6  |  62 |  14 |    3.4285714285714286
     2016-01-05         |    9  |  71 |  18 |    2.9444444444444444
     2016-01-06         |    3  |  74 |  27 |    1.7407407407407407
     2016-01-07         |    4  |  78 |  36 |    1.1666666666666667
     2016-01-08         |    7  |  85 |  42 |    1.0238095238095238
     2016-01-09         |    3  |  88 |  50 | 0.7600000000000000000
     2016-01-10         |    3  |  91 |  56 | 0.6250000000000000000
     2016-01-11         |    4  |  95 |  62 | 0.53225806451612903226
     2016-01-12         |    6  | 101 |  71 | 0.42253521126760563380
     2016-01-13         |    9  | 110 |  74 | 0.48648648648648648649
     2016-01-14         |    6  | 116 |  78 | 0.48717948717948717949
     2016-01-15         |    6  | 122 |  85 | 0.43529411764705882353
     2016-01-16         |   11  | 133 |  88 | 0.51136363636363636364
     2016-01-17         |    8  | 141 |  91 | 0.54945054945054945055
(22 rows)
```

Now that you have considered both the launch timing and the suggested retail price of the scooter as possible causes of the reduction in sales, it is time to direct your efforts to other potential causes, such as the rate of opening marketing emails. Does the marketing email opening rate influence sales growth throughout the first 3 weeks? You will find out in the next exercise.

> **NOTE**
>
> The solution for this activity can be found on page 480.

EXERCISE 9.04: ANALYZING SALES GROWTH BY EMAIL OPENING RATE

In this exercise, you will analyze the sales growth using the email opening rate. To investigate the hypothesis that a decrease in the rate of opening emails impacted the **Bat** Scooter sales rate, you will again select the **Bat** and **Lemon** Scooters and compare the email opening rates.

Perform the following steps to complete this exercise:

1. Load the **sqlda** database from psql.

2. Firstly, look at the **emails** table to see what information is available. Select the first five rows of the **emails** table:

```
SELECT
   *
FROM
   emails
LIMIT
   5;
```

The following result displays the email information for the first five rows:

```
email_id | customer_id |        email_subject        | opened | clicked
| bounced |        sent_date        | opened_date | clicked_date
----------+-------------+-----------------------------+--------+--------
-+----------+-------------------------+-------------+--------------
   175138 |         575 | Like a Bat out of Heaven | f      | f
| f       | 2019-05-19 15:00:00 |             |
   175484 |        1074 | Like a Bat out of Heaven | f      | f
| f       | 2019-05-19 15:00:00 |             |
   177740 |        4229 | Like a Bat out of Heaven | f      | f
| f       | 2019-05-19 15:00:00 |             |
   177826 |        4359 | Like a Bat out of Heaven | f      | f
| f       | 2019-05-19 15:00:00 |             |
   180518 |        8197 | Like a Bat out of Heaven | f      | f
| f       | 2019-05-19 15:00:00 |             |
(5 rows)
```

To investigate your hypothesis, you need to know whether an email was opened, when it was opened, as well as who the customer was who opened the email, and whether that customer purchased a scooter. If the email marketing campaign was successful in maintaining the sales growth rate, you would expect a customer to open an email soon before a scooter was purchased. The period in which the emails were sent, as well as the IDs of customers who received and opened an email, can help you determine whether a customer who made a sale may have been encouraged to do so following the receipt of an email.

3. To determine this hypothesis, you need to collect the **customer_id** column from both the **emails** table and the **bat_sales** table for the **Bat** Scooter, the **opened**, **sent_date**, **opened_date**, and **email_subject** columns from the **emails** table, as well as the **sales_date** column from the **bat_sales** table. Since you only want the email records of customers who purchased a **Bat** Scooter, you will join the **customer_id** column in both tables. Then, you will insert the results into a new table—**bat_emails**:

```
SELECT
    emails.email_subject,
    emails.customer_id,
    emails.opened,
    emails.sent_date,
    emails.opened_date,
    bat_sales.sales_date
INTO
    bat_emails
FROM
    emails
INNER JOIN
    bat_sales
ON
    bat_sales.customer_id=emails.customer_id
ORDER BY
    bat_sales.sales_date;
```

You will obtain the following output:

```
SELECT 40190
```

4. Select the first 10 rows of the **bat_emails** table, ordering the results by
    sales_date:

```
SELECT
    *
FROM
    bat_emails
ORDER BY
    sales_date
LIMIT
    10;
```

The following table shows the first 10 rows of the **bat_emails** table ordered by
sales_ date:

```
                        email_subject            | customer_id | opened
    |       sent_date       |      opened_date      | sales_date
-------------------------------------------------+-------------+-------
-+---------------------+---------------------+-----------
    Black Friday. Green Cars.                     |       31307 | f
    | 2020-07-21 15:00:00 |                         | 2019-06-07
    25% off all EVs. It's a Christmas Miracle!    |       24125 | f
    | 2019-07-23 15:00:00 |                         | 2019-06-07
    Like a Bat out of Heaven                      |       42213 | f
    | 2019-05-19 15:00:00 |                         | 2019-06-07
    A New Year, And Some New EVs                  |       40250 | f
    | 2021-09-03 15:00:00 |                         | 2019-06-07
    Shocking Holiday Savings On Electric Scooters |       24125 | f
    | 2016-07-26 15:00:00 |                         | 2019-06-07
    25% off all EVs. It's a Christmas Miracle!    |       42213 | f
    | 2019-07-23 15:00:00 |                         | 2019-06-07
    We Really Outdid Ourselves this Year          |       31307 | t
    | 2019-09-12 15:00:00 | 2019-09-13 22:03:20 | 2019-06-07
    Save the Planet with some Holiday Savings.    |       24125 | f
    |·2021-07-20 15:00:00 |                         | 2019-06-07
    We Really Outdid Ourselves this Year          |        4319 | f
    | 2019-09-12 15:00:00 |                         | 2019-06-07
    A Brand New Scooter...and Car                 |       24125 | f
    | 2016-12-31 15:00:00 |                         | 2019-06-07
(10 rows)
```

Here, you can see that there are several emails unopened, over a range of sent
dates, and that some customers have received multiple emails. Looking at the
subjects of the emails, some of them do not seem related to the ZoomZoom
scooters at all.

5. Select all rows where the **sent_date** email predates the **sales_date** column, order them by **customer_id**, and limit the output to the first 22 rows. This will help you find out which emails were sent to each customer before they purchased their scooter. Write the following query to do so:

```
SELECT
  *
FROM
  bat_emails
WHERE
  sent_date < sales_date
ORDER BY
  customer_id
LIMIT
  22;
```

The following table lists the emails that were sent to customers before the date in the **sales_date** column:

| | email_subject | | | customer_id | opened |
	sent_date		opened_date		sales_date	
25% off all EVs. It's a Christmas Miracle!				7	t	
2019-07-23 15:00:00	2019-07-24 03:55:30	2021-12-20				
A Brand New Scooter...and Car				7	f	
2016-12-31 15:00:00		2021-12-20				
We Really Outdid Ourselves this Year				7	f	
2019-09-12 15:00:00		2021-12-20				
Tis' the Season for Savings				7	f	
2018-07-23 15:00:00		2021-12-20				
Save the Planet with some Holiday Savings.				7	f	
2021-07-20 15:00:00		2021-12-20				
Shocking Holiday Savings On Electric Scooters				7	f	
2016-07-26 15:00:00		2021-12-20				
Like a Bat out of Heaven				7	f	
2019-05-19 15:00:00		2021-12-20				
The 2013 Lemon Scooter is Here				7	f	
2015-10-27 15:00:00		2021-12-20				
An Electric Car for a New Age				7	t	
2017-11-26 15:00:00	2017-11-27 15:10:55	2021-12-20				
We cut you a deal: 20%% off a Blade				7	t	
2017-05-15 15:00:00	2017-05-16 15:11:17	2021-12-20				
A New Year, And Some New EVs				7	f	
2021-09-03 15:00:00		2021-12-20				
Zoom Zoom Black Friday Sale				7	f	
2017-07-25 15:00:00		2021-12-20				
Black Friday. Green Cars.				7	f	
2020-07-21 15:00:00		2021-12-20				

```
An Electric Car for a New Age              |         22 | f
| 2017-11-26 15:00:00 |                     | 2020-04-10
The 2013 Lemon Scooter is Here             |         22 | f
| 2015-10-27 15:00:00 |                     | 2020-04-10
Zoom Zoom Black Friday Sale                |         22 | t
| 2017-07-25 15:00:00 | 2017-07-26 11:31:03 | 2020-04-10
A Brand New Scooter...and Car              |         22 | t
| 2016-12-31 15:00:00 | 2017-01-01 13:31:23 | 2020-04-10
Shocking Holiday Savings On Electric Scooters |      22 | f
| 2016-07-26 15:00:00 |                     | 2020-04-10
Like a Bat out of Heaven                   |         22 | f
| 2019-05-19 15:00:00 |                     | 2020-04-10
Tis' the Season for Savings                |         22 | f
| 2018-07-23 15:00:00 |                     | 2020-04-10
We Really Outdid Ourselves this Year       |         22 | f
| 2019-09-12 15:00:00 |                     | 2020-04-10
25% off all EVs. It's a Christmas Miracle! |         22 | f
| 2019-07-23 15:00:00 |                     | 2020-04-10
(22 rows)
```

6. Delete the rows of the **bat_emails** table where emails were sent more than six months prior to production. As you can see, there are some emails that were sent years before the transaction date. You can easily remove some of the unwanted emails by removing those sent before the **Bat** Scooter was in production. In the **products** table, the production start date for the **Bat** Scooter is **2019-06-07**:

```
DELETE FROM
  bat_emails
WHERE
  sent_date < '2019-06-07';
```

> **NOTE**
>
> In this exercise, you are removing information that you no longer require from an existing table. This differs from the previous exercises, where you created multiple tables: each with a slightly different information from the others. The technique you apply will differ, depending on the requirements of the problem being solved. Do you require a traceable record of analysis, or are efficiency and reduced storage the key?

7. Delete the rows where the sent date is after the purchase date since they are not relevant to the sales:

```
DELETE FROM
   bat_emails
WHERE
   sent_date > sales_date;
```

8. Delete those rows where the difference between the transaction date and the sent date exceeds 30 since you only want emails that were sent shortly before the scooter purchase. An email 1 year before is probably unlikely to influence a purchasing decision, but one that is closer to the purchase date may have influenced the sales decision. You will set a limit of 1 month (30 days) before the purchase. Write the following query to do so:

```
DELETE FROM
   Bat_emails
WHERE
   sales_date-sent_date > '30 days';
```

9. Examine the first 22 rows again, ordered by **customer_id**, by running the following query:

```
SELECT
   *
FROM
   bat_emails
ORDER BY
   customer_id
LIMIT
   22;
```

The following table shows the emails where the difference between the transaction date and the sent date is less than 30 days:

```
               email_subject              | customer_id | opened |
sent_date        |      opened_date       | sales_date
------------------------------------------+-------------+--------+-
--------------------+----------------------+------------
 25% off all EVs. It's a Christmas Miracle! |        129 | t      |
2019-07-23 15:00:00 | 2019-07-24 06:31:37 | 2019-07-26
 A New Year, And Some New EVs             |         145 | f      |
2021-09-03 15:00:00 |                      | 2021-09-16
 Black Friday. Green Cars.                |         150 | f      |
2020-07-21 15:00:00 |                      | 2020-08-15
 Black Friday. Green Cars.                |         173 | f      |
2020-07-21 15:00:00 |                      | 2020-08-01
 We Really Outdid Ourselves this Year     |         196 | f      |
2019-09-12 15:00:00 |                      | 2019-09-20
 We Really Outdid Ourselves this Year     |         319 | f      |
2019-09-12 15:00:00 |                      | 2019-09-26
 25% off all EVs. It's a Christmas Miracle! |        418 | f      |
2019-07-23 15:00:00 |                      | 2019-08-18
 A New Year, And Some New EVs             |         560 | t      |
2021-09-03 15:00:00 | 2021-09-04 15:56:14 | 2021-09-25
 We Really Outdid Ourselves this Year     |         600 | f      |
2019-09-12 15:00:00 |                      | 2019-09-15
 A New Year, And Some New EVs             |         660 | t      |
2021-09-03 15:00:00 | 2021-09-04 23:37:03 | 2021-09-04
 A New Year, And Some New EVs             |         681 | f      |
2021-09-03 15:00:00 |                      | 2021-09-09
 Black Friday. Green Cars.                |         806 | t      |
2020-07-21 15:00:00 | 2020-07-22 16:59:40 | 2020-07-26
 A New Year, And Some New EVs             |         881 | t      |
2021-09-03 15:00:00 | 2021-09-04 21:07:28 | 2021-09-18
 25% off all EVs. It's a Christmas Miracle! |        934 | t      |
2019-07-23 15:00:00 | 2019-07-24 09:22:45 | 2019-08-21
 25% off all EVs. It's a Christmas Miracle! |        983 | f      |
2019-07-23 15:00:00 |                      | 2019-07-27
 A New Year, And Some New EVs             |        1060 | f      |
2021-09-03 15:00:00 |                      | 2021-09-23
 25% off all EVs. It's a Christmas Miracle! |       1288 | f      |
2019-07-23 15:00:00 |                      | 2019-08-08
 25% off all EVs. It's a Christmas Miracle! |       1317 | f      |
2019-07-23 15:00:00 |                      | 2019-08-10
 A New Year, And Some New EVs             |        1400 | t      |
2021-09-03 15:00:00 | 2021-09-04 15:01:00 | 2021-09-06
 Save the Planet with some Holiday Savings. |       1417 | f      |
2021-07-20 15:00:00 |                      | 2021-07-23
 Save the Planet with some Holiday Savings. |       1433 | f      |
2021-07-20 15:00:00 |                      | 2021-08-19
 Black Friday. Green Cars.                |        1529 | f      |
2020-07-21 15:00:00 |                      | 2020-07-25
(22 rows)
```

At this stage, you have reasonably filtered the available data based on the dates the email was sent and opened. Looking at the preceding `email_subject` column, it also appears that there are a few emails unrelated to the **Bat** Scooter (for example, `25% of all EVs. It's a Christmas Miracle!` and `Black Friday. Green Cars`). These emails seem more related to electric cars than scooters, so you can remove them from your analysis.

10. Select the distinct value from the `email_subject` column to get a list of the different emails that were sent to customers:

```
SELECT
  DISTINCT(email_subject)
FROM
  bat_emails;
```

The following table shows a list of distinct email subjects:

```
                email_subject
-----------------------------------------------
 A New Year, And Some New EVs
 Save the Planet with some Holiday Savings.
 We Really Outdid Ourselves this Year
 Black Friday. Green Cars.
 25% off all EVs. It's a Christmas Miracle!
(5 rows)
```

11. Delete all the records that have **Black Friday** in the email subject. These emails do not appear to be relevant to the sale of the **Bat** Scooter:

```
DELETE FROM
  bat_emails
WHERE
  position('Black Friday' in email_subject)>0;
```

> **NOTE**
>
> The `position` function in the preceding example is used to find any records where the **Black Friday** string is anywhere in the **email_subject** column. Thus, you are deleting any rows where **Black Friday** is in the email subject. For more information on the PostgreSQL `position` function, refer to the following documentation regarding string functions: https://www.postgresql.org/docs/current/functions-string.html.

12. Delete all rows where **25% off all EVs. It's a Christmas Miracle!** and **A New Year, And Some New EVs** can be found in the **email_subject** column:

```
DELETE FROM
   bat_emails
WHERE
   position('25% off all EV' in email_subject)>0;


DELETE FROM
   bat_emails
WHERE
   position('Some New EV' in email_subject)>0;
```

13. At this stage, you have your final dataset of emails that were sent to customers. Count the number of rows that are left in the sample by writing the following query:

```
SELECT
   count(sales_date)
FROM
   bat_emails;
```

You can see that **319** rows are left in the sample:

```
count
-------
319
(1 row)
```

14. Now, you will compute the percentage of emails that were opened relative to sales. Count the emails that were opened by writing the following query:

```
SELECT
   count(opened)
FROM
   bat_emails
WHERE
   opened='t';
```

You can see that **83** emails were opened:

```
count
-------
83
(1 row)
```

15. Count the customers who received emails and made a purchase. You can determine this by counting the number of unique (or distinct) customers that are in the **bat_emails** table:

```
SELECT
    COUNT(DISTINCT(customer_id))
FROM
  bat_emails;
```

You can see that **314** customers who received an email made a purchase:

```
count
-------
314
(1 row)
```

16. Count the unique (or distinct) customers who made a purchase by writing the following query:

```
SELECT
    COUNT(DISTINCT(customer_id))
FROM
  bat_sales;
```

The following is the output of the preceding code:

```
count
-------
6659
(1 row)
```

17. Calculate the percentage of customers who purchased a **Bat** Scooter after receiving an email:

```
SELECT 314.0/6659.0 AS email_rate;
```

The output of the preceding query is as follows:

```
email_rate
-------
0.04715422736146568554
(1 row)
```

> **NOTE**
>
> In the preceding calculation, you can see that you included a decimal place in the figures (for example, **314.0** instead of a simple integer value of **314**). This is because the resulting value will be represented as a fraction that is less than 1. If you excluded these decimal places, the SQL server would have completed the division operation as integers and the result would be **0**.

Just under 5% of customers who made a purchase received an email regarding the **Bat** Scooter. There is a strong argument to be made that actively increasing the size of the customer base who receive marketing emails could increase **Bat** Scooter sales. But how likely is it that this argument is correct? You must compare this number to the effectiveness of other products' email campaigns, which is called a control or comparison group. Now that you have examined the performance of the email marketing campaign for the **Bat** Scooter, you need a control or comparison group to establish whether the results were consistent with that of other products. Without a group to compare against, you simply do not know whether the email campaign of the **Bat** Scooter was good, bad, or neither. You will investigate performance in the next exercise.

> **NOTE**
>
> To access the source code for this specific section, please refer to https://packt.link/b3wRQ.

EXERCISE 9.05: ANALYZING THE PERFORMANCE OF THE EMAIL MARKETING CAMPAIGN

In this exercise, you will investigate the performance of the email marketing campaign for the **Lemon** Scooter to allow for a comparison with the **Bat** Scooter. Your hypothesis is that if the email marketing campaign's performance of the **Bat** Scooter is consistent with another, such as the 2016 **Lemon**, then the reduction in sales cannot be attributed to differences in the email campaigns.

Perform the following steps to complete this exercise:

1. Load the **sqlda** database with **psql**.

2. In *Activity 9.02, Analyzing the Difference in the Sales Price Hypothesis*, you tried to compare the sales of the **Lemon** Scooter against the **Bat** Scooter, to find the impact of pricing. In this exercise, you will compare the sales of the **Lemon** Scooter against the **Bat** Scooter from another angle, which is the effectiveness of the email campaign. So, first drop the existing **lemon_sales** table, which contains information not related to this exercise:

```
DROP TABLE IF EXISTS lemon_sales;
```

3. The 2016 **Lemon** Scooter is **product_id=3**. Select **customer_id** and **sales_transaction_date** from the **sales** table for the 2016 **Lemon** Scooter. Insert this information into a table called **lemon_sales**. Here, the **TIMESTAMP** column **sales_transaction_date** is converted into the **DATE** column **sales_date**:

```
SELECT
  customer_id,
  sales_transaction_date::DATE as sales_date
INTO
  lemon_sales
FROM
  sales
WHERE
  product_id=3;
```

4. Select all the information from the **emails** database for customers who purchased a 2016 **Lemon** Scooter. Place this information in a new table called **lemon_emails**:

```
SELECT
    emails.customer_id,
    emails.email_subject,
    emails.opened,
    emails.sent_date,
    emails.opened_date,
    lemon_sales.sales_date
INTO
    lemon_emails
FROM
    emails
INNER JOIN
    Lemon_sales
ON
    emails.customer_id=lemon_sales.customer_id;
```

5. Identify the date when the production of the 2016 **Lemon** Scooter started, to remove all the emails that were sent before:

```
SELECT
    production_start_date
FROM
    products
WHERE
    product_id=3;
```

The following table shows the **production_start_date** column:

```
production_start_date
---------------------
2015-12-27  00:00:00
(1 row)
```

6. Now that you know the production start date, you can delete the emails that were sent before the start of production of the 2016 **Lemon** Scooter:

```
DELETE FROM
   lemon_emails
WHERE
   sent_date < '2015-12-27';
```

7. Remove all the rows where the sent date occurred after the date in the **sales_date** column:

```
DELETE FROM
   lemon_emails
WHERE
   sent_date > sales_date;
```

8. Remove all the rows where the sent date occurred more than 30 days before the date in the **sales_date** column:

```
DELETE FROM
   lemon_emails
WHERE
   (sales_date - sent_date) > '30 days';
```

9. Remove all the rows from **lemon_emails** where the email subject is not related to the **Lemon** Scooter. Before doing this, you will search for all distinct emails:

```
SELECT DISTINCT
   email_subject
FROM
   lemon_emails;
```

The following table shows the distinct email subjects:

```
                      email_subject
-------------------------------------------------
  Tis' the Season for Savings
  25% off all EVs. It's a Christmas Miracle!
  A Brand New Scooter...and Car
  Like a Bat out of Heaven
  Shocking Holiday Savings On Electric Scooters
  Save the Planet with some Holiday Savings.
  We cut you a deal: 20%% off a Blade
```

```
An Electric Car for a New Age

We Really Outdid Ourselves this Year

Black Friday. Green Cars.

Zoom Zoom Black Friday Sale

(11 rows)
```

10. Delete the email subjects not related to the **Lemon** Scooter using the **DELETE** command:

Exercise9.05.sql

```
1 DELETE FROM
2  lemon_emails
3 WHERE
4  POSITION('25% off all EVs.' in email_subject)>0;
5
6 DELETE FROM
7  lemon_emails
8 WHERE
9  POSITION('Like a Bat out of Heaven' in email_subject)>0;
10
11 DELETE FROM
12  lemon_emails
13 WHERE
14  POSITION('Save the Planet' in email_subject)>0;
15
```

Please find the complete code at https://packt.link/QNwRU.

11. Now, check how many emails to the **lemon_scooter** customers were opened:

```
SELECT
   COUNT(opened)
FROM
   lemon_emails
WHERE
   opened='t';
```

You can see that **127** emails were opened:

```
count
-------
127
(1 row)
```

12. List the number of customers who received emails and made a purchase:

```
SELECT
   COUNT(DISTINCT(customer_id))
FROM
   lemon_emails;
```

The following result shows that **498** customers made a purchase after receiving emails:

```
count
-------
498
(1 row)
```

13. Calculate the percentage of customers who opened the received emails and made a purchase:

```
SELECT 127.0/498.0 AS email_rate;
```

You can see that 25% of customers opened the emails and made a purchase:

```
email_rate
----------------------
0.25502008032128514056
(1 row)
```

14. Calculate the number of unique customers who made a purchase:

```
SELECT
    COUNT(DISTINCT(customer_id))
FROM
    lemon_sales;
```

You can see that **13854** customers made a purchase:

```
count
-------
13854
(1 row)
```

15. Calculate the percentage of customers who made a purchase having received an email. This will enable a comparison with the corresponding figure for the **Bat** Scooter:

```
SELECT 498.0/13854.0 AS email_sales;
```

The preceding calculation generates a 36% output:

```
email_sales
----------------------
0.03594629709831095712
(1 row)
```

You can see that 25% of customers who opened an email made a purchase, which is similar to that figure for the **Bat** Scooter (83/314=26%). You have also calculated that about 3.6% of customers who purchased a **Lemon** Scooter were sent an email, which is much lower than almost 5% of **Bat** Scooter customers.

> **NOTE**
>
> To access the source code for this specific section, please refer to https://packt.link/b3wRQ.

In this exercise, you investigated the performance of an email marketing campaign for the **Lemon** Scooter to allow for a comparison with the **Bat** Scooter using various SQL techniques. Now, you will review all the exercises and activities you have done in this chapter and see whether you can draw some meaningful conclusions.

CONCLUSIONS

Now that you have collected a range of information about the timing of the product launches, the sales prices of the products, and the marketing campaigns, you can make some conclusions regarding your hypotheses:

- In *Exercise 9.03*, *Launch Timing Analysis*, you gathered some evidence to suggest that launch timing could be related to the reduction in sales after the first 2 weeks, although this cannot be proven.

- There is a correlation between the initial sales rate and the sales price of the scooter, with a reduced sales price trending with a high sales rate (*Activity 9.02*, *Analyzing the Difference in the Sales Price Hypothesis*).

- The number of units sold in the first 3 weeks does not directly correlate to the sales price of the product (*Activity 9.02*, *Analyzing the Difference in the Sales Price Hypothesis*).

- There is evidence to suggest that a successful marketing campaign could increase the initial sales rate, with an increased email opening rate trending with an increased sales rate (*Exercise 9.04*, *Analyzing Sales Growth by Email Opening Rate*). Similarly, for the customers receiving email trends, there is an increase in the number with increased sales (*Exercise 9.05*, *Analyzing the Performance of the Email Marketing Campaign*).

IN-FIELD TESTING

At this stage, you have completed your post hoc analysis (that is, data analysis completed after an event) and have evidence to support a couple of theories as to why the sales of the **Bat** Scooter dropped after the first 2 weeks. However, you cannot confirm these hypotheses to be true, as you cannot isolate one from the other, such as pricing difference or email campaign effectiveness.

This is where you need to turn to another tool in your toolkit: in-field testing. As the name suggests, in-field testing is testing hypotheses in the field (for instance, while a new product is being launched or existing sales are being made).

One of the most common examples of in-field testing is A/B testing, whereby you randomly divide your users or customers into two groups (A and B) and provide them with a slightly modified experience or environment and observe the result. For example, you randomly assigned customers in group A to a new marketing campaign and customers in group B to the existing marketing campaign. You could then monitor sales and interactions to see whether one campaign was better than the other.

Similarly, if you wanted to test the launch timing, you could launch in Northern California, for example, in early November, and Southern California in early December, and observe the differences.

The essence of in-field testing is that unless you test your post hoc data analysis hypotheses, you will never know whether your hypothesis is true. To test the hypothesis, you must only alter the conditions to be tested—for example, the launch date. To confirm your post hoc analysis, you could recommend that the sales teams apply one or more of the following scenarios and monitor the sales records in real-time to determine the cause of the reduction in sales:

- Release the next scooter product at different times of the year in two regions that have a similar climate and equivalent current sales records. This would help determine whether launch timing had an effect.

- Release the next scooter product at the same time in regions with equivalent existing sales records at different price points and observe this for differences in sales.

- Release the next scooter product at the same time and the same price point in regions with equivalent existing sales records and apply two different email marketing campaigns. Track the customers who participated in each campaign and monitor the sales.

SUMMARY

You have just completed your first real-world data analysis problem using SQL. In this chapter, you developed the skills necessary to develop hypotheses for problems and systematically gather the data required to support or reject them. You started this case study with a reasonably difficult problem of explaining an observed discrepancy in sales data and discovered two possible sources (launch timing and marketing campaign) for the difference while rejecting one alternative explanation (sales price).

While being a required skill for any data analyst, being able to understand and apply the scientific method in your exploration of problems will allow you to be more effective and find interesting threads of investigation. In this chapter, you used the SQL skills you have developed throughout this book, from simple **SELECT** statements to aggregating complex data types, as well as windowing methods. After completing this chapter, you will be able to continue and repeat this type of analysis in your own data analysis projects to help find actionable insights.

You have reached the end of this book. Throughout these chapters, you have learned about data and how you can find patterns within it. You have also learned how SQL's powerful functionality can be used to organize data, process it, and identify interesting patterns. Additionally, you saw how SQL can be connected to other systems and optimized to analyze at scale. This all culminated in using SQL on a case study to help improve a business.

However, these skills are only the beginning of your work. Relational databases are constantly evolving, and new functionality is being developed all the time. There are also several advanced statistical techniques that this book did not cover. So, while this book may serve as a guide to data analytics and an invaluable tool in the form of SQL, it is only the first step in what is hopefully a rewarding journey.

APPENDIX

CHAPTER 1: UNDERSTANDING AND DESCRIBING DATA

ACTIVITY 1.01: CLASSIFYING A NEW DATASET

Solution:

1. The unit of observation is a car sale.

2. **Date** and **Sales Amount** are quantitative, while **Make** is qualitative.

While there could be many ways to convert **Make** into numeric data, one commonly accepted method would be to map each of the **Make** types to a number. For instance, **Ford** could map to **1**, **Honda** could map to **2**, **Mazda** could map to **3**, **Toyota** could map to **4**, **Mercedes** could map to **5**, and **Chevy** could map to **6**.

ACTIVITY 1.02: EXPLORING DEALERSHIP SALES DATA

Solution:

1. Open Microsoft Excel to a blank workbook.

2. Go to the **Data** tab and click on **Get Data | From File | From Text/CSV**.

3. Find the path to the **dealerships.csv** file and click on **Import**.

4. In the file import window, click on **Load**. The following table is what you will see when the file loads.

Location	Net Annual Sales	Number of Female Employees
Millburn, NJ	150803012	27
Los Angeles, CA	110872084	17
Houston, TX	183945873	22
Miami, FL	156355396	18
San Mateo, CA	143108603	17
Seattle, WA	142755480	33
Arlington, VA	144772604	28
Portland, OR	179608438	32
Reno, NV	145101244	19
Chicago, IL	171491596	24
Atlanta, GA	198386988	27
Orlando, FL	180188054	24
Jacksonville, FL	158479693	32
Round Rock, TX	181820474	27
Phoenix, AZ	95512810.7	18
Charlotte, NC	199653776	32
Philadelphia, PA	193111679	31
Kansas City, MO	176816637	35
Dallas, TX	168769837	33
Boston, MA	350520724	20

Figure 1.38: The dealerships.csv file loaded

A histogram of the results may vary a little bit depending on what parameters are chosen, but it should look similar to *Figure 1.38*:

Number of Female Employees

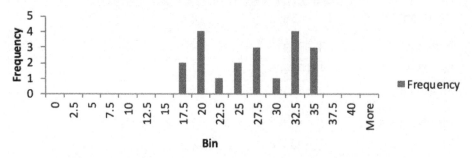

Figure 1.39: A histogram showing the number of female employees

5. Calculate the mean and median by following all the steps in *Exercise 1.03, Calculating the Central Tendency of Add-On Sales*. The mean sales are calculated to be $171,603,750.13 and the median sales are calculated to be $170,130,716.50.

6. Using steps similar to those found in *Exercise 1.04, Dispersion of Add-On Sales*, the standard deviation of the sales is calculated to be $50,152,290.42.

7. The Boston, MA dealership is an outlier. This can be shown graphically or by using the IQR method.

8. You should get the following four cut points for quintiles (five-quantiles):

n-Quintile	Value
1	144439803.80
2	157629974.20
3	177933357.40
4	185779034.20

Figure 1.40: Quintiles and their values

9. Removing the outlier of Boston, you should get a correlation coefficient of 0.55. This value implies that there is a strong correlation between the number of female employees and the sales of a dealership. While this may be evidence that having more female employees leads to more revenue, it may also be a simple consequence of a third effect. In this case, larger dealerships have a larger number of employees in general, which also means more women will be at these locations as well. There may be other correlational interpretations as well.

CHAPTER 2: THE BASICS OF SQL FOR ANALYTICS

ACTIVITY 2.01: QUERYING THE CUSTOMERS TABLE USING BASIC KEYWORDS IN A SELECT QUERY

Solution:

Here is the solution for *Exercise 2.01*, *Running Your First SELECT Query*:

1. Open **pgAdmin**, connect to the **sqlda** database, and open SQL query editor. Examine the schema for the **customers** table from the schema drop-down list. Make sure you are familiar with the names of the columns, just like you did in *Exercise 2.02*, *Querying the salespeople Table Using Basic Keywords in a SELECT Query*, for the **salespeople** table.

2. Execute the following query to fetch customers' emails in the state of Florida in alphabetical order:

```
SELECT email
FROM customers
WHERE state='FL'
ORDER BY email;
```

The following is the output of the preceding code:

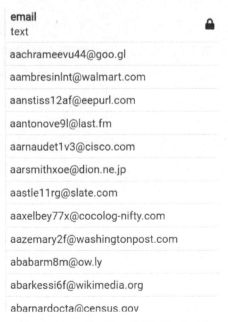

email text 🔒
aachrameevu44@goo.gl
aambresinlnt@walmart.com
aanstiss12af@eepurl.com
aantonove9l@last.fm
aarnaudet1v3@cisco.com
aarsmithxoe@dion.ne.jp
aastle11rg@slate.com
aaxelbey77x@cocolog-nifty.com
aazemary2f@washingtonpost.com
ababarm8m@ow.ly
abarkessi6f@wikimedia.org
abarnardocta@census.gov

Figure 2.47: Emails of customers from Florida in alphabetical order

3. Execute the following query to pull all the first names, last names, and email addresses for ZoomZoom customers in New York City, New York. The customers should be ordered alphabetically, with the last name followed by the first name:

```
SELECT first_name, last_name, email
FROM customers
WHERE city='New York City' AND state='NY'
ORDER BY last_name, first_name;
```

The following is the output of the preceding code:

first_name text	last_name text	email text
Nell	Abdy	nabdyec4@fema.gov
Thomasine	Absolon	tabsolonomk@forbes.com
Ram	Acheson	racheson1ai@bloglovin.com
Pru	Achrameev	pachrameev2sr@example.com
Jandy	Adamowicz	jadamowiczb1w@clickbank.net
Kati	Adrian	kadrianeem@51.la
Orly	Aers	oaersx61@redcross.org
Bradney	Aglione	baglionee5n@usgs.gov
Mellicent	Ainslee	mainsleeir0@abc.net.au
Fergus	Aireton	fairetonq16@yellowpages.com
Ugo	Aldam	ualdamhnc@wikimedia.org

Figure 2.48: Details of customers from New York City in alphabetical order

4. Execute the following query to fetch all customers that have a phone number ordered by the date the customer was added to the database:

```
SELECT *
FROM customers
WHERE phone IS NOT NULL
ORDER BY date_added;
```

The following is the output of the preceding code:

customer_id bigint	title text		first_name text	last_name text		suffix text	email text		gender text	ip_address text		phone text
2625	[null]		Binky	Dawtrey		[null]	bdawtrey20w@shareasale.com		M	15.75.236.78		804-99
17099	[null]		Pearla	Halksworth		[null]	phalksworthd6y@cyberchimps.com		F	114.138.82.24		541-19
13390	[null]		Danika	Lough		[null]	dloughabx@skype.com		F	188.19.7.207		212-76
6173	[null]		Danila	Gristwood		[null]	dgristwood4rg@furl.net		F	254.239.58.108		832-15
18685	[null]		Ingram	Crossman		[null]	icrossmanef0@weebly.com		M	207.145.1.202		503-35
7486	[null]		Ciro	Ferencowicz		[null]	cferencowicz5rx@ucoz.ru		M	8.151.167.184		786-45
35683	[null]		Betteanne	Rulf		[null]	brulfrj6@jalbum.net		F	52.208.248.90		503-39
30046	[null]		Nanete	Hassur		[null]	nhassurn6l@alibaba.com		F	232.115.170.92		209-36
34189	[null]		Devlin	Barhems		[null]	dbarhemsqdo@shareasale.com		M	180.175.21.245		240-89
38885	[null]		Bridget	Blankenship		[null]	bblankenshipu04@techcrunch.com		F	203.187.66.59		517-97
22640	[null]		Shana	Nugent		[null]	snugenthgv@ask.com		F	207.239.127.188		202-37

Figure 2.49: Customers with a phone number ordered by the date
the customer was added to the database

The output in *Figure 2.30* will help the marketing manager to carry out campaigns and promote sales.

ACTIVITY 2.02: CREATING AND MODIFYING TABLES FOR MARKETING OPERATIONS

Solution:

Here is the solution for *Exercise 2.02, Creating and Modifying Tables for Marketing Operations*:

1. Open pgAdmin, connect to the **sqlda** database, and open SQL query editor.

2. Run the following query to create the table with New York City customers:

```
CREATE TABLE customers_nyc AS (
SELECT *
FROM customers
WHERE city='New York City'
AND state='NY'
);
```

3. Run the following code to see the output:

```
SELECT * FROM customers_nyc;
```

This is the output of the code:

customer_id bigint	title text		first_name text		last_name text		suffix text	email text		gender text	ip_address text		phone text
52	[null]		Giusto		Backe		[null]	gbacke1f@digg.com		M	26.56.68.189		212-959-91
162	[null]		Artair		Betchley		[null]	abetchley4h@dagondesign.com		M	108.147.128.250		[null]
374	[null]		Verge		Esel		[null]	veselad@vistaprint.com		M	58.238.20.156		917-653-23
406	[null]		Rozina		Jeal		[null]	rjealb9@howstuffworks.com		F	50.235.32.29		917-610-25
456	Rev		Cybil		Noke		[null]	cnokecn@jigsy.com		F	5.31.139.106		212-306-60
472	[null]		Rawley		Yegorov		[null]	ryegorovd3@google.es		M	183.199.243.74		212-560-12
496	[null]		Layton		Spolton		[null]	lspoltondr@free.fr		M	108.112.8.165		646-900-82
1028	[null]		Issy		Andrieux		[null]	iandrieuxsj@dell.com		F	199.50.5.37		212-206-78
1037	[null]		Magdalene		Veryard		[null]	mveryardss@behance.net		F	93.201.129.213		[null]

Figure 2.50: Table showing customers from New York City

4. Run the following query statement to delete users with the postal code 10014:

```
DELETE FROM customers_nyc
WHERE postal_code='10014';
```

5. Execute the following query to add the new **event** column:

```
ALTER TABLE customers_nyc
ADD COLUMN event text;
```

6. Update the **customers_nyc** table and set the **event** column to **thank-you party** using the following query:

```
UPDATE customers_nyc SET
event = 'thank-you party';
```

7. Run the following code to see the output:

```
SELECT *
FROM customers_nyc;
```

The following is the output of the code:

	street_address text		city text		state text	postal_code text	latitude double precision	longitude double precision	date_added timestamp without time zone		event text
959-9172	6 Onsgard Terrace		New York City		NY	10131	40.7808	-73.9772	2013-03-02 00:00:00		thank-you party
488-5351	3475 Kedzie Plaza		New York City		NY	10280	40.7105	-74.0163	2014-01-30 00:00:00		thank-you party
975-0572	2222 Killdeer Park		New York City		NY	10175	40.7543	-73.9798	2019-04-30 00:00:00		thank-you party
}	124 3rd Trail		New York City		NY	10160	40.7808	-73.9772	2012-12-24 00:00:00		thank-you party
865-8370	63 Waywood Center		New York City		NY	10150	40.7808	-73.9772	2017-01-09 00:00:00		thank-you party
862-7926	6 Florence Point		New York City		NY	10090	40.7808	-73.9772	2013-03-27 00:00:00		thank-you party
}	5 Mallory Road		New York City		NY	10009	40.7262	-73.9796	2017-04-26 00:00:00		thank-you party
}	80 Kedzie Drive		New York City		NY	10045	40.7086	-74.0087	2020-06-05 00:00:00		thank-you party
829-3123	59 Carey Park		New York City		NY	10004	40.6964	-74.0253	2018-11-01 00:00:00		thank-you party
179-2827	5682 1st Trail		New York City		NY	10160	40.7808	-73.9772	2013-11-18 00:00:00		thank-you party

Figure 2.51: The customers_nyc table with event set to thank-you party

8. Delete the **customers_nyc** table as asked by the manager using **DROP TABLE**:

```
DROP TABLE customers_nyc;
```

This will delete the **customers_nyc** table from the database.

CHAPTER 3: SQL FOR DATA PREPARATION

ACTIVITY 3.01: BUILDING A SALES MODEL USING SQL TECHNIQUES

Solution:

1. Open **pgAdmin**, connect to the **sqlda** database, and open the SQL query editor.

2. Use **INNER JOIN** to join the **customers** table to the **sales** table:

```
FROM sales s
JOIN customers c
ON s.customer_id = c.customer_id
```

   Note that the SQL in *Steps 2*, *3*, and *4* is not complete SQL that you can run in **pgAdmin**. They are part of the **FROM...JOIN** clause on which the full **SELECT** statement will be built. They are created to guide you through the process of forming a complex dataset using **JOIN**. If you want to test the SQL, you can make it complete by adding **SELECT** * at the start.

3. Use **INNER JOIN** to join the **products** table to the **sales** table:

```
FROM sales s
JOIN customers c
ON s.customer_id = c.customer_id
JOIN products p
  ON s.product_id = p.product_id
```

4. Use **LEFT JOIN** to join the **dealerships** table (right table) to the **sales** table (left table):

```
FROM sales s
LEFT JOIN dealerships d
  ON d.dealership_id = s.dealership_id
JOIN customers c
  ON s.customer_id = c.customer_id
JOIN products p
  ON s.product_id = p.product_id
```

5. Return all columns of the **customers** table and the **products** table:

```
SELECT
  c.*, p.*
FROM sales s
```

```
LEFT JOIN dealerships d
   ON d.dealership_id = s.dealership_id
JOIN customers c
   ON s.customer_id = c.customer_id
JOIN products p
   ON s.product_id = p.product_id;
```

6. Return the **dealership_id** column from the **sales** table, but fill in **dealership_id** in **sales** with **-1** if it is **NULL**:

```
SELECT
COALESCE(s.dealership_id, -1) sales_dealership,
c.*, p.*
FROM sales s
LEFT JOIN dealerships d
ON d.dealership_id = s.dealership_id
JOIN customers c
ON s.customer_id = c.customer_id
JOIN products p
ON s.product_id = p.product_id;
```

7. Add a column called **high_savings** that returns **1** if the sales amount was **500** less than **base_msrp** or lower. Otherwise, it returns **0**. Please make sure that you perform the query on a joined table:

```
SELECT
   COALESCE(s.dealership_id, -1) sales_dealership,
   CASE
WHEN sales_amount < base_msrp - 500 THEN 1
     ELSE 0
   END high_savings,
   c.*, p.*
FROM sales s
LEFT JOIN dealerships d
   ON d.dealership_id = s.dealership_id
JOIN customers c
   ON s.customer_id = c.customer_id
JOIN products p
   ON s.product_id = p.product_id;
```

CHAPTER 4: AGGREGATE FUNCTIONS FOR DATA ANALYSIS

ACTIVITY 4.01: ANALYZING SALES DATA USING AGGREGATE FUNCTIONS

Solution:

1. Open **pgAdmin**, connect to the **sqlda** database, and open SQL query editor.

2. Calculate the total number of unit sales the company has made:

```
SELECT
    COUNT(*)
FROM
    sales;
```

The result is as follows:

Figure 4.29: Result of COUNT(*) for sales units

Note that because each sales transaction contains a product ID, there is no **NULL** value in the **product_id** column. So, **COUNT(product_id)** will also work. Similarly, **COUNT(sales_amount)** will also work.

3. Calculate the total sales amount in dollars for each state:

```
SELECT
    c.state,
    SUM(s.sales_amount)::DECIMAL(12,2)
FROM
    sales s
JOIN
    customers c
ON
    s.customer_id = c.customer_id
GROUP BY
    c.state
ORDER BY
    1;
```

The result is as follows:

state text	sum numeric (12,2)
AK	1124268.78
AL	4820333.79
AR	1487923.59
AZ	4109364.45
CA	27942722.04
CO	5377388.31
CT	3038361.32

Figure 4.30: Result of sales by state

4. Identify the top five best dealerships in terms of the most units sold (ignore internet sales).

The most common approach to getting the top/bottom **N** rows is to run the **SELECT** statement with **ORDER BY**, then use **LIMIT** to only get the first **N** rows. In this activity, you can use **LIMIT 5** together with **ORDER BY DESC** to generate the top five dealerships. However, if there is a tie between the 5th and 6th elements, **LIMIT 5** will cut off between the 5th row and 6th row, regardless of whether you want both items or not. In the real world, you need to check the boundary condition carefully, that is, check the value below the limit to make sure there is no tie.

For this question, if you just aim at getting the dealership ID, the following SQL is good enough. However, if you would like to have the dealership details, you need to select the information from the dealerships table, with a filter on the dealership IDs from the following query:

```
SELECT
    s.dealership_id,
    COUNT(*)
FROM
    sales s
WHERE
```

```
    channel <> 'internet'
GROUP BY
  s.dealership_id
ORDER BY
  2 DESC
LIMIT
  5;
```

Here is the output:

dealership_id 🔒 double precision	count 🔒 bigint
10	1781
7	1583
18	1465
11	1312
1	1297

Figure 4.31: Result of top five dealerships by sales

5. Calculate the average sales amount for each channel, as shown in the **sales** table, and look at the average sales amount, first by **channel** sales, then by **product_id**, and then both together:

```
SELECT
  channel,
  product_id,
  AVG(sales_amount)
FROM
  sales
GROUP BY grouping sets (
  (channel),
  (product_id),
  (channel, product_id)
);
```

The result is as follows. Note that in this screenshot (the order of rows in your result may vary), row 22 and above are grouped by both **channel** and **product_id**. Rows 23 and 24 are grouped by **channel** only, and row 25 and beyond are grouped by **product_id** only. In other words, there are three different sets here, one is grouped by both **channel** and **product_id**, the other two by one of these two columns respectively, and all three sets are eventually joined together:

	channel text	product_id bigint	avg double precision
19	internet	5	670.2934545454501
20	internet	6	62751.56862745098
21	internet	4	109910.18518518518
22	dealership	4	109822.27488151658
23	dealership	[null]	7939.331320759544
24	internet	[null]	6413.115404120134
25	[null]	12	334.3621042780715
26	[null]	3	477.16463214168124

Figure 4.32: Result of GROUPING SETS

6. Calculate the ratio of sales transactions that have a **NULL** dealership:

```
SELECT
  1 - COUNT(dealership_id) * 1.0 / COUNT(*)
FROM
  sales
```

The result is as follows:

Figure 4.33: Ratio of NULL values of dealership in sales

7. Calculate the percentage of internet sales the company has made for each year. Order the year in a timely fashion and you will get time series data. Does this time series suggest something?

```
SELECT
  TO_CHAR(sales_transaction_date, 'yyyy'),
  SUM(sales_amount)
FROM
  sales
WHERE
  channel = 'internet'
GROUP BY
  1
ORDER BY
  1;
```

The result is as follows:

to_char 🔒 text	sum 🔒 double precision
2012	30199.245000000043
2013	418470.3899999968
2014	454268.64299999515
2015	79288.10300000005
2016	898982.0199999923
2017	17559807.96100031
2018	47974666.75799742
2019	59233516.51599967
2020	65767340.349996954
2021	69130589.87699932
2022	5706307.722000072

Figure 4.34: Internet sales by year

From the result data, you can see that there was a significant increase in sales starting in 2015. The upward trend is continuing into 2022, which is still at the beginning of the year at the point of data collection (the last sales transaction date is 2022-01-25). But does this increase occur in the overall sales of ZoomZoom, or does it only happen to the internet sales channel? If it is the former, internet sales and non-internet sales should have a similar amount of increase. There are many ways to measure and compare these two increases. You will use the simplest form by listing the internet sales and non-internet sales side by side. The SQL will be as follows:

```
SELECT
  TO_CHAR(sales_transaction_date, 'yyyy'),
  SUM(
CASE
      WHEN channel = 'internet' THEN sales_amount
      ELSE 0
END
  ) AS internet_sales,
  SUM(
CASE
      WHEN channel <> 'internet' THEN sales_amount
      ELSE 0
END
  ) AS non_internet_sales
FROM
  sales
GROUP BY
  1
ORDER BY
  1;
```

The result is as follows:

to_char text	internet_sales double precision	non_internet_sales double precision
2012	30199.245000000043	0
2013	418470.3899999968	0
2014	454268.64299999515	0
2015	79288.10300000005	0
2016	898982.0199999923	0
2017	12723375.26600071	4836432.695000121
2018	28066730.801999394	19907935.956000257
2019	30320153.7679995	28913362.74799954
2020	30919075.69400037	34848264.65600043
2021	28768943.799996857	40361646.07699914
2022	2399962.0260000015	3306345.696000024

Figure 4.35: Internet and non-internet sales by year

CHAPTER 5: WINDOW FUNCTIONS FOR DATA ANALYSIS

ACTIVITY 5.01: ANALYZING SALES USING WINDOW FRAMES AND WINDOW FUNCTIONS

Solution:

The solution to this activity is as follows:

1. Open **pgAdmin**, connect to the **sqlda** database, and open SQL query editor.

2. Calculate the total sales amount by day for all the days in the year 2021 (that is, before the date January 1, 2022).

3. The query for this step will be:

```
SELECT
    sales_transaction_date::date,
    SUM(sales_amount) sales_amount
FROM
    sales
WHERE
    sales_transaction_date::date BETWEEN '20210101' AND '20211231'
GROUP BY
    sales_transaction_date::date;
```

The result is:

sales_transaction_date 🔒 date	sales_amount 🔒 double precision
2021-01-01	320739.70100000006
2021-01-02	248239.73599999998
2021-01-03	213419.72799999994
2021-01-04	378919.7169999999
2021-01-05	331084.6939999999
2021-01-06	90089.649
2021-01-07	426449.7289999998
2021-01-08	183449.789
2021-01-09	513254.7929999999
2021-01-10	307994.72699999984

Figure 5.18: Daily Sales of 2021

4. Calculate the rolling 30-day average for the daily number of sales deals. The query for this step will be:

`Activity5.01.sql`

```
1  WITH
2  daily_sales as (
3    SELECT
4      sales_transaction_date::date,
5      SUM(sales_amount) sales_amount
6    FROM
7      sales
8    WHERE
9      sales_transaction_date::date BETWEEN '20210101' AND '20211231'
10   GROUP BY
11     sales_transaction_date::date
12 )
13 SELECT
14   sales_transaction_date,
15   sales_amount,
```

You can find the complete code here: https://packt.link/f3bEp

The result is:

sales_transaction_date date	sales_amount double precision	moving_avg double precision
2021-01-01	320739.70100000006	[null]
2021-01-02	248239.73599999998	320739.70100000006
2021-01-03	213419.72799999994	284489.7185
2021-01-04	378919.7169999999	260799.72166666668
2021-01-05	331084.6939999999	290329.7205
2021-01-06	90089.649	298480.7152
2021-01-07	426449.7289999998	263748.8708333333
2021-01-08	183449.789	286991.85057142854
2021-01-09	513254.7929999999	274049.092875
2021-01-10	307994.72699999984	300627.50399999996
2021-01-11	432599.66599999997	301364.2263

Figure 5.19: Daily Sales Moving 30-Day Average

5. Note that the moving average for 2021-01-01 is NULL here because there are no daily sales from 2020 in the **daily_sales** common table expression. So, the 30-day preceding window is empty. For 2021-01-02, the 30-day preceding window contains only one row, which is the daily sales for 2021-01-01. As it goes down the order of dates, more and more days join the window. Eventually, after 2021-01-31, it became a true 30-day preceding window.

This activity intentionally applies the **sales_transaction_date::date BETWEEN '20210101' AND '20211231'** filter to the **daily_sales** common table expression to provide you with an illustration of what might happen for the first few rows in the moving average window creation.

In reality, a better way is to include the last 30-day sales of 2020 in the **daily_sales** common table expression so that you can still calculate the moving average properly for days in January 2021 and use a 2021 date range in the main query to only display the 2021 data.

6. Calculate which decile each date would be in compared to other days based on their daily 30-day rolling sales amount.

PostgreSQL does not have a **DECILE** function, but it has a more general **NTILE()** function that you can use. **NTILE(10)** is the equivalent of **DECILE()**.

7. The query for this step will be:

Activity5.01.sql

```
 1 WITH
 2   daily_sales as (
 3     SELECT
 4       sales_transaction_date::date,
 5       SUM(sales_amount) sales_amount
 6     FROM
 7       sales
 8     WHERE
 9       sales_transaction_date::date BETWEEN '20210101' AND '20211231'
10     GROUP BY
11       sales_transaction_date::date
12   ),
13   moving_avg AS (
```

You can find the complete code here: https://packt.link/f3bEp

The result is:

sales_transaction_date 🔒 date	sales_amount 🔒 double precision	moving_avg 🔒 double precision	decile 🔒 integer
2021-01-02	248239.73599999998	320739.70100000006	1
2021-01-12	164189.76699999996	313294.72081818176	1
2021-01-11	432599.66599999997	301364.2263	1
2021-01-13	12829.790999999997	300869.30799999996	1
2021-01-10	307994.72699999984	300627.50399999996	1
2021-01-06	90089.649	298480.7152	1
2021-02-06	50389.734999999986	293352.5650333333	1
2021-01-05	331084.6939999999	290329.7205	1
2021-02-02	161009.56200000003	288809.9029333333	1
2021-02-03	275539.70199999993	287062.8974	1
2021-01-08	183449.789	286991.85057142854	1

Figure 5.20: Dealership Deciles Based on Max Daily Sales Moving 30-Day Average

CHAPTER 6: IMPORTING AND EXPORTING DATA

ACTIVITY 6.01: USING AN EXTERNAL DATASET TO DISCOVER SALES TRENDS

Solution:

1. Before you can begin the rest of the analysis, you will need to properly load the dataset into Python and export it to your database. First, download the dataset from GitHub using the link provided: https://packt.link/l058E. If you are a Linux user, you can use the **wget** command like this:

```
wget https://github.com/PacktPublishing/SQL-for-Data-Analytics-Third-
Edition/blob/main/Datasets/public_transportation_statistics_by_zip_
code.csv
```

Alternatively, you can navigate to the link via the browser. Once you navigate to the web page, click on **Save Page As**... using the menus on your browser:

Figure 6.31: Saving the public transportation .csv file

2. Next, create a new Jupyter notebook. Launch Jupyter Notebook from Anaconda Navigator. In the browser window that pops up, create a new Python 3 notebook. In the first cell, type in the standard **import** statements and the connection information (replacing **_X** with the appropriate parameter for your database connection):

```
from sqlalchemy import create_engine
import pandas as pd
%matplotlib inline


cnxn_string = ("postgresql+psycopg2://{username}:{pswd}@
{host}:{port}/{database}")
print(cnxn_string)
```

Here is the output of the code:

```
postgresql+psycopg2://{username}:{pswd}@{host}:{port}/{database}
```

In the next cell, type the following code, which will create the **SQLAlchemy** engine:

```
engine = create_engine(
    cnxn_string.format(
        username="postgres",
        pswd="your_password",
        host="localhost",
        port=5432,
        database="sqlda"
    )
)
```

3. Read the data using a command such as the following (replacing the path specified with the path to the file on your local computer):

```
data = pd.read_csv(
    "c:\\Users\\Public\\public_transportation_statistics_by_ zip_
code.csv",
    dtype={'zip_code':str}
)
```

4. Check that the data looks correct by creating a new cell, entering data, and then hitting *Shift + Enter* to view the contents of the data. You can also use **data. head()** to see only the first five rows:

```
data.head()
```

Here is the output of the code:

	zip_code	public_transportation_pct	public_transportation_population
0	01379	3.3	13
1	01440	0.4	34
2	01505	0.9	23
3	01524	0.5	20
4	01529	1.8	32

Figure 6.32: Reading the public transportation data into pandas

5. Next, transfer data to the database using **data.to_sql()**. Using the **psql_insert_COPY** function, you can speed this up considerably; however, it is not necessary:

Activity6.01.py

```
1 import csv
2 from io import StringIO
3
4 def psql_insert_COPY(table, conn, keys, data_iter):
5     # gets a DBAPI connection that can provide a cursor
6     dbapi_conn = conn.connection
7     with dbapi_conn.cursor() as cur:
8         s_buf = StringIO()
9         writer = csv.writer(s_buf)
10         writer.writerows(data_iter)
11         s_buf.seek(0)
12
13         columns = ', '.join('"{}"'.format(k) for k in keys)
14         if table.schema:
15             table_name = '{}.{}'.format(table.schema, table.name)
```

Please find the complete code here: https://packt.link/4RAFd

Alternatively, you could have just performed the slower version of this:

```
data.to_sql(
    'public_transportation_by_zip',
    engine,
    if_exists='replace'
)
```

At this stage, you now have your data in your database, ready for querying.

6. Execute the **max()** function to see the maximum value in the DataFrame. As explained before, this function will return the maximum values of all columns in this DataFrame:

```
data.max()
```

```
[21]:  ▶| data.max()

Out[21]: zip_code                          99929
         public_transportation_pct        100.0
         public_transportation_population  35139
         dtype: object
```

Figure 6.33: Output of the pandas Data Frame max() method

7. Execute the **min()** function to see the minimum value in the DataFrame. As explained before, this function will return the minimum values of all columns in this DataFrame:

```
data.min()
```

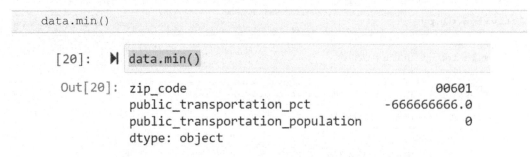

Figure 6.34: Output of the pandas DataFrame min() method

8. To see the range of **public_transportation_pct** values, you can simply query this from the database. First, you need to query the database:

```
engine.execute("""
    SELECT
        MAX(public_transportation_pct) AS max_pct,
        MIN(public_transportation_pct) AS min_pct
    FROM public_transportation_by_zip;
""").fetchall()
```

You get the following result from your query:

max_pct	min_pct
100	-666666666

Figure 6.35: Showing the minimum and maximum values

Looking at the maximum and minimum values, you will see something strange: the minimum value is **-666666666**. You can assume that the values are missing, and you can remove them from the dataset.

9. Calculate the requested sales amounts by running a query in your database. Note that you will have to filter out the erroneous percentages that are less than 0 based on your analysis. There are several ways to do this; however, the following solution is a single succinct query:

Activity6.01.py

```
1 engine.execute("""
2     SELECT
3         (public_transportation_pct > 10) AS                    4 is_high_
public_transport,
5         COUNT(s.customer_id) * 1.0 / COUNT(DISTINCT
6 c.customer_id) AS sales_per_customer
7     FROM
8         customers c
9     INNER JOIN
10        public_transportation_by_zip t
11        ON t.zip_code = c.postal_code
12     LEFT JOIN
13        sales s
14        ON s.customer_id = c.customer_id
```

Please find the complete code here: https://packt.link/4RAFd

Here is an explanation of this query:

- You first identify customers living in an area with public transportation by joining the **customer** table and the **public transportation** table.

- Then, you look at the public transportation data associated with their postal code. If **public_ transportation_pct > 10**, then the customer is in a high usage public transportation area. This expression will either return **True** or **False** for each customer.

- You then group customers by this expression to identify the customers that are or are not in a high-usage public transportation area. One catch is that you need to exclude all zip codes where **public_transportation_pct** is less than **0** so that you exclude the missing data (denoted by **-666666666**).

- You then look at sales per customer by joining the **customers** table with the **sales** table. You will first count the number of sales from the **sales** table **(COUNT(s.customer_id))** and divide it by the unique number of customers **(COUNT(DISTINCT c.customer_id))**. You want to make sure that you retain fractional values, so you can multiply by **1.0** to cast the entire expression to a float: **COUNT(s.customer_ id) * 1.0 / COUNT(DISTINCT c.customer_id)**. The result is the sales per customer.

- Now that you know how to calculate both the sales per customer and the high public transportation flag per customer, you need to join your customer data to the public transportation data, and then, finally, to the sales data, to calculate them all in one single query. Once you put them side by side, you can aggregate the sales per customer by the high transportation flag to see the difference in customer behavior between different groups of public transportation availability.

  Eventually, you end up with the following output:

  ```
  is_high_public_transport |    sales_per_customer
  -------------------------+-------------------------
   f                       | 0.71703932151117964534
   t                       | 0.80502739284563325814
  (2 rows)
  ```

  Figure 6.36: Calculating the requested sales amount

  From this, you see that customers in high public transportation usage areas have 12% more product purchases than customers in low-usage public transportation areas.

10. Read this data from your database and add a **WHERE** clause to remove the outlier values. You can then plot the results from this query:

```
data = pd.read_sql_query("""
    SELECT
        *
    FROM
        public_transportation_by_zip
    WHERE
        public_transportation_pct > 0
    AND
        public_transportation_pct < 50
""", engine)
data.plot.hist(y='public_transportation_pct')
```

You will obtain an output similar to the following:

```
In [13]: data = pd.read_sql_query("""
         SELECT *
         FROM public_transportation_by_zip
         WHERE public_transportation_pct > 0
         AND public_transportation_pct < 50""", engine)
         data.plot.hist(y='public_transportation_pct')

Out[13]: <matplotlib.axes._subplots.AxesSubplot at 0x1193ef160>
```

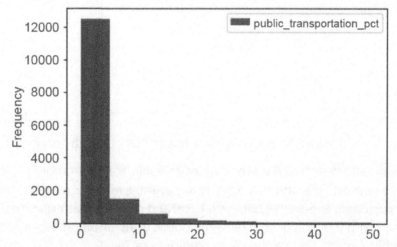

Figure 6.37: Jupyter notebook with an analysis of the public transportation data

11. Rerun your command from *Step 5* to get the timing of the standard **to_sql()** function:

```
%time data.to_sql('public_transportation_by_zip', engine, if_
exists='replace', method=psql_insert_COPY)

%time data.to_sql('public_transportation_by_zip', engine, if_
exists='replace')
```

The following is the output of the code:

```
In [4]: import csv
        from io import StringIO

        def psql_insert_copy(table, conn, keys, data_iter):
            # gets a DBAPI connection that can provide a cursor
            dbapi_conn = conn.connection
            with dbapi_conn.cursor() as cur:
                s_buf = StringIO()
                writer = csv.writer(s_buf)
                writer.writerows(data_iter)
                s_buf.seek(0)

                columns = ', '.join('"{}"'.format(k) for k in keys)
                if table.schema:
                    table_name = '{}.{}'.format(table.schema, table.name)
                else:
                    table_name = table.name

                sql = 'COPY {} ({}) FROM STDIN WITH CSV'.format(
                    table_name, columns)
                cur.copy_expert(sql=sql, file=s_buf)
```

```
%time data.to_sql('public_transportation_by_zip', engine, method=psql_insert_copy, if_exists='replace')

CPU times: user 102 ms, sys: 21.1 ms, total: 123 ms          With COPY: ~1 Second
Wall time: 1.2 s
```

```
In [5]: %time data.to_sql('public_transportation_by_zip', engine, if_exists='replace')

CPU times: user 4.58 s, sys: 4.16 s, total: 8.75 s           Without COPY: ~9 minutes
Wall time: 9min 15s
```

Figure 6.38: Inserting records with COPY is much faster

12. Group customers based on their zip code public transportation usage rounded to the nearest 10%, and then look at the average number of transactions per customer. Export this data into Excel and create a scatterplot to better understand the relationship between public transportation usage and sales. For this analysis, you can tweak the query from *Step 9*:

`Activity6.01.py`

```
1 data = pd.read_sql_query("""
2     SELECT
3         10 * ROUND(public_transportation_pct/10) AS                    4
public_transport,
5         COUNT(s.customer_id) * 1.0 / COUNT(DISTINCT          6    c.customer_id)
AS sales_per_customer
7     FROM
8         customers c
9     INNER JOIN
10        public_transportation_by_zip t
11        ON t.zip_code = c.postal_code
12    LEFT JOIN
13        sales s
14        ON s.customer_id = c.customer_id
```

Please find the complete code here: https://packt.link/4RAFd

First, you want to put your query results in a Python variable data so that you easily write the result to a **CSV** file later.

Next is the tricky part: you want to aggregate the public transportation statistics somehow. What you can do is round this percentage to the nearest 10%, so 22% would become 20%, and so on. You can do this by dividing the percentage number (represented as 0.0-100.0) by 10, rounding off, and then multiplying it back by **10**: **10 * ROUND(public_transportation_pct/10)**.

The logic for the remainder of the query is explained in *Step 9*.

Next, you open the **sales_vs_public_transport_pct.csv** file in Excel:

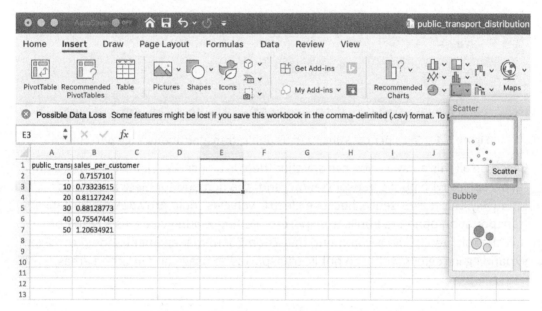

Figure 6.39: Excel workbook containing the data from your query

After creating the scatterplot, you get the following result, which shows a clear positive relationship between public transportation and sales in the geographical area:

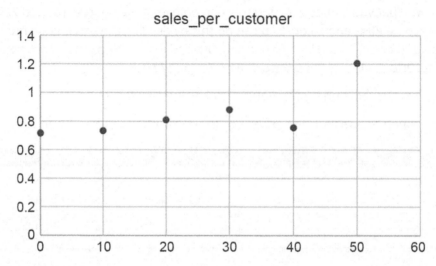

Figure 6.40: Sales per customer versus public transportation usage percentage

Based on all this analysis, you can say that there is a positive relationship between "geographies with public transportation" and "the demand for electric vehicles." Intuitively, this makes sense, because electric vehicles could provide an alternative transportation option to public transport for getting around cities. As a result of this analysis, you would recommend that ZoomZoom management should consider expanding in regions with high public transportation usage and in urban areas.

CHAPTER 7: ANALYTICS USING COMPLEX DATA TYPES

ACTIVITY 7.01: SALES SEARCH AND ANALYSIS

Solution:

1. First, create the materialized view on the **customer_sales** table. If a view with the same name already exists but is not up to date, execute the **DROP IF EXISTS** statement prior to the **CREATE** statement:

```
DROP MATERIALIZED VIEW IF EXISTS customer_search;

CREATE MATERIALIZED VIEW customer_search AS (
  SELECT
    customer_json -> 'customer_id' AS customer_id,
    customer_json,
    to_tsvector('english', customer_json) AS search_vector
  FROM
    customer_sales
);
```

This gives you a table of the following format (output shortened for readability):

```
SELECT * FROM customer_search LIMIT 1;
```

The following is the output of the code. Note that the output cells are too large to fit onto a screen so only the first few words are shown in the screenshot:

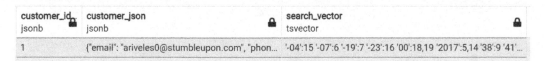

customer_id jsonb	customer_json jsonb	search_vector tsvector
1	{"email": "ariveles0@stumbleupon.com", "phon...	'-04':15 '-07':6 '-19':7 '-23':16 '00':18,19 '2017':5,14 '38':9 '41'...

Figure 7.28: Sample record from the customer_search table

2. You can now search records based on the salesperson's request for a customer named Danny who purchased a Bat scooter using the following query with the **Danny Bat** keywords:

```
SELECT
  customer_json
FROM
  customer_search
WHERE
  search_vector @@ plainto_tsquery('english', 'Danny Bat');
```

This results in eight matching rows:

customer_json
jsonb

{"email": "darundale87e@nytimes.com", "phone": null, "sales": [{"product_id": 8, "product_name": "Bat Limited Edition", "sales_amount": 69⸱

{"email": "dsinkins8vv@theatlantic.com", "phone": null, "sales": [{"product_id": 7, "product_name": "Bat", "sales_amount": 599.99, "sales_tra

{"email": "dfalkusrnr@mysql.com", "phone": "360-138-1212", "sales": [{"product_id": 7, "product_name": "Bat", "sales_amount": 599.99, "sal⸱

{"email": "dtyddwax@weebly.com", "phone": "626-781-3263", "sales": [{"product_id": 7, "product_name": "Bat", "sales_amount": 479.992, "s⸱

{"email": "dberthelmotxt5@jigsy.com", "phone": "559-535-5099", "sales": [{"product_id": 8, "product_name": "Bat Limited Edition", "sales_an⸱

{"email": "ddanev1b5@geocities.com", "phone": "415-491-7645", "sales": [{"product_id": 7, "product_name": "Bat", "sales_amount": 479.992⸱

{"email": "dlamondpy0@soundcloud.com", "phone": "585-779-9709", "sales": [{"product_id": 7, "product_name": "Bat", "sales_amount": 599⸱

{"email": "dmagister113r@canalblog.com", "phone": "860-336-0719", "sales": [{"product_id": 8, "product_name": "Bat Limited Edition", "sale⸱

Figure 7.29: Resulting matches for your Danny Bat query

3. In this complex task, you need to find customers who match with both a scooter and an automobile. That means you need to perform a query for each combination of scooter and automobile. To get every unique combination of scooter and automobile, you can perform a simple cross join:

```
SELECT DISTINCT
  p1.model,
  p2.model
FROM
  products p1
CROSS JOIN
  products p2
WHERE
  p1.product_type = 'scooter'
AND
  p2.product_type = 'automobile'
AND
  p1.model NOT ILIKE '%Limited Edition%';
```

This produces the following output:

```
      model       |       model
------------------+------------------
 Bat              | Model Chi
 Bat              | Model Epsilon
 Bat              | Model Gamma
 Bat              | Model Sigma
 Blade            | Model Chi
 Blade            | Model Epsilon
 Blade            | Model Gamma
 Blade            | Model Sigma
 Lemon            | Model Chi
 Lemon            | Model Epsilon
 Lemon            | Model Gamma
 Lemon            | Model Sigma
 Lemon Zester     | Model Chi
 Lemon Zester     | Model Epsilon
 Lemon Zester     | Model Gamma
 Lemon Zester     | Model Sigma
(16 rows)
```

Figure 7.30: All combinations of scooters and automobiles

4. Transform the output into a **tsquery** object:

```
SELECT DISTINCT
  plainto_tsquery('english', p1.model)
    &&
    plainto_tsquery('english', p2.model)
FROM
  products p1
CROSS JOIN
  products p2
WHERE
  p1.product_type = 'scooter'
AND
  p2.product_type = 'automobile'
AND
  p1.model NOT ILIKE '%Limited Edition%';
```

This produces the following result:

```
'bat' & 'model' & 'chi'
'bat' & 'model' & 'sigma'
'blade' & 'model' & 'chi'
'lemon' & 'model' & 'chi'
'bat' & 'model' & 'gamma'
'blade' & 'model' & 'sigma'
'lemon' & 'model' & 'sigma'
'bat' & 'model' & 'epsilon'
'blade' & 'model' & 'gamma'
'lemon' & 'model' & 'gamma'
'blade' & 'model' & 'epsilon'
'lemon' & 'model' & 'epsilon'
'lemon' & 'zester' & 'model' & 'chi'
'lemon' & 'zester' & 'model' & 'sigma'
'lemon' & 'zester' & 'model' & 'gamma'
'lemon' & 'zester' & 'model' & 'epsilon'
(16 rows)
```

Figure 7.31: Queries for each scooter and automobile combination

5. Query your database using each of these **tsquery** objects and count the occurrences for each object:

Activity7.01.sql

```
1  SELECT
2    sub.query,
3    (
4      SELECT
5        COUNT(1)
6      FROM
7        customer_search
8      WHERE
9        customer_search.search_vector @@ sub.query
10   )
11 FROM (
12   SELECT DISTINCT
13     plainto_tsquery('english', p1.model)
14       &&
15       plainto_tsquery('english', p2.model) AS query
```

Please find the complete code here: https://packt.link/TVvPy

The following is the output of the preceding query:

```
                    query                    | count
---------------------------------------------+-------
 'lemon' & 'model' & 'sigma'                 |   340
 'lemon' & 'model' & 'chi'                   |   331
 'bat' & 'model' & 'epsilon'                 |   241
 'bat' & 'model' & 'sigma'                   |   226
 'bat' & 'model' & 'chi'                     |   221
 'lemon' & 'model' & 'epsilon'               |   217
 'bat' & 'model' & 'gamma'                   |   153
 'lemon' & 'model' & 'gamma'                 |   133
 'lemon' & 'zester' & 'model' & 'chi'        |    28
 'lemon' & 'zester' & 'model' & 'epsilon'    |    22
 'blade' & 'model' & 'chi'                   |    21
 'lemon' & 'zester' & 'model' & 'sigma'      |    17
 'blade' & 'model' & 'sigma'                 |    12
 'lemon' & 'zester' & 'model' & 'gamma'      |    11
 'blade' & 'model' & 'epsilon'               |     4
 'blade' & 'model' & 'gamma'                 |     4
(16 rows)
```

Figure 7.32: Customer counts for each scooter and automobile combination

While there could be a multitude of factors at play here, you see that **lemon scooter** and the **model sigma** automobile is the combination most frequently purchased together, followed by the **lemon** and **chi** models. **bat** is also fairly frequently purchased with both of those models, as well as the **epsilon** model. The other combinations are much less common, and it seems that customers rarely purchase the **lemon zester**, the **blade**, or the **gamma** model.

CHAPTER 8: PERFORMANT SQL

ACTIVITY 8.01: QUERY PLANNING

Solution:

1. Open PostgreSQL with **psql** and connect to the **sqlda** database.

2. Use the **EXPLAIN** command to return the query plan for selecting all available records within the **customers** table:

```
EXPLAIN
SELECT *
FROM customers;
```

3. Read the output of the plan and determine the total query cost, the setup cost, the number of rows to be returned, and the width of each row.

   The output is as follows:

```
Seq Scan on customers   (cost=0.00..1535.00 rows=50000 width=140)
```

   As such, the total query cost is **1535.00**, the setup cost is **0.00**, the number of rows to be returned is **50000**, and the width of each row is **140**. Your result may have numbers that are slightly different. But the general concept of measurements should be the same.

4. Repeat the query from *step 2* of this activity, this time limiting the number of returned records to **15**. Review the updated query plan and compare its output against the output of the previous step, paying special attention to how many steps are involved in the query plan and what the cost of the limiting step is:

```
EXPLAIN
SELECT *
FROM customers
LIMIT 15;
```

   The output is as follows:

```
Limit   (cost=0.00..0.46 rows=15 width=140)
   ->   Seq Scan on customers   (cost=0.00..1535.00 rows=50000
width=140)
```

The lower line in this output is the same as the output of *step 3*, in which the total query cost is **1535.00**, the setup cost is **0.00**, the number of rows to be returned is **50000**, and the width of each row is **140**. For the upper line, the total query cost is **0.46**, the setup cost is **0.00**, the number of rows to be returned is **15**, and the width of each row is **140**.

5. Update the SQL to select all rows where customers live within a latitude of **30** and **40** degrees. Generate the query plan. Compare the total plan cost as well as the number of rows returned by the query to the numbers from previous steps:

```
EXPLAIN
SELECT *
FROM customers
WHERE latitude BETWEEN 30 AND 40;
```

The output is as follows:

```
Seq Scan on customers   (cost=0.00..1785.00 rows=26369 width=140)
   Filter: ((latitude >= '30'::double precision) AND (latitude <=
'40'::double precision))
```

The plan in this output has only one step, in which the total query cost is **1785.00**, the setup cost is **0.00**, the number of rows to be returned is **26369**, and the width of the rows is still **140**. Since there is additional filtering involved, the total cost increased but the starting cost remains at zero as there is nothing to prepare in a sequential scan.

ACTIVITY 8.02: IMPLEMENTING INDEX SCANS

Solution:

Here are the steps to follow:

1. Use the **EXPLAIN** and **ANALYZE** commands to profile the query plan to search for all records with an IP address of **18.131.58.65**:

```
EXPLAIN ANALYZE
SELECT *
FROM customers
WHERE ip_address = '18.131.58.65';
```

The result is as follows:

```
Seq Scan on customers   (cost=0.00..1660.00 rows=1 width=140) (actual
time=0.098..13.626 rows=1 loops=1)
   Filter: (ip_address = '18.131.58.65'::text)
```

```
     Rows Removed by Filter: 49999
Planning Time: 0.199 ms
Execution Time: 13.659 ms
```

Here, the planning and execution times are **0.199 ms** and **13.659 ms**, respectively.

2. Create a generic index based on the IP address column:

```
CREATE INDEX ix_ip ON customers(ip_address);
```

3. Rerun the query in *step 1*. How long does the query take to plan and execute?

The result is as follows:

```
Index Scan using ix_ip on customers   (cost=0.29..8.31 rows=1
width=140) (actual time=0.099..0.101 rows=1 loops=1)
   Index Cond: (ip_address = '18.131.58.65'::text)
Planning Time: 0.791 ms
Execution Time: 0.131 ms
```

Now the planning and execution times are **0.791 ms** and **0.131 ms**, respectively.

4. Create a more detailed index based on the IP address column with the condition that the IP address is **18.131.58.65**:

```
CREATE INDEX ix_ip_less ON customers(ip_address)
WHERE ip_address = '18.131.58.65';
```

5. Rerun the query in *step 1*:

```
Index Scan using ix_ip on customers   (cost=0.29..8.31 rows=1
width=140) (actual time=0.026..0.027 rows=1 loops=1)
   Index Cond: (ip_address = '18.131.58.65'::text)
Planning Time: 0.338 ms
Execution Time: 0.055 ms
```

Now it takes the query **0.338 ms** and **0.055 ms** to plan and execute. As you add more and more restraints to the index definition, the time spent on planning increases because PostgreSQL needs more time to review the index definitions and determine which index to use. But as indexes are defined with further details, the execution time became much less.

6. Use the **EXPLAIN ANALYZE** commands to profile the query plan to search for all records with a suffix of **Jr**:

```
EXPLAIN ANALYZE SELECT * FROM customers WHERE suffix = 'Jr';
```

The result is as follows:

```
Seq Scan on customers  (cost=0.00..1660.00 rows=100 width=140)
(actual time=0.075..10.694 rows=102 loops=1)
  Filter: (suffix = 'Jr'::text)
  Rows Removed by Filter: 49898
Planning Time: 0.191 ms
Execution Time: 10.732 ms
```

7. Create a generic index based on the suffix address column:

```
CREATE INDEX ix_suffix ON customers(suffix);
```

8. Rerun the query in *step 6*:

```
Bitmap Heap Scan on customers  (cost=5.07..302.60 rows=100 width=140)
(actual time=0.072..0.170 rows=102 loops=1)
  Recheck Cond: (suffix = 'Jr'::text)
  Heap Blocks: exact=98
  -> Bitmap Index Scan on ix_suffix  (cost=0.00..5.04 rows=100
width=0) (actual time=0.056..0.056 rows=102 loops=1)
        Index Cond: (suffix = 'Jr'::text)
Planning Time: 0.676 ms
Execution Time: 0.212 ms
```

Compared to the original execution time of **10.732 ms**, this **0.212 ms** execution time is a huge improvement. The increase in plan time from **0.191 ms** to **0.676 ms** is almost negligible compared to the reduction in execution time.

ACTIVITY 8.03: IMPLEMENTING HASH INDEXES

Solution:

In this activity, you will follow these steps:

1. Use the **EXPLAIN** and **ANALYZE** commands to determine the planning time and cost, as well as the execution time and cost, of selecting all rows where the email subject is **Shocking Holiday Savings on Electric Scooters**.

The SQL you use is as follows:

```
EXPLAIN ANALYZE
SELECT * FROM emails
WHERE email_subject='Shocking Holiday Savings On Electric Scooters';
```

The result is as follows:

```
Gather  (cost=1000.00..10480.81 rows=18789 width=79) (actual
time=237.847..936.473 rows=19873 loops=1)
  Workers Planned: 2
  Workers Launched: 2
  ->  Parallel Seq Scan on emails  (cost=0.00..7601.91 rows=7829
width=79) (actual time=410.903..633.642 rows=6624 loops=3)
        Filter: (email_subject = 'Shocking Holiday Savings On
Electric Scooters'::text)
        Rows Removed by Filter: 132762
Planning Time: 157.116 ms
Execution Time: 937.329 ms
```

2. Create a hash scan on the **email_subject** column:

```
CREATE INDEX ix_subject ON emails USING HASH(email_subject);
```

3. Repeat *step 1*. Compare the output of the Query Planner without the hash index to the output with the hash index:

```
Bitmap Heap Scan on emails  (cost=605.61..6264.48 rows=18789
width=79) (actual time=1.223..12.319 rows=19873 loops=1)
  Recheck Cond: (email_subject = 'Shocking Holiday Savings On
Electric Scooters'::text)
  Heap Blocks: exact=290
  ->  Bitmap Index Scan on ix_subject  (cost=0.00..600.92 rows=18789
width=0) (actual time=1.073..1.073 rows=19873 loops=1)
        Index Cond: (email_subject = 'Shocking Holiday Savings On
Electric Scooters'::text)
Planning Time: 0.936 ms
Execution Time: 13.078 ms
```

The hash index clearly has a positive impact on the performance of the two queries.

4. Create a hash scan on the **customer_id** column:

```
CREATE INDEX ix_customer_id ON emails USING HASH(customer_id);
```

5. Use **EXPLAIN** and **ANALYZE** to estimate how long it would take to select all rows with a **customer_id** value greater than **100**:

```
EXPLAIN ANALYZE SELECT * FROM emails WHERE customer_id>100;
```

The result is as follows:

```
Seq Scan on emails   (cost=0.00..10650.98 rows=417346 width=79)
(actual time=0.067..105.158 rows=417315 loops=1)
  Filter: (customer_id > 100)
  Rows Removed by Filter: 843
Planning Time: 0.548 ms
Execution Time: 117.899 ms
```

You can see that PostgreSQL decided to use a sequential scan instead of a hash index because a hash index can only be used with the = comparison, not any other operators.

ACTIVITY 8.04: DEFINING A LARGEST SALE VALUE FUNCTION

Solution:

Perform the following steps:

1. Connect to the **sqlda** database.

2. Create a function called **max_sale** that does not take any input arguments but returns a numeric value called **big_sale**:

```
CREATE FUNCTION max_sale() RETURNS integer AS $big_sale$
```

3. Declare the **big_sale** variable and begin the function:

```
DECLARE big_sale numeric;
BEGIN
```

4. Insert the value of the largest sale into the **big_sale** variable:

```
SELECT MAX(sales_amount) INTO big_sale FROM sales;
```

5. Return the value for **big_sale**:

```
RETURN big_sale;
```

6. End the function with the **LANGUAGE** statement:

```
END; $big_sale$
LANGUAGE PLPGSQL;
```

7. Call the function to find out what the value of the largest sale in the database is:

```
SELECT * FROM max_sale();
```

The output is as follows:

```
Max
--------
115000
(1 row)
```

ACTIVITY 8.05: CREATING FUNCTIONS WITH ARGUMENTS

Solution:

These are the steps to follow:

1. Create the function definition for a function called **avg_sales_window** that returns a numeric value and takes two **DATE** values to specify the from and to dates in the form **YYYY-MM-DD**:

```
CREATE FUNCTION avg_sales_window(from_date DATE, to_date DATE)
RETURNS numeric AS $sales_avg$
```

2. Declare the return variable as a numeric data type and begin the function:

```
DECLARE sales_avg numeric;
BEGIN
```

3. Select the average sales amount as the return variable where the sales transaction date is within the specified date:

```
SELECT AVG(sales_amount)
FROM sales
INTO sales_avg
WHERE sales_transaction_date > from_date
AND sales_transaction_date < to_date;
```

4. Return the function variable, end the function, and specify the **LANGUAGE** statement:

```
RETURN sales_avg;
END; $sales_avg$
LANGUAGE PLPGSQL;
```

5. Use the function to determine the average sales values between 2020-04-12 and 2021-04-12:

```
SELECT avg_sales_window('2020-04-12', '2021-04-12');
```

The output is as follows:

```
avg_sales_window
----------------
7663.13305937025
(1 row)
```

ACTIVITY 8.06: CREATING A TRIGGER TO TRACK AVERAGE PURCHASES

Solution:

Here are the steps to follow for this activity:

1. Connect to the **sqlda** database.

2. Create a new table called **avg_qty_log** that is composed of an **order_id integer** field and an **avg_qty numeric** field:

```
CREATE TABLE avg_qty_log (order_id integer, avg_qty numeric);
```

3. Create a function called **avg_qty** that does not take any arguments but returns a trigger. The function computes the average value for all order quantities (**order_info.qty**) and inserts the average value, along with the most recent **order_id**, into **avg_qty**:

```
CREATE FUNCTION avg_qty() RETURNS TRIGGER AS $_avg$
DECLARE _avg numeric;
BEGIN
  SELECT
    AVG(qty)
  INTO
    _avg
  FROM
    order_info;
  INSERT INTO
    avg_qty_log (order_id, avg_qty)
  VALUES
    (NEW.order_id, _avg);
  RETURN NEW;
END; $_avg$
LANGUAGE PLPGSQL;
```

4. Create a trigger called **avg_trigger** that calls the **avg_qty** function after each row is inserted into the **order_info** table:

```
CREATE TRIGGER avg_trigger
AFTER INSERT ON order_info
FOR EACH ROW
EXECUTE PROCEDURE avg_qty();
```

5. Insert some new rows into the **order_info** table with quantities of **6**, **7**, and **8**:

```
SELECT insert_order(3, 'GROG1', 6);
SELECT insert_order(4, 'GROG1', 7);
SELECT insert_order(1, 'GROG1', 8);
```

6. Look at the entries in **avg_qty_log**:

```
SELECT * FROM avg_qty_log;
```

The result is as follows:

```
 order_id |        avg_qty
----------+----------------------
     1625 | 4.7500000000000000
     1626 | 5.0000000000000000
     1627 | 5.3000000000000000
(3 rows)
```

You can see that the average quantity is gradually increasing.

CHAPTER 9: USING SQL TO UNCOVER THE TRUTH: A CASE STUDY

ACTIVITY 9.01: QUANTIFYING THE SALES DROP

Solution:

Perform the following steps to complete this activity:

1. Load the **sqlda** database with psql.

2. Using the **OVER** and **ORDER BY** statements, compute the daily cumulative sum of sales. This provides you with a discrete count of sales over a period of time on a daily basis. Insert the results into a new table called **bat_sales_growth**:

```
SELECT
  *,
  sum(count) OVER (ORDER BY sales_date)
INTO
  bat_sales_growth
FROM
  bat_sales_daily;
```

3. Compute a seven-day **lag** of the **sum** column, and then insert all the columns of **bat_sales_daily** and the new **lag** column into a new table, **bat_sales_daily_delay**. This **lag** column indicates the sales amount a week prior to the given record, allowing you to compare sales with the previous week:

```
SELECT
  *,
  lag(sum, 7) OVER (ORDER BY sales_date)
INTO
  bat_sales_daily_delay
FROM
  bat_sales_growth;
```

4. Inspect the first 15 rows of **bat_sales_growth**:

```
SELECT
  *
FROM
  bat_sales_daily_delay
ORDER BY
  Sales_date
LIMIT
  15;
```

The result is as follows:

```
 sales_date | count | sum | lag
------------+-------+-----+-----
 2019-06-07 |     9 |   9 |
 2019-06-08 |     6 |  15 |
 2019-06-09 |    10 |  25 |
 2019-06-10 |    10 |  35 |
 2019-06-11 |     5 |  40 |
 2019-06-12 |    10 |  50 |
 2019-06-13 |    14 |  64 |
 2019-06-14 |     9 |  73 |    9
 2019-06-15 |    11 |  84 |   15
 2019-06-16 |    12 |  96 |   25
 2019-06-17 |    10 | 106 |   35
 2019-06-18 |     6 | 112 |   40
 2019-06-19 |     2 | 114 |   50
 2019-06-20 |     5 | 119 |   64
 2019-06-21 |     6 | 125 |   73
(15 rows)
```

5. Compute the sales growth as a percentage, comparing the current sales volume to that of a week prior. Insert the resulting table into a new table called **bat_sales_delay_vol**:

```
SELECT
  *,
  (sum-lag)/lag AS volume
INTO
```

```
    bat_sales_delay_vol
FROM
    bat_sales_daily_delay;
```

6. Compare the first 22 values of the **bat_sales_delay_vol** table to ascertain a sales drop:

```
SELECT * FROM bat_sales_delay_vol LIMIT 22;
```

The result is as follows:

```
sales_date | count | sum | lag |         volume
-----------+-------+-----+-----+------------------------
2019-06-07 |     9 |   9 |     |
2019-06-08 |     6 |  15 |     |
2019-06-09 |    10 |  25 |     |
2019-06-10 |    10 |  35 |     |
2019-06-11 |     5 |  40 |     |
2019-06-12 |    10 |  50 |     |
2019-06-13 |    14 |  64 |     |
2019-06-14 |     9 |  73 |   9 |    7.1111111111111111
2019-06-15 |    11 |  84 |  15 |    4.6000000000000000
2019-06-16 |    12 |  96 |  25 |    2.8400000000000000
2019-06-17 |    10 | 106 |  35 |    2.0285714285714286
2019-06-18 |     6 | 112 |  40 |    1.8000000000000000
2019-06-19 |     2 | 114 |  50 |    1.2800000000000000
2019-06-20 |     5 | 119 |  64 | 0.85937500000000000000
2019-06-21 |     6 | 125 |  73 | 0.71232876712328767123
2019-06-22 |     9 | 134 |  84 | 0.59523809523809523810
2019-06-23 |     2 | 136 |  96 | 0.41666666666666666667
2019-06-24 |     4 | 140 | 106 | 0.32075471698113207547
2019-06-25 |     7 | 147 | 112 | 0.31250000000000000000
2019-06-26 |     5 | 152 | 114 | 0.33333333333333333333
2019-06-27 |     5 | 157 | 119 | 0.31932773109243697479
2019-06-28 |     3 | 160 | 125 | 0.28000000000000000000
(22 rows)
```

While the count and cumulative **sum** columns are reasonably straightforward, why do you need the **lag** and **volume** columns? That is because to look for a drop in sales growth, you need to first calculate the growth. Growth is calculated by comparing the daily sum of sales to the same values 7 days earlier (the lag). By subtracting the sum and lag values and dividing by the lag, you obtain the volume value and can determine sales growth compared to the previous week of the sales transaction. Then, you will observe the trend in growth and identify possible drops.

Notice that the sales volume on **2019-06-14** is **700%** greater than the launch date of **2019-06-07**. By **2019-06-17**, the volume has doubled compared to the week prior. As time passes, this relative difference begins to decrease dramatically. By the end of June, the volume is **28%** higher than the week prior. At this stage, you can observe and confirm the presence of a reduction in sales growth after the first 2 weeks. In the next exercise, you will attempt to explain the causes of the reduction.

ACTIVITY 9.02: ANALYZING THE DIFFERENCE IN THE SALES PRICE HYPOTHESIS

Solution:

Perform the following steps to complete this activity:

1. Load the **sqlda** database from psql.

2. Select the **sales_transaction_date** column for 2016 **Lemon** model sales and insert the column into a table called **lemon_sales**:

```
SELECT
    sales_transaction_date
INTO
    lemon_sales
FROM
    sales
WHERE
    product_id=3;
```

3. Count the sales records available for the 2016 **Lemon** model:

```
SELECT
    count(sales_transaction_date)
FROM
    lemon_sales;
```

The result is as follows:

```
count
-------
 16558
(1 row)
```

4. Display the latest **sales_transaction_date** column:

```
SELECT
  max(sales_transaction_date)
FROM
  lemon_sales;
```

The result is as follows:

```
        max
---------------------
 2021-08-23 19:12:10
(1 row)
```

5. Convert the **sales_transaction_date** column into a **date** type:

```
ALTER TABLE
  lemon_sales
ALTER COLUMN
  sales_transaction_date TYPE DATE;
```

6. Count the number of sales per day within the **lemon_sales** table and insert the data into a table called **lemon_sales_count**:

```
SELECT
  sales_transaction_date,
  COUNT(sales_transaction_date)
INTO
  lemon_sales_count
FROM
  lemon_sales
GROUP BY
  sales_transaction_date
ORDER BY
  sales_transaction_date;
```

7. Calculate the cumulative sum of sales and insert the corresponding table into a new table labeled **lemon_sales_sum**:

```
SELECT
  *,
  sum(count) OVER (ORDER BY sales_transaction_date)
INTO
  lemon_sales_sum
FROM
  lemon_sales_count;
```

8. Compute the seven-day **lag** function on the **sum** column and save the result to **lemon_sales_delay**:

```
SELECT
  *,
  lag(sum, 7) OVER (ORDER BY sales_transaction_date)
INTO
  lemon_sales_delay
FROM
  lemon_sales_sum;
```

9. Calculate the growth rate using the data from **lemon_sales_delay** and store the resulting table in **lemon_sales_growth**:

```
SELECT
  *,
  (sum-lag)/lag AS volume
INTO
  lemon_sales_growth
FROM
  lemon_sales_delay;
```

10. Inspect the first 22 records of the **lemon_sales_growth** table by examining the **volume** data:

```
SELECT
  *
FROM
  lemon_sales_growth
ORDER BY
```

```
      Sales_transaction_date
LIMIT
  22;
```

The expected output is as follows:

```
sales_transaction_date | count | sum | lag |       volume
-----------------------+-------+-----+-----+---------------------
   2015-12-27          |   6   |  6  |     |
   2015-12-28          |   8   | 14  |     |
   2015-12-29          |   4   | 18  |     |
   2015-12-30          |   9   | 27  |     |
   2015-12-31          |   9   | 36  |     |
   2016-01-01          |   6   | 42  |     |
   2016-01-02          |   8   | 50  |     |
   2016-01-03          |   6   | 56  |  6  |    8.3333333333333333
   2016-01-04          |   6   | 62  | 14  |    3.4285714285714286
   2016-01-05          |   9   | 71  | 18  |    2.9444444444444444
   2016-01-06          |   3   | 74  | 27  |    1.7407407407407407
   2016-01-07          |   4   | 78  | 36  |    1.1666666666666667
   2016-01-08          |   7   | 85  | 42  |    1.0238095238095238
   2016-01-09          |   3   | 88  | 50  | 0.76000000000000000000
   2016-01-10          |   3   | 91  | 56  | 0.62500000000000000000
   2016-01-11          |   4   | 95  | 62  | 0.53225806451612903226
   2016-01-12          |   6   | 101 | 71  | 0.42253521126760563380
   2016-01-13          |   9   | 110 | 74  | 0.48648648648648648649
   2016-01-14          |   6   | 116 | 78  | 0.48717948717948717949
   2016-01-15          |   6   | 122 | 85  | 0.43529411764705882353
   2016-01-16          |  11   | 133 | 88  | 0.51136363636363636364
   2016-01-17          |   8   | 141 | 91  | 0.54945054945054945055
(22 rows)
```

Now that you have collected data to test the two hypotheses of timing and cost, what observations can you make and what conclusions can you draw?

The first observation that you can make is regarding the total volume of sales for the three different scooter products. The **Lemon** Scooter, over its production life cycle of 4.5 years, sold **16558** units, while the two **Bat** Scooters, the original and Limited Edition models, sold **7328** and **5803** units, respectively, and are still currently in production, with the **Bat** Scooter launching about 4 months earlier and with approximately 2.5 years of sales data available.

Looking at the sales growth of the three different scooters, you can also make a few different observations:

- The original **Bat** Scooter, which launched on **2019-06-07** at a price of **$599.99**, experienced a 700% sales growth in its second week of production and finished the first 22 days with 28% growth and a sales figure of 160 units.

- The **Bat Limited Edition** Scooter, which launched in **2019-10-13** at a price of **$699.99**, experienced 450% growth at the start of its second week of production and finished with 96 sales and 66% growth over the first 22 days.

- The 2016 **Lemon** Scooter, which launched in **2015-12-27** at a price of **$499.99**, experienced 830% growth in the second week of production and ended its first 22 days with 141 sales and 55% growth.

Based on this information, you can make different conclusions:

- The initial growth rate starting in the second week of sales correlates to the cost of the scooter. As the cost increased to **$699.99**, the initial growth rate dropped from 830% to 450%.

- The number of units sold in the first 22 days does not directly correlate to the cost. The **$599.99 Bat** Scooter sold more than the 2016 **Lemon** Scooter in that first period, despite the price difference.

- There is some evidence to suggest that the reduction in sales can be attributed to seasonal variations, given the significant reduction in growth and the fact that the original **Bat** Scooter was the only one released in June. So far, the evidence suggests that the drop in sales can be attributed to the difference in launch timing.

Before you draw the conclusion that the difference can be attributed to seasonal variations and launch timing, ensure that you have extensively tested a range of possibilities. Perhaps marketing work, such as email campaigns (that is, when the emails were sent) and the frequency with which the emails were opened, made a difference.

HEY!

Jun Shan

Matt Goldwasser

Upom Malik

Benjamin Johnston

We are Jun Shan, Matt Goldwasser, Upom Malik, and Benjamin Johnston the authors of this book. We really hope you enjoyed reading our book and found it useful for learning SQL.

It would really help us (and other potential readers!) if you could leave a review on Amazon sharing your thoughts on *SQL for Data Analytics, Third Edition*.

Go to the link https://packt.link/r/180181287X.

OR

Scan the QR code to leave your review.

Your review will help us to understand what's worked well in this book and what could be improved upon for future editions, so it really is appreciated.

Best wishes,

Jun Shan, Matt Goldwasser, Upom Malik, and Benjamin Johnston

INDEX

Made in United States
North Haven, CT
07 March 2024